SPACES OF MODERNITY

Mappings: Society/Theory/Space
A Guilford Series

APPROACHING HUMAN GEOGRAPHY: An Introduction to
Contemporary Theoretical Debates
Paul Cloke, Chris Philo, and David Sadler

THE POWER OF MAPS
Denis Wood (with John Fels)

POSTMODERN CONTENTIONS: Epochs, Politics, Space
John Paul Jones III, Wolfgang Natter, and Theodore R. Schatzki, Editors

TRAVEL, GENDER, AND IMPERIALISM: Mary Kingsley and
West Africa
Alison Blunt

WRITING WOMEN AND SPACE: Colonial and
Postcolonial Geographies
Alison Blunt and Gillian Rose, Editors

LAW, SPACE, AND THE GEOGRAPHIES OF POWER
Nicholas K. Blomley

GROUND TRUTH: The Social Implications of Geographic
Information Systems
John Pickles, Editor

INDIFFERENT BOUNDARIES: Spatial Concepts of Human Subjectivity
Kathleen M. Kirby

LOGICS OF DISLOCATION: Models, Metaphors, and Meanings of
Economic Space
Trevor J. Barnes

SPACE, TEXT, AND GENDER: An Anthropological Study of the
Marakwet of Kenya
Henrietta L. Moore

EMANCIPATING SPACE: Geography, Architecture, and Urban Design
Ross King

REPLACING CITIZENSHIP: AIDS Activism and Radical Democracy
Michael P. Brown

THE PLACE OF MUSIC
Andrew Leyshon, David Matless, and George Revill, Editors

SPACES OF MODERNITY: London's Geographies, 1680–1780
Miles Ogborn

Spaces of Modernity
London's Geographies, 1680–1780

MILES OGBORN

Department of Geography
Queen Mary and Westfield College
University of London

THE GUILFORD PRESS
New York   London

© 1998 The Guilford Press
A Division of Guilford Publications, Inc.
72 Spring Street, New York, NY 10012
http://www.guilford.com

Printed in the United States of America

This book is printed on acid-free paper.

Last digit is print number: 9 8 7 6 5 4 3 2 1

Library of Congress Cataloging-in-Publication Data

Ogborn, Miles.
    Spaces of modernity : London's geographies, 1680–1780 / Miles Ogborn.
        p.   cm.
    Includes bibliographical references and index.
    ISBN 1-57230-343-3. — ISBN 1-57230-365-4 (pbk.)
    1. London (England)—History—18th century.   2. Architecture, Modern—17th–18th centuries—England—London.   3. London (England)—History—17th century.   4. London (England)—Historical geography. 5. Public spaces—England—London—History.   I. Title.
DA682.O33   1998
942.1'07—dc21   98-13000
                                                              CIP

Contents

List of Figures   ix

Acknowledgements   xi

Chapter One   **Spaces of Modernity**   **1**

Debating Modernity   2
Retaining Modernity?   6
Reworking Modernity   12
   Contextual Histories of Modernity   13
   Difference, Power and Modernity   14
   Geographies of Modernity   17
Eighteenth-Century Modernities   22
Locating Modernity   28

Chapter Two   **The Magdalen Hospital**   **39**

Introduction: Modernity and Identity   39
The Problem of Prostitution   45
   Prostitution and Population   46
   Prostitution and the City   49
Modern Morality Tales: *The Histories of*   53
   Some of the Penitents
   Lost Selves   54
   Remaking Selves   58

The Magdalen Hospital: Order,   60
Self-Reflection and Solitude
A Simple, Regular and Laborious Life   61
Reflection, Prayer and the Space of Solitude   66
Rationality, Autonomy and Domesticity   70
Conclusions   73

Chapter Three   **The Street**   **75**

Introduction: Modernity in the Streets   75
Theorising the Public Sphere   77
The Imagined Geographies of   79
Political Philosophy
Shaftesbury   79
Bernard Mandeville   84
David Hume   87
Making Public Space: Paving Westminster   91
Representing the Pedestrian   104
Presenting the City   106
Class and Gender in the Streets   110
Dirt and Disorder   111
Conclusions   104

Chapter Four   **The Pleasure Garden**   **116**

Introduction: Learning from Vauxhall   116
A Tour of Vauxhall Gardens in the 1750s   119
Commodification, Commercialisation   122
and Luxury
Dreaming of Sex and Money at the   128
Ridotto al Fresco
The True Orthodox Tread upon Fairy   133
Ground: Locating the Macaroni
Imperial Vauxhall   142
Gazing upon Madam Hartley   148
Vision in Vauxhall   150
Conclusions   155

Chapter Five   **Excise Geographies**   **158**

Introduction: The Capacities of the   158
Modern State
Charles Davenant's Political Arithmetic   163

Shaping the Excise, 1683–1689   170
Interpreting *The Excise Man*   185
The Excise in Eighteenth-Century London   194
Conclusions   199

Chapter Six   **The Universal Register Office**   **201**

Introduction: Time, Space and Modernity   201
The Universal Register Office   211
    The World Together in One Place   211
    The Vigorous Circulation of the   219
     Civil Power
    The Register Office: Tricks, Villainy   223
     and Chicanery
    Conclusions   229

Chapter Seven   **Maps of Modernity**   **231**

Notes   **239**

Bibliography   **305**

Index   **334**

List of Figures

Figure 1:   Rocque's Map of London, 1740s (John Rocque,   29
Plan of the Cities of London and Wesminster. By
permission of the British Library, Crace III.106)

Figure 2:   Ground Plan of the Magdalen Hospital, 1769   62
(Magdalen Hospital, *An Account of the Rise,
Progress and Present State.* By permission of the
British Library, 1578/102)

Figure 3:   Frontispiece from Jonas Hanway's *Thoughts on the*   63
Plan for a Magdalen House, 1758.(By permission of
the British Library, 8285.e.46)

Figure 4:   Frontispiece from Jonas Hanway's *Reflections,*   69
1761. (By permission of the British Library,
4404.h.34)

Figure 5:   John Gwynn's Proposed Improvements for Part   102
of Westminster, 1766. (John Gwynn, *London and
Westminster Improved.* By permission of the British
Library, 191.a.19)

Figure 6:   Title Page Illustration from John Gay's *Trivia,*   105
1716. (By permission of the British Library,
12330.f.26)

Figure 7:   The Maccaroni Sacrifice, 1773. (*The Vauxhall*   117
                 Affray. By permission of the British Library,
                 1414.e.28)

Figure 8:   A General Prospect of Vauxhall Gardens, 1751.   121
                 (By permission of the British Museum)

Figure 9:   Spring Gardens, Vauxhall, 1741. (By permission   130
                 of the Duchy of Cornwall Office)

Figure 10:   Vaux Hall, c. 1741. (By permission of the Duchy   131
                 of Cornwall Office)

Figure 11:   The Noviciate of a Macaroni. Ranelagh, 1772.   135
                 Published by M. Darly. (By permission of the
                 British Museum)

Figure 12:   A Mungo Macaroni. Published by M. Darly.   136
                 (By permission of the British Museum)

Figure 13:   Modello for *The Humanity of General Amherst,*   146
                 Francis Hayman, 1760. (By permission of The
                 Beaverbrook Foundation)

Figure 14:   Modello for *Lord Clive Receiving the Homage of*   147
                 the Nabob Francis Hayman, c. 1761–1762. (By
                 courtesy of the National Portrait Gallery,
                 London)

Figure 15:   The Geometry of Casks, 1739. (Charles   159
                 Leadbetter, *The Royal Gauger.* By permission of
                 the British Library, 1609/4499)

Figure 16 a–e: Charles Davenant's Travels, November 1683   173
                 to September 1685

Acknowledgements

The research presented here was made possible by the staff at the British Library, the Duchy of Cornwall Archive, the British Museum's Department of Prints and Drawings, the Guildhall Library, the Bodleian Library and the Minet Library. I have also been given help with languages by David Noy and Ian Jones. The maps in Chapter 5 were drawn by Edward Oliver.

I have been fortunate to have had comments on earlier versions of the material that appears here from Stephen Daniels, Philip Howell, Roger Lee, Lynda Nead, Jerry Brotton, Rachel Holmes, David Weed, David Solkin, John Allen, David Patton, Charles Withers, Jeremy Stein, David M. Smith, Derek Gregory, Michael Dear and the publisher's readers. I can only repeat Louis Chambaud's comment to Dr Ward in 1753 that 'Your judicious animadversions confirm me in my opinion that no Author ought to send his performance to the press before it has been read by . . . judicious and knowing person[s],' and add that the faults that remain are my responsibility alone.

This book also owes much to encouragement from Felix Driver, Charlie Smith, Nicholas Robson and Jane Ogborn. However, my greatest debt is to Catherine Nash who has read and improved the whole thing, and has even been able to make some writing a pleasure.

CHAPTER ONE

Spaces of Modernity

We are already in the modern world, the world of banks and cheques, budgets, the stock exchange, the periodical press, coffee houses, clubs, coffins, microscopes, shorthand, actresses and umbrellas.[1]

Modernity is most often a matter for grand theory and for portentous pronouncements heralding either its origin or its demise. It can, however, also be a matter of close investigations of the spaces and places of the past—and of the banks, newspapers, actresses and umbrellas that fill them—that try to connect these geographies to deep and wide social transformations. It is in this light that this book takes a series of historical geographies of London in the period 1680–1780 and interprets them through the lens provided by theories of modernity.[2] My aim in doing this is to provide a series of specific and detailed readings of changes that reshaped this period, this city, and the multitude of other places to which it was connected. I have, therefore, tried to offer historical geographies of processes—individualisation, the formation of 'the public sphere,' commodification, bureaucratic rationalisation, state formation, and the transformations of time and space through communications innovations—that are crucial to the period and, in various ways, mark it as 'modern.' Yet even as these studies celebrate contextual detail and local particularity, they run against the stream of much of the theorising about modernity. This work often presents it in ways that threaten to ride roughshod over the histories and geographies that could be written of modernity in different places at different times, ignoring

1

tricky issues of context, specificity, difference and contingency. One of
the key questions that this introduction addresses is whether historical
geographies of modernity can be written that are not simply about the
march of the modern. Another question is whether allowing in these
complexities means having to abandon the seemingly totalising concept
of modernity altogether. In trying to answer these questions—a search
for workable versions of modernity somewhere between totalisation
and difference—I cannot claim to sort out once and for all the theoretical tangle that anyone writing about modernity must enter. Instead, I
want to think alongside those who have pursued their theorising
through writing some of modernity's histories and sketching some of
its geographies.[3] In doing so, I will argue that these geographies—what
I have called, borrowing from Griselda Pollock and others, 'spaces of
modernity'—can be part of projects concerned with specific places,
times, and social transformations such as those detailed in the following
chapters and, perhaps, can also be a way of understanding modernity
that sidesteps some of the pitfalls of 'grand' theory.[4] This book is, therefore, both about eighteenth-century London, addressing issues crucial
to that period and place, and about how writing contextual historical
geographies can change the ways we theorise modernity. This chapter
seeks to set out the groundwork for writing the studies that follow—of
the Magdalen Hospital, the paved and lit streets of Westminster, Vauxhall's pleasure gardens, excise taxation, and the Fieldings' Universal
Register Office—by discussing the problems attendant upon the concept of modernity.

DEBATING MODERNITY

Paradoxically, the literature on modernity is full of both ambiguity and
totalisation. There is certainly no agreed-upon definition. Its periodisations, geographies, characteristics and promise all remain elusive.[5] In
part, this is the point. The notion of modernity is used to explore a
world of crises, confusions and contradictory processes and experiences
'made up of equal parts of certainty and uncertainty, seriousness and su-
perficiality.'[6] It denotes both a world in which rational beings are caught
within an iron cage of their own making, and one where all that is solid melts into the air of dramatic and disruptive transformation.[7] Consequently, an enormous variety of processes, institutions and experiences
are claimed as modern even though they seem to have little in common.

Combined with this ambiguity are totalisations. The claims made for modernity are grand ones. Indeed, it seems that in these otherwise antitotalising times it is the one totalisation that is still allowed. Inevitably, this poses the problem that 'such an operation of necessity homogenizes and represses, reduces or forgets, certain forms of difference.'[8] In part this reduction is due to thinking of modernity as a particular relationship to time and history whereby the 'modern' is simply the 'new,' the contemporary, marking a separation from the past and offering reimaginings of the future. It is, therefore, understood as a 'historical self-consciousness' that produces 'a totalizing temporalization of history' that puts a gulf between the new and the old.[9] As Philibert Secretan has it:

> Newness, artificiality, emancipation: these three aspects of modernity begin to present a unity of meaning which is totally antithetical to the trilogy of tradition, nature, establishment.[10]

Yet even this brief summary begins to suggest that modernity cannot simply be reduced to what is chronologically new. Understandings of time and history are shaped and reshaped by new and changing experiences, relationships and institutions. Capitalism, bureaucracy, imperialism and disciplinary power all remake time and give content to understandings of what is historically new. They 'fill the form of the modern' and shape modern lives in ways that feed into, but are not reducible to, philosophical meditations on time and history.[11] As Paul Gilroy puts it—combining both 'form' and 'content' within an attention to social theory—'Modernity is understood as a distinct configuration with its own spatial and temporal characteristics defined above all through the consciousness of novelty that surrounds the emergence of civil society, the modern state, and industrial capitalism.'[12]

Yet these social theories of modernity are still frequently couched in totalising terms that posit a well-defined historical break—a 'Big Ditch'—between premodern and modern societies.[13] And the break that institutes modernity is based most frequently either upon forms of rationality, or modes of production and consumption. In terms of rationality, the problem is posed of a 'modern' world in which human action is newly liberated and enabled to transform the world by being based upon reason (as opposed, conventionally, to tradition), but is simultaneously destabilised because instrumental rationality—'the "hallmark of modernity"'—offers no ethical or moral basis on which to act.[14] The modern world can be ordered, but it cannot be made meaningful.[15]

The sources of these transformational forms of rationality are frequently traced to the scientific revolutions of the early seventeenth century; Tilo Schabert, for example, identifies 1620 and the publication of Francis Bacon's *Novum Organum* as 'the zero year of the modern age.'[16] The implications are also worked out in many other realms where rationality and rationalisation transform lives, spaces and practices. The classic locus for this is, of course, Max Weber's discussion of 'the specific and peculiar rationalism of Western culture,' where he begins to set out the difference between the West and the rest of the world in terms of the forms of reason embodied in everything from music to science to capitalism. His assessment of the consequences of this disenchantment of the world are also well known.[17] More recently this version of modernity has been used to good effect by Zygmunt Bauman in a series of sociological and philosophical writings that also assess the consequences of instrumental reason and rational ordering.

For Bauman, modernity offers both promises and dangers. It is 'a rebellion against fate and ascription, in the name of the omnipotence of design and achievement.'[18] But the 'adventure' inaugurated with the dissolution of traditional powers, certainties and constraints by the greater transformational resources of rationality and planning is also a cause for concern.[19] Bauman's account concerns 'modern rational societ[ies]' that are industrial and bureaucratic. He deals with states that have 'audacious engineering ambitions'—plans to produce rationally ordered societies 'purified of the last shred of the chaotic, the irrational, the spontaneous, the unpredictable'—and the means to effect them: a 'monopoly of the means of violence' and the ethically blind 'modern bureaucratic mode of rationalisation.'[20] He calls this 'the modern "gardening" state'—one that understands the society it rules 'as an object of designing, cultivating and weed-poisoning'—and he conceptualises it in terms of power and knowledge.[21] For Bauman, 'Empires of unconfined and unchallenged sovereignty, and the truth of unlimited and uncontested universality[,] were the two arms with which modernity wished to remould the world according to the design of perfect order.'[22] Modernity's power, but also its threat, lies in this potent combination of monopolised power and rational ordering. The precise delineation and classification of people, things and practices both transforms the world and leads to terrible industrialised and bureaucratised slaughter as ambiguity and difference are eradicated.

For many, this is enough to damn modern rationality.[23] Others seek to retain a sense of the benefits of reason, and argue for ways of conceptualising rationality that avoid some of the problems outlined by its critics.[24] Elsewhere, however, different conceptions of modernity stress not reason and order but flow, flux and change. They argue that modernity's potentials and problems spring from rather different sources, ones that have more to do with the logic and instrumental rationality of turning a profit than with those of state and science. This is expressed by Marshall Berman:

> There is a mode of vital experience—experience of space and time, of the self and others, of life's possibilities and perils—that is shared by men and women all over the world today. I will call this body of experience 'modernity.' To be modern is to find ourselves in an environment that promises us adventure, power, joy, growth, transformation of ourselves and the world—and, at the same time, that threatens to destroy everything we have, everything we know, everything we are.[25]

Here modernity is again a threat and a promise, but its locus now is the transformations wrought by what Allan Pred and Michael Watts call 'the maelstrom of capitalist modernization' and its 'creative destruction' of time, space and being.[26] In this version of modernity, the search for profit and the imperative of the maximum development of all productive forces lead to the continual making and remaking of land, labour and capital. Continual 'modernisation' transforms lives and landscapes. New cities arise, old ones are torn down; classes are formed, enriched and pauperised; canals are dug, roads are thrown across space, and ships are set in motion across oceans; homes are built, destroyed, or refigured for new purposes of consumption and reproduction. The globe becomes united in its experience of modernity, 'but it is a paradoxical unity, a unity of disunity.'[27]

There is clearly a danger here of totalising modernity and reducing it to capitalism. Berman reruns the same story of capitalist modernisation and urban transformation in Paris, St. Petersburg and New York, flattening the differences in the specific and localised experiences of its reconfigurations as he does so.[28] Others judge modernity only by the degree of capitalist transformation.[29] Indeed, Pred and Watts realise the dangers of assuming capitalism to be the sole agent of modernity. Although, for them, the prime generator of the 'new' is '[t]he revolutionary capacity of capital,' which has 'precipitated a multiplicity of modernities' and a multitude of resistances, they do acknowledge modernity's multiplicity in other ways. Their version of it as 'complexly multilinear' and characterised 'by simultaneity—by simultaneous diversity' at least admits the claims of bureaucratic rationality alongside those of capitalism:

> [I]t must be understood that our focus on the complex articulations of
> capitalism, culture and modernity is not to suggest that the experiences of
> modernity are *all* situated within this nexus. Localised experiences of
> modernity also derive from, among other things, new incursions of bu-
> reaucratic rationality. However, the intricate, context-dependent articula-
> tions that emerge among specific bureaucratic rationalities, culture and
> modernity are beyond our purview, deserving a lengthy treatment of
> their own.[30]

Combining the claims of (bureaucratic) rationality and capitalism—and
in many versions, including those of Weber and Marx, they are not easily separable at all—might help to capture the peculiar combination of
routinisation and dynamic change characteristic of modernity.[31] It
would certainly help us to begin to address some of the material and
symbolic transformations indexed by theories of modernity. Yet it is not
capable of capturing the multiplicity of modernities that might be included, the multiplicity of modern processes that transform places and
spaces at all scales. The desirability of doing so, and the considerable
problems it raises for continuing to use the term 'modernity,' can be
seen by considering the issue of periodisation.

RETAINING MODERNITY?

Differences over what modernity is mean that there can be no agreement on its chronology.[32] The many histories and geographies that can
be drawn, depending upon which ideas, relations or experiences are
taken to be the important ones, mean that there is no periodisation
consonant with Gellner's 'Big Ditch' or with the idea that Bruno Latour
characterises as 'The Great Divide.'[33] As Stephen Toulmin argues:

> Raise these questions, and ambiguity takes over. Some people date the
> origin of modernity to the year 1436, with Gutenberg's adoption of
> moveable type; some to A.D. 1520, and Luther's rebellion against Church
> authority; others to 1648, and the end of the Thirty Years' War; others to
> the American or French Revolution of 1776 or 1789; while modern
> times start for a few only in 1895, with Freud's *Interpretation of Dreams* and
> the rise of 'modernism' in the fine arts and literature.[34]

Indeed, within any of these histories there are also 'complex filiations'
between past and present that displace 'the metaphors of discontinuity'
and suggest other histories.[35] Taking this further, and insisting that

modernity might be irreducible to a single definition and a single temporality, suggests that close attention to chronologies might end the problem of understanding modernity by dissolving the notion altogether. For Bauman, '[O]nce the effort of dating starts in earnest, the object itself begins to disappear. Modernity, like all other quasi-totalities we want to prise off from the continuous flow of being, become elusive: we discover that the concept is fraught with ambiguity, while its referent is opaque at the core and frayed at the edges.'[36] Its retention cannot be based upon simple claims that it describes a demonstrable historical period, it has to be a matter of thinking carefully about what and how 'modernity' helps to understand and explain.

One way in which the notion of modernity has been retained is through the ways in which the concept itself has been imagined and deployed as part of discursive contests over the meanings of past, present and future. Rita Felski, for example, holds onto the concept in order 'to unravel the complexities of modernity's relationship to femininity through an analysis of varied and competing representations.' She wishes to retain a sense of the multiplicity of definitions of modernity in order to pay attention to 'the mobile and shifting meanings of the modern as a category of cultural consciousness.'[37] Modernity can certainly be multiple when it is a matter of multiple and contested meanings and representations. It is in this sense that Bruno Latour questions the notion of 'The Great Divide' between 'rational' modern societies and 'irrational' premodern ones. He suggests that 'modernity' denotes a version of history offered by the West that sets apart its supposedly 'rational' knowledges from the 'local' and 'particular' knowledges characteristic of the past and the rest of the world. This, he argues, paints history in the colours of both destiny and tragedy and permits all sorts of actions and interventions. Yet, for him, it can only be sustained by ignoring the particular contexts and conditions within which 'rational' knowledges are produced. These reveal, if examined closely, that there are not different 'nature–cultures' that can be described as 'premodern' and 'modern' on the basis that the latter keeps nature and culture separate, mediated only by rational science, and that the former has nature and culture bound together by animist magic. His argument is that '[w]e have never been modern,' but we think we have. 'The Great Divide' is an invention of the moderns that hides the continuities between past and present, and between here and there. Modernity is simply a way of conceptualising history and geography and, for Latour, a very partial conceptualisation since '[a] whole supplementary work of sorting out, cleaning up and dividing up is required to obtain the impression of a modernization that goes in step with time.' It is, however, a way of thinking that 'provided the moderns with the daring to mobilise things and people on a scale they would otherwise have disallowed,' and discursively produced the 'traditional' and the 'premodern' as well as the 'modern.'[38]

However, while Latour and Felski are interested in the rhetorics of 'modernity,' their understandings of change are not limited to the discursive realm. For Felski, '[M]odernity is not a homogenous Zeitgeist which was born at a particular moment in history, but rather . . . it comprises a collection of interlocking institutional, cultural and philosophical strands which emerge and develop at different times and which are often only defined as "modern" retrospectively.'[39] For Latour, the differences between the forms of knowledge and practice that have been labeled 'premodern' and 'modern' are not a matter of wholesale transformations in ways of thinking—some sort of break to modern rationality—but a matter of the extensions of what he calls 'networks' of people, practices, knowledges and objects so that they involve more and more actors at more and more sites. These 'networks' are the tracks along which knowledge and power run, and the grooves in which they have to run in order to be circulated and accumulated. The more extensive the networks, the more likely that certain knowledges and practices are to be taken as true and 'rational,' while others, in less extensive networks, become 'local,' 'traditional,' and, significantly, 'premodern.'[40] Thus, for Latour, the overblown dramatic tragedy of any break to modernity can be denied by figuring change as the gradual extension of some networks and the accumulation of knowledge and power in certain centres that eventually creates an asymmetry that can be (mis)interpreted as 'The Great Divide.' As he puts it, 'To be sure, the innovation of lengthened networks is important, but it is hardly a reason to make such a great fuss.'[41]

Latour's argument that 'the differences are sizeable, but they are only of size' usefully counters notions of a radical and wholesale disjuncture on the basis of rationality.[42] It does not, however, mean rejecting all other versions of modernity. What is intriguing here are the similarities, alongside very real differences that should not be downplayed, between Latour and Anthony Giddens. Giddens, unlike Latour, understands modernity as a discontinuity. His 'first approximation' is that '"modernity" refers to modes of social life or organisation which emerged in Europe from about the seventeenth century onwards and which subsequently became more or less worldwide in their influence.' Consequently, he argues that 'modern social institutions are in some respects unique—distinct in form from all types of traditional order.'[43] Yet this is a discontinuist history that allows for some continuities—for Giddens realises the danger of overly schematic contrasts of 'traditional' and 'modern'—and avoids any notion of an abrupt shift or precise peri- odisation by conceptualising what is 'modern' in quantitative as much as qualitative terms. For Giddens, the differences are that 'in' modernity the pace of change is faster, the scope of change is wider, and, while in- sisting that '[s]ome modern social forms are simply not found in prior historical periods—such as the political system of the nation-state, the wholesale dependence of production upon inanimate power sources, or the thoroughgoing commodification of products and wage labour,' the delineation of their modernity is as much about their extent and degree of organisation and coordination as about the fact of their existence.[44] Most tellingly, Giddens's understanding of modernity hangs on what he calls 'time–space distanciation,' that is, the ways in which modern social forms organise larger and larger spans of space and time: nation-states effectively organising surveillance across their whole territories, or capi- talist production operating in a global market. For Giddens, the differ- ences are sizeable *and* they are of size, since what he is interested in is the workings of the sorts of institutions that are capable of disembed- ding themselves from face-to-face interaction to operate on a large scale, and the experience of living in a world organised by them.

This leads Giddens to theorize that '[m]odernity . . . is multidi- mensional on the level of institutions,' and it is capitalism, industrialism, surveillance, and the control of the means of violence that are the 'insti- tutional dimensions of modernity' that he identifies as crucial. In turn, this means focusing down on the nation-state and systematic capitalist production, 'institutions' that, he argues, '[b]oth have their roots in spe- cific characteristics of European history and have few parallels in prior periods or in other cultural settings' and that have 'in close conjunction with one another . . . swept across the world . . . because of the power they have generated.'[45] This concentration on modernity as a singularly Western project; the characteristically careful and systematised symme- try of Giddens's 'institutional dimensions'; his reduction of them back to the classic Marxist and Weberian terrain of capitalism and the na- tion-state; and the schematic nature of the discussions that his theoreti- cal agenda permits, means that the histories and geographies of moder- nity that he produces are hardly complex and contextual ones attentive to difference and contingency.[46] However, he points some way toward an analysis of modernity that combines a concern for institutional and experiential transformations while also recognising the multiplicity of those transformations. He may describe modernity as a 'juggernaut' but, as he notes, '[i]t is not an engine made up of integrated machinery, but one in which there is a tensionful, contradictory, push-and-pull of different influences.'[47] It is certainly worth considering how modernity might be multidimensional in less systematic and schematic ways.

Indeed, others have retained the notion of modernity by treating it, if not exactly theorising it, as a complex multiplicity of institutions, experiences and transformations in an attempt to incorporate both the contingencies of the particular histories and geographies involved and a sense of wider and deeper transformations. For Paul Gilroy, modernity is 'the fatal intermediation of capitalism, industrialisation, and a new concept of political democracy' which he uses to weave the histories and biographies of black writers and activists who were simultaneously inside it and outside.[48] Similarly, Roger Friedland and Deirdre Boden, following Giddens, 'treat modernity simply as the intertwined emergence of capitalism, the bureaucratic nation-states, and industrialism, which, initiating in the West but now operating on a global scale, has also entailed extraordinary transformations of space and time.'[49] More expansively, Barbara Marshall argues that, '[a]gainst the backdrop of the Enlightenment, modernity is associated with the release of the individual from the bonds of tradition, with the progressive differentiation of society, with the emergence of civil society, with political equality, with innovation and change. All of these accomplishments are associated with capitalism, industrialism, secularisation, urbanisation and rationalisation.'[50] Elsewhere, in all sorts of writing on modernity, instances crowd in to realise a multiple modernity that is not readily reducible to any single definition, or even set of definitions. Understandings of pornography, identity, city life and exhibitions, as well as more overtly theoretical accounts, insist that modernity is made of complex conjunctions of, among other things, commodification, print culture, public spheres, scientific rationalities, gender differentiation, surveillance and fashion.[51] By crowding in processes, institutions and experiences, they all undermine any simple totalisation and seek to retain a notion of modernity as useful for understanding a whole series of different histories and geographies. Each of these accounts suggests differences, changes and transformations that cannot be reduced to questions of discourse and meaning (although these undoubtedly play a key part), but that are material alterations of lives, geographies and histories identified, in various ways, as 'modern.'

Again the question has to be raised of whether totalising conceptions of modernity can be undermined without abandoning the concept itself. Is it possible and useful to understand modernity as multiple and still retain the term as a meaningful one? Rita Felski has argued that it is. Her first argument is that 'modernity' is a term that 'serves to draw attention to long-term processes of social change, to the multidimensional yet often systematic interconnections between a variety of cultural, political, and economic structures.'[52] As such, it deals directly in multiplicity since what is 'modern' is never a matter of a single dimension—capitalism, bureaucracy, or democracy—and it always opens the question of their connection even if that cannot be ultimately resolved. The danger in the heyday of modernisation theory was that these connections were presented in a celebratory rather than a critical light, and that 'modernity' was understood to be both coherent and to appear, inevitably and everywhere, in the image of the West. Any reworking of the notion of modernity must attend to difference and to the fissures and contradictions which that involves both between and within modernities.[53]

Felski's second argument is that modernity 'refers not simply to a substantive range of sociohistorical phenomena—capitalism, bureaucracy, technological development, and so on—but above all to particular (though often contradictory) experiences of temporality and historical consciousness.'[54] Undoubtedly and unsurprisingly, it is the experience of time that has attracted most attention for theorists of modernity. Indeed, Peter Osborne has posed the problem of modernity with which this chapter deals in exactly those terms, arguing that 'the main difficulty with the concept and the source of its enduring strength . . . [is] its homogenization through abstraction of a form of historical consciousness associated with a variety of socially, politically and culturally heterogeneous processes of change.'[55] As a result, both Osborne and Felski argue that it is in this problematic intersection of institutional change and temporal experience that the value of the concept of 'modernity' lies. The point can, I think, be broadened. As I have argued above, the experience of modernity is not simply the experience of a particular form of temporality or historicity, but the experience of living in worlds organised and transformed by certain, if multiple, sorts of 'institutional' arrangements. These arrangements shape how temporality and historical consciousness are lived, but that does not exhaust the experience of modernity. In particular, this book argues that attention needs to be paid to the experiences of space and to the transformations of spaces, places and landscapes; but it is also the case that the notion of 'modernity' usefully denotes the more general intersection of these material changes and experiences of them. It is, as Berman has it, a matter

of the 'open-ended development of self and society, incessant transformation of the whole inner and outer world.'[56] Inner and outer worlds,
social process and subjective experience, cannot and should not be separable. It is in this vein that Elizabeth Wilson wants to speak of modernity rather than capitalism, since 'the word "modernity" attempts to
capture the essence of both the cultural and the subjective experience
of capitalist society and all its contradictions. It encapsulates the way in
which economic development opens up, yet simultaneously undercuts
the possibility both of individual self-development and of social co-op-
eration.'[57] Modernity, therefore, can draw attention to the inseparability
of the 'structural' and the experiential, emphasising that neither accounts for the shape of 'the modern' alone and that these experiences
are differentiated ones.

To return to Latour, I would argue that a retention of the notion
of modernity on the basis set out above would certainly not insist on a
"Great Divide" between the premodern and the modern either in
terms of scientific rationality or, indeed, any neat periodisation. However, I would argue that there are significant transformations, and while I
emphasize that it is not possible to identify any clear break, I believe
that it is possible to both mark the differences that modernity makes
and to explore those differences in terms of the ways they shape lives,
spaces and times. The argument here is for ways of thinking that enable
discussion of substantive, dramatic, long-term and far-reaching changes
in a whole variety of arenas of life and experience—changes that all
those who use the term 'modernity' are calling to mind, even if they
would not agree with each other if called to make precise definitions of
importance, connection and causation—without losing touch with the
local and specific character of these changes. There needs, therefore, to
be a recognition of the ways in which the multiplicity of modernity is
also a matter of its contextualisation. I want to suggest that one way forward in thinking about these multiple modernities is through contextualising their historical geographies and considering the production of a
variety of 'spaces of modernity.'

REWORKING MODERNITY

If, as Nicholas Rengger suggests, modernity should be understood as a
'constellation'—'a "juxtaposed rather than integrated cluster of changing elements that resist reduction to a common denominator, essential

core or generative first principle"'—then there is no single history and no unitary geography of capitalism realising value, reason disenchanting, the iron cage of bureaucracy dropping down, disciplinary society animating its puppet bodies, or of the advent of individual freedom sowing both liberation and anxiety.[58] Instead there is the possibility of writing many histories and geographies, large and small, all of which can lay claim to versions of modernity's 'complexly multilinear' time and space.[59] In addition, there are different ways in which the writing of these histories and geographies have been begun: through contextualisation, through attention to difference and power, and through understandings of modernity's geographies. I want to learn lessons from each of them.

Contextual Histories of Modernity

The overly schematic 'histories' of modernity that characterise its presentation in much of the philosophical and sociological literature can be contrasted with the contextual history of modernity attempted by Stephen Toulmin.[60] Toulmin's project is still one of philosophical or intellectual history, and therefore somewhat different from many of my own more material and everyday concerns, but his method is interesting. He argues that modernity has two contrasting strands. However, it is the legacy of the 'seventeenth-century pursuit of mathematical exactitude and logical rigor, intellectual certainty and moral purity'—the rationality of Descartes and Newton—that has set the tone rather than the alternative, tolerant, sceptical and humanist strand characteristic of sixteenth-century thinkers such as Erasmus, Shakespeare, Rabelais and Montaigne.[61] His task is, therefore, to provide a contextual history of the triumph of these restricted notions of 'science' and 'reason.' It is, ironically, a contextual history of how rationality became 'decontextualised' though 'four changes of mind—from oral to written, local to general, particular to universal, timely to timeless.'[62] His method, therefore, is to take what are all too often seen as transcendent features of modernity—certain forms of rationality and the geometric world of universal laws that they conjure—and to contextualise them in order to render them partial and contingent.

In caricature, Toulmin's argument is that clarity and absolute 'geometrical certainty' appealed to Europeans in the aftermath of the carnage and uncertainty of the Thirty Years' War. He argues that the '"Quest for Certainty" was no mere proposal to construct abstract and timeless intellectual schemas, dreamed up as objects of pure, detached intellectual study. Instead, it was a timely response to a specific historical challenge—the political, social and theological chaos embodied in the Thirty Years' War.' There was no place for scepticism, rhetoric, and, in particular, context in a search for absolute answers through a process that attempted 'to "purify" the operations of human reason, by decontextualising them.' Yet, recontextualising these processes himself, Toulmin argues that they should be understood in terms of the relationships both between nation-states—where his example is Leibnitz's work toward a universal language—and within them—where he examines the political ontology of Newtonian principles of 'stability' and 'hierarchy.'[63] Toulmin shares with Latour, and many other historians of science, the desire to show that 'Western rationality' is contextual too. However, he does so in ways that also retain a place for the 'newness' and specificity of forms of rationality and politics that can be thought of as 'modern.'[64]

Toulmin, I argue, offers a way into dealing with modernity by writing contextualised histories of it. While the form of this in *Cosmopolis* remains problematically androcentric and Eurocentric, he does offer the possibility of multiple contextual histories of modernity that take grand historical and theoretical themes and ground them in the dirty work of society, politics and culture. The challenge here lies in moving from the realm of philosophical statements to the more messy ground of histories and geographies. It means trying to situate modernity in its particular transformations and locations, undermining totalisations without underestimating the degree of change. Others who have begun to do this have shown, in a variety of ways, that it means thinking carefully about difference.

Difference, Power and Modernity

Those who have attended to questions of gender and race have argued that the experience of modernity is not a unitary one, and that any totality is, at least, a fractured and fissured one. Paul Gilroy, writing against the tendency to homogenise and sanitise modernity's histories through the presentation of unexamined and homogenous categories such as 'the modern self' or 'the modern city,' asserts that '[t]he possibility that the modern subject may be located in historically specific and unavoidably complex configurations of individualisation and embodiment— black and white, male and female, lord and bondsman—is not entertained.' He argues that the suggestion 'that an all-encompassing modernity affects everyone in a uniform and essentially similar way . . . runs contrary to my own concern with the variations and discontinuities in modern experience and with the decentred and inescapably plural nature of modern subjectivity and identity.'[65] Admitting these issues raises questions of 'difference'—Whose experiences are being discussed? Whose modernity is this?—and questions of power that would put the 'Enlightened' science in scientific racism and racial terror under question and would use the histories of plantation slavery to force a reassessment of accounts of capitalism, bureaucracy and industrialisation.[66] Similarly, feminist scholars have shown how understanding modernity in explicitly gendered terms changes the basis on which we understand it, and challenges theories of it to get to grips with both difference and the implicit but unrecognised genderings that have structured social theory.[67] This is a matter of exploring how notions of modernity are themselves saturated with the metaphorics of gender and how gender shapes 'distinctive feminine encounters with various facets of the modern,' while also recognising 'the multiplicity and diversity of women's relations to historical processes.'[68] Power and difference structure the institutions and experiences of modernity so that while attention must be paid to 'assessing the differing, uneven, and often contradictory impact of such processes on particular social groups,' these histories are not somehow separate from the main event.[69] These are the histories of modernity.

These authors have, therefore, begun to differentiate modernity and to rework it in terms of issues of difference, power and position. They have shown the usefulness of thinking through notions of modernity—and there are substantial differences between the ways in which they conceptualise it—while questioning and fragmenting it in various ways. In part, doing so has meant dealing with histories of modernity somewhat similar to Toulmin's in order to remobilise conceptual categories. As Barbara Marshall argues:

> I have emphasized the need to historicize, to make gender visible, the dualistic categories which underlie theories of modernity—public/private, individual/society, family/economy. Once historicized in this fashion, they appear not as ossified structures, but as shifting and fluid mechanisms of regulating identities—to make legitimate the public expression of some identities, but to exclude others. I have also suggested that we need to take up the question of the subject, and in particular, gendered subjects, as a crucial level of analysis.[70]

Similarly, Gilroy and Felski's contextualised histories reveal different 'countercultures of modernity' that, as positioned simultaneously 'inside' and 'outside' modernity, offer renewed perspectives on it.[71] Significantly, these histories of power, difference and modernity are often prosecuted through a rethinking of its geographies.

Paul Gilroy's rewriting of the histories of modernity in terms of 'people in but not necessarily of the modern, western world' suggests their 'double consciousness'—resulting in action to make modernity live up to its promises of democracy, equality and liberation and attempts to reveal its contradictions and fissures—and prompts a reworking of the geographies of modernity. Instead of a single and expanding global modernity, or of nationally bounded modernities, or even a punctiform set of urban modernities, Gilroy—influenced in part by maritime histories of the eighteenth century—offers 'the rhizomatic, fractal structure of the transcultural, international formation I call the black Atlantic.'[72] This complex geography of fracture and connection suggests a way of conceptualising modernity in terms of power and difference. He himself uses it to trace a complex historical geography of race politics that relates both ambitious modern projects of emancipation and renewal and a scepticism about modern promises and hopes.

Griselda Pollock also fractures the homogenous geography of modernity to discuss the gendered politics of Parisian modernism. She argues that modernity's spaces and sites are differently experienced and differently represented by men and women as well as being structured by class. Through a discussion of Manet and Degas's representations of theatres, parks, cafes, folies and brothels, she argues that these 'spaces of modernity are where class and gender interface in critical ways, in that they are the spaces of sexual exchange.' Thus, women painters like Cassatt and Morisot operated in and through a different but intersecting set of spaces. This is not simply to argue that understanding gender means seeing Paris as a city of separate spaces, separate spheres and separate modernities, but that 'the social process defined by the term modernity was experienced spatially in terms of access to the spectacular city which was open to a class and gender-specific gaze.'[73] Modernity's spaces are spaces of power and difference. Indeed, similar concerns have structured other discussions of the gendering of the *flâneur* and of urban space more generally. Here a concern with 'the historical and the local' is used to demonstrate the 'unreflective, malestream construction' of 'dominant theoretical accounts of space, modernity and the urban' and to open the possibility of beginning to tell 'other stories of modernity.'[74] Each of these investigations of power and difference recomposes the geographies of modernity in different ways, and suggests that attention to space is necessary alongside the more conventional concern for time.[75]

Geographies of Modernity

New geographies of modernity have, therefore, been important in efforts to rethink it in terms of power, identity and difference. In what follows I want to suggest that there are three further ways in which attention to modernity's geographies offers alternative ways of understanding it: through investigating the forms in which the spatial is written into theories of modernity; by acknowledging the ways in which there are different modernities in different places; and by conceptualising modernity as a matter of the hybrid relationships and connections between places. Together these continue to challenge the idea of a singular and totalised modernity without denying the relevance of it as a concept. In doing so, they offer, through attention to the multiple processes of the production of modern space, ways of attending to the intricate, deep-rooted and widespread changes that modernity has brought. This concern for the production of space serves to introduce the contextualised historical geographies of spaces of modernity for which I want to argue.

An attention to space has already been shown for Paul Gilroy and Griselda Pollock. It is also true of Marshall Berman's endeavours to understand attempts 'to create a totally modernized space' that combines the disorientations of the urban transformations that he chronicles and 'the ways [in which modern people] . . . act and interact in these spaces in the attempt to make themselves at home.'[76] Moreover, in the sociological formulations of Anthony Giddens, Zygmunt Bauman and Peter Wagner the spatial relations of modernity are crucial to understanding its characteristics.[77] Giddens, as I argued above, devotes much attention to the ways in which time–space distantiation—the disembedding of institutions and their 'stretching' across space and time—means that 'the very tissue of spatial experience alters, conjuring proximity and distance in ways that have few close parallels in prior ages.'[78] He is, therefore, concerned with the distinctive geographies of 'modern' institutions. For example, his discussion of the modern state offers a sense of the specificity of the ways in which surveillance is ordered across space:

[T]he concentrated focusing of surveillance as 'governmental' power is largely, if not completely, a phenomenon of the modern state. As such, it

is inherently involved in the capability of the state to co-ordinate its administrative scope in a precise fashion with the bounds of a clearly delim-
ited territory. All states have a territorial aspect to them but, prior to the
advent of the nation-state, it is unusual for the administrative power of
the state apparatus to coincide with defined territorial boundaries. In the
era dominated by the nation-state, however, this has become virtually
universal.[79]

For Giddens, modernity has a new geography bound up, in this case,
with the spatial organisation of surveillance. For him, only modern
states 'govern' in the sense of maintaining 'regularised administration of
the overall territory claimed as its own.'[80]

Zygmunt Bauman's 'geographies' are less concrete and more elusive. On the one hand, in Bauman's view, modern life is dis-placed—it is
'an in-between life: in between in space, in between in time, in between
all fixed moments and settled places that, thanks to their fixity, boast an
address, a date or a proper name.'[81] On the other hand, his concern is
with the intersection of knowledge and power in the modern state's attempts to impose order on this lack of fixity. This is understood in
terms of the centralisation and monopolisation of power, 'the social
production of distance' that dulls 'moral inhibitions' in the exercise of
that power, and 'the urgency and ferocity of the boundary-drawing and
boundary-defining drive' that guarantees control.[82] This distinctively
modern insistence on classification and order renders modernity 'an era
of particularly bitter and relentless war against ambivalence' as boundaries and classifications are devised and imposed.[83] The language of order that Bauman finds at the heart of modernity is a spatial one. Indeed,
in all of these cases modernity is spatialised in different ways, from Anthony Giddens's attention to territory to Paul Gilroy's concern with
fractal fragmentation. In doing so, it is argued that the geographies of
modernity are a crucial part of how the specific nature of its processes
are conceptualised.

However, this attention to the spatiality of modernity's processes
needs to be combined with an attention to different modernities in different places, that is, with the ways in which modernities are shaped by
context. This is suggested in Marshall Berman's explorations of the experience of modernity in the literature of three cities. However, as
Derek Gregory argues, he does not quite succeed since '[f]or all his finely textured portraits of particular cities (Paris, St. Petersburg, New
York), Berman uses them as a kind of spatial palette from which to
compose an undifferentiated, almost timeless representation of moder-

nity . . . more or less indifferent to spatio–temporal context.'[84] This
problem is also only partially addressed by the global histories and sociologies of modernity often associated with forms of modernisation
theory. These attend to how different responses in different societies
and cultures to a seemingly unitary, and generally Western, set of
processes 'have engendered a wide variety of modern or modernizing
societies.'[85] While such an approach allows for some sorts of comparative historical geographies of modernity, they only operate on national
or international scales and generally treat modernity as an external
force. So while paying due attention to 'national modernities' is useful,
particularly given the role of nation-states in shaping space, it is clear
that modernising processes cannot be captured within such a limited
geographical frame.[86] In part, this is to argue for very localised geographies of modernity, and for the sorts of 'local modernities' and 'place-
specific experiences of modernity' explored by Pred and Watts.[87] Yet it
is also to think about the ways in which modernity has both created
and confounded spatial scales. It has to be understood as transforming
the intimate geographies of everyday life and animating grand transformations on a national or global scale at the same time, bringing different
spatialities and temporalities together in previously unlikely juxtaposi-
tions. Doing so emphasises the multiplicity of modernities and shows
that they are shaped by context in more than just the ways in which local particularities deflect universalised processes in different directions.
This means that processes like individualisation, commodification and
bureaucratisation need to be examined in the particular places and
spaces that they make and that make them. It also means that this will
be a matter of contextual and geographical histories of a multiplicity of
modernities that cannot remain at any single scale as local, regional, national and global relations are combined and recombined.

Modernity's geographies are not, therefore, place-specific in any
singular sense. These differentiated geographies are made in the relationships *between* places and *across* spaces. Again, this has tended to be
understood as the 'exportation' of modernity from centre to periphery,
both for metropole and empire and for city and country. This conceptualisation, however, ignores the crucial ways in which these geographies of connection are moments in the making of modernities rather
than being matters of their transfer or imposition. As Peter Osborne argues, it was 'the spatial unification of the globe through European colo-
nialism [that was] . . . the geopolitical condition for the development of
the concept of modernity: the marker not just of a new historical present, but a new temporalisation of history itself.'[88] Modernity, as a mode

of understanding history, was and is a way of making powerful differentiations between localities, regions, nations and vast areas of the globe. Notions of the modern and the primitive, traditional or backward were ways in which these encounters and differentiations were justified and dramatised, ways in which connections were minimised in favour of emphasising the gap that existed and had to be crossed between 'rationality' and 'irrationality' or between 'democracy' and 'despotism.' Such notions of modernity describe a geography of purity rather than of hybridity, one where there are no rural or non-Western modernities, and where modernity is a pristine metropolitan invention for good or ill.[89] Questioning that assumption means seeing modernities as made within the relationships and connections between places, and understanding them as producing material transformations in the places and spaces that they connect and create. The modern world is a hybrid and cosmopolitan one forged from a multiplicity of flows and networks of people, material objects and ideas, and their power-laden and inventive conjunctions and transformations in the places they circulate through and between. In the chapters that follow, commodification is understood as inseparable from new, often global, geographies of trade that create problematically hybrid people and places; states and bureaucracies, as they are formed, are seen to connect together urban, rural and imperial spaces into vast and complex networks; and processes of individualisation are contextualised within the making of mercantile empires.

Together with the possibilities for contextualised histories and an attention to difference and power, this attention to the geographies of modernity begins to offer ways in which it can be understood through accounts of the varied spaces that it makes and within which modernity is constituted. Attempting to write contextualised historical geographies of various 'spaces of modernity' certainly offers a sense of the multiplicity of modernities. There are, quite simply, a series of 'multiple and contradictory' spaces and places at all scales and taking many different forms: imagined geographies, territorialisations, networks, or hybridisations that combine the local and the global.[90] It also offers a sense of the partiality of modernity that concentrates attention on the contours of geographies that are shaped in specific ways by particular intersections of people, processes and practices. There is no singular definition of modernity's geography. However, this does not mean denying that there are important material changes to practices, institutions and experiences. Studying these geographies of modernity means being attentive to the ways in which they are produced. It means being concerned about their conditions of emergence and existence, and about the social relations through which they are constituted, while retaining a sense of the abstracted processes—such as commodification and bureaucratisation—of which they are a part.

In some ways this attention to the production of these spaces of modernity has affinities with Henri Lefebvre's notions of the production of space which also explore how commodification and bureaucratisation produce geographies. It cannot, however, be collapsed onto Lefebvre's delineation of the making of 'abstract space.' On the one hand, Lefebvre's version is too narrow where the production of space is primarily interpreted in terms of capitalism.[91] On the other hand, while the processes of abstraction that he details connect with interpretations of modernity—particularly those organised around the distanced gaze and geometrical rationalities—Lefebvre's notion of abstract space is simply too broad to capture the differentiated and contextualised geographies of modernity's spaces that are argued for here. Each of these spaces needs careful investigation to understand its contours and conditions of existence. However, Lefebvre is surely right when he says that 'social space, and especially urban space, emerged in all its diversity— and with a structure far more reminiscent of flaky *mille-feuille* pastry than of the homogeneous and isotropic space of classical (Euclidean/Cartesian) mathematics.'[92] What is needed are investigations of this combination of varied, multiform and hybrid spaces rather than the assumption that modernity's geography is simply a planned, rational and panoptic space.[93]

There are, therefore, many ways in which modernity's spaces are produced, and each of these processes of production and emergence warrant investigation as a way into modernity's material and symbolic transformations. Many more geographies could be written of the re-makings of spaces, places and landscapes, from the local to the global, that are consequent on capitalism's convulsive circuits. There are also more accounts to be constructed of the experience of modernity and modernism in the streets, built environments and representations of a wider range of cities than has yet been considered. More attention should also be paid to the constitution of modern 'publics' and to the new forms of politics and culture that they encourage. Elsewhere, the work of charting the making of rational grids of power and knowledge, and the networks through which they can be imposed, has only just begun and needs to be continued in mapping exploration, imperialism, science and state formation from the minute spaces of the laboratory to the carving up of the globe.[94] Indeed, both the ordered geographies of rationality and the more febrile geographies of commodification and commerce find a place in the chapters that follow. Together they sketch out a historical geography of modernity that deals with the conditions of production of closely defined private territories, ordered public spaces, unstable worlds of fantasy and imagination, and widespread networks of people, power and information. Each traces a different story of the production of space in modernity, yet they all acknowledge that what is being written are 'local' and contextualised historical geographies, and perhaps—as Stephen Toulmin, Paul Gilroy, or Griselda Pollock might argue—that that was what was always being written even when accounts of modernity were being presented in their grandest guise. These contextual accounts of identity, power and the production of space are rooted both in theoretical claims about modernity and in the details of the transformation and reshaping of lives, practices and places in, in this case, eighteenth-century London.

EIGHTEENTH-CENTURY MODERNITIES

Debating modernity in the eighteenth century disturbs many of its conventional periodisations. This is not the modernity of late-nineteenth- and early-twentieth-century Paris, Vienna or Stockholm, where modernity and modernism mingle in a heady brew of social, spatial and artistic disruptions and recompositions, and where whole social formations seem to be remodeled as modern from top to bottom in manifold ways by the cultural forces of the market and the machine.[95] However, it does repeat other periodisations. An eighteenth-century modernity might well be the modernity of Enlightenment rationalism: of the discoverers, classifiers and encyclopedists whose universalisation and systematisation of knowledge is taken as both modernity's greatest danger and as a project to be reformulated and continued.[96] What I want to do here is to tread a path between them by emphasising, as suggested above, the variety of eighteenth-century modernities that cannot simply be contained by singular notions of the Enlightenment, even though they may contain and extend some of its notions of rationality, knowledge and power. In doing so, I will argue that investigating modernity in the eighteenth century, and the eighteenth century in terms of modernity, helps us to better understand both. I also want to insist again that these questions concerning historical periods and periodisations involve considerations of the geographies of modernity.

In many ways the debate over the history of eighteenth-century

Britain has been staged in terms of the emergence of modernity. For Plumb, the century was characterised by enclosures, roads, canals, newspapers and commercial entertainments, all 'vital and very visible changes, all novel, all speaking of modernity.'[97] It was a century dominated by the 'idea of progress,' the superiority of the 'moderns' over the 'ancients,' which engendered a 'broad spirit of improvement, openness to change, and excitement about innovation as Britain entered, indeed created, the modern world.'[98] Plumb, therefore, connects these changes of mind—movements away from the 'Providence-dominated world of early modern and medieval Europe'—to science, rationality and the commercial and industrial revolutions:

> During the eighteenth century extraordinary economic and social changes swept through Britain and brought into being the first society dedicated to ever-expanding consumption based on industrial production. For this to succeed required men and women to believe in growth, in change, in modernity; to believe that the future was bright, far brighter than the past; to believe, also, that what was new was desirable, whether it was the cut of a dress, the ascent of a balloon, or a new variety of auricula.[99]

Yet this identification of the eighteenth century as 'essentially modern'—as composed of commerce, rationality, innovation, and the questioning of traditional authorities and established religions—has been challenged by Jonathan Clark, who casts the period 1688 to 1832 as England's ancien regime, sturdy and stable on three cornerstones: 'monarchy, aristocracy, Church.'[100] Clark's complaint is against reductionist and teleological histories of the eighteenth century that ignore or caricature religion and politics in favour of notions of economic change (or industrial revolution) and class conflict. Clark criticizes histories that, in setting 'bourgeois modernity' against aristocratic reaction, mean that '[t]he "eighteenth century" is consequently coupled to an industrial–democratic engine of change and drawn off into "the future."'[101]

Clark's attempt to rewrite this period's history in the colours of patriarchalism and deference, politics and religion, have prompted a strong reaction. This has come from those who would seek to catch him out by understanding aristocratic agrarian capitalism, and its enclosures and 'improvements,' as the apotheosis of eighteenth-century modernity, aided and abetted, rather than hindered, by archaic state forms and paternalist ideologies.[102] It has also come from those who would, albeit in different ways, temper the strength of the contrasts

drawn between 'ancien regime' and 'modern world,' and who argue that
singular claims to encompass whole periods under the blankets of either
tradition or modernity are hard ones to sustain.[103] As Peter Mathias
once put it, working with a rather different sense of the 'modern,'

> When did the eighteenth-century world die? When does modern histo-
> ry begin? The economic historian might prefer to give the evasive an-
> swer, 'at different times in different places.'[104]

It might even be preferable to say 'at different times *and* in different
places.' The need to choose between either modernity or its opposite
seems to rest on the sorts of assumptions about totalising theories that
have been subject to scrutiny in the earlier parts of this chapter. These,
as histories, become locked into singular claims about whole periods
and delineations of 'hegemonic' structures of social and cultural power,
rather than thinking about social or geographical difference.[105] Indeed,
where these histories argue from is crucial. Grounding arguments in
north or south; city, town or country; Parliament or manufactory;
counting house, clerk's desk or church pulpit, is to make particular arguments about the period and to play others down. '[T]here was,' as
Linda Colley stresses in reviewing its historiography, 'more than one
eighteenth-century Britain.'[106]

There are, therefore, histories that explore how the eighteenth
century 'presented a mix of traditional and modern features,' and attempt to depict its diversities and contradictions.[107] Both Roy Porter
and Paul Langford have provided detailed and wide-ranging explorations of the entanglements of commerce and politeness, oligarchic
politics and landed property, religion and science, and individualism and
deference. Both stress the widespread and dramatic social changes in
English society and the stability of a 'fundamental configuration of
power and politics [that] was inegalitarian, hierarchical, male dominated, heritable, and reverential and referential to the past.'[108] For Porter,
during the eighteenth century Britain became the foremost capitalist
society in Europe, but was still, in terms of power and politics, conduct-
ing 'business as usual.'[109] There are, therefore, attempts to check the assumption that 'tradition' and 'modernity' can be simply identified and
their opposition used as historical explanation. For example, Tom
Keymer has explored the very different responses of Smollett and Defoe
to commercial modernity in Scotland; John Money has sensitively interrogated the ways in which 'old' ideas may be learned and circulated
in 'modern' ways and applied in 'modern' situations; and, finally, Roy

Porter has suggested that the ideological cohesion and imperial military strength that underpinned oligarchic power may have been maintained through new technologies and new forms of bureaucratisation and pro-fessionalisation.[110]

All of this opens up room for an investigation of eighteenth-cen-tury modernities that stresses their multiplicity and recognises both their importance and, at the same time, their partiality and specificity. It is clear, however, that, on this basis, this book cannot claim to offer a historical geography of eighteenth-century Britain. It should also be clear that this is not an argument that claims that the 'origins'—if such things can ever be found—of modernity are in eighteenth-century London. What it does claim is that, because of the historical debates outlined above, the eighteenth century provides a terrain that demands that modernity be carefully theorised if it is to be part of explanations of this complex historical geography. Moreover, this book claims that rethinking modernity along these lines helps reinterpret the ways in which eighteenth-century Britain is not simply part of an 'old' world or the herald of a 'new' one. In these ways, and by working through ac-counts of eighteenth-century modernities, I hope to begin to address what Lynn Hunt calls one of 'the "classic" historical questions'—'why and how does the eighteenth century lay the foundations for moderni-ty in its various aspects?'[111]

One of the few historians of eighteenth-century Britain who has tried to retheorise the concept of modernity is Kathleen Wilson. She argues that the problems in doing so revolve around avoiding totalisa-tions that produce ahistorical accounts:

> Among more positivistic social scientists and historians, for example, modernity has been conceived as the story of 'modernization'—the structures and texture of 'modern' life: urbanization, industrialization, de-mocratization; bureaucracy, scientism and technology. Although heuristi-cally useful in sketching in some fundamental shifts in Western culture, the 'modernity as modernization' perspective is a conceptual dead end for historians less interested in structural determinacy than in the specific meanings, ambiguities, and significance of a period's configurations.[112]

Yet this does not mean rejecting the concept. Wilson argues that, in-stead of a checklist of 'modern structures,' the textures of modern life and 'the notion of modernity' can be conceptualised 'as an unfolding set of relationships—cognitive, social, and intellectual as well as economic and technological—which, however valued or construed, are seen as producing the modern self and its expectations of perfection or progress.'[113] This integration of experience and modernity's institutional structures is given a critical twist by poststructural and postmodern readings of the legacies of eighteenth-century forms of knowledge and power. There is, she argues, the possibility of theorising modernity in more sensitive ways:

> [M]odernity need not be seen as *one* particular moment, whose 'origins' and characteristics can be identified with certainty and mapped onto a specific temporality between the sixteenth and twentieth centuries. . . . Modernity in this sense is not one moment or age, but a set of relations that are constantly being made and remade, contested and reconfigured, that nonetheless produce among their contemporaneous witnesses the conviction of historical *difference*. Such conceptualisation opens up whole new grounds for theorizing and understanding our histories without denying the specificity of a period's configurations or reducing the eighteenth century to the status of the great primordial swamp of a more 'modern' world.[114]

There is much here that chimes with what has already been said in this chapter about theorising modernity: a sense of the utility for contextual accounts of a term often associated with grand philosophical or sociological debates; a concentration on understanding the connections between institutions (or structures) and the experiences of modernity; a concern to write critical accounts of modernity without reducing it to a unitary caricature. Yet for Wilson these concerns are all historical ones. What is at issue is the specificity and complexity of a period of time, and finding ways of not reducing that span of years to a unitary story of progress, stability or decline. This is undoubtedly an important issue, but another implication of these arguments is that if what is important is 'stressing the complexity, heterogeneity, and hybridity of modernity at the moments of its various historical articulations,' then this must be done by being attentive to its geographies, to what I have called the 'spaces of modernity.'[115]

Returning to the ways in which the modernity of the eighteenth century is often constructed around the Enlightenment can illustrate these points. Recent scholarship has begun to argue that there are many histories of the Enlightenment that might be written, to the extent that 'The Enlightenment' should become 'Enlightenments.'[116] In part this pluralisation comes from a recognition of the many geographies of Enlightened knowledges: the different ways in which they were involved in the complexities of colonial encounters; different national trajectories; and the specificity of the sites—including museums, laboratories and botanical gardens—for the production and transfer of knowledge. Yet it is also about the partiality of Enlightenment knowledges. They only traveled in certain circuits among certain people and for certain purposes. They were also in circulation with, alongside and against other, often seemingly incompatible, knowledges that might nonetheless find easy or uneasy reconciliations in minds both polite and the popular.[117] And if this was a geography of production, circulation and negotiation, it was also a matter of the spaces figured within the forms of knowledge themselves. For example, Barbara Maria Stafford has staged a history of eighteenth-century knowledges that contrasts the 'radical linear emptiness' and 'violent intellectual simplification' of the Enlightenment epistemologies of schematisation, codification, classification and quantification—an essentially geometrical world—with the 'extravagant chromatic complexity' and intricate geographies of coexisting polyphonic, Epicurean and libertine—even rococo and romantic—epistemologies.[118] Understanding these Enlightenments means showing how these various geographies of knowledge intersect to produce a complex, heterogeneous and hybrid modernity whose investigation is as much about tracing geographies as about problematising social structures and periodisations.

The task, therefore, is to begin to draw out maps of these differentiated geographies of modernity. This is not done to somehow finally chart modernity, since its historical geography will always be an unfinished project. The aim is to detail a complex, heterogeneous and hybrid modernity sensitive to the intricacies of its eighteenth-century articulations by showing how its multiple, overlapping and contradictory spaces—Lefebvre's *mille feuille*—are constituted. This will rework modernity in terms of its eighteenth-century context, and the eighteenth century in terms of a more sensitive conceptualisation of modernity.

Accounts of these spaces—or constructions of these 'maps,' of eighteenth-century modernities—must, therefore, be attentive to the specificity of the period's configurations. They must be contextualised. Yet, in many ways, the spaces that are considered here—the prostitutes' penitentiary, the newly paved street, the pleasure garden, the bureaucratic network, and the Universal Register Office's web of commercial transactions—have been chosen precisely because they fit somewhat uneasily into their supposed 'contexts.' The variegated terrains of modernity in eighteenth-century Britain mean that these spaces are ones that stand out as different. Through their geographies they signaled, both for contemporaries and for later interpreters, what Wilson calls 'the conviction of historical *difference*.'[119] They were, in short, something new. They were part of the reason why 'foreigners came to England to see Modernity,' and this raises the question of what contexts they should be considered in relation to.[120] In part, the context must be the tensions around uneven processes like commercialisation or state formation and the ways in which they reshaped relations of class and gender. It is also the case, however, that these spaces are always part of the ways in which modernity is a 'project,' albeit a complex and hetero-geneous one.

As a 'project' modernity is less a realised set of relationships, insti-tutions and experiences than a series of claims and attempts to make and remake the future.[121] It judges the future as something that is to be constructed by setting itself in opposition to 'the divinely ordained world,' one 'that just *was*—without ever thinking how to make itself to be.'[122] Read in this way the 'spaces of modernity' considered here might be seen as anachronisms: spaces that were self-consciously novel, spaces that didn't fit, spaces that sought to constitute a different future. Just as modernity involves a transformation of space, these were its spaces of transformation, spaces where change was possible and desirable. It is, therefore, a matter of constructing contextual historical geographies of anachronistic spaces. As Allan Pred says of the three exhibitions he chronicles, 'Each of these spaces was a crucible in which the new crys-tallized out of the ongoing.'[123]

LOCATING MODERNITY

The case that I have made for understanding the geographies of moder-nity is partly about locating modernity and understanding it through its spaces and places, but it is not a matter of mapping and fixing the loca-tions of modernity once and for all. Like its chronologies, modernity's geographies are shifting ones and, as I have emphasised above, they are also geographies that stress the hybrid connections between places and spaces as well as grounding institutions, experiences and practices in particular locations. They are the points where arguments begin rather than where they end. So, why begin with eighteenth-century London and, more specifically, why interrogate the Magdalen Hospital, the street, Vauxhall Gardens, the Excise and the Universal Register Office?

It is appropriate to start with the whole city. Figure 1 shows Lon-don in the late 1740s.[124] It was drawn from a survey started in 1737 by

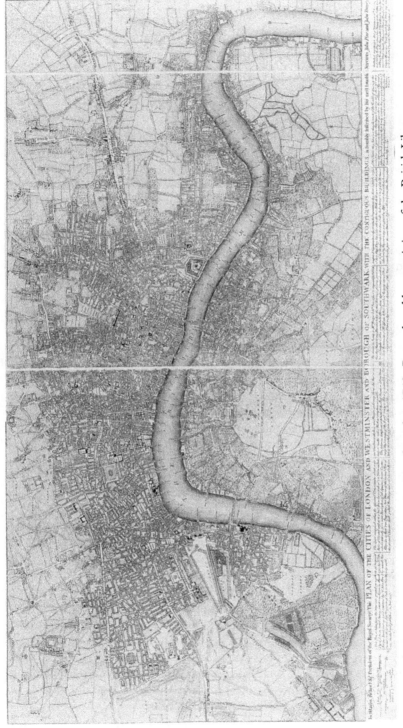

Figure 1 Rocque's Map of London, 1740s. Reproduced by permission of the British Library.

John Rocque, and originally published in 1746 as twenty-four imperial sheets. These were to be put together to make a final map that was thirteen feet wide, and six and a half feet deep, and sold for eight guineas. At a scale of 200 feet to the inch, with an alphabetical index of streets and significant buildings, and based on the first systematic survey of London since William Morgan's in 1682, it must have come as a revelation to the public to see the mid-eighteenth-century city displayed all at once and in so much detail. What is shown here is one of the cheaper, smaller editions that attempted to retain the accuracy of the survey while sacrificing some of its clarity. As well as allowing an understanding of the geography of the city as a whole, within which the development of London and the spaces dealt with in subsequent chapters can be located, Rocque's map can itself be situated in terms of the production of the spaces of modernity.

The map was produced within the period 1660 to 1760 that saw 'independent English schools of artists, engravers and cartographers, superseding those of the Netherlands.'[125] It was part of the changes in printing and publishing identified by John Brewer as crucial to the making of English culture in the eighteenth century as books, images and performances were produced for a commercial market and a wide public rather than under the narrow auspices of court and church (see Chapter 4).[126] Its surveyor exemplifies these changes. John Rocque was a Huegenot emigré who cut his teeth as a *desinateur de jardins,* surveying the royal and aristocratic gardens around London. However, despite the support of Frederick, Prince of Wales, and the Duke of Cumberland, his map of London was not to be a courtly commission. Pursued in conjunction with the engraver John Pine, a governor of the Foundling Hospital and a friend of William Hogarth, and the successful printmaker John Tinney, who put up the money needed to get the survey finished, it was more akin to his later work as a print and map seller. It was a scheme that offered itself to a broad public. Financial and practical support came from the lord mayor, Sir Richard Hoare, and from the court of aldermen; the survey's methods were complimented in print by two distinguished members of the Royal Society; and the majority of the funding came from four hundred subscribers, including Horace Walpole, Hans Sloane and the Duke of Richmond, as well as government offices (including the Excise Office), academic institutions and City companies. Financing such an enterprise by subscription, thought impossible by William Maitland in the 1730s, had become possible by the 1740s and, as Brewer notes, marked the transformation from the personal patron who commissioned and controlled cultural production to the production of texts and images for a market within which each subscriber was 'one of its consumers, a conspicuously identified member of the reading public.'[127]

Its origins are observable in the form and content of Rocque's map. Its design, and this is even more evident in the large-scale version, intended a stern practicality. It was an imaging of the city without artifice or interpretation that we may also trace in the work of Defoe. As Max Byrd has argued, Defoe's presentation of the city in his novels and other writings was produced for men of business and, as a result, London 'emerges as curiously featureless, as a collection of names—of streets, buildings, squares—but not as a realised picture.' And while Rocque's map of this busy commercial city does conjure a picture of the whole, it also replicates Defoe's writings in that 'in the end London exists for us only as a network of traffic, a gigantic system for comings and goings: . . . an "abstract civic space."'[128] That this map was a representation of London as a city born of the connections between commerce and liberty is as evident in the mapping of the streets in Figure 1 as it is on the original version in terms of the allegorical figures of Plenty, Liberty and Global Commerce that framed the cartouche and the merchant ships depicted riding at anchor on the Thames.[129]

In keeping with this mercantile and civic practicality, Rocque and Pine stressed the practical intentions of the project. They showed that these pointed in two directions since the map was to be 'a sure Guide to the Street-Traveller, and an accurate Scale to the political Calculator.'[130] The first, which they also linked to the precise establishment of parish and property boundaries, was met by the intricacy of the detail, the accuracy of the survey (both in terms of the measurements and the trigonometric calculations necessary to combine them), and the care with which place-names had been ascertained.[131] The second—by which they meant to provide the means for comparing the extent of London to other contemporary cities, particularly Paris, as part of the political arithmetic of national wealth and power (see Chapter 5)—demanded an overview of the whole city. As such, and in its concentration on the connections between liberty, commerce and mercantile power, this map takes its place within the array of works of history, literature and art that attempted to depict the character of the city. Within this context, Rocque's map offers a positive and optimistic view of London's prosperous modernity.[132]

However, the conjoint demands of both accurate detail and a complete overview rendered the map so large as to be useless for all but a limited set of purposes. It certainly could not be used for getting around the city; and only those with sufficient money, space and interest to be able to follow the recommendation to set it up on a roller that could be let down from the wainscot by a pulley, could study the whole in all its glory.[133] Roque's map, therefore, while offering a vision of the whole city, also usefully demonstrates the partiality of that overview. It is a reminder that understanding London as a single entity is important, but that it gives only one view of a heterogenous city that can be seen in very different ways from different locations. Moreover, it was a view that was produced under certain conditions. As a commercial enterprise for a broad public, it mobilised the claims of science and technology in its favour and sought to facilitate trade, travel and the claims of political arithmetic. Thus, although it represents all of London, it only offers a partial view of a place that had a variety of other geographies. It is in this way that Rocque's map can provide a guide to understanding the city's modernity.

Taken as a whole, the city that Rocque surveyed could be said to offer itself as a hinge to the modern world. It became, as his comparisons showed, Europe's largest city at midcentury and, fed by migration and trade, retained that position into the nineteenth century. For E. A. Wrigley, its huge market and 'rational' rather than 'traditional' ways of life and thought provided one of the key motors propelling the economy into the industrial revolution and society into modernity.[134] In a rather different theoretical language, Peter Linebaugh describes London as the 'world centre of the modes of production' that organised labour and capital across the globe from the 1690s. In its docks, streets and buildings were brought together the produce and the workers of the world.[135] Yet there are problems in simply locating modernity in the big cities of the 'West,' in London, Paris and Berlin. As I have argued above, the West's modernities are entangled with those of other places and other people through trade, imperialism and slavery. Accounts of these modernities cannot be histories and geographies of pristine origins and subsequent global exportation. Also, modernity is not simply a matter for city people. Town, village and countryside—and again the scope is global—have their modernities—agrarian transformations, 'improvements' and utopian visions—that are often connected to those of cities near and far but are not limited by them.[136] Thus any understanding of London's modernities must be one that appreciates both the particularities of location and the connections to other spaces and other places. Indeed, the accounts presented in the following chapters soon spill out of the conventional boundaries of the city: the solitary cell of the penitent prostitute cannot be understood outside the exigencies of global trade; the bureaucratic spaces and routines of excise taxation in the capital need to be understood in terms of a national system of rules, regulations and practices that were anchored in the countryside's market towns and were dedicated to gathering funds for worldwide wars; and the pleasures and dangers of Vauxhall Gardens are shown to involve spectacles of empire and its spoils. Modernity was not simply born in London, but London was transformed by modernity as its positions in the regional, national and global geographies that tied it in various ways to other places were reconfigured.

In many ways London was made important by these reconfigurations.[137] The long eighteenth century 'proved epochal for London.' It was the period when 'London became the wonder city.'[138] In 1500 the city's population was about 50,000. It was about a third the size of Paris or Naples and not even one of the twenty largest European cities. Its most dramatic population increases brought it to a population of 400,000 by 1650 and, although its growth then slowed, it was, at 575,000 people, as large as Paris by 1700. During the eighteenth century London continued to grow—to 900,000 by 1801—becoming during that century the largest city in Western Europe, almost twice the size of Paris. In global terms only Edo, Peking and Constantinople were larger. What was different about London was not simply its absolute size. In 1750 11% of England's population lived in London. This compared with the 2.5% of the French population who lived in Paris, a figure that had not changed since 1650 when London already contained 7% of England's people. It was far larger than the next largest towns in the urban hierarchy and, although this primacy decreased during the century, it has been estimated that around one in six people in England had experienced living in London.[139]

London was central in many ways, built as it was upon national politics and overseas trade: '[I]t was not only the seat of government in England, and the chief residence of the court: it was also the head of an expanding overseas empire; an international port and finance centre; an immense market and centre for inland trade; the location for a number of substantial manufacturing industries; and a social resort with a winter season of much magnificence.'[140] Its flourishing artistic and literary life drew in talents looking for a national stage. It had more doctors and lawyers than the rest of the country put together. Its banking and finance houses brought with them an army of factors, jobbers and brokers. Its expanding governmental, business and legal machines 'churned out more and more paper' and gave employment to an expanding lower middle class who lived by the pen and benefited from England's exceptional economic and political centralisation.[141] Its shopkeepers stocked their new windows with an expanding array of goods for increasingly fashion-conscious consumers. Many of these goods were shipped into the city by the sailors who inhabited the riverside parishes when not traveling the world, and were moved by the army of porters who made a living fetching and carrying bales, bundles and boxes. It was also Europe's biggest industrial city, based on an economy primarily made up of small workshops driven by the hand not by the machine, and shaken by periodic slumps and depressions caused by weather, war and the London Season. While the basic structures of this economy were not fundamentally transformed until the 1860s, neither did they stay entirely still. Services became more prominent; guilds, apprenticeships and the small workshops were weakened by subdivision of the production process; and, as Peter Linebaugh has argued, many, and often the poorest, bore the brunt of reconfigurations of the capital–labour relation that sought to sweep away customary perquisites and practices in favour of the money wage whose compulsions were backed by Tyburn's gallows.[142] If London was 'above all a metropolis of merchandise' at the heart of a world of goods, this had different implications for different people.[143] There were livings, good and bad, to be made by the light-fingered as well as the nimble-fingered, and the quick-witted as well as the well-connected.

The shape of London also changed in ways that are visible on Rocque's map. It was, as Dorothy George had it, 'growing more rapidly in bricks and mortar then in population as people left the crowded lanes of the City for the newer parts of the town.'[144] Most growth was north of the river, with the south only being opened up by the new bridges at Westminster (shown on Figure 1 even though it was not opened until 1750) and Blackfriars (1769). As the city grew, the social differences between west and east which had first appeared in the sixteenth century widened and gave London a new geography which set out in parks and squares, and courts and alleys, the vast differences in wealth that the city contained. The West End—serving court and Parliament, and increasingly becoming the home of City merchants too—was 'an innovation in urban living.'[145] Its squares began to give the metropolis a new texture that 'in a hundred years . . . wrapped all London in a net of pavements and covered hundreds of acres of meadow and marsh.'[146] This shape and texture was produced without any of the overall planning that defined the absolutist capitals of Paris and Berlin. Instead, it proceeded in waves of building activity stirred and halted by economic fluctuations and the fortunes of war. It was a landscape produced in an unstable financial environment by aristocratic landowners and speculative builders eager for profit. It was shaped by old landholding patterns, new leasing arrangements, and men like Nicholas Barbon whose buildings were a testament to standardisation, mass production and an eye for the market. There was little place for great public buildings in the built environment of these 'propertied patricians.'[147] Instead, public spaces were made and animated by a culture of sociability driven by the commercialisation of leisure:

> Georgian public life increasingly revolved around the town itself, its streets, public spaces, and entertainments. For citizens and visitors alike the urban environment, enhanced by commercial facilities like taverns, shops and pleasure gardens, set the scene for passing the time: sauntering, shopping, sitting, strutting, staring.[148]

Elsewhere, however, life was different. The poorest areas north and east of the City were densely populated, dirty and dangerous. People were crowded into poorly built and decaying houses in a labyrinthine cluster of courts and alleys that covered any spare ground behind the main streets. Short leases and the absence of guild restrictions meant that foreign immigrants crowded into areas like Spitalfields, while the dominance of the docks and wharves in the east's riverside parishes made them into a separate urban world, as well as one of the places where the world entered London. For much of the eighteenth century London's mortality rates were much higher than those in the rest of the country. Deaths outpaced births, and the city only grew through a continual inflow of migrants. Chances were worst for infants, immigrants and the inhabitants of these poor areas, and the situation only began to improve after 1780.[149] If Dorothy George is right that the history of London life in the eighteenth century was one of 'a gradually improving state of things,' then this improvement was experienced very differently in different quarters.[150]

London was also changed in ways not so readily seen on Rocque's map. It had an increasingly global reach. Merchants based in London sent ships and their sailors round the world to complete transactions that would bind City financiers to slave traders, plantation owners and thousands of consumers across the Atlantic world (see Chapter 6). Political decisions made in London also prompted battles, the redrawing of maps of colonial possessions, and power-laden negotiations on the other side of the world. The docks and the government buildings are there on the map of the city, but they cannot easily show the depth of transformation that Britain's commercial empire brought. As James Walvin has argued, the imperial combination of power, profit and tropical staples such as tea, coffee, sugar and tobacco wrought transformations in the spaces of production, distribution and consumption: by spreading plantations across Europe's empires, by opening up not only trade routes but also shops where before there had only been fairs and higglers, and by reworking the social relations of tea tables and coffeehouses in ways that defined new modes of masculinity and femininity and new notions of Britishness.[151] These transformations connected the global and the intimate, reshaping spaces and lives in ways not easily captured on Pine's engraved city. Together with the regional and national geographies that London animated as a political capital and economic powerhouse, and that also shaped its spaces at all scales, these changes point toward geographies that must be traced with the help of other sorts of 'maps.'

London—transformed in the eighteenth century by commerce, capital and fashion, as well as by charity and, in some more limited ways, by the state—was a fractured and heterogenous city. While it was reshaped by the forces of modernity, this was never anything like a wholesale transformation. Again, therefore, there is a place for a differentiated historical geography of modernity here. Indeed, it is important that such multiple histories and partial geographies of modernity are written for those places that are otherwise too easily assumed to be central to these processes and whose modernity is in danger of being taken as somehow unproblematic. I want, therefore, to set alongside the projects of those who have questioned the centrality and singularity of urban, Western modernities a series of historical geographies of one such context that is attentive to the multiplicity, partiality and hybridity of its modernities.

I have attempted to do this by discussing in detail in the five chapters that follow the historical geographies of some of eighteenth-century London's 'spaces of modernity.' My account is far from exhaustive. There are other histories and geographies of these spaces, as well as many other spaces and places that could have been considered. There is little here about production, residential spaces and the family, and there perhaps should have been more that would have made London's global role much more explicit. What I have tried to do is to provide accounts of the production of a variety of spaces that reveal the different conditions within which they emerged and the ways in which they crystallised, albeit in different ways, processes and transformations that marked them and, in some ways, London as 'modern.' As such, these are all transformative spaces that are part of the 'project' of modernity. In Chapter 2 the rationales for and regimes of the Magdalen Hospital for penitent prostitutes, particularly the disciplinary discourse of solitude and self-reflection within a separate cell, are considered in relation to individualisation and modern forms of reflexive subjectivity. Chapter 3 explores the newly paved and lit streets of Westminster through debates over the making of new public spheres that investigate how they were structured and disrupted by the tensions between public and private; and Chapter 4 understands Vauxhall Gardens's pleasures as part of processes of commodification that reveal them to be a problematic and hybrid space where identities became confused. In contrast, Chapter 5 offers an account of attempts to produce stability and certainty through a consideration of the rationalised and routinised spaces and practices of excise taxation in terms of the formation of modern states. That this in-volved the careful management of information across spaces beyond that of the city itself provides a connection to Chapter 6, where the Universal Register Office, a place where all commodities and services could be exchanged, is worked through as part of modernity's transfor-mations of time, space and social relations.

Each of these studies is an essay on an aspect of modernity that grounds it in the production of a particular geography, whether this is a bounded space, an imagined landscape, or a far-flung network. The danger is, of course, that the different processes through which 'mod-ern' spaces are produced may come to be seen as somehow separate from each other. The benefit is that each process can be grounded in a particular history and geography that situates modernity in context, dis-cussing it without denying the specificity of period or place. This means that the spaces discussed are very particular to eighteenth-centu-ry London. They do not necessarily herald dramatic transformations or mark the start of linear histories. They cannot be projected into the fu-ture to find the nineteenth century or any later modernity, and they may not be found elsewhere in the same forms. I have interrogated spaces around which modernity's reconfigurations of the world can best be interpreted for London in the eighteenth century. Spaces like the Magdalen Hospital, Vauxhall Gardens, or the Universal Register Office have little resonance for later periods or for other places, although I would argue that the processes that animated them and that were con-stituted through them do. It is also the specificity of these spaces that has governed the temporal limits set for this book. I have moved back as far as the 1680s only in order to understand the geographies of taxation and, while most of the transformations that I deal with cluster around midcentury, I have taken 1780 as a convenient cutoff point that marks the differences that the 1790s made to many of the processes discussed.

What, then, does this add up to? It certainly cannot be a full account of the eighteenth century, nor even of eighteenth-century London. The aim is much more specific than that. Each chapter develops arguments about aspects of modernity—about the contradictory nature of modern subjectivity, or about the pleasures and dangers, hopes and fears, attendant upon commodification or time–space distanciation— that might stand on their own and contribute to a range of interdisciplinary debates. Taken together, they aim to provide a sense of the variegated topography of modernity in eighteenth-century London. Its transformations were crucial in shaping lives, but they were always partial, working in different ways in different places, sometimes affecting many people, sometimes only a few. Inasmuch as this presents a 'map' of parts of eighteenth-century London, it also continues the task of rethinking modernity. This task is one that involves understanding the ways in which lives, institutions, experiences and geographies were transformed, but it also involves fracturing modernity as a totality by contextualising it in terms of specific histories and geographies. In short, I want to use eighteenth-century London to speak to these wider questions without losing sight of the historical geographies of the city itself. This dual aim is a problematic one. No doubt those who like their theory neat and tidy will feel that the attempt to write about modernity has been hamstrung by the attention to the contingencies and specifics of geographies and histories large and small. Others will feel that history (or historical geography) should not be written this way, and that the attempt to relate the details of some London lives and local geographies is damaged by attempts to understand them with as nebulous a constellation of ideas as those around 'modernity.' In answer I would offer a reminder that writing about the past and offering theoretical accounts of social relations are only separable in debates that reify 'History' and 'Theory.' I would also offer the hope that I have trodden a path that uses often abstract theories of modernity to interrogate quite particular spaces and contexts, and that allows these detailed cases to readdress 'grand' theoretical issues. I am not convinced that there is any other way in which historical geographies of modernity can be written.

CHAPTER TWO

The Magdalen Hospital

INTRODUCTION: MODERNITY AND IDENTITY

The modern self seems to wear two faces: the first presents willed individuality, controlled autonomy and reasoned self-development; the second presents rootlessness, fracturing and constant transformation. 'Ultimately,' writes Peter Wagner, 'modernity is about the increase of individualism and individuality' since '[m]odern discourse constructed the human being as capable of teleological action, controlling his [*sic*] body and nature . . . as autonomous towards his fellow human beings' and as responsible for 'his' own fate.[1] Modernity brings with it 'a conception of the individual as the ultimate source and container of social power.' These 'isolated, self-centred individual[s]' are locked into bodies that have a distinct singularity since within 'the "new bodily canon" of rationalist ideology, the body is rendered impermeable, "merely one body; no signs of duality have been left. It is self-sufficient and speaks in its name alone. All that happens within it concerns it alone, that is, only the individual, closed sphere."'[2] Some of the histories and geographies of this subject and of this body have been traced by Michel Foucault, Norbert Elias and Donna Haraway, all of whom understand it in relation to modern configurations of power and knowledge, but it is also central to the parallel modern histories of capitalism and Marxism.[3] Marshall Berman tells us that through 'the desire for *development*'— which merges both economic development and self-development into a single project—the 'psychic gain and growth' and freedom of action of each self-made individual becomes a central theme of both modern capitalism and Marx's thoroughly modern social theory.[4] Here, as else-where, the account of this figure is both a celebration of its power and freedom and a critique of its limitations. Likewise, Stephen Toulmin urges us to free ourselves from the 'prison walls of Descartes' solipsistic Mind,' and Peter Wagner shows us the 'cold universe' that these mascu-line monads inhabit, a world where the promise of individual liberty comes at the expense of treating others in objective and instrumental ways.[5]

There is, however, a parallel discussion of modernity—the one that presents its second face—which reminds us that, for good or ill, this 'self' is a project that is never realised, and that the processes of its con-struction bring their own threats and dangers. Here the modern self cannot be stable, it must be fluid. Berman argues that '[i]n order for people, whatever their class, to survive in modern society, their person-alities must take on the fluid and open form of this society.' They must yearn for change and the transformation of themselves and their world.[6] On this reading, 'the modern self' is never finally *made,* it is in-stead always undergoing the volatility of transformation. Part of this volatility is the realisation that selves that are made can also be unmade, and moreover that there is no sound basis for choosing the models ac-cording to which they are constructed.[7] This, for Bauman, means that 'the modern human condition' combines 'homelessness, rootlessness and the necessity of self-construction.'[8] Modernity displaces identity:

> All individuals are displaced, and displaced permanently, existentially— wherever they find themselves at the moment and whatever they may happen to do. They are *strangers* everywhere and, their efforts to the con-trary notwithstanding, at all places. There is no single place in society at which they are truly at home and which can bestow upon them a natur-al identity. Individual identity becomes therefore something to be yet at-tained (and presumably to be created) by the individual involved and never securely and definitively possessed—as it is constantly challenged and must be ever anew negotiated.[9]

This displacement—a product of modernity's global upheavals and its remakings of economies, polities, societies and cultures—has long been associated with the modern metropolis, and has not infrequently been diagnosed as an urban condition.[10] For Georg Simmel, writing in and of the early twentieth century, 'the deepest problems of modern life' are associated with 'the attempt of the individual to maintain the independence and individuality of his [*sic*] existence' against the fracturing and hardening of life by the division of labour and monetary exchange and the metropolis's 'rapid telescoping of changing images.'[11] Modern selves are in danger of dissolution.

Taking these two versions of the self together means that understanding the subjectivities associated with modernity means understanding them as self-constructions in a rapidly changing world. This, in turn, means thinking about them in terms of a series of oppositions: unification and fragmentation, power and powerlessness, rationality and confusion.[12] In this chapter I want to explore an episode in the history and geography of these subjectivities in order to show how specific versions of the self and particular techniques of self-construction arise in response to peculiarly modern threats, dangers and promises. This, however, must be carried out in the context of how the histories of eighteenth-century subjectivities have been written.

Debates over changing understandings of selves and identities have an important place in interpretations of eighteenth-century England. This is particularly clear in discussions that have used notions of 'individualism' to connect the economics, politics and culture of the period in the portrayal of an 'atomized and individualized society,'[13] or to assert the rise of 'affective individualism' and its transformation of familial social relations, at least among certain classes.[14] More generally, Colin Campbell argues that the eighteenth century saw the extensive spread of a new understanding of the self as a 'psychic inner world' containing 'the power of agency and emotion' and subject to 'willed control.' The 'growth of self-consciousness' that this change prompted was, he says, 'a uniquely modern ability.'[15]

There are, however, others who would deny individualism—or, more specifically, 'bourgeois individualism'—any place in the history of the eighteenth century. Jonathan Clark, as I have shown in the previous chapter, 'argue[s] against the familiar picture of eighteenth-century England as the era of bourgeois individualism' and for an 'ancien regime' society and culture organised in terms of a hegemonic aristocratic patriarchalism until at least 1832. His main aim is to deny the significance of Lockeian notions of understanding and property and to refute the interpretation 'that society as a whole is aptly seen through the categories of utilitarian psychology and contract theory.'[16] Another challenge to understanding the English eighteenth century in terms of individualism has been mounted by Alan Macfarlane, who claims that we may push the 'origins' of 'English individualism' so far back into the distant past as to refute any transformation in its nature at any time from the fourteenth century onward.[17]

Instead of arguing for or against wholesale definitions of societies, cultures and periods as 'individualist' or not, I want to stress two rather different issues: space and gender. Both raise questions of difference that these broader arguments inevitably tend to deny. First, selves and subjectivities have geographies as well as histories. Space, place and landscape have a role in the formation of subjects and the consequent variation in the nature of their subjectivities.[18] Part of this concern with geography must be a concern for the specific sites in which subjects are formed. Hence part of the argument of this chapter is that investigations of modern subjectivities should involve understanding the geographies of modernity within which they are shaped. Indeed, this work has already been begun by John Bender in his immensely suggestive *Imagining the Penitentiary* on which many of the themes and arguments of this chapter depend. Bender discusses the development of reflexive and narrativised selves in relation to the spaces and powers of the modern city, the planned disciplinary spaces of the late-eighteenth-century prison, and, most importantly, their earlier realisations in the fictions of Defoe, Gay and Fielding.[19] I want to extend this discussion by thinking through some of the antecedents to the penitentiaries of the 1780s on which Bender concentrates and the earlier historical geography of the idea of 'solitude in imprisonment' that is so central to his analysis.[20] In part, this means understanding some of the spaces and subjectivities that were thrown up within the experience of the modern metropolis. It also means thinking about gender.

That 'modern' subjectivities, like all subjectivities, are gendered is clear. Making connections between masculinity, rationality and the notion of the unitary self is now commonplace, and the genderings of the fragmented, metropolitan self have also been explored.[21] Perhaps more intriguing is Nancy Armstrong's claim that 'the modern individual was first and foremost a woman.'[22] She makes this claim within an interpretation of the forging of modern forms of self-consciousness in the novel and their interiorisation in terms of sensibility and sexuality as part of the development of new forms of class and gender politics. What is doubly interesting here is that her arguments about gender are also arguments about space. According to Armstrong, fiction 'helped to formulate the ordered space we now recognise as the household, made that space totally functional, and used it as the context for representing normal behavior.'[23] Indeed, these connections have also been made by others. While Barker-Benfield disagrees with Armstrong's identification of the first 'moderns,' his concern with the gendering of sensibility and individualism also leads to a consideration of the particular spaces and practices that fostered it:

> Here, behind hardwood 'doors embellished with brass locks,' they [women] dressed themselves, read, and wrote letters in newly private 'closets,' sitting on more comfortable chairs, activities and spaces historians see as the generators of individualism.[24]

These novel practices figured a range of spaces. If they shaped a particular 'inner world' and the domestic space of the houses of the 'middling sort,' they also reached out to connect these women to the wider world through their reading, writing and consuming.[25] Their structuring by class and gender also meant that the forms of identity associated with the privacy and solitude that the 'closet' implied were mobilised across social boundaries in contexts where they eventually became politicised. Armstrong resituates the domestic spaces and identities figured in fiction within 'the middle-class struggle for dominance'; and Barker-Benfield works through their association with sensibility to argue that in the making of gendered identities 'one finds women's [sic] shaping themselves by expressing their own wishes combined with their necessary awareness and internalization of the powerful wishes of men.'[26] What I argue here is that they were also mobilised in attempts to remake the selves of working-class women.

To explore the gendered geographies of modern subjectivity I want to consider a particular institution: the Magdalen Hospital. This was a charitable reformatory for prostitutes which opened on the eastern edge of London in Goodman's Fields, Whitechapel, on 10 August 1758. It was, according to Stanley Nash, 'exemplary of an early stage in the evolution of modern techniques of state authority' in that it anticipated almost all the practices of the penitential prisons of the 1780s.[27] Like them, its regime of strict segregation and a disciplined life of work and prayer was established in opposition to the existing bridewells and houses of correction, which Jonas Hanway—a Russia Company merchant, tireless pamphleteer and philanthropist, and one of the Magdalen's founders—referred to as 'houses of *corruption,* not of *reformation.*'[28] Hanway also differentiated the Magdalen from other earlier disciplinary institutions that might have provided a model, particularly the Amsterdam *Spinhuis.* This was an innovative place of confinement for women established in 1597 alongside the male *Rasphuis* (opened in 1595) and based on religious education and, as the names suggest, hard and compulsory physical labour: the women spun thread and the men sawed Caribbean logwood for dyes. The Spinhuis, which spawned imitators in Gouda (1610), Delft (1628), Schieden (1644) and Middelburg (1642), as well as in Germany and Batavia (1641), held prostitutes, beggars and petty offenders sent there by the courts or, in the case of prostitutes, gathered up during the supervisors' sweeps of inns and taverns.[29] It also held women who had transgressed sexual mores—wives who had committed adultery and uncontrollable daughters—who were incarcerated by the courts or at the request of their husbands or fathers. For foreign visitors, paying to see these women at work was one of the most popular sights of seventeenth-century Amsterdam's golden age.[30]

However, by the 1750s discipline in the Spinhuis had become lax, with one visitor reporting of the inmates that 'it is customary for them to entertain their visitors with such abominable discourses and indecent actions, as are shocking to men of any sense or morality.'[31] Because of this, but mainly because of the practice of allowing visitors to pay to see the women at all, Hanway explicitly rejected the Spinhuis model of the primacy of labour and corporal punishment while learning some useful lessons from it.[32] In this way the making of the Magdalen Hospital was part of the process whereby the 'penitentiary' began the replace the 'house of correction' at the cutting edge of penal practice in eighteenth-century Britain.[33] Indeed, the novelty of the Magdalen was the belief that women's inner lives could be transformed through its new regime.[34] However, as Nash also points out, it did not involve a key feature of the later penitentiaries: the reformative use of solitude via confinement in separate cells.[35] While acknowledging that this was the case, I want to argue that the notions of the self that 'solitude in imprisonment' relied upon were central to the Magdalen's regime, and that it needs to be seen as an important moment in the conjoint historical geographies of the shaping of the modern prison and the making of modern subjectivities. If Jonas Hanway was the originator of the notion of solitude as a reformatory device, then these ideas were first explored within the walls of the Magdalen Hospital in relation to working-class women.[36] Primarily, then, what is interpreted here is the often idealised vision of the Magdalen Hospital presented in the writings of its founders. My aim is not an assessment of the actuality of the institution, but of its contours as a scheme or project.[37]

In dissecting the Magdalen Hospital as a 'space of modernity,' this chapter begins by exploring the ways in which prostitution was understood as a problem in London in the late 1750s. The modernity of this problem and of the proposed solutions to it are then explained in relation to the ways in which the social relations of the modern city were seen to throw the self into danger by removing autonomy and control. The Magdalen regime is then interpreted as a set of carefully calibrated spaces and practices for the remaking of a willed, autonomous self and, in turn, for attempting to counter the problems that this form of self-hood threw up in relation to women. I begin, then, with the flurry of pamphlets on the reformation of prostitutes that led to the foundation of the Magdalen.

THE PROBLEM OF PROSTITUTION

The debate over prostitution that led to the Magdalen's foundation began in 1751 when Robert Dingley, another Russia Company merchant, mentioned an idea for a reformatory to his business associate, Jonas Hanway. At around the same time a letter in the periodical *The Rambler* had also addressed the issue in terms that suggested that it was charity, pity and sympathy that should suggest new solutions. Yet it was only in 1758 that discussion really took off. It was prompted by the Society for the Encouragement of Arts, Science and Commerce, which offered its gold medal for the best plan for a charity 'to receive and employ such common Prostitutes as are desirous to forsake their evil Courses.'[38] Proposals were put forward by several men, including members of the Society itself. Robert Dingley and Jonas Hanway submitted schemes, as did John Fielding—the half brother of Henry Fielding, a Bow Street magistrate from 1754, and later knighted—and Saunders Welch, born of pauper parents and brought up in the workhouse, but later a successful grocer, Henry Fielding's right-hand man as high constable of Holborn, and a magistrate alongside John Fielding from 1755.[39] Their proposals, which wove together in various ways the discourses of political economy and those of sentiment suggested by the letter in *The Rambler,* both included and prompted a range of comments that extended the debate over how the problem of prostitution was to be defined and, if possible, solved.[40]

The arguments put forward stressed the novelty of the problem and, in the case of plans for a reformatory, the 'modernity' of the solution. The new institutional 'experiment' was to mark a break from the institutional solutions of the past.[41] As Hanway said, '[N]o subject has come before us, for a long time, so *new* as this, and yet so *interesting*.'[42] These reformers were responding to new forms of prostitution thrown up in the eighteenth century by changing marriage patterns and rapid

urbanisation.[43] Moreover, the modernity of the issue is also signaled by
the two contexts within which prostitution appeared as a problem in
the 1750s: the regulation of population and the ordering of urban
space. Together these were identified under the heading 'police.' Indeed,
this period was precisely the time when earlier notions of the term 'police' as the good ordering of the capacities of the state were being
joined by new understandings of 'police' as a bureaucratically organised
and state-sanctioned body of officials with a monopoly on finding and
apprehending those who committed crimes.[44] The latter meanings
would ultimately replace the former ones, but both coexisted at midcentury as part of a set of charitable and state-financed practices concerned with ordering space, time, people and activities in forms suitable
to an imperial political economy, a commercial urban society, and the
middling classes that benefited from them. For them, if not for others,
'the prominent and public sexual culture,' including street prostitution,
was a problem, and it was a problem because it raised crucial and connected questions about the bases of social order and individual action.[45]

Prostitution and Population

Eighteenth-century mercantilist imperialism defined political space in
terms of the boundaries of states competing for trade routes and markets. It defined political strength in terms of the ability of those states to
build empires by waging war, and therefore their capacity to produce, to
trade and to raise taxes (for a fuller examination of this see Chapter 5).
In turn, geopolitical power was seen to be dependent upon the quantity, quality and employment of the state's population. Thus, each state's
'policy' was to ensure the maintenance or, if possible, an improvement
in the rate and nature of the production and reproduction of their population. Solutions to the problem of prostitution were understood in
terms of the dangers of 'the want of inhabitants' and 'the properest
means of saving as many lives as possible.'[46] Hanway, while stressing his
religious motivation, pointed out that:

> [P]oliticians should remember, that there was nothing more in view than
> *political* prudence, with regard to the increase of the species, and the good
> order of the state, there is the utmost reason to check this species of iniq-
> uity. For as *matrimony* is the most certain means of augmenting the num-
> ber of the people, and the truest cement of *civil* society, though we can-
> not suppress whoredom, it is surely no small object to *discourage* it.[47]

Proposals for a reformatory should, therefore, be understood within a whole complex of charitable endeavours which, particularly in the 1740s and 1750s, were the British response to these imperial demands.[48] This charitable response was organised through new institutional forms that mirrored successful business practices. It was orchestrated by a well-defined group of mercantile donors, many of whom were connected through the Russia Company, among whom Jonas Hanway was the central figure. Among the 'imperial charities' that they founded were the Foundling Hospital (1740), which saved unwanted babies for the nation; the Lock Hospital (1746), which cured venereal diseases; the Lying-In Hospital (1749) and the Lying-In Charity (1757), which sought to increase the numbers of women and children who survived birth; the Marine Society (1756), which trained poor boys for a life at sea; and the Asylum for the Reception of Orphaned Girls (1759), which sought to prevent girls from becoming prostitutes.[49]

For these philanthropists, prostitution was a problem because of its negative effects on population. Saunders Welch argued that 'those who understand political arithmetic must allow this to be no less a national than a moral evil.'[50] Prostitutes disordered the state and threatened the empire.[51] Robert Dingley wrote that their activity 'diffuses the contagion, even through both sexes, propagating profligacy, and spreading ruin, disease, and death . . . almost through the whole human species.'[52] The issue was, in part, a medical one. Preventing venereal disease would, Hanway suggested, 'save a number of subjects to the state.'[53] Yet this was always understood in moral terms. Welch reported that '[y]outh are debilitated, their constitutions are destroyed, and their morals are corrupted.'[54] These boys would not grow up to be healthy, productive men. More directly, prostitutes did not produce children themselves and they destroyed marriages by 'alienat[ing] the mind from matrimony.'[55] This threat to demographic productivity was matched by a lack of economic productivity. As Marchant asked, '[I]s it not a crime of the blackest Dye, to deprive their Country of the Benefit of their Labours, and them of the Advantage of the Gifts and Talents which God and Nature has so liberally bestowed upon them?'[56] Consequently, each reformatory scheme included some provision for putting the women to what was seen as appropriate work. For Hanway, their efforts in making carpets or weaving for import substitution and export promised 'a great increase in national wealth,' and the plans of Fielding and Massie were entirely based on industry.[57] Fielding proposed 'a public Laundry . . . to reform those Prostitutes whom Necessity has drove into the Streets, and who

are willing to return to Virtue and obtain an honest Livelihood by severe Industry.' His regime of reading, sewing, washing, ironing and religion would make housewives or domestic servants of them.[58] Massie's
proposals aimed to deal with the problem of coordinating London's
large migrant labour supply and its growing economy. He suggested a
new rate to support migrants until they found work. Alongside that he
proposed draconian measures to be used against those who turned to
begging or crime, and a range of charitable institutions—including the
reformatory for prostitutes—to deal with those who could not work.
The reformatory would retrain women for a changing economy, teach
them the harsh lessons of free wage labour, and set them to contributing to a favourable balance of world trade via a carefully calculated intervention in mercantile geopolitics.[59] Whether via demographics or
economics, each proposal was a political intervention, and all the proposers were 'politicians' acting in the state's interest by transforming
these women into 'useful members of society.'[60] This, however, meant
understanding the problem of population at an individual level as well
as at the level of state and empire.

     In general terms, the forms of governance identified as 'police'
were always concerned with individuals. Foucault called these forms
'the new techniques by which the individual could be integrated into
the social entity' and argued that they both produced and governed the
political notion of the individual as a 'live, active and productive man
[sic]' whose way of life could enhance or undermine the strength of the
state. In this way the regulation of 'population' always raised the question of individual practices and capacities, whether they were economic
or, in this case, sexual.[61] In part, this was a matter of distinguishing between productive and unproductive sexual acts. Because 'it remains
largely true that ethico-sexual attitudes in the eighteenth century were
obsessively haunted by the often asserted need for a booming demogra-
phy,' it meant that 'private sexual conduct was held to have a profound
effect on the state of the nation.'[62] As a result, the demographic and
economic arguments set out above were presented within an account of
the 'proper' conduct of the individual that understood sexuality through
a morally charged religious language, and also sought to fix the relationship between 'charity and policy' so as not to promote vice.[63] Significantly, these issues were raised much more forcefully in relation to women.
Women's sexuality—and what they chose to do with it—was understood within political arithmetic as the foundation of national and imperial strength and wealth. Their private activities had public consequences, and therefore had to be regulated:

> *Private vices are public injuries.* This is strongly verified in the *lawless commerce* of the sexes. A general depravity in this instance, would bring on a general confusion: for at the same time we untie the knot of *conjugal love,* we rob the state of its best support and security, and impiously dare to abrogate one of the plainest injunctions of the *divine legislator.* The happiness of society can have no other stable foundation than the *virtue of individuals.* If the whole body were corrupt, the dissolution of it would inevitably ensue.[64]

This explicitly anti-Mandevillean sentiment (see Chapter 3) justified both the regulation of deviant sexualities and the charitable actions and institutions through which they were regulated by tying tight the knot between the desires, needs and actions of individuals and 'the good order of the state.'[65] The concern was with women because they were understood to hold both 'the threat of unregulated sexuality and the promise of maternity.'[66] These concerns with individual vices and social and political order were also present within the other strand of 'police,' the ordering of the city's spaces.

Prostitution and the City

The eighteenth-century transformation of London involved both the disruption of existing social relations and the geographies that went with them, and the making of new relationships and new spaces. The transformation of public spaces and the ordering of the transactions and interactions that went on within them was a matter of 'police' in both the senses outlined above (see Chapters 3 and 6). As imposers of this new urban order, the pamphleteers of the late 1750s saw a disorderly city.[67] Moreover, it was a city where disorder was ordered by class and gender. For example, in 1757–1758 three-quarters of those indicted for vagabondage were women. Prostitutes were a disorderly presence on all counts.[68]

Through his examinination of parish judicial records Anthony Henderson has been able to sketch out the geography of prostitution in eighteenth-century London and to detail the complex negotiations between women, men and officers of the law that defined the social relations of prostitution on the street. There was no strict segregation of street prostitution, but it was concentrated in specific districts: in the east around Smithfield, Whitechapel and Shadwell; in the west around Drury Lane, the Strand and Covent Garden, as well as in the streets around Pall Mall, Haymarket and Piccadilly; and to the south on Tooley

Street and Dover Street in Southwark. These patterns were shaped by the abundant supply of cheap lodging houses and willing clients that these entertainment areas afforded, and the extent of prostitution expanded with the growing city. They were also shaped by the uneven enforcement of the law. There was no explicit legal prohibition of streetwalking, which meant that policing, organised by a variety of fragmented parochial bodies, was left to traditional usage and custom, the discretion of the watchmen and magistrates, and the inevitable informal compromises between the forces of order and those of disorder as they met daily on the streets of the capital. The '[f]lexibility, compromise, and absence of system [that] were almost the defining characteristics of the policing of street prostitution' and the 'very public nature of prostitution in the capital' were the main dimensions of its geography and were the key concerns of the reforming pamphleteers.[69]

This is particularly clear in the writings of the magistrate Saunders Welch. His main objection to prostitution was simply that it was public:

> Prostitutes swarm in the streets of this metropolis to such a degree, and bawdy-houses are kept in such an open and public manner, to the great scandal of our civil polity, that a stranger would think that such practices, instead of being prohibited, had the sanction of the legislature, and that the whole town was one general stew.[70]

Welch and Hanway held prostitutes responsible for subverting the desirable relations of the public sphere. Their 'infamous' behaviour—'a certain *effrontery* in which *modesty* has no *share*'—drove 'modest women' from the streets and debauched youths.[71] Prostitutes also threatened the hierarchies and equalities that the public sphere sought to construct:

> Shall we not become fearful of our own *domestics,* or our *children,* and yet more terrified at the faces of each other, when we meet in the streets or roads, even under a meridian sun?[72]

What mattered about this 'sexual geography' was visibility.[73] For Welch, '[T]here is a wide difference between vice hiding its head and skulking in corners, and vice exposing its face at noon-day.' It was this visibility that corrupted young men 'into whose minds lewdness would not have found its way, had not the temptation been placed in this barefaced manner before their eyes.'[74] Off the streets, prostitution corrupted through its invisibility. Welch and others figured 'bawdyhouses' as particularly problematic sites of disorder. They were where a dark underworld of hidden connections between whores and thieves was forged, and the site of moral transgressions and unwanted transformations where 'the Apprentice and Journeymen first broach their Morals, and are soon taught to change their Fidelity and Integrity for Fraud and Felony; here the Tradesman, overcome with Liquor, is decoyed into a Snare, injurious to his Property, fatal to his Constitution, destructive to his Family, and which frequently puts a Period to his Peace of Mind.'[75]

Welch's response was through the judicial apparatus. That there was '*no police*' was due to ineffective laws that depended upon neighbours' complaints rather than the autonomous actions of the authorities.[76] He suggested making street prostitution a crime, increasing the powers of arrest for constables, and supplementing the powers of justices of the peace by enabling them to suppress bawdy houses, to commit women to his proposed 'Hospital' for a year or more, and to transport to the colonies those who persisted in a life of prostitution. His 'Hospital' would become an adjunct to the courts. Half of it would be an agreeable retreat for voluntary penitents, but the more important half would function as a place of punishment, a reformed bridewell backed by strong legal powers. Moreover, all this would fit within a system of 'police' that sought to put the whole city under surveillance by singling out each individual within it for scrutiny and by documenting their movements. Along with proposing the reorganisation of the lighting and watching of all public streets (see Chapter 3), and suggesting that all migrants be required to have a certificate from their home parish stating personal details, character reference and reasons for migration, Welch argued that '[s]ome method of rendering low mechanics, servants, and labourers in this town, known, would be of the utmost consequences to the good government of it, as by this means it might be ascertained where to find them, and how . . . their time is employed. In a place so extensive, its inhabitants so numerous, various and fluctuating, it seems almost impossible to fix this with any tolerable certainty.' His solution was to divide London into districts of thirty houses. Each district was to be under the care of a 'conservator' who would record everyone's details and amend the files when changes occurred.[77] These proposals would fix every individual, and enclose the city, within a network of writing, policemen and judicial authority.

It was not, however, Welch's version of the policed individual that triumphed. Hanway urged caution in putting too much power in the hands of magistrates and too much faith in the law. New laws might well 'drive prostitutes from the public streets, and remove every dangerous temptation from the unwary youth,' but magistrates could never be the agents of penitence and reformation. Moreover, there was a great danger that new, effective laws would endanger cherished constitutional freedoms.[78] As a result, Hanway understood his project as having 'a quite different œconomy' from that required by 'coercive laws.' For him, 'true politics'—the state's security and the civility of the public sphere—and 'true religion' depended less upon laws and more upon 'the virtue of individuals.'[79] Individuals must choose virtue and liberty rather than have 'morality' forced upon them:

> [T]here are many *inconveniences* that *free-born* subjects will submit to, *of their own choice*, that the notion of *law* would render insupportable. So far as *reason* and *religion* have any power over the *mind*, your good work may be accomplished, without the authority of the *civil magistrate:* and surely no body can pretend to say, it *is not possible* that reason and religion can produce the end proposed. Would *human laws* be of sufficient force, to prevent mankind from degenerating into a species of *unnatural brutes*, were *religion*, and the *persuasive* calls of *humanity*, quite out of the question? . . . A vigorous exercise of power in a legislature, and the *attention* of good magistrates to their duty, do marvellous things, towards the reforming of the *manners* of a people; but the remedy against prostitution is one of those circumstances, which . . . depends so much on the virtue of *individuals*.[80]

Again, the problem of prostitution is understood in terms of the relationship between individual morality and social order. Each depends upon the other. As Markman Ellis and Sarah Lloyd have pointed out, this involved not only paying attention to the political economy of the city, the nation, and the empire, but also refiguring the prostitute as a virtuous woman seduced and coerced into prostitution. As a 'sentimentalised subject,' understood within the discourses of sensibility and seduction, the prostitute became a fit object for charity, and the possibility of her returning to the sort of individual virtue that Hanway stressed was opened.[81]

In short, mid-eighteenth-century prostitution emerged as an issue at the intersection of the problematics of population and urban order. To borrow from Janet Wolff, it can be said that '[m]odernity breeds, or makes visible' the prostitute within the writings of Hanway, Fielding, Welch and Dingley on empire and urbanisation.[82] This meant that the meanings of prostitution and prostitutes were constructed in specific ways, which also shaped the solutions. What mattered at one level was demographic and economic productivity and public order. At another, intimately connected, level, what mattered was 'individual virtue' figured through the discourse of sensibility as the choice of a good life defined by sexual and religious practice. What I want to do next is to explore this idea of 'individual virtue' in terms of how the founders of the Magdalen Hospital understood the characters, actions, rationalities and choices of the women who found themselves within its walls. This involves reading some fiction.

MODERN MORALITY TALES: *THE HISTORIES OF SOME OF THE PENITENTS*

The artful construction of sentimental fictions that took feeling and emotion as a guide to moral action was a crucial weapon in the pamphleteer's armoury and, as such, was part of the making of the Magdalen Hospital and the production of new definitions of prostitution. Hanway asked his readers to imagine the destruction of first a son and then a daughter by prostitution and attempted to orchestrate those readers' emotions as he did so. Other reformers' accounts of how women became prostitutes, and of their subsequent lives, are indistinguishable from novelistic narratives. Moreover, the fictionalised testimony of 'Magdalens' was used to promote the charity by sentimentalising its objects.[83] The examples that I want to concentrate on here are two volumes that appeared in 1759 entitled *The Histories of Some of the Penitents in the Magdalen House, as Supposed to Be Related by Themselves* and a later volume entitled *The Magdalen*.[84] *The Histories* presented four narratives, four 'harlot's progresses' that ended within the walls of the Magdalen Hospital. Like Hogarth's series of pictures, they are part of a new understanding of such lives in terms of a structured 'progress,' and a recognition that this needed to be thought about in terms of choice and constraint.[85] It is how this was conceived that concerns me here.

The author of *The Histories* is unknown. What we do know is that the author was a woman, an acquaintance of Lady Barbara Montagu and Sarah Scott, and that Lady Barbara enlisted the novelist Samuel Richardson to ensure the book's publication. Richardson was already a contributor to the Magdalen Hospital, and he had also been involved in Lady Barbara's other charitable projects including a set of 'educational and amusing' cards 'to teach painlessly geography, chronology, and history.' He was certainly very enthusiastic about the moral value of the stories and showed them to Robert Dingley, by then a member of the Magdalen's governing committee, who reciprocated with some letters he had received from women who had been in the Hospital.[86] Sentimental writings bound the charitable together through the emotions that they provoked.

These 'histories' present themselves as fictions, albeit ones that claim access to harsh realities. The novel form, while appealing to a readership that might be expected to make charitable donations, permitted the exploration of morally ambiguous territory. It allowed a more nuanced discussion of what might happen after 'a fall' than any religious or philanthropic tract could permit.[87] Yet this ambiguity was also potentially threatening, so the Preface, suggested by Richardson, sought to guide readers' interpretations:

> If I may be permitted to be so methodical, upon that species of writing which seems so generally to owe its rise to the wild wanderings of the wildest of things, the imagination; I will venture to give directions for reading of Novels.[88]

It was explained that novels without clear morals 'are certainly very pernicious,' but then announced that these tales were moral fables, fictions to be read for their moral messages: 'Though the facts may be imaginary, the consequences drawn from them may be real.'[89] Indeed, reader and characters were to be bound together through inhabiting the same moral universe:

> We are all prompted by the same motives, all deceived by the same fallacies, all animated by hope, obstructed by danger, entangled by desire, and seduced by pleasure.[90]

This suggests a characteristically tangled relationship between fictions and actions. The stories were intended to prepare the path for charitable giving, but they also shaped conceptions of character and conduct, offering a training in morality through the detailed description of immorality.[91] As Price says, 'Art is imitating life, and life, not quite certain what its models for morality should be, imitates art.'[92] They are, therefore, part of 'the remarkable convergence between novelistic discourse and reformist practice at mid-century,' and can be read for an understanding of the moral world of the Magdalen Hospital as they present tales of characters lost and re-formed.[93]

Lost Selves

In each of the histories the female protagonist is represented as telling her own story. True to their genre, these narratives transparently present as real and immediately available 'thoughts, subjective responses and sensations.' Each of these consciousness-centred novels stages 'the illusion of entry into the consciousness of fictional characters' as if it were 'a full and authentic report of human experience,' and each follows the transformation of a single individual.[94] This is emphasised by the patterning of relationships. Each woman undergoes an early separation from her family. In the first history the mother and father die in the opening chapter and the protagonist has to leave her sister to go into service. In the second the woman elopes and cuts herself off from parental support. In the third history she is adopted. In the fourth she is alienated from her parents when they force her to marry against her will. Throughout the stories the protagonists' relationships with other people are presented as transient and flimsy. The women's sexual relationships with men never last. No close friendships, especially between women, are struck. With only some exceptions (see below), the relationships portrayed are merely instrumental. The one woman-to-woman friendship made (in the fourth history) is with a young girl, but it is facilitated by money and only struck in order to help the protagonist to escape from the house where she is being held captive by her husband. This sense of facing the world alone is further enhanced by the lack of any support from official authority. The law is presented as riddled with corruption, and therefore a hindrance rather than a help. One woman is told that because she has no money 'there is no law for you.'[95] Established religion is absent. In the fourth history the woman is married while she is unconscious. As with Hogarth's progresses, the reader is presented with a representation of 'the social behavior of the isolated self.'[96] Moreover, this is achieved through seemingly direct access to their changing consciousness.

Each of the histories is also presented as a strict chronological sequence. This starkly shows the changes in character, fortunes and circumstances and dramatises the 'progress.' It also relates to the way in which the stories present the morality of choice and compulsion. Can the women be blamed for 'falling'? On the one hand, they are blamed. There are bad mistakes and bad choices—often choices of men—that are made early on, and the consequences of those choices are reaped in the end. As the central character in *The Magdalen* says, 'I have exposed all my crimes and follies, and given a strong proof, how much evil one bad action draws along with it.'[97] Yet things are not quite that simple. The choices made are, in part, excused through the assumed frailties of women in general and, more importantly, the conditions under which these choices are made.[98] Each history shows that after 'the first step into that way of life' a multiplicity of other choices and contingencies crowd in to shape the path taken.[99] The 'wierdly complex plotting' of the histories does not present a road running straight to hell but, in-stead, a picaresque path marked by frequent, and often bizarre and dra-matic, detours.[100] Terry Castle, drawing on the work of Tony Tanner, argues that in many eighteenth-century novels the plot depends upon the central character leaving the father's home and entering the 'pi-caresque' spaces of the Road or of the City, and that the 'narrative ur-gency' of these passages and the 'potentially disruptive or socially unsta-bilized energy' of the characters within them can work to undermine the stated morality of the novel as a whole.[101] Certainly, within *The Histories,* the opportunity is taken to discuss, if not at length, female de-sires and the thrills of dangerous forms of attraction, and to play on the arousal associated with 'virtue in distress.'[102] All of this can be read as potentially destabilising the stories' morality.

These winding routes also serve to set out a litany of forces be-yond the control of the central characters. Men and bawds are scheming against them, and seduction and deception are keys to the 'recurrent sentimental narrative' of the 'fall.'[103] Economic necessity also forces ac-tions that would not otherwise occur. As one women says, '[W]hat lib-erty can a person in the utmost want boast of possessing? Necessity is the worst bondage; it forces our wills, and enslaves our bodies; it obliges us to do things most contrary to our choice.'[104] Unpredictable occur-rences also shape the histories in important ways. Some of these are economic. In the first history the woman's arrest, the collapse of her haberdashery business, and her financial entrapment by a bawd are all the consequence of debts her former lover had amassed without her knowledge. She, like the woman in the second story, is also unable to find work due to the saturation of the labour market.[105] Other occur-rences are seemingly random. Chance encounters stud the narratives, and unforeseen events mean that the stories take dramatic turns. Again, in the second history, the protagonist is robbed by her servant just after she has decided to move to the country to lead a Christian life, and she finds that the only man who can help her has left London. In the fourth history the destitute central figure has just agreed to marry the sea cap-tain who is bringing her back from Gibraltar, where the man she was living with had died, when the ship is attacked by a French man-of-war. Although the battle is won, the ship's captain is killed. Eventually, in one way or another, all other options are closed off until only one is left: prostitution.

Choice, then, is blurred. It is also contextual. The ease with which people can make 'good' choices is dependent on *where* they are making those choices. There are places presented within the narratives that are so ordered that 'good' choices become hard to make and 'bad' choices become rational. In the third history the protagonist comes under the influence of a London bawd who pretends to be her mother. She proceeds, within her bawdy house, to try and persuade her 'daughter' that a particular customer will become her husband and that, according to the 'customs' of the fashionable world, she should sleep with him before marriage.[106] She is only just saved by what is left of her sense of virtue. This critique of higher class moralities is also pursued in the first history, where the central character is in service in the dissipated household of Sir George and Lady Markland and their rakish son. The family play cards on Sundays and avoid worship to the extent that she does 'not know whether the family I lived in was Jew, Mohometan, or Christian.'[107] In this place she gradually discards her own religion and becomes receptive to the advances of the son, who is given free rein by his parents and aided by immoral servants.

In a more general sense it is London—the city—that is the problematic place. In the first history it is the site of the protagonist's fall. In the second it is where the woman elopes to. In the third it is where she is entrapped by a bawd, having made the mistake of assuming that the city was just like her village and thinking that everyone there would know her mother and that no one would deceive her. In the final story London is where the woman goes to hide from her husband when her reputation is finally lost. As she says, 'the busiest place being judged the fittest for concealment,' and, moreover, it was a place where the only thing that mattered was whether you could pay the rent, for 'nothing else in one could merit their attention.'[108] In the city moral choices are problematic.

These women are, therefore, presented, at least in part, as victims of deception, seduction and circumstance. As a consequence they can become the worthy recipients of charity. They are not to blame for 'falling' because life is unpredictable and not amenable to control.[109] More importantly, it is modern, urban life that is unpredictable and uncontrollable. As Ronald Paulson remarks of the first picture in Hogarth's 'Harlot's Progress' series—in which Moll Hackabout arrives in London to be met by indifference from those who could save her and attention from those who seek to deceive her—'how minimal is free will in modern times.'[110] In what is presented as a world of strangers, potential deceivers and unpredictable events, economic and otherwise—a world where the skeins of social relations spin out far beyond the limits of control—notions like 'individual virtue' become deeply problematic and the moral principles on which they are based start to unravel.[111] The solution, as presented in *The Histories* and in the Magdalen Hospital, is a remaking of the individual through a reordering of space.

Remaking Selves

There are other aspects of *The Histories* that speak to this re-forming of selves. Each history is presented as being told by the central character to the other women, who also tell their stories, while sitting together one evening in the Hospital. *The Magdalen* is presented as a women telling her story by letter to her benefactress. In each case the retellings are charged with the intimacy and privacy of these contexts and the privilege of hearing the stories. The Magdalen Hospital's rules forbade 'every kind of discourse that may lead to discoveries which the parties themselves do not chose to make' and, after 1772, each ward had a notice bearing the legend "Tell your story to no one."[112] That the stories fulfill Hanway's injunction that they were to remember the past only to repent of it means that they are shaped by the controlled space of the reformatory rather than by the disorder of the city.[113] The effect of this controlled retelling is to present a reflexive self—a consiousness that is able to observe itself as if from the outside and to judge itself. That this judgment is retrospective is crucial. Each narrator speaks from the position of penitential self-reflection. They are relating their histories in the light of the clear moral vision that comes with repentance. They see themselves anew, and their own stories take on new meaning. For example, in the second story the protagonist recognises her own vain self-deception:

> I . . . felt myself of as great consequence, and with as much reason, as she who with conscious dignity struts about Bedlam with a straw scepter and paper crown, convinced that she is the sovereign of that place.[114]

Yet this moral vision and the self-reflection that it permits is clearly something that springs from the telling, not from the doing. The women are generally represented as presenting themselves as incapable of moral self-reflection at the time of the events narrated. This self-reflection is only present in two ways within the narratives. The first is through the representation of sexual passion as a battle for the self. In the first history the woman relates her feelings as she was about to give in to the Marklands' son:

Sensible of my weakness, and how everyone was combined for my destruction, I had still virtue enough left to wish that I could find some refuge against myself; but I could see none unless I could obtain it of my Lady.[115]

This appeal to the hierarchical relations of age, class and employment fail her, of course, and she succumbs, or, as she puts it, 'My heart took advantage of this opportunity and . . . silenced my reason and my principles.'[116] The fourth history presents the same combination of forces. It also makes the more general point that 'A woman who hopes to preserve her virtue after she has laid aside decorum, is as foolish as a man would be, who should expect to defend a town, whose fortifications and outworks are destroyed, against a powerful enemy; especially if there is treachery within.'[117] Passion and sexuality are pitted against reason in a battle for the self and for self-control. Sexuality is identified as a site where self-reflection is prompted.

The second point where a clear moral vision is evident is in characters who act as the external observers of these women's interior worlds. They do the job of surveillance that should be done by the women themselves, and in doing so they prompt the self-reflection that leads to penitence and to the gates of the Magdalen Hospital. These are the exceptional, noninstrumental relationships that I mentioned earlier.[118] What is important is that these characters are all distillations and representatives of the relations of heterosexual, monogamous and reproductive love, marriage and family.[119] In the last story penitence is prompted by the protagonist's young son's deathbed speech. In the second history Mr Senwill, the woman's former lover, is morally transformed when he realises his duty to his father. He repents and becomes the agent for the 'fallen' woman's repentance. In the first story, the central figure's sister, who is leading an almost blameless life, periodically appears to remind her 'that your present and eternal happiness depend on the proper regulation of your affections.' The sister's penetrating moral gaze becomes so unbearable that the woman says 'I longed to be removed from the eyes I feared.' When they meet again, via a chance encounter thrown up by the city, the protagonist tells of being 'almost suffocated by the struggle in my breast, between the various passions that affected me.'[120] Finally, in the third history, the agent of moral vision is Mrs Lafew. She is the perfect wife in the perfect marriage, sharing 'the pleasures of mutual love.' Her happiness is disrupted by the arrival of the central character (Fanny) as a servant. Fanny has already 'fallen' and soon disrupts the household to such an extent that virtually everyone falls ill. By the time they have been nursed back to health, a process that involves Fanny saving the life of the Lafew's daughter, the husband is in love with her. She is hastily shuttled off to a lovenest, where she falls ill. She is nursed by Mrs Lafew, the woman she has wronged, who also writes love letters for her to Mr Lafew, crying all the time. When asked why she has acted in this way, seemingly so contrary to her own interests, she says she did not want to hurt her husband in any way, and notes that 'I had sometimes been tempted to envy, till I reflected on the greater eligibility of my situation, with mortified affections, disappointed love, but a clear conscience, than that of one, whose pleasures must be embittered with self-reproaches here, and punished with unspeakable torments hereafter.'[121] She has moral self-reflection on her side as well as marriage. Fanny suddenly sees things this way too. Mrs Lafew teaches her religion and repentance and she goes into the Magdalen Hospital while Mr and Mrs Lafew are reunited. The path to penitence is paved with self-reflection.

These moments of penitence, and the self-reflection on which they depend, are represented as a form of exertion of control over the self. In the face of anxieties about a world of chance and risk where the future was both changeable and unpredictable, where social and personal certainties, relationships and identities could be created or eroded without warning, and where individuals' biographies were formed in the infinite, and often anonymous, intersection of people, places, objects and institutions, the response was to look 'inward' toward the government of the self as an arena in which some control could be exerted through self-reflection and discipline. This, however, was not simply a freeing of the individual but was suffused with hierarchical power relations. It also depended upon remaking the self within a new, ordered space that promised to make social relations systematic and predictable, but that also repeated, and in many ways increased, the contextual dependence of self upon environment. With the penitents at the doors of the Magdalen Hospital I want to show how these ways of understanding the subject underpinned the Magdalen's regime and how they shaped its spaces and the lives that were lived within them.

THE MAGDALEN HOSPITAL: ORDER, SELF-REFLECTION AND SOLITUDE

The Magdalen Hospital started in 'a commodious House' between Prescott Street and Chambers Street in Goodman's Fields, Whitechapel, which had previously been used by the London Hospital (see Figure 1).[122] Although only six women were admitted on the first day, there had been 1,500 admissions by 1769. The building offered 'space, air, and privacy, at a moderate expence,' and the experience of the first few years was to be used to show what was needed from a purpose-built structure.[123] Once Blackfriars Bridge had been built in 1769, it allowed the development of parts of Southwark and their full integration into the city. The Magdalen Hospital was to be part of this. The governors took advantage of cheaper land and a new site on the edge of the city to move away from Goodman's Fields—which was becoming hemmed in by buildings and had long been a notorious area for prostitution—and to design and build a much larger new hospital in St George's Fields (see Figures 1 and 2). The inmates and staff moved there in 1772.[124]

From its inception the Magdalen was run as an 'associated' charity by 'men of business, zeal, and piety.' Marking its distance from contemporary penal institutions, it employed a salaried, full-time staff and had a set of formal, written rules.[125] Women were admitted to the Magdalen for a stay of three years and, on leaving, the governors aimed to see them reconciled to their families and friends, entering a good marriage, a trade, or emigrating to America.[126] Between the times of entering and leaving the institution attempted to effect a personal transformation, to build an ordered form of self that was rational and accountable, a self built on self-control. My argument is that the Magdalen was designed to effect this transformation—through regimes of the mind and body that anticipated later penitential prisons in their construction of a disciplined, unitary, solitary and self-reflecting subject—and also to try to constrain it through notions of the gendered relations of rationality, autonomy and accountability. To make this argument I want to interpret another 'fiction,' the frontispiece of Jonas Hanway's *Thoughts on the Plan for a Magdalen House* of 1758 (see Figure 3). Examining this image, and its disposition within a single room of a dietary, a spinning wheel, books, light and a solitary, kneeling woman, will help show what lay within Hanway's scheme to 'rescue their *bodies* and *their souls.*'[127]

A Simple, Regular and Laborious Life

Creating a reformatory space meant separating the women in the institution from the city on whose edge it stood. At Whitechapel the windows overlooking the street were concealed from prying eyes by wooden blinds.[128] At Southwark a boundary wall surrounded the Hospital. Although Massie's proposals for a country site and armed guards were

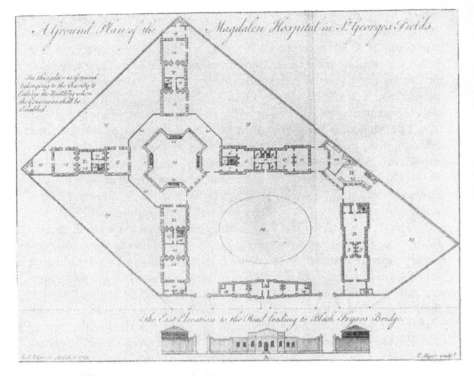

Figure 2 Ground Plan of the Magdalen Hospital, 1769. Reproduced by permission of the British Library.
Key:
A   Offices for male servants
B   Committee rooms
C   Household apartments
D,E, F   Rooms for women (with eating, working, and matron's assistants' [15] rooms on the ground floor and dormitories above)
G   Chapel
H   Washing, baking and laundry

not followed, the boundary was strictly regulated.[129] No letter or message was to pass in or out 'without the Knowledge and Inspection of the Matron,' who was also to hold the keys to the wards.[130] '[N]o-one whatever [was to] be permitted to see, or have any Conversation with them [the women] without a leave first had and sign'd, by the President, or two of the Committee.'[131] The physician, the surgeon, and the apothecary were required to attend the sick themselves in the presence

Figure 3 Frontispiece from Jonas Hanway's *Thoughts on the Plan for a Magdalen House,* 1758. Reproduced by permission of the British Library.

of the matron. Their pupils, apprentices and servants were forbidden access to the wards. The steward, porter and messenger were to have no 'Communication' with the wards, and none of the women were allowed out without special leave in writing signed by the treasurer or chairman and two members of the committee.[132] Everything that crossed the boundary—money, people, information and commodities—was subject to strict accounting procedures.[133]

The day-to-day running and 'good Order' of the Magdalen Hospital was in the hands of a matron. The days were strictly timetabled and this order was mapped out onto a functional space. The new building, which would hold two hundred women, was designed to allow both the clear segregation of activities and their coordination.[134] This can be seen in the centrality of the chapel (crucial for worship and fundraising), the arrangements for supplying the wards with food, and the effective segregation of different classes of women (see Figure 2).[135] This 'superiority or preference of wards' was central to the working of the institution, which classified the women 'according to the appearance, deportment and education of the persons admitted.'[136] While this was in part a matter of social gradation, women were also to be promoted (or demoted) between the wards and to receive a set of rewards 'according to the Progress they made in Reformation.'[137] Women entering the Magdalen were to be kept segregated for a month both to ensure that their penitence was sincere and to evaluate them for assignment to the proper ward. In this way the progressive development of the reformation of character was built into the plan of the institution.

Hanway's frontispiece (Figure 3) presents an imaginary space that did not exist in the institution as it was constructed. Yet the precise orderliness of this plain, sparse, clean room can be read in terms of the institution's intimate ordering of social relations. Hanway sought to counter a general human 'propensity to sensual gratification,' and he argued that '*idleness* and *debauchery*' could be subdued by 'a submission to a regular œconomy' within a '*simple, regular* and *laborious* life.'[138] For him, 'a life of *piety* and *industry*' was 'that kind of life which renders *virtue* most easy to be acquired.'[139] The key to this acquisition was a Lockeian understanding of 'habit':

> *Habit* is the axis on which life turns. To acquire *good habits,* and to correct *bad* ones, is the sum and the amount of life. By habit we act as if we were in *earnest* with *God* and *men;* and by *habit* we become *triflers* in our commerce with heaven and earth. Nay more, by habit we abandon ourselves to the gratification of sense and appetite, and even exceed the bounds

which are prescribed to brutes: and by *habit* we are led to act agreeably to the dignity of our own nature, and to pursue what is fit to be done for the attainment of our proper happiness.[140]

For Hanway, 'these unhappy women are enslaved by their *bad habits*' and could only be freed via the disciplined repetition of 'proper' mental and physical actions that would then become 'both habitual and pleasurable.'[141] As he put it, by 'learning *decency* in their *external behaviour* [they] will become *pure in heart*.'[142] This depended, therefore, on their '*confinement*' within the impermeable boundaries of the institution where all influences could be controlled, and on their submission to the disciplined regime signaled by Figure 3. They would be discharged when 'they shall have acquired such habits as promise fair to secure them from the fatal effects of idleness.'[143]

Food was a key part of the regime. Hanging on the wall of the Magdalen's room (Figure 3) is a 'Table of Diet' which needs to be read as a mechanism for regulating morality and behaviour:

> Our passions and appetites depend much on our *senses*, and our senses depend very much on our *aliment*. She who with *simple plain diet*, without excess in *quantity*, might have continued *chaste*, supposing the temptations equal; with *another kind of diet* may have become a *prey to incontinency*.[144]

The food was to be 'very clean and healthy,' perhaps much the same as Hanway allowed himself.[145] Another vital part of the regime was work. The women were required to undertake the domestic tasks of the Magdalen Hospital. Although they were paid, partly to teach them the lessons of wage labour, and the work was to be improving rather than imposed as hard labour, if they didn't work they didn't eat.[146] This program was underpinned by an understanding of the morality and virtue of work which, through the exercise of their bodies, made those poor people who are compelled to labour happier than the rich. As Hanway put it:

> I cannot too often inculcate this rule, that the *hands* of these women must be employed as well as their *hearts*; for if *piety* is not duly supported, it will lose ground, and will not be able to keep them within bounds. If they were inclosed within walls of brass idleness would corrupt them.[147]

The Magdalen's spinning wheel signals a form of work that was gendered, traditional and individualised. If labour was a lesson, then hard work was a sign of repentance and virtue.[148] However, the disciplines of food and work were not enough to effect reformation. This also required another, less material, range of technologies and geographies of the self.

Reflection, Prayer and the Space of Solitude

The Magdalen Hospital was built upon the belief that change in 'character' was possible. As with the contemporary literature on masturbation, the emphasis was on building 'that degree of self-control which allows it [the self] to function in society.'[149] To achieve this self-control, the old self had first to be cast off. The women who entered the Magdalen Hospital could conceal their identities by using only first names and, where necessary, numbers or newly adopted names. In addition, the uniform of light-grey shalloon gowns, 'as plain and neat as possible,' 'and exactly alike,' aimed at anonymity as well as being a tactic deployed against vanity.[150]

The women also had to be kept under a variety of forms of surveillance. They were watched by the staff. The chaplain submitted a monthly report on each woman. This was set alongside the weekly reports from the matron and her assistants, who also slept in rooms adjacent to each of the wards (see Figure 2).[151] Details of their work and character—'with regard to piety, good manners, and gentleness of disposition'—were to be recorded in a ledger, or 'register,' which would be used to judge their readiness for discharge and would be rewritten as a character reference when they eventually left.[152] They also watched over each other. In each ward it was ordered that 'one shall be Appointed to preside and be accountable for the Conduct and Behaviour of the rest.'[153] These, however, were all supports to the central injunction to 'let your first concern be to watch YOURSELF.'[154]

Hanway believed that all people were constantly in a 'probational state' and that 'Whilst you think in this manner you will take care of your steps, and reflect maturely on what you are to *yourselves,* and to *others,* in the several relations in which you stand, and above all, what it is you owe to HIM, to whom you are indebted to for your very existence.'[155] The Magdalen offered a new home for women 'long accustomed to *banish reflexion*' on the understanding that they were truly penitent and recognised that they were only at the start of a long process of repentance. They had to acknowledge that 'some *time,* and some *reflection* are necessary, to *learn truly how to repent*' and that 'To fly from the *world,* is not to fly from yourself.'[156]

In fact, the case was quite the reverse. In the Magdalen Hospital self-reflection became a way of life:

> To form a true judgement of ourselves, we should constantly attend to the motions of our own hearts, nor even in the intervals between sleeping and waking, should we leave ourselves *unguarded*. There is a *lurking spirit* within us, which is ever watchful of all opportunities, of diverting our thoughts from the true objects of our happiness.[157]

The sense that 'we have enemies, powerful enemies *within,* as well as *without,* to encounter and subdue' was to be permanently installed via the constant injunction that God—the ultimate external observer of the inner self—was watching at all times.[158] That inmates were encouraged to imagine that 'the eye of infinite purity is full upon you' is represented in Figure 3 by the light that illuminates the Magdalen from outside and above her room.[159] This external 'eye' was to be voluntarily internalised:

> Teach me to cast mine eyes *within,* and *examine* my *conscience,* that I may contemplate the *state of my soul,* and meditate on *the life to come!*[160]

The crucial mechanism for this internalisation of self-reflection was prayer.[161] The Magdalen Hospital employed a full-time chaplain who conducted morning and evening prayers and a Sunday service that all the women were required to attend. Indeed, Sundays and holy days were entirely devoted to prayer and the reading of approved moral and religious texts. However, it was a more intimate and private relationship to prayer that was most important. It was understood to operate on the self through language. Using the 'proper words'—saying the right prayers—acted 'as a fortress of the soul.'[162] The open prayer book in the Magdalen's room and the Bible on which it rests signify this relationship (Figure 3). Yet, for Hanway, prayer also worked through the body:

> [A]s the *whole man* consists of *body* and *soul* together, you must *glorify* him in *both;* and, considering their natural union and *sympathy,* you must take such heed to every gesture and posture of your body, as that they will be such as will best express your humility, reverence, and earnestness, and keep up *suitable* thoughts and affections in your soul.[163]

Indeed, if control of the body and appropriate gesture and posture were important for everyone, they were vital in the Magdalen Hospital:

Strict order and *discipline* are, indeed, essential to all undertakings, but more particularly in such as this; and it ought to be presumed, that such as the *deportment* of these women is, in the *public worship of their Maker,* such is their *behaviour* at their *labor,* and at the common refreshments of life.[164]

This attention to gesture, posture and deportment is made clear in Figure 4 where the contrast between past and present, moral and immoral, dissipated and reformed, is dramatised and performed through the women's bodies and dress.[165] It is also present in Figure 3 where the Magdalen adopts the most suitable posture for glorifying God—kneeling—and prays in solitude following Hanway's recommendation 'to *retire* when we *pray*.'[166]

However, the connection between self-reflection, reformation and solitude is not a simple one. As I pointed out above, the space depicted in Hanway's frontispiece is an imaginary one. The women did not each have a separate room for work and prayer, and the penitent in the picture is further mythologised through a form of dress that was certainly not the institutional uniform.[167] Within the wards they were all to have separate beds with a curtain to allow them to create a space for 'private devotion' and to 'promote the greater delicacy of manners' without blocking ventilation or permitting concealment for 'any evil purpose.'[168] Solitude did play a role since solitary confinement for up to twelve hours was used as a punishment and solitary reflection was offered as a reward: 'a small Closet or Apartment is to be provided for the Retirement of the most Serious and best behaved in the Intervals of their Employment, and these also considered the Reward of good Conduct.'[169] Yet, whether there were separate 'cells' or not, I want to claim that the key features of Jonas Hanway's notion of reformative 'solitude in imprisonment'—'precise material circumstances,' the penitential introspection of an 'isolated self-consciousness,' and its re-forming of the self—were present in the Magdalen Hospital.[170] Separate cells were not necessary since each penitent's self was to be, under the conditions Hanway set out, her own separate cell.

It might be objected that the women in the Magdalen Hospital had repented and had entered voluntarily on the course of reformation. Whereas those in prison had to be brought unwillingly to change themselves, the Magdalen did not attempt the 'difficult task' of trying to 'amend the human heart, in opposition to its own inclinations.'[171] Indeed, one of Hanway's later discussions of 'solitude in imprisonment' hinges on a contrast between the iniquities of the imprisonment of women in the Bridewell and the regime in the Magdalen Hospital. In

Figure 4 Frontispiece from Jonas Hanway's *Reflections*, 1761. Reproduced by permission of the British Library.

the former they must be kept separate since solitude is 'the only effectual means of calling forth *reflection,* and preventing *disgrace* and *infamy.*' In
the latter the women can live in wards of twenty or thirty together because they already direct their gazes inward and pose no threat to each
other.[172] Yet the idea of a reformation that springs unbidden from solitude is also present in the Magdalen Hospital. By 1758 Hanway was already arguing that repentance could be taught. *The Histories* suggested
that the regime might perform a more thoroughgoing transformation
than expected and, moreover, under conditions that faithfully foreshad-
owed the penitentiaries of the 1780s:

> [W]hen every distraction from reflexion, and every impediment to con-
> viction, is removed, the whisperings of conscience will be heard, and she,
> whose only design extended no further than the reformation of her con-
> duct, will find her heart amended, and, from a decent behaviour, will pro-
> ceed to purity of mind.[173]

This is what later became expected of the prison: that solitude would
prompt a chain of self-reflection that would lead to reformation at the
same time that regulated and disciplined behaviour shaped moral action. This is also what prompted Jonas Hanway to put more faith in
building prisons than in building churches.[174] Ultimately, the Magdalen
Hospital shows that transformation of the self is a matter of order, discipline, reflection and application rather than 'any wonder-working power.'[175] However, the meanings of these modern selves were always unstable ones.

Rationality, Autonomy and Domesticity

The Magdalen Hospital was a machine for creating selves. The conditions of their production encapsulate the two faces of the modern self
since the Magdalen's regime attempted to deal with the opacity of
those social relations that stretched beyond and threatened to fragment
the self by constructing a space within which an autonomous, self-re-
flexive and individualised subjectivity could be made. This was to be a
self that could make choices, control, project and act. For Hanway, this
moderate, reasoning subjectivity was equally necessary for the governors as for the 'penitents,' and was best developed by the 'more sober
part of mankind of the *middle* stations in life.'[176] There were, however,
problems when it came to women.

Hanway believed that people were free to make choices—indeed, that they had to make them—and that God would judge them on those choices. Since they would be held accountable, everyone 'must learn what it is to act like *accountable* beings!' They must, therefore, make themselves and their worlds so 'that *reason* should prevail over *passion* and *appetite*.'[177] Women were not exempt from this injunction, even if they were 'governed,' as some said, 'only by *fashion* and *caprice*.' For him, 'women are *rational* and accountable, the same as men.' So, like men, they could and should avoid the '*slavery*, and . . . *confinement*' of being ruled by '*violent passions*' through exercising rationality.[178] As he said, 'The mind is . . . only *free*, when its choice is directed by the natural motive of *right reason*, and not by the violent *force* of a *blind* and headstrong *passion*.' This rationality would lead them to '*think* well and act right' since '*reason* declares against everything we believe to be *vicious*,' including a life of prostitution.[179] The women in the Magdalen were, as penitents, to cultivate free and rational selves.

This combination of rationality, accountability, self-possession and solitude would become, in the hands of women like Mary Wollstonecraft—who opposed 'Asylums and Magdalens' on the grounds that 'It is justice not charity, that is wanting in the world'—a powerful part of calls for women's freedoms.[180] Hanway, however, attempted to still any such possibilities by insisting on a strict hierarchy of gender and strong, external codes of moral propriety:

> If *virtue* is the supreme happiness of accountable beings, that state of life which renders virtue the most easy, is the *best*. Therefore if *fear*, and a sense of *shame*, operate as strongly as any other passions, it must follow, that in proportion as *women* are more awed by *fear* and *shame*, than *men*, they are more *happy* than men.[181]

And if fear can be happiness, then subordination can be freedom:

> *Women* are undeniably made as *free* as *men*, though *subordination* is essential to the well being of life. . . . If we allow the *woman* to be as *free* as the *man*, we must adhere to the doctrine of *one to one*, or renounce our superiority over *brutes* in the instance of the continuation of our species.[182]

The price of freedom and rationality was domesticity. The consequences of not locking women into reproductive heterosexual monogamy were 'infinite calamities,' the undermining of 'the best security of the state,' and the unleashing of 'a total subversion of all government.'[183] The personal was certainly political and the cost of a new free and rational selfhood for women was that it could only be exercised within the patriarchal family, 'the source of almost every relation that is dear and sacred.'[184] This, for Hanway, was the only choice that women could 'rationally' make. It was also the model for the Magdalen Hospital. This was to be a caring haven from the world organised as a 'well-regulated private family' with its 'natural Distribution of the Business' between men and women.[185] Indeed, Fielding's plan was to have it run by a group of men calling themselves 'Fathers,' and the matron was seen as 'a good mother to all her little family.'[186] For a woman, entering the Magdalen Hospital was seen to be a 'return to her *obedience* to the *parent of mankind*,' a reconciliation with 'her *natural* father' through the '*power* of religion' and 'the force of *parental love*.'[187] Yet, because this confinement within the family was rationally chosen, it was not to be understood as being limiting. For Hanway these were 'restraints as naturally produce the true and real freedom of the mind.'[188] Like truly modern selves, the 'Magdalens' were to be confined in the name of liberty.[189]

However, as Sarah Lloyd has argued, 'the meanings attached to the penitent prostitute were fundamentally unstable,' and even Hanway's logic could not still them. In part, this was a matter of the detailed attention to the penitents' sexuality and to the processes of passion and seduction that structured the Magdalen Hospital and the attentions of the charitable chapel-goers. In part, it relates to the limitations of a model of penitence that meant that almost half of the women admitted to the Magdalen Hospital in the 1760s were discharged for 'misbehaviour' or as unsuited to hospital life. It was also, however, a matter of 'successful' self-possession and self-control. In discussing the representation of the penitent used by the Magdalen Hospital (Figure 4), Lloyd argues that the woman's gaze disrupts the recommendation by William Dodd, the Magdalen's chaplain, that they adopt 'the humble, meek and downcast look' of the truly penitent. 'Such a direct look,' she notes, 'undermines her neat costume and demure pose. The penitent prostitute was an emblem of the charity's benevolence, and her challenging expression was probably intended to appeal to the philanthropic, but it also recalled the gestures of her disreputable past.'[190] Even more problematic, it was the direct, unswerving gaze of the self-controlled and self-possessed woman that the institution had produced that recalled the autonomy of the prostitute, denied the 'meek and downcast look,' and destabilised the meanings of penitence. All Hanway's domestic ideology could not fix the meanings of the subject that returned the gaze from the pages of his own 'Reflections.'

CONCLUSIONS

The transformations wrought by the Magdalen Hospital were seen as something novel. It was not just that these women's characters could be 're-formed,' but that the institutional structures that dealt with them were too. As the rules stated, 'To consider what they were, and what they now appear to be, a change of manners of this kind is not less *strange* than *new*; and with pleasure we behold an effect which we once thought next to *impossible*.'[191] In this chapter I have interpreted these transformations in terms of a peculiarly modern alchemy of subjectivity: that selves can be made, unmade and remade. Moreover, they are made, unmade and remade in specific spaces. I have tried, therefore, to connect the particular fictionalised spaces of the metropolis and the disciplinary institution's solitary cell—two spaces of modernity—to the making of the contradictory modern subjectivities identified at the outset. This prompts a number of conclusions.

Understanding the notions of the modern self as either a willed, autonomous individual or as a fragmented, fractured and displaced identity or, indeed, both, means interpreting the spaces within which they emerged or were made. It would of course be quite wrong to claim that the Magdalen Hospital was the only site where this happened. However, I have tried to show that it is certainly one site, and one that can lay claim to a significant position in the interconnections within modernity between discipline, solitude, urbanity and subjectivity. Its significance lies, in part, in its anticipation of what would later become more generalised disciplinary techniques and geographies—including the notion of reformation through solitude—that can be shown to both attempt the production of particular forms of subject and to be a response to their dissolution and fragmentation in the modern city. However, fitting the Magdalen Hospital into this history, or historical geography, of disciplinary technologies also disrupts it in some ways. I have shown the ways in which prostitution emerged as a problem at the intersection of understandings of 'police' as population regulation and urban order, and how that posed a question about both social order and individual conduct to which the Magdalen Hospital was an answer, albeit one that could never really work. This means constructing an understanding of modernity's disciplinary armoury and its characteristic subjectivities that gives full weight to gender and sexuality— and to the spaces of the home, the street and the reformatory—alongside the class relations and the link between the factory and the prison that have generally structured historical accounts.[192] Perhaps, in this

sense, the first modern individuals—with all the ambivalences that im-
plies—*were* women.

Clearly, to tie the sorts of statements that the theorists of modernity make about 'modern selves' to the more specific claims of particular
histories and geographies, and to the claim that these selves and spaces
are gendered, is also to disrupt them by questioning their generality.
Understanding and, in part, grounding them within the multiple spaces
of their emergence is to search for differences—perhaps in terms of
gender, class, race or location—among modern subjectivities and experiences of modernity. For example, I have tried to show how the notions of solitude, individuality and rationality that underpin some conceptions of modern subjects have histories that are shaped by class and
gender, and that cannot be separated from the, albeit multiple, spaces
within which they were constituted and lived. Here that has meant
concentrating on the ways in which the Magdalen Hospital's founders
envisaged remaking other selves, a dream of disciplinary control that
could never be realised in full. However, it is also true that these men
were continually in the process of shaping themselves, and often in similar ways.[193] That Jonas Hanway is 'said to have been the first man who
made a practice of using an umbrella while walking in the streets of
London' speaks to both the questions of urbanity and individualisation
that have animated this chapter and to the notions of modernity as a
transformation of the public sphere that are the concern of the next.[194]

CHAPTER THREE

The Street

INTRODUCTION: MODERNITY IN THE STREETS

In 1741 Lord Tyrconnel addressed the House of Lords on the condition of the streets of Westminster:

> The filth, sir, of some parts of the town, and the inequality and rugged-
> ness of others, cannot but in the eyes of foreigners disgrace our nation
> and incline them to imagine us a people, not only without delicacy, but
> without government—a herd of barbarians, or a colony of Hottentots.
> The most disgusting part of the character given by travellers, of the most
> savage nations, is their neglect of cleanliness, of which, perhaps, no part of
> the world affords more proof than the streets of London, a city famous
> for wealth, commerce, and plenty, and for every other kind of civility and
> politeness; but which abounds with such heaps of filth, as a savage would
> look on with amazement.[1]

It is these concerns, which were shared by many others, that I want to
deal with in this chapter. More importantly, it is the terms that Tyrconnel used in framing the nature of the problem of dirty streets that help
to set out the terrain on which I want to work. How can we understand
the connections that are made in his speech between the order or disorder of public space—a disorder expressed through a racialised discourse
of savagery—and the issues of 'government,' 'delicacy,' 'civility and politeness,' and 'wealth, commerce, and plenty'? How, to translate, does the
cleanliness of the urban built environment become a matter of political
authority, polite sociability, self-control and commodity exchange?

In order to provide some answers to these questions, I want to concentrate on the spaces that exercised Lord Tyrconnel: the streets of Westminster that were gradually planned and extended west from the City of London as the geometry of the city's squares gave a new shape to urban space (see Figure 1). The historiography of urban improvement makes it clear that the streets themselves, like other streets in other towns and cities throughout Britain, were also changing in the eighteenth century.[2] Moreover, it is apparent that they were changing in a particular direction. The street surface (or 'pavement') was becoming more smooth and uniform, more solid, and more subject to regular and thorough cleaning. In places, what we now call pavements (or sidewalks)—separate, often elevated, 'footwalks' for pedestrians—were coming into being. The streets were becoming brighter and safer. They were better lit, and lit for longer periods, by new techniques of street lighting, and they were under the eye of newly organised forms of watching (or policing). Streets were also being ordered and straightened. They were losing some of their crookedness and clutter as the jumble of shop signs and house fronts was tidied away to provide clear sight-lines. When new streets were constructed, they were spaces that contained all or some of these 'mark[s] of urban modernity.'[3] It was within these processes of smoothing, cleaning, brightening, ordering and straightening that dirt became such an issue. Why it became an issue of cultural politics in the specific senses that Lord Tyrconnel expressed is what this chapter seeks to explain.

The interpretative framework that I want to use is the notion of the rise of 'the bourgeois public sphere.'[4] Jürgen Habermas has argued that the eighteenth century witnessed the emergence of a realm of critical and rational public debate situated between the private realms of the nuclear family and the capitalist economy, on the one hand, and the public realms of state and court, on the other. Working though these ideas, which have been taken up in a variety of different ways by historians, allows the investigation of eighteenth-century London as part of a wider 'historical geography of modernity' that connects public spaces and public spheres.[5] More specifically, the way this chapter proceeds is via a short discussion of the ways that the public sphere has been theorised. This attempts to establish its usefulness for understanding the geographies of the street in terms of the notion of the 'bourgeois public sphere' as a matter of 'private people come together as a public.'[6] This notion is then taken up within a series of different contexts within which urban public spaces are an issue. First, I offer a reading of the works of contemporary political philosophers of various stripes—

Shaftesbury, Mandeville and Hume—to demonstrate that conceptions of urban public space were a vital element in attempts to define the relationship between private individuals and public interests within modern, commercial economies and polities. Indeed, some of the ways in which the cultural politics of the city were understood, particularly by Hume, can be seen again within the competing notions of public and private interests that were played out in the second context: the plans for the transformation of urban public space, especially those for the paving of Westminster in the 1760s. However, it is also evident in the politics of paving, and in the third context, which interprets contemporary representations of urban public space, that the ways in which private individuals were conceptualised, and the ways that they came together as a public, were not unproblematic, and depended, as did Humean notions of the 'public,' upon both governing and limiting the public sphere in various ways.

THEORISING THE PUBLIC SPHERE

Discussion of the public sphere has been shaped by Jürgen Habermas's *Structural Transformation of the Public Sphere,* an historical investigation of the emergence of a particular form of politics that is also part of his work on normative political theory and the legacy of modernity's rationalising processes.[7] In it Habermas understands the 'authentic' public spheres of letters and politics as emerging in the eighteenth century from the private spheres of commodity exchange and the bourgeois family, and as separated from the older public realms of the state and the court.[8] The new public sphere emerges through the modern development and elaboration of capitalist social relations and the creation of territorial states under absolutism. These states, in their attempts to 'police' processes of production, reproduction and consumption within families and commodified relations of work and exchange, effectively create 'civil society' as their object of intervention. For Habermas, the 'authentic public sphere' develops in the critical zone between the state and the private realm such that 'private people' become engaged in public debate as 'the addressees' of state authority.[9] They come together in critical, rational debate, often in print, to assess and respond to state authority. This is done in ways that do not spring simply from private interests but involve the 'bracketing' of the differences between the participants to create a theoretically inclusive public sphere that readdresses the state. Indeed, it is this positive legacy of Enlightenment rationality

that he seeks to rescue; and in his more recent work he has continued to
address the conditions for these potentially democratic forms of politics.[10]

Other interpreters of the histories of the public sphere have been
more critical than Habermas of the ways in which its 'publics' were
constituted through class and gender difference.[11] This also relates to
how class and gender structure 'a public sphere constituted by private
people.'[12] Here privatised individuals are understood as property owners—formed within the sphere of commodity exchange—and as individualised subjectivities 'originating in the interiority of the conjugal
family.'[13] For Habermas, the public sphere that is constructed allows
these individuals to maintain a private identity while 'coming together'
to form a public either in the world of letters or of politics.[14] There are
several connected issues here. These political subjects are constituted as
classed and gendered through the power relations of property and the
patriarchal family. It is, however, by no means certain that any rigid separation between fixed definitions of public and private, or any stable
gendering of those terms, can be assumed for the eighteenth century.[15]
Instead, it is in the process of private individuals coming together to
form a public that definitions of public and private—of privatised individuals and public spheres—are constituted. Each helps to define the
other. Therefore, privatised individuals are 'made' within the confines of
the family and the economy, but they are also defined 'in public' and
along with 'the public.'[16] It is this problematic issue of the formation of
a public of privatised individuals that is the main concern of this chapter.

Lawrence Klein has argued that one way forward here is through
considering space and language. However, understanding Habermas's
ideas in terms of space is problematic.[17] It cannot simply be a matter of
identifying the public spaces that somehow correspond to 'public
spheres,' although discussions of coffeehouses and salons have often
been conducted in that way.[18] It would certainly be wrong to claim that
the street was the space for critical-rational debate, particularly when its
politics often took the form of 'mob' riot and elite spectacle.[19] I want to
argue, however, that these spaces can be considered as part of the problematic constitution of new publics of privatised individuals. Habermas
himself argues that the twentieth-century 'changes in the function of
streets and squares due to the technical requirements of traffic flow'
have closed off political potential since '[t]he resulting configuration
does not afford a spatially protected private sphere, nor does it create
free space for public contacts and communications that could bring pri-

vate people together to form a public.'[20] Richard Sennett has also tied a novel, eighteenth-century sense of 'public life' to the ways in which 'the public geography of a city is civility institutionalised.' Within this new public life he explicitly includes, and understands as 'modern,' 'the first attempts at making streets fit for the purpose of pedestrian strolling as a form of relaxation.'[21] More recently, such connections between a new public civility, politics and modern city spaces have helped to illuminate the gendering of space, male sexuality, and the production of eighteenth-century painting.[22] In this vein this chapter seeks to consider the question of the conjoint formation of 'privatised individuals' and conceptions of the 'public' in eighteenth-century London in relation to the spaces that this new public of privatised individuals both relied upon and transformed. I want to show that in three different arenas—the spaces imagined within political philosophy, the organisational arrangements for paving Westminster, and the representations of London's public spaces—the mutual constitution of public and private was a problematic issue that could only be resolved by regulating individuals and publics in specific ways.

THE IMAGINED GEOGRAPHIES
OF POLITICAL PHILOSOPHY

From the mid-seventeenth century political philosophy had to grapple with the problem of defining the relationships between commercialised economies and public interests. What I want to show is that within several different, if connected, approaches to the question of private interests and public benefits—those of Shaftesbury, Mandeville and Hume—this problem is discussed in relation to a series of imaginary geographies of the city that situate the relationship between public and private. In each case the city's streets are, as they were for Lord Tyrconnel, a matter of government, civility and self-control, although each of the three thinkers understood the connections between power, space and identity in a different way. They are, therefore, all figuring imaginary urban geographies in order to understand the problems and possibilities of publics composed of privatised individuals.

Shaftesbury

Anthony Ashley Cooper—the third Earl of Shaftesbury—built his political and aesthetic philosophies around the notion of an 'innate "moral sense"'[23] in humans that could intuitively distinguish between vice and virtue on the basis of public benefit:

> We have found, that to deserve the name of *Good* or *Virtuous,* a Creature must have all his Inclinations and Affections, his Dispositions of Mind and Temper, suitable, and agreeing with the Good of his *Kind,* or of that *System* in which he is included, and of which he contributes a PART. To stand thus well affected, and to have one's Affections *right* and *intire,* not only in respect of one's self, but of Society and the Publick: This is *Rectitude, Integrity,* or VIRTUE.[24]

For Shaftesbury, any 'more than ordinary Self-Concernment, or Regard to private Good, which is inconsistent with the Species or Publick' was to be regarded as vicious. Indeed, such selfishness was to be regarded as ultimately against the 'happiness and Welfare' of the individual, and it would, he argued, be 'A strange Constitution' where public and private interests were opposed.[25]

This philosophically defined coincidence of public and private interests required explanation. For Shaftesbury, people were bound together by 'social affections' without which they could not themselves be happy. These were 'Natural, Kindly, or Generous Affections strong and powerful towards the Good of the Publick,' among which he listed 'Love, Gratitude, Bounty, Generosity, Pity, Succour, or whatever else is of a social or friendly sort.'[26] These he opposed to the 'unnatural affections'—inhumanity, petulancy, misanthropy, superstition, and perversions—which he argued characterised both 'Tyrants' and 'the more savage nations,' and which, in 'civilised nations,' effected an '*inward Banishment* . . . from human Commerce.'[27] His argument was with philosophers who proposed the hegemony of private interests:

> You have heard it (my Friend!) as a common Saying, that *Interest governs the World.* But, I believe, whoever looks narrowly into the Affairs of it, will find, that *Passion, Humour, Caprice, Zeal, Faction,* and a thousand other Springs which are counter to *Self-Interest,* have as considerable a part in the Movements of this Machine. There are more Wheels and *Counter-Poises* in this Engine than are easily imagin'd. 'Tis of too complex a kind, to fall under one simple View, or be explain'd thus briefly in a word or two. The Studiers of this *Mechanism* must have a very partial Eye, to overlook all other Motions besides those of the lowest and narrowest Compass. 'Tis hard, that in the Plan or Description of this Clock-work, no Wheel or Ballance shou'd be allow'd on the side of the better and more enlarg'd Affections; that nothing shou'd be understood to be done in

Kindness or *Generosity;* nothing in *pure good-Nature* or *Friendship,* or thro any *social* or *natural Affection* of any kind: when, perhaps, the main Springs of this Machine will be found to be either these very *natural Affections* themselves, or a compound kind deriv'd from them, and retaining more than one half of their Nature.[28]

For Shaftesbury, both private interests and social affections were at work. The key was to regulate the former. In 'a civil STATE or PUBLICK' it was one of the tasks of 'a virtuous Administration' to adjust the distribution of rewards and punishments so that it would be 'of the highest service; not only by restraining the Vicious, and forcing them to act usefully to Society; but, by making Virtue to be apparently the Interest of every one.'[29] Private interest was also to be subject to 'Self-Inspection' and control for the benefit of both the public and the individual.[30] So the search for private wealth was acceptable as long as it was 'moderate and in reasonable degree.' For Shaftesbury, 'if it occasion no passionate Pursuit, nor raises any ardent Desire or Appetite, there is nothing in this Case but what is compatible with Virtue, and even suitable and beneficial to Society.' Desires had to have their limits and private interests could not be indulged 'beyond a moderate degree' without corroding the natural affections.[31]

Shaftesbury's vision was, therefore, one in which sociability and publicity held centre-stage. For him, 'the highest Pleasures and Enjoyments' were social, and social interaction, guided by these natural affections, was to be conducted according to the dictates of civility and politeness.[32] Polite manners were vital in providing the basis for a new sociability. Solitude, in contrast, was dangerous to one and all:

> For whoever is unsociable, and voluntarily shuns Society, or Commerce with the World, must of necessity be morose and ill-natur'd. He, on the other side, who is with-held by force or accident, finds in his Temper the ill Effects of this Restraint.[33]

Yet the nature of the 'society' to which these 'affections' could be felt also had to be specified. For Shaftesbury, 'UNIVERSAL Good, or the Interest of *the World in general*' was a 'remote Philosophical Object' that 'falls not easily under the Eye.' Even 'National Interest, or that of a whole People, or Body Politick' was too large. He had in view, then, 'a more contracted Publick' within which the participants could know and be known, and it is these limitations on his 'public' that are my concern here.[34]

Shaftesbury's ideas are to be understood in terms of the problematic relationship between his anglicised version of civic humanism or classical republicanism and the moral dilemmas of a commercial society.[35] Within this problematic he has been interpreted in various ways. For Stephen Copley, Shaftesbury presents an 'exclusively aristocratic [and gentlemanly] polite culture' that is so threatened by market forces that he goes to 'considerable effort . . . to define the domain of politeness as being outside commerce and commodity exchange altogether.' It was only with Joseph Addison and Richard Steele's *Spectator* and, ultimately, with Hume, that commerce and 'civic humanism' were brought together in the form of a 'commercial humanism.'[36] David Solkin's presentation of Shaftesbury is similar in many ways. John Barrell summarises his analysis of a portrait of Shaftesbury by John Closterman as portraying '[t]he true citizen as envisaged in the English version of classical republicanism: a gentleman philosopher, the owner of landed property, who looks at the world with a disinterested and benevolent concern for the public interest and a wise distrust of commerce.'[37] Here Shaftesbury takes land to be the only possible basis of independent and virtuous political action and thought, and these landed gentleman-philosophers as the only 'disinterested masculine citizens,' whose sociable and polite conversation is the sole way to develop truths "independent of opinion and above the world."[38] However, Solkin argues that Shaftesbury's attempts to negotiate the new economic and political forces of the late seventeenth century allowed the possibility for polite public conversation to be used as a way of understanding commercial transactions and, therefore, the possibility of rendering those transactions virtuous. It was Shaftesbury's reworking of politeness away from its courtly connotations of dangerous luxury and his conceptualising of it in terms of liberty and virtue that was crucial. As Solkin says, '[W]hile philosophy was busy negotiating with politeness, commerce has sneaked in by the back door.' So Shaftesbury's relationship to commerce was a reluctant one such that '[a]lthough the Earl included modernity within his sociable embrace, he never admitted commercial men into his company of virtue, nor even into the ranks of the truly polite.'[39] Shaftesbury was a modern but only despite himself.

In marked contrast, Lawrence Klein presents Shaftesbury as directly endorsing the world of commerce. He groups Shaftesbury with Addison and Steele as 'Whig cultural ideologists' engaged in showing how politeness and virtue could be reconciled as part of 'an attempt to perform the delicate negotiations between traditional and classical notions of virtue and the commercial society.'[40] However, whether one agrees with Klein that '"Politeness" was not a form of nostalgia, but a program for modernity,' or with Solkin that 'Shaftesbury describes his ideal society as an hierarchical republic ruled by . . . autonomous men of public virtue who stand above and apart from the interdependent world of corrupt and commercial modernity,' it can be agreed that it was the relationship between virtue and commerce that exercised his mind.[41] Moreover, in demonstrating how this political philosophy was predicated upon a particularly limited and homosocial public, and by arguing that defining a space for that public involved imagining a particular sort of city, Shaftesbury's ambivalence toward modernity becomes apparent.

Shaftesbury's 'public,' whether limited to landed philosophers or including a wider sphere of 'politeness,' was certainly male and, as with his notions of the scale of a 'society' within which natural affections could be felt, it appears as a gentleman's club. For him the key liberty to be defended was 'the Liberty of *the Club,* and of that sort of freedom which is taken amongst *Gentlemen* and *Friends,* who know one another perfectly well.'[42] His public was a circumscribed space with strict rules of entry. Within this space the 'essence of freedom was "amicable collision," friendly interaction, the sort embodied in conversation and expected in the club of gentlemen.'[43] In part this version of a polite 'public' fitted uneasily with both the histories and the realities of the urban spaces in response to which Shaftesbury wrote. There are shadows of both ancient Rome and contemporary London in the following passage:

> We see the enormous Growth of Luxury in capital Citys, such as have been long the Seat of Empire. We see what Improvements are made in Vice of every kind, where numbers of Men are maintain'd in lazy Opulence, and wanton Plenty. 'Tis otherwise with those who are taken up in honest and due Imployment, and have been well inur'd to it from their Youth. This we may observe in the hardy remote Provincials, the Inhabitants of smaller Towns, and the industrious sort of common People; where 'tis rare to meet with any Instances of those Irregularitys, which are known in Courts and Palaces, and in the rich Foundations of easy and pamper'd Priests.[44]

This was not a simple antiurbanism, but a plea for a particular arrangement of urban space appropriate to classical notions of republicanism. As Klein points out, Shaftesbury made notes for a comparison of ancient Athens and modern London where the point of comparison was to be 'publicity, . . . public space and public discourse.'[45] The beauty and

importance of Athens lay in its public places:'Its citizens, equal and un-
intimidated, were all pedestrians. They walked on foot in a city, "*propre,
paisible, spatieuse.*"' The problem with London was that it had no '*places
publiques.*' Shaftesbury characterised the metropolis as 'an accumulation
of private spaces linked only by noisy streets overrun with carriages.' So
his philosophy figured a 'politeness' that was 'urban and urbane' and a
city that was '*propre, paisible, spatieuse.*' It was, however, a classical city that
he could not find in the contemporary world and, more significantly, it
was an imaginary city whose public spaces were only occupied by male
philosopher-citizens engaged in conversations that seamlessly merged
the individual and the public.[46] His understanding of this space is part
of a more general appeal in his work to 'a mythical golden age of public
debate' that was always part of the politics of civic humanism, and
which entailed a denial of the modern world of circulating commodities even while it may have been a way of imagining other modernities.[47] What is intriguing is that just as Shaftesbury's political philosophy
can be said to have opened up the possibility of making commerce and
self-interest virtuous through polite conversation, so his trinity of urban
values—'*propre, paisible, spatieuse*'—signaled the improvements that were
to come.

Bernard Mandeville

Mandeville, a Dutch doctor who had emigrated to Britain, was notorious as the propounder of a political philosophy quite antithetical to
Shaftesbury's. Famously, his *Fable of the Bees* stated that 'private vices'
were 'public virtues,' a formulation that ran counter not only to polite
Whiggish republicanism but also to the contemporaneous reformation-
of-manners campaigns that sought to forge a connection between private and public virtue.[48] Instead of, and against, these ideas, Mandeville
provided 'a morally paradoxical defence of commercial modernity'
that sought to celebrate commerce while pointing to the contradictions
that arise when attempting 'to reconcile plenty with morality.'[49] In
doing so he punctured Shaftesbury's 'idealistic fallacies' of innate principles and natural affections with a sharp empirical materialism that
stressed the rootedness of prosperous commercial societies in grubby
self-interest and 'worldly and sensual' pleasures.[50] His opening paragraph picks through the slime of bodily interiors for a visceral image of
civil society to contrast to the clean wheels and balances of Shaftesbury's machine:

Laws and Government are to the Political Bodies of Civil Societies, what the Vital Spirits and Life itself are to the Natural Bodies of Animated Creatures; and as those that study the Anatomy of Dead Carcasses may see, that the chief Organs and nicest Springs more immediately required to continue the Motion of our Machine, are not hard Bones, strong Muscles and Nerves, nor the smooth white Skin that so beautifully covers them, but small trifling Films and little Pipes that are either overlook'd, or else seem inconsiderable to Vulgar Eyes; so they that examine into the Nature of Man, abstract from Art and Education, may observe, that what renders him a Sociable Animal, consists not in his desire of Company, good Nature, Pity, Affability, and other Graces of a fair Outside; but that his vilest and most hateful Qualities are the most necessary Accomplishments to fit him for the largest, and according to the World, the happiest and most flourishing Societies.[51]

Sociability is built on selfishness, and Mandeville's construction of a 'public' was one that is composed purely of private interests. In his fable the 'hive' is a prosperous commercial society, but riddled with vice. Each trade is stocked with cheats; each individual is self-seeking. Pride, luxury, vanity and envy are the ruling passions. His aim was to show that the two were connected, that commercial prosperity is impossible without vice:

> T'enjoy the World's Conveniencies,
> Be fam'd in war, yet live in ease
> Without great Vices, is a vain
> EUTOPIA seated in the Brain.[52]

So when the hive's inhabitants convince their gods to banish vice, its economy declines into inactivity and poverty. Mandeville's argument was that it is these private 'vices' that drive commercial societies on to the prosperity that is their public virtue. For example, he argued that luxurious consumption and pride provide employment for millions, and that through the individualistic desires for emulation and competition fickle envy and vanity provide the motors of fashion in food, furniture and clothes that keep production and exchange moving:

> Thus every Part was full of Vice,
> Yet the whole Mass a Paradise;
> Flatter'd in Peace, and fear'd in Wars,
> They were th'Esteem of Foreigners,
> And lavish of their Wealth and Lives,

The Ballance of all other Hives.
Such were the Blessings of that State;
Their Crimes conspir'd to make them Great:
And Virtue who from Politicks
Had learn'd a Thousand cunning Tricks,
Was, by their happy Influence,
Made Friends with Vice: And ever since
The worst of all the Multitude,
Did something for the Common Good.[53]

Contra Shaftesbury, this position decried moderation. Mandeville wanted boundaries to be exceeded and dissolved since 'if the wants of men
are innumerable, then what ought to supply them has no bounds.'[54]
Trade was, therefore, to be expanded as far as possible. This distrust of
moderation and regulation also extended to the state and self-control.
While he saw the necessity for the balance of trade to be under state
control along with laws, punishments, foreign affairs and warfare, he argued that the self-government of appetites and passions was a trick
played by rulers on the ruled. Government and self-government were
knitted together because the distinction between vice and virtue was a
political construction that worked in the interests of the powerful. Instead of being innate principles embedded in religion, 'Moral Virtues
are the Political offspring which Flattery begot upon Pride.'[55] Indeed,
his empirical materialism sought to reveal as political constructions
many aspects of human societies that others presented as natural.[56] His
aim was to question all controls of private interests.

This political philosophy was again worked out through an imaginary geography of the city. The *Fable*'s Preface contains a discussion of
London that depicts its public spaces as shaped by private interests, and
that parallels the searching out of the little films and pipes as the key elements of the body:

There are, I believe, few People in *London,* of those that are at any times
forc'd to go a foot, but what could wish the Streets of it much cleaner
than generally they are; whilst they regard nothing but their own Cloaths
and private Conveniancy; but when once they come to consider, that
what offends them is the result of the Plenty, great Traffick and Opulen-
cy of that mighty City, if they have any Concern in its Welfare, they will
hardly ever wish to see the Streets of it less dirty. For if we mind the Materials of all sorts that must supply an infinite number of Trades and
Handicrafts, as are always going forward; the vast quantity of Victuals,
Drink and Fewel that are daily consum'd in it, and the Waste and Super-

fluities that must be produc'd from them; the multitudes of Horses and other Cattle that are always dawbing the Streets, the carts, Coaches and more heavy carriages that are perpetually wearing and breaking the Pavement of them, and above all the numberless swarm of People that are continually harrassing and trampling through every part of them. If, I say, we mind all these, we shall find that every Moment must produce new Filth, and considering how far distant the great Streets are from the River side, what Cost and Care soever be bestow'd to remove the Nastiness almost as fast as it is made, it is impossible London should be more cleanly before it is less flourishing. Now would I ask if a good Citizen, in consideration of what has been said, might not assert that dirty streets are a necessary Evil inseparable from the Felicity of London.[57]

This filthy city, where the coming together of private interests in the streets creates both muck and brass, parallels and exemplifies Mandeville's philosophy. The private vices of luxury, vanity, pride and avarice produce, through exchange and commerce, the public benefit of commercial prosperity, a benefit far greater than clean public spaces would provide. Removing the dirt, like removing vice, would render London less flourishing. If private vices are public benefits, then 'dirty streets are a necessary Evil inseparable from the Felicity of London.'

While there could be no simple reconciliation between Shaftesbury and Mandeville, it is possible to trace a set of philosophical manoeuvres that employed elements of each in an attempt to balance the claims of land and commerce, to render 'luxury as consistent with virtue,' and to rework the ways in which privatised (and acquisitive) individuals could be constructed and could construct a public.[58] I want to illustrate this, and the ways in which it also imagined another sort of city, by considering David Hume.

David Hume

Hume was an admirer of Shaftesbury, and while he was a critic of Mandeville's all-encompassing notion of self-interest, he had to admit the force of his analysis of the benefits that 'vice'—especially luxury—brought for commerce.[59] Hume, unlike Shaftesbury, also explicitly stressed that 'the *landed* and *trading* interest in *England*' were 'not really distinct,' and in many ways he sought to connect the two by developing a moralised conception of luxurious consumption that might render trade more virtuous.[60] The key here was forging a distinction between 'luxury' and 'refinement' that would allow a differentiation to be made between those private vices that were virtuous and those that were not.

Within a conception of refined consumption, commercial transactions could, using the language of politeness, be understood as civilised conversation, an understanding that rendered them virtuous to the extent that they were conducted with, and in the name of, taste and civility. In this way private interests might be morally grounded in their service to the public.[61]

For Hume, however, these nice distinctions, and the possibilities that they opened for harmoniously bringing together public and private interests, could only be ensured through the government of private individuals in various ways. First, individuals must be governed by the state. His discussions of forms of government in the *Essays* are both alert to questions of liberty and democracy and keen to explain how state forms influence 'the humors and tempers of men.'[62] More particularly, the state has a duty to ensure the coincidence of private and public interests. For Hume, 'Municipal laws are a supply to the wisdom of each individual; and, at the same time, by restraining the natural liberty of men, make the private interest submit to the interest of the public.'[63] Indeed, good government is where 'private interest must necessarily, in its operation, concur with the public,' and, as Hume concludes, there must be some form of public power since 'men could not live at all in society, at least in a civilised society, without laws, and magistrates and judges, to prevent the encroachments of the strong upon the weak, of the violent upon the just and equitable.'[64] Yet a reliance on magistrates is not enough. It must be accompanied by a second form of government: self-control.

Hume argued that each 'man' must govern his own private interests, holding himself in check through self-reflection and the realisation that pure self-interest would dissolve society. For him, 'A man who loves only himself, without regard to friendship or merit, is a detestable monster; and a man, who is only susceptible of friendship, without public spirit, or a regard to the community, is deficient in the most material part of virtue.'[65] The ideal individual, counterposed to 'the wildest savage,' is '*he* who governs his appetites, subdues his passions, and has learned from reason to set a just value on every pursuit and enjoyment,' exercising control of the body and desires, including avarice, not unlike that required of the women in the Magdalen Hospital.[66] Indeed, the gendering of these techniques of the self is crucial. It was men who were required to exercise self-government. Women had a different role that arose within the forms of sociability or publicity that established the third form of government: the regulation of men's private interests through heterosocial interaction or 'conversation':

What better school of manners, than the company of virtuous women; where the mutual endeavours to please must insensibly polish the mind, where the example of the female softness and modesty must communicate itself to their admirers, and where the delicacy of that sex puts everyone on his guard, lest he give offence by any breach of delicacy. [67]

Men are refined, Hume argues, by conversation or 'commerce' with women in public, and nothing 'embellishes, enlivens and polishes society' better.[68] But what sort of role does this give women in Hume's public sphere? It clearly did not confine them to domestic spaces. It also made them essential to polite conversation, as the genderings of public talk endorsed the female voice.[69] It is also true that Hume's requirements of women in public were more than just 'good manners' and 'vivacity in her turn of wit.'[70] The sort of 'furnished' mind he required demanded education. However, it is also clear in his *Essays* that it was women's effect on men that was important, and that while men might become refined, women should not become less so.[71] Any notions that he had of the 'nearness of rank, not to say equality, which nature has established betwixt the sexes' were rooted in a strong sense of gender difference, and Hume's public was always strictly defined in terms of these differences as well as through exclusions on the basis of race and class.[72]

In short, while admitting that a certain degree of luxury, avarice, pride and emulation were necessary to animate people to industry and improvement, and while arguing that commercial societies could not and should not follow a Spartan model, Hume's political philosophy required the regulation and control of private interests by a set of higher powers: the state, the reasoning self, and civilised, feminised sociability.[73] Without these controls the modern, progressive society that Hume thought could be built would fail. The future was fragile yet it also promised more than anything which had gone before.[74] This virtuous and prosperous social order, produced through the managed coincidence of public and private interests—a public formed of privatised individuals—was elaborated through an imaginary urban space:

The more these refined arts advance, the more sociable do men become; nor is it possible, that, when enriched with science, and possessed of a fund of conversation, they should be contented to remain in solitude, or live with their fellow-citizens in that distant manner which is peculiar to ignorant and barbarous nations. They flock into cities; love to receive and communicate knowledge; to show their wit or their breeding; their taste in conversation or living, in cloaths or furniture. Curiousity allures the wise; vanity the foolish; and pleasure both. Particular clubs and societies are everywhere formed: both sexes meet in an easy and sociable manner; and the tempers of men, as well as their behaviour, refine apace. So that, besides the improvements which they receive from knowledge and the liberal arts, 'tis impossible but they must feel an increase of humanity, from the very habit of conversing together, and contributing to each other's pleasure and entertainment. Thus *industry, knowledge* and *humanity,* are linked together by an indissoluble chain, and are found, from experience as well as reason, to be peculiar to the more polished and luxurious ages.[75]

This civilised city is the urban environment of a thriving and polite commercial society. It is built on the solid foundations of free government and spiced with a little innocent luxury. It offered up a cultural and political space both similar to and different from those figured by Shaftesbury and Mandeville. While Hume, like Shaftesbury, prioritised refined conversation, the participants, now both men and women, step outside the confines of the gentleman's club. They may not have stepped into the agora of classical Athens, but they were understood as inhabiting a space that was not an impossible one rooted in a mythological past. Yet, while private interests were not denied, neither was this the cynically materialist social space of Mandeville's filthy city. It was refined and polite, and within it commerce and virtue, public and private interests, were reconciled as 'conversation' and ordered through the governmental practices of state, self and society.

Each of these political philosophies, therefore, concerns itself with the nature of 'public spheres' and 'public spaces' and, in defining them, also defines how 'private individuals' should be conceptualised: as naturally harmonising with the public, as viciously inclined but publicly beneficial, or as orchestrated into a 'public' through various forms of government. What is intriguing is the way in which each of these political philosophies was understood through the cultural spaces of the public sphere—as the classical city, the filthy city, and the civilised city—and how each of them were explicitly or implicitly concerned with the qualities of those public spaces and the activities that took place within them. In each case they can be seen to address the problematic, also addressed by Habermas, of how private individuals come together to form a public through the space of the city. Moreover, I want to argue that understanding urban improvement means thinking through the Humean notions of the civilised city—with its constitution of various polite public spaces—since it is only there that the public streets of the contemporary city were valued enough to have them paved, cleansed, lit, made safe—in short, 'civilised'—and presented for use by a new public that was both expanded and limited in various ways. It was also Hume's notions of the governing of private interests that helps to connect these ideas to the next realm within which I want to explore the formation of private individuals and their new publics: the paving of Westminster.

MAKING PUBLIC SPACE: PAVING WESTMINSTER

The question of how 'private individuals' were constructed in and into publics can be approached by considering the making of one of the public spaces—the newly improved streets—within which this happened. What I want to argue here is that this process, like the political ideas discussed above, was also a matter of the conjoint, and problematic, conceptualisation of political authorities and 'privatised individuals.' As a consequence, what interests me is less the extent or 'success' of paving than what the plans, projects and legislation devoted to paving reveal about the cultural politics of the construction of spaces, identities and powers. That the seemingly mundane world of paving and lighting can reveal a realm of politics is made most evident in the differences between the plans for Paris and those for London. In absolutist Paris paving and lighting schemes, heavily laden with political symbolism, were 'centrally organised and financed by a new tax' as early as 1638. Nonabsolutist London ordered things differently and improvements did not come to fruition until a century later.[76] Within this history Westminster's importance is that its innovations in paving were copied by the City of London, Southwark, and 'most of the great cities and towns in th[e] kingdom,' and that the changes that were wrought were understood by contemporaries as a dramatic modernisation of urban space.[77] For John Pugh, commenting in 1787 on Jonas Hanway's involvement in promoting Westminster's paving, it was 'an undertaking which has introduced a degree of elegance and symmetry into the streets of the metropolis, that is the admiration of all Europe and far exceeds anything of the kind in the modern world.'[78]

The seventeenth-century paving and cleansing of Westminster was governed by custom and tradition dating from at least the early fifteenth century and was a matter for householders grouped together under the authority of the wards or parishes that provided scavengers and rakers to clear away the dirt those inhabitants swept into piles.[79] These arrangements were codified by legislation under Charles II. While he appointed commissioners to attend to the paving of some specific streets around Piccadilly, he left most of the city's streets in the hands of those who lived in them:

> [E]very of the said Householders to repair and pave, and to keep repaired and paved, the Streets, Lanes or Allies before his house, and so far as his Housing, Walls or Building extend, unto the Channel, or middle of the same Street, Lane or Alley.[80]

The penalty for not doing so was a fine. Lighting was organised in a similar manner, with every householder 'whose house adjoyns unto, and is next the Street' required every night from dusk until 9:00 P.M. from Michaelmas to Ladyday to 'set or hang out Candles or Lights in Lanthorns, in some part of his house next the street, to enlighten the same for passengers.'[81] This extension of the old duty to carry a torch after dark probably provided no more than a series of navigation points, and certainly did not amount to a systematic brightening of the streets.[82]

These arrangements of parochial and householder duties were repeated for paving and repairing under William and Mary in 1690. Householders were also required to sweep the streets in front of their properties on Wednesdays and Saturdays. This, along with restrictions on vehicles' wheel sizes, urban pig-keeping, and dumping, was designed to keep the streets both whole and wholesome. Most power over the pavement was held by householders and the vestries that ran the parishes. However, to ensure that paving and repairs took place, enforcement powers were also given to justices of the peace.[83] Under the 1690 act they could order the inhabitants of new-made roads to pave the areas outside their properties. The JPs' powers were extended in 1728 when legislation permitted JPs and vestries to appoint 'Surveyors of the Streets' to make a report to the justices concerning those areas needing repairs and the names of the householders responsible for them. This was to be checked and read out at the quarter sessions and, if necessary, in the parish church. Those whose names were announced were to make the required repairs within twenty days. After that time elapsed the repairs would be made by the Surveyor and the householder would be liable for the cost.[84] Paving powers were shared out among the courts, the parish and the household.

While this arrangement of powers and spaces might, particularly for magistrates and vestrymen, figure a suitable and workable level of local and parochial responsibility and authority, for others it signaled disorder. A bill read before Parliament on 22 May 1751 that sought to appoint commissioners empowered to pave, cleanse and light Pall Mall as 'an experiment towards the paving, cleansing, enlightening and keeping in repair of the streets of the City and Liberty of Westminster' argued that the current arrangements meant that private action, or inaction, was unconstrained by public authority. According to the proposers, 'the Neglect of Paving is chiefly occasioned by the Inhabitants being obliged to pave before their own Houses without being limited either as to Time, Materials, or Method of doing it.'[85] The bill constructed the inhabitants as privatised individuals unregulated by any higher authority and, at the same time, as problematic. In doing so, the parochial 'public' was seen as no public at all. The bill was not passed, but the issue did not die. A petition to Parliament in 1753 claimed that Westminster had outgrown the framework set out in the 1690 act. The petitioners argued that it was expensive, it was not being enforced, and that what was needed was not the sporadic punishment of offenders by the courts but a regular and continuous system of administration that would prevent the deterioration of the streets.[86] A set of proposals that would meet these complaints were put forward by John Spranger, a gentleman of Covent Garden, in 1754.[87] Examination of Spranger's plan and the legislation that followed it reveals the beginnings of a new organisation of space and power, and a new way of figuring a public authority within which private individuals could participate in the construction of an urban public sphere.[88]

Spranger's whole plan was conceived in terms of coordinating the individual and the public, and in doing so he constituted them both in particular ways:

> Every sensible Man, who lives under our most happy System of Government, must naturally be interested in all Things, that concern the Public; because he, though an Individual, sooner or later, more nearly or remotely, must be affected by every Degree of prosperity or Adversity, that attends the Community, of which he is a Member. This it is, that has made our political Constitution the chief Object of the Admiration, and Envy of the best Politicians on the Continent: That it is, that gives us a certain Connection, a Regard to the public Good, which is unknown in most other Countries; and whilst we are duly touch'd with a Sense of our Duty to the Public, every man in his Sphere will be ready and solicitous to promote the common Emolument, of which he is always sure to share.[89]

He announced his adherence to the doctrine that the purpose of English legal and political authority was the protection of the 'Rights and Liberties' of 'every Individual, of what Rank soever,' and that the laws that prevented official tyranny were the 'inalienable' property of even the 'Meanest' inhabitant. He also announced with the practised rhetoric of a projector that 'my sole Motive is the Service of the Public,' and proclaimed the openness of a sphere of political action 'in which the Ears of the *King and Parliament* are open to all the Petitions and Remonstrances of the *People*' and that, therefore, 'it must . . . be our own Faults, if any Thing be wanting to compleat the public Weal.' Consequently, his plan to adjust a matter of 'defective' 'political œconomy' was to be made '*Public,* that every One may make such Objections, or offer such Amendments, as Reason and good Policy shall direct.' Paving politics was part of a critical and rational debate over state and society in the public sphere, and Spranger planned to appeal to 'every sensible and public-spirited Inhabitant' by whom his plan would 'be candidly received, and accurately consider'd . . . abstractedly from any private Motives, Interests, or Prejudices.'[90]

He also couched his specific proposals in the language of a commercial political economy (familiar from the discussion of David Hume) that understood economic prosperity in terms of the circulation of people, money and things:

> In all well-governed Countries, the first Care of the Governors hath been to make the Intercourse of the Inhabitants, as well as of Foreigners, sojourning in the Country, safe, easy and commodious, by open, free and regular *Highways*. This is more especially incumbent on *Trading* Nations, as, without a free and safe Intercourse between Place and Place by Land as well as by water, *trade* cannot subsist, much less flourish.[91]

The turnpikes had provided the appropriate infrastructure for a commercial nation, but Westminster was still a hellhole of 'scarcely passable' streets whose 'Foulness and Darkness' and 'broken or irregular Pavements' rendered them unpleasant and unsafe. Spranger summoned all the perils of urban darkness and danger to his aid—losing one's footing, losing one's way, disease, death, and the 'Ruffians that infest our Streets'—and promised to dispel them with a rational set of solutions.[92]

He proposed that a number of inhabitants from each parish, suitably qualified via the ownership of property, should be elected by the ratepayers to act as commissioners. They would be empowered to do what the magistrates and vestries could not do via legislation which would permit them to make by-laws, to raise and use funds, to hear complaints and grievances, and to punish offenders (although the JPs would remain the final arbiters). These commissioners and, for their local knowledge, the churchwardens were also to appoint one or more 'creditable Householders . . . as Surveyors of the Streets and Lights for one Year' for appropriate divisions of each parish.[93] The aim was to ensure uniformity in pavement and administration. Spranger was, however, keenly aware of the problems that new rates and new powers would pose. So he suggested that the old forms should be put to new uses.[94] On the information of the surveyors everyone would be ordered, via notices published in the churches, to repave the streets in front of their property, as the legislation currently required them to, but this time they would all be required to do it in the same way:

> In all public Streets, Lanes &c. where Carriages pass, with broad Purbeck Stone Paving, or with Purbeck Squares, in the Paths or foot Ways, between the Houses and the Posts; and with good Pebbles, or other Stones, laid on a solid substantial Foundation and cover'd with Thames Sand, or binding Gravel, between the Posts and the Denter Stones; and in all Courts and other Places, where Carriages do not or cannot pass, with broad Purbeck Paving, or Purbeck Squares.[95]

Where possible the new streets would take the form we are now familiar with: a convex road surface with side gutters and raised 'Purbeck Pavement[s]' for walking on. The commissioners' additional powers 'to amend, take away and alter Gutters, Channels, and . . . Encroachments of Stalls, Sheds, Bulks, and other irregular Buildings' would help to produce a smooth, clean and regular urban landscape.[96]

In general the commissioners were simply to do for both paving and cleansing what the vestries and JPs had done in the past, but now they would also ensure that policy was uniform and coordinated for the whole of Westminster. Householders were still required to make the repairs (or to pay for them), but they now had no choice as to materials or method. For lighting, the commissioners were to respond to the contracting out of street lighting by inhabitants to private companies since the 1690s.[97] Spranger proposed:

> That said Commissioners shall . . . measure and mark out, at equal Distances, throughout their respective Parishes, the Places, which shall be thought most fit and expedient, for the erecting of Lamps or Lights, and shall cause globular Lamps to be erected on wooden Pedestals of [blank] Feet in Heighth, even with the Posts of the Streets, (where the Breadth of

the Streets will admit of it) or else upon the Walls of the several Houses, within the Distance of [blank] Feet from each other; and be so situated or placed, that the Lamps on one Side shall stand opposite to the Center of the Vacancies of the other; and Surveyors, with the Consent of the Commissioners, shall be empowered to contract and agree with proper persons, for lighting the same.[98]

These lamps were to be lit from sunset to sunrise throughout the year. Urban darkness was to be regularly dispelled by public authority. There were to be no more dark times or dark corners. The city would be opened up by clean, uniformly paved streets, street lamps, and clearly marked street names. This was to be done via a new arrangement of powers. While Spranger retained the parish as part of his system, his suspicion of the 'Partiality' of vestry politics led to the suggestion that the commissioners be directly elected by the householders rather than simply appointed.[99]

Spranger's call for public debate was, unsurprisingly, taken up by Jonas Hanway in an enthusiastic endorsement of his proposals. As well as offering detailed suggestions on the form of paving, the design of scavangers' carts, and on legislation over the width of cartwheels, he also understood paving and lighting as a political issue that led him into a broader discussion of 'police.' In addition, he interpreted the separation of 'footwalks' from the road using posts as a sign of the comparative liberty of the English:

> It is true they occupy a considerable space, but if, we compare the streets of London with those of Paris, this distinction seems, upon the comparison, to carry with it a *kind* of proof, that we are a *free* people, and that the French are *not so*. The *Gentleman,* as well as the *Mechanic,* who walks the streets of *Paris,* is continually in danger of being run over, by every careless or imperious coachman, of whom there are many; and in fact these accidents frequently happen in that city, in so much that few people of distinction ever walk in the streets.

The salubrity of the streets was also a signal of the 'fate of nations.' Hanway rejected Mandeville's logic that wealth meant dirt, noting that 'the more trade you have, surely the more capable you are of taking care of your *police,*' and argued that although the cleanliness of London's private spaces in comparison to its public places suggested 'a people ... thoughtless of the public welfare,' this should not be too readily assumed. He declared that '[t]he hearts of *all* the people are not influenced by motives of vicious self-interest,' and noted that there was plen-

ty of evidence of people being 'ready to pro ote the common interest.'
As a result, he urged Spranger to be less areful of supposed '*rights,*
which one would imagine no subject coul possess, when the interest
and welfare of the whole community came 'n competition with it' and
to admit the existence of 'a coercive power.' [00]

Indeed, the legislation that followed Sp anger's plan did go further
than he had proposed. A parliamentary com ittee appointed to consider the matter agreed that the paving proble was caused by 'the Inhabitants paving before their own Houses, with ut being limited, either in
Time, Materials, or Method of doing it,' and resolved that the whole 'be
put under the Management of Commission rs' who would have particular powers, responsibilities and funds for th new paving that the committee saw as more vital than continued repairs.[101] Having passed
through the procedures of both Houses as a bill, with petitions from
objectors being heard, the proposals were assed into law.[102] It was, as
Dorothy George notes, the beginning of 'a ew era.'[103]

The new legislation aimed to replace the older 'ineffectual' laws
and to achieve 'properly laid and regula d' pavements throughout
Westminster by appointing named 'Comm ssioners Paviour.'[104] These
men were to be propertied and to have no personal interest in any of
the contracts that they made. Indeed, it wa their 'high birth and large
possessions' that were to 'render them mo e faithful and disinterested
trustees for the public.'[105] Their meetings re to be fully minuted and
they were to be financially accountable to arliament. They were empowered to order that any street 'be paved repaired, raised or altered,
cleansed and lighted,' or for nuisances or o structions to be removed,
and then to contract for the work to be d ne. To help them in these
tasks, they were empowered to appoint salaried and independent surveyors to inspect the streets and the works. Beyond an initial £5000
from the king to begin to pay for the new paving, works were to be financed by a quarterly rate of not more than 1s 6d in the pound levied
on the local inhabitants on the basis of the assessments of property
made for the parochial poor rate. This was to be calculated for each inhabitant from the parishes' books, and then collected by the commissioners' receivers. Any appeals, financial or otherwise, against the commissioners' decisions were to be made to the justices of the peace. All in
all, the legislation had everything that was necessary to resolve the problem of the noncoincidence of private and public interests (newly defined in terms of clean streets for the whole of Westminster), and to
achieve the uniformity that Spranger had called for. In removing the
control of paving, cleansing and lighting from the vestries, the aim was

to operate in an area large enough to equalise the tax burden so that both rich and poor streets and districts could be paved.[106] This created a new political body, a new layer of tax-raising and active authority, which dealt directly with 'private inhabitants' and refigured their relation to the public.[107] In short, instead of operating as householders sporadically required by the parish to repair the street in front of their houses, inhabitants were now addressed by an authority that operated in relation to a much larger area, and only addressed itself systematically and regularly to individualised ratepayers through a new set of channels that bypassed the church and, where possible, the courts.[108]

This political challenge did not pass uncontested. The amendments to the act had to reword sections to ensure that the commissioners' powers extended to the places Parliament intended, and to institute penalties for obstructing officers in the course of their duties. More significantly, legislation was needed to prohibit parishes from charging fees for the consultation of their rate books by the commissioners' receivers.[109] Yet there were also signs of approbation. One significant amendment was designed to hurry the process of new paving along via an 'optional clause' that allowed the inhabitants of any street or square to raise the money for new paving themselves and to give it to the commissioners after a suitably advertised public meeting had ended with the agreement in writing of three-quarters of the qualified inhabitants.[110] Indeed, the whole scheme was applauded by Charles Walcot, MP, as successful in creating durable, clean and safe streets with 'an elegant uniform appearance,' and he deplored the old order with 'every one consulting his own interest, or gratifying his own fancy, without the least regard to order, or the safety of convenience of the public.'[111] Walcot and others sought new sources of funds for the commissioners, including a lottery and turnpike tolls.[112] The debates over paving eventually became so heated and so public that they were a suitable medium for satire.[113]

What was at stake for the 'pavers' is well illustrated by John Gwynn's (1766) *London and Westminster Improved*. Gwynn was an architect, draughtsman and bridge designer whom James Boswell described as 'a fine, lively, rattling fellow.'[114] His argument was that 'publick elegance' was 'a publick good' and he proposed the remaking of the city according to 'a well regulated plan' that would give 'publick direction' to 'the rage of building,' and which, he hoped, could be carried through despite 'the old cry of private property and the infringement on liberty.'[115] Indeed, his whole scheme was predicated on arguing for the 'public good' over and above the objections of 'interested individuals' on the grounds that the public benefits would be reaped in the long term and should not be sacrificed to short-term private losses. He particularly argued for the benefits of public elegance and magnificence:

> Publick magnificence may be considered as a political and moral advantage to every nation; politically, from the intercourse with foreigners expending vast sums on our curiosities and productions; morally, as it tends to promote industry, to stimulate invention and to excite emulation in the polite and liberal arts. . . . The English are now what the Romans were of old, distinguished like them by power and opulence, and excelling all other nations in commerce and navigation. Our wisdom is respected, our laws are envied, and our dominions are spread over a large part of the globe.
>
> Let us, therefore, no longer neglect to enjoy our superiority; let us employ our riches in the encouragement of ingenious labour, by promoting the advancement of grandeur and elegance.[116]

Public magnificence, as expressed in the space and face of the imperial city, was to promote 'a love of elegance . . . among all ranks and degrees of people,' producing a 'refinement of taste' in the nobleman and, in the mechanic, 'at least cleanliness and decorum.'[117] National improvements in morals and trade would be the results of urban improvements.

So far, Gwynn argued, London had missed the boat. The rejection of Sir Christopher Wren's plan for the rebuilding of the city after the Great Fire had meant that although London was improved, it 'by no means answered to the characters of magnificence or elegance.' There was so much to do. The Thames, from Chelsea to Blackwall on one side and from Battersea to Greenwich on the other, had 'not one convenient, well-regulated spot either for business or elegance in that whole extent.' Wapping, Rotherhithe and Southwark were 'all entirely destitute of that useful regularity, convenience and utility, so very desirable in commercial cities.' The Custom House, which should have been grand and magnificent, was 'the worst contrived heap of absurdity and inconvenience that could possibly be put together'; Westminster Bridge was a wasted opportunity; and St James's Palace was 'universally condemned' as 'a house so ill-becoming the state and grandeur of the most powerful and respectable monarch in the universe.' He argued that every chance had to be taken to have 'publick' improvements made to land when it became available so that 'streets might be opened, avenues widened, publick edifices made conspicuous, and passages to and from places of the greatest resort for public business rendered safe, commodious and elegant.'[118] Streets like the ones that Spranger and the commissioners planned were clearly part of John Gwynn's vision. Indeed, he specifically applauded their efforts:

> It becomes necessary in this place to take particular notice of the very elegant, useful and necessary improvement of the city of Westminster, and its liberties, by the present method of paving and enlightening it; an improvement which every one who is doomed to walk feels in the most sensible manner; to say that the streets are thereby rendered safe and commodious would be saying too little, it may without exaggeration be asserted, that they are not only made safe and commodious, but elegant and magnificent. . . . [T]here never was in any age or country a publick scheme adopted which reflects more glory upon a government, or does greater honour to the person who originally proposed or supported it.[119]

Yet, characteristically, Gwynn felt that they had not gone far enough. In part this was a matter of specific criticisms about the removal of noxious businesses, but it was also because he had a grander scheme for the capital. In the abstract this relied upon a set of general principles. The 'grandeur and convenience' of capital cities were best served, he believed, by 'a square or circular form . . . in the center of which in a spacious opening the King's palace should be situated; in which case he would be surrounded by his subjects, and the whole, if the expression may be allowed, would resemble a hive of bees.' In turn, this 'hive' was to be a geometrically ordered one since '[i]t is to be wished that, the ground-plans of all great cities and towns were composed of right lines, and that the streets intersected each other at right angles, for except in cases of absolute necessity, acute angles ought for ever to be avoided, as they are not only disagreeable to the sight, but constantly waste the ground and spoil the buildings.'[120] London was clearly a disappointment. It was a place where 'right lines have hardly ever been considered,' producing 'so much confusion . . . in the disposition of the streets.' His scheme was to put this right by imposing a new plan on the city:

> Such a vast city as that of London ought to have had at least three capital streets which should have run through the whole, and at convenient distances been intersected by other capital streets at right angles, by which means all the inferior streets would have an easy and convenient communication with them. . . . [A] quiet and easy communication from place to place is of the utmost consequence to the inhabitants of a great commercial city.[121]

Gwynn effectively redrew the map of London as he thought it should be and published his amended version with an explanation (see Figure 5, which presents his plans for a section of Westminster). He wanted a new royal palace on a raised mound in Hyde Park surrounded by formal lakes and drives; a whole new set of public buildings from which the city and the country could be properly governed; and a string of residential squares, modeled on Grosvenor Square, which would run from Hyde Park to the British Museum. He also proposed one—King's Square—for where Trafalgar Square was later built. This planning was also a matter of detail. Gwynn paid attention to each street and intersection. The bold lines on his plans showed how roads could be widened, straightened and made to meet at right angles (e.g., where Gerrard Street meets Windmill Street). His new geometrical plan 'improved' on the faint, ghostly, dotted lines of the crooked city he was leaving behind. His immediate aims were both the elegance and magnificence of the public spaces of the city and meeting the needs of private interests as manifested in traffic flows and property values. What ultimately drove this plan was what was also evident in the laying of the 'new manner of paving' which, Gwynn argued, 'gives a determined and regular line to build from.'[122] All these small straightenings of the urban landscape were part of the making of a new social order. As Gwynn argued, '[I]t must be allowed that publick works of real magnificence, taste, elegance and utility, in a commercial city, are of the utmost consequence.'[123] They produced and reproduced the appropriate, and appropriately civilised, cityscape for a prosperous commercial society within which the private interests of individuals could be appropriately realised.

Despite the building of London's squares, Gwynn's plan remained largely unrealised, and the arguments over new legislation were more concerned with local accountability and the politics of the powerful 'close' vestries of Westminster than with grand schemes.[124] As well as debating the source and level of the rate, in the context of the commission's problematic finances, opponents of the commissioners argued for the addition of vestry-appointed commissioners—who would have to be householders—and for the parish to be both the unit of rate-raising and spending.[125] The key issue was residence. Being a householder or not was regarded as 'so fundamental a Distinction, that it must affect the *Mind* as it does the *Interest,* of every Individual.'[126] This reassertion of local identities and local political affiliations was bound into a debate over the conduct of vestry politics that represented 'private interest' as both positive and negative. On the one hand, 'Friends to the new Pavement' argued that a return to the parish level would bring higher costs

Figure 5 John Gwynn's Proposed Improvements for Part of Westminster, 1766. Reproduced by permission of the British Library.

and 'continual confusion in the Progress and Execution of the Acts' as parishes and individuals acted in their own interests.[127] On the other hand, it was argued that only householders organised through parishes could tax and spend; that they represented the only legitimate interests. This 'running warfare' between the parishes and the commission ended in a reassertion of vestry power.[128]

Legislation in 1771 empowered vestrymen and inhabitants to appoint additional commissioners to represent each parish. These were required to be resident householders and to have the same property qualification as before. This was, after all, a revolt of the propertied. They were also empowered to appoint a committee of between seven and twenty-one 'resident householders' for their parish. These committees were interposed between the commission and the local ratepayers. They set and collected a parish rate, they made and oversaw the local performance of contracts, they heard complaints, and they appointed local supervisors and collectors. The commission, who still appointed their own inspectors, decided where was to be paved and lit and how it should be done. Their continued presence ensured uniformity in the production of the built environment.[129] Unfortunately, reopening the door to vestry power signaled the decline of the Paving Commission. One by one, from 1782, the vestries were able to secure local acts withdrawing them from the jurisdiction of the commission even against the will of Parliament. By 1800 the Paving Commission controlled only a few streets. Its legacy, however, lived on rather more successfully in the improvements it had inspired elsewhere.[130]

The making of a public sphere, whether in the imaginations of John Spranger and John Gwynn or in the practical proposals and political structures of paving legislation, once again involved the conjoint construction of public authorities and private individuals. In Westminster there were conflicting constructions of the notion of the 'private householder' and their self-interest. On the one hand, this was a crucial part of the local politics of the vestry and was bound to the setting of rates—with a low rate being understood as the greatest public benefit— and the notion of the parish as the public sphere. On the other hand, there was a more formalised construction of the relationship between public authority and the privatised individual ratepayer in the making of public space. Conceptualising urban public space across Westminster as a whole meant understanding parochial interests as a barrier to the realisation of the 'public' benefits of clean, clear roads, or even of magnificence and elegance in the built environment. It is also apparent that it was very much within the public debate over paving plans that notions of the private individual, the legitimacy of their interests, and the conceptualisation of their relationship to the public were formed. How private individuals were to come together as a public in the making of the 'polite' spaces of a commercial city was the problematic that shaped paving politics. This process of the defining and redefining of public and private also surfaces in representations of the city's spaces and those who were out in them.

REPRESENTING THE PEDESTRIAN

Figure 6 reproduces the image from the title page of John Gay's poem *Trivia; or, The Art of Walking the Streets of London,* which was published in 1716.[131] It shows an urban scene, and a scene of urban improvement. The clean, clear lines of building and pavement are organised to frame a church in the distance, and also to situate the men and women, well dressed and generally alone, who are strolling through the scene, and whose 'arts' the poem celebrates. The prominence of these walkers is counterposed to the carriage in the background, and to the working man, framed by the arch of the building to the right, who is carrying his load out of the picture. However, the central position in the image is taken by two pavers who are hard at work constructing the pavement that floors this improved urban landscape. Gay's *Trivia,* and this image, offer a representation of the civilised city and the paved public spaces discussed above, albeit one that presents it in comic and mock-heroic terms. Indeed, in Penelope Corfield's review of the literature of the eighteenth-century urban odyssey, Gay's poem is described as both 'a crucial moment in the history of urban literature' and 'far from unique.'[132] Unlike Corfield's extensive survey of views of the street, I want to compare the representation of urban life—and particularly the figure of the walker and the arts of walking—that Gay's *Trivia* constructs to other forms of urban representation. This is done in order to argue that Gay's poem presents a quite specific, if not necessarily unique, mode of apprehending and being in the city that can be connected back to the problematics within the political philosophies and paving practices discussed above.

The comparisons that I want to make are with Ned Ward's *The London Spy* (1698–1700)[133] and the anonymous *A Brief Description of the Cities of London and Westminster* (1776).[134] Ned Ward's eighteen-part account of London high and low life in a mix of prose and poetry was originally published monthly from November 1698 as a highly success-

Figure 6 Title Page Illustration from John Gay's *Trivia*, 1716. Reproduced by permission of the British Library.

ful sixpenny journal. Ward, a prolific writer of satires, is argued to have 'pioneered the exploration, representation and study of the life and character of the city as a literary science.' *The London Spy's* scatological and canting refusal to conform to a polite literary language represents a city that is both filthy and vibrant, dangerous and exciting.[135] In contrast, the *Brief Description* was a decorous visitor's guide to London that described the city in general terms and then listed and outlined its key sites. Although it had appended to it some comments on metropolitan crimes that were ascribed to Sir John Fielding, he denied any connection with the book.[136] Given that these are disparate types of writing about London separated by over three-quarters of a century of urban transformation, differences between them are not surprising. However, by considering these differences in terms of the ways in which the city is represented, the classed and gendered subjectivities that the texts present, and the relationships to urban dirt and disorder that they figure, I want to argue that they each work through different notions of the experience of inhabiting urban space, and that it is Gay's walker who resonates most clearly with the tensions that structure the problematic of private individuals coming together to form a public.

Presenting the City

Ward's *The London Spy* presents the city through a series of journeys around the capital and, toward the end, the 'microcosmography' of a series of specific urban characters such as the beau, the banker and the stockjobber.[137] These journeys are presented as undertaken by 'the Spy'—an 'innocent' countryman come to town—and his knowledgeable urban acquaintance. This boisterous pair '"ramble," "stumble," "stroll" and "blunder" around the capital' like, as Ward says, 'a couple of runaway apprentices, having confined ourselves to no particular port, uncertainty being our course and mere accident our pilot.'[138] In part this is a sight-seeing trip in which the Spy's companion extends to him 'the common civility of a London inhabitant to a country friend or acquaintance' and shows him 'the tombs at Westminster, the lion in the Tower, the rogues in Newgate, the mad people in Bedlam, and the merchants upon the 'Change, with the rest of the Town rarities worth a country fool's admiring,' before leaving him to his own devices.[139] In part it is a trip from tavern to tavern, coffeehouse to coffeehouse, and sight to sight, satisfying desires for food, drink, diversion and entertainment.

This itinerary and the stated aim of revealing the city's iniquities—

'to expose the vanities and vices of the town' in order to help people to 'avoid those snares and practised subtleties which trepan many to their ruin'—leads the pair into seeking diversion among the 'mobility.'[140] They weave their way through the dark corners of the city—in Billingsgate, the taverns of Wapping, Bedlam, Poultry Compter, the Bridewell, the May Fair, the 'astonishing confusions' of Bartholomew Fair and at the Rag Fair—as well as through its official and established settings, such as the Inns of Court and St Paul's.[141] Their journey is mapped onto the topography of the city in a way that both emphasises its subtle differentiations and draws high and low together. In doing so the city is presented as the locus of corrupt pleasures, dirty dealing and self-interest. Ward shows 'how all ranks and sexes prey upon one another's needs and weaknesses' as he depicts, among others, corrupt constables, gambling rakes, idle soldiers, dissipated flagellants, tricky lawyers and narcissistic courtiers.[142] Even the supposed reformers of these urban vices are as driven by self-interest as the merchants 'who love nobody but themselves' and operate 'as if plain dealing was a crime and cozenage a virtue.'[143] Yet this is no reforming tract. It is all laid out with glee in the bad language of the back alleys. There is a delight in bodily excesses, in grotesque figures, and in a ribald humour that is most evident in the pleasure that all classes take in the customary privilege of Thames watermen and their passengers to deliver lovingly crafted volleys of scatological invective between boats afloat on the river.[144] The city is deliciously dangerous.

Gay's metropolitan georgic, *Trivia,* which presents urban space both from and to the perspective of a solitary walker, is also concerned with the city's dangers:

> Now venture, Muse, from home to range the town,
> And for the publick safety risque thy own.[145]

However, by representing the everyday perils of the modern metropolis through an elevated poetic language they also become comic.[146] In this way Gay warns urban pedestrians that they might be run over, robbed, pushed into the gutter by people or carts, or caught out by barrels, low benches or open cellar doors; and he offers advice on how to proceed through the city by day and at night:

> Let constant vigilance thy footsteps guide,
> And wary circumspection guard thy side;
> Then shalt thou walk unharm'd the dang'rous night,

Nor need th' officious link boy's smoaky light.[147]

All of this is mapped out across London giving, for example, advice about which streets to take and which to avoid. This presentation of a series of urban knowledges and techniques, both specific to London and more general, is part of the definition of a 'personal etiquette of acceptable street behaviour' that seems to have increasingly shaped the custom and practice of the 'respectable' in the eighteenth century. There were, for instance, conventions on right of way, it was considered rude to stare or to look into private houses, and spitting, swearing, drunkenness and urinating in public were discouraged.[148]

For Gay's solitary pedestrian this is woven into a specific quality of relations in public that mixes both an interest in others and an anonymity provided by the city's streets:

> But sometimes let me leave the noisie roads,
> and silent wander in the close abodes
> Where wheels ne'er shake the ground; there pensive stray,
> In studious thought, the long uncrouded way.
> Here I remark each walker's diff'rent face,
> And in their look their various bus'ness trace.[149]

This solitary strolling and looking, being part of the city through simply walking its streets, can be set against the roistering companionship that structures *The London Spy*, whose narrator, when he is left to his own devices, talks of 'Being . . . left to range the Town by myself like a man-hater that loved no company, or like a hangman that could get none.'[150] But they both share an apparent aimlessness, a shaping of their sinuous paths by whim and the contingencies of the city, that contrasts to the method of the *Brief Description*.

A Brief Description of the Cities of London and Westminster was a commercial venture that promised that all those in the city 'either native or foreigner, who shall take this work for his guide . . . may, without vanity, boast, (which hitherto but few could) that he possesseth a true and adequate knowledge of this surprising metropolis.' This total geographical vision was to be used 'to examine more effectually the wealth, beauty, and magnificence, of the great city.' It would guide the reader through a dynamic and exciting space. London was described as 'a huge magazine of men, money, ships, horses, and ammunition, of all sorts of commodities necessary or expedient for the use or pleasure of mankind: the nightly rendezvous of nobility, gentry, courtiers, divines, physicians, merchants, seamen, and all kind of excellent artificers: of the most refined wits, and the most amiable beauties.'[151] The relationship this guide establishes to the city is one of spectator to spectacle.

The metropolis was presented as a series of sites to be visited. Alongside the main attractions—Westminster Abbey, the Tower, the Monument, St Paul's—which are described in some detail, are churches, the houses of nobles, hospitals, parks, squares and bridges. All, even those in private hands, were made public by treating them as sights. The descriptions of them are primarily about what can be seen from the street, about architecture, views and vistas. The city becomes, above all else, something to look at, and this looking reveals the city's greatness: hospitals are signs of 'charity and public spirit'; company halls signal 'the thriving condition of our internal trade and manufactures'; and parliament buildings represent constitutional freedoms.[152] Moreover, these particular sights are located within a framework that offers the reader the freedom of the city as a public space. Within the book sites are presented in alphabetical order from, for example, the Admiralty to York House. This classificatory imitation of 'the Botanic Writers' is supplemented by 'an alphabetical account of all the streets, lanes, courts, alleys, etc. by which the stranger with a very little enquiry, may easily find his way to any particular street, square, court, alley, or place, in the cities of London and Westminster, and the suburbs thereof.'[153] This was an enterprise that chimed with Spranger's earlier proposals for the transparency and legibility of public space:

> [W]ere the Names of Streets cut on white Stones, the Letters blacken'd, and set up at every Corner, the greatest Strangers might, with the Assistance of a small pocket Map, find his Way into any Part of these contiguous Cities and their extended Liberties, without being at the Pain and Trouble of enquiring his Way of a Populace, not the most remarkable for their Politeness to Strangers, or such as do not speak their Language in the native Accent.[154]

These techniques and practices meant that the city could be understood, and presented to the individual, as a public space open to the wanderings and gaze of the walker. The journeys they took would be constructed across a known and open terrain.[155] Indeed, the *Brief Description* celebrated the urban improvements that created 'wide, airy and straight' streets lit to 'charm the eye' and opened up to give 'a surprising air of pleasantness and freedom to the whole.'[156] These public spaces would be laid open to, and could be read by, anyone who owned the

book. Who this walker might be, however, is a question that needs to be
asked of all three texts.

Class and Gender in the Streets

While the streets were more 'democratically accessible' than many other
public spaces it is necessary to consider the constitution of the urban
travelers in these texts.[157] In *The London Spy* the companions are positioned not so far above the crowd that they can't enjoy its dirty pleasures and the challenges it offers to authority, but are distanced from it
enough to move at will, to spend freely, and to look down upon the
mob as superiors and, at times, with disgust.[158] They are also male.
Women appear mainly as whores and drawers of drink. They may be
objects of desire, they may also be powerful, but this comes through
gossip or a voraciousness that means that they are not to be trusted.[159]
Gay's *Trivia* also positions the pedestrian in terms of class and gender
but this time through the categories of civility rather than libertinism.
The walker here is a sturdy man of the middling sort:

> Let due civilities be strictly paid.
> The wall surrender to the hooded maid;
> Nor let thy sturdy elbow's hasty rage
> Jostle the feeble steps of trembling age:
> And when the porter bends beneath his load,
> And pants for breath; clear then the crouded road.
> But above all, the groping blind direct,
> And from the passing throng the lame protect.
> You'll sometimes meet a fop, of nicest tread,
> Whose mantling peruke veils his empty head,
> At ev'ry step he dreads the wall to lose,
> And risques, to save a coach, his red-heel'd shoes,
> Him, like the miller, pass with caution by,
> Lest from his shoulder clouds of powder fly.[160]

Elsewhere the walker's 'strong cane' is compared to the 'amber tipt' stick
or 'gilded chariot' of the club- or court-bound beau, and his honesty,
charity and virtuous morality are contrasted with the lavishness and
'gaudy pride' of men and women in carriages.[161] This theme also appears in the *Brief Description* whose assumptions of leisure and literacy
are accompanied with a set of solid, bourgeois public values through
which the urban scene is to be understood. The nobility and gentry are
aligned with magnificence and elegance, but also with luxury and cor-

ruption, while mercantile men 'are persons of great humanity, sobriety and industry, of open generosity and extensive credit.' Their pedestrian publicity is opposed to carriage-borne selfishness:

> He must frequently expect to see ambition and self-interest through the glare of equipage and the splendour of a numerous retinue. He will be grieved sometimes to find conceit and confidence bearing down sense and merit. [162]

While the *Brief Description*'s warnings and salutations are primarily addressed to men, there is an anticipation and expectation that public space is open to both men and women, and that women will also use the book. The tone, however, is parallel to Hume's notions of women's role in the public sphere:

> The women here have the most engaging charms, the most wit and the most beauty of any women in the world; yet the greatest latitude of freedom and behaviour is indulged to them. They frequent all public places of entertainment; make parties of pleasure; pay and receive visits to and from those of either sex without restraint . . . ; and all this with perfect innocence and an irreproachable character.[163]

Women and other classes are not, and could not be, excluded from the public streets, but each of the texts is centred on a middling-sort masculinity. For *Trivia* and the *Brief Description,* this is structured through the codes of public civility that organise these subjects' relations to others in the streets through differentiations based on class and gender. In doing so, these codes claim the public streets as the locus of these valued and civilised identities. The emphasis on individualised subjectivities is clear in both texts, but it is also clear that these are formed in public and through the making of a public sphere of urban interactions. This is most readily shown through their representations of the dirt and disorder of the city.

Dirt and Disorder

Unsurprisingly, Ned Ward's *London Spy* both revels in and reviles the disorderly city it represents. It combines its delight in filthy stories of dirty bodies and the murky pleasures of the fair with complaints about uneven pavements and foul sights.[164] It is a place where high and low are not readily separable. The money that binds the city together is dirt, 'that filthy dross which defiles the virgin, corrupts the priest, contaminates the fingers of the judge, is the cause of every ill, and the very seed of human misery.'[165] It is a world that is often upside-down: Bedlam becomes the home of truth; constables work 'like so many footpads'; and doctors are little different from quacks and mountebanks. Indeed, in his account of the lord mayor's pageant the Spy is amused by the mob slinging mud, shit and a dead cat at the unwary and he wilfully misinterprets the allegories in the parade as representing the vices and immorality of the City.[166]

In contrast, the *Brief Description* warns its readers of London's disorders. The city's magnificence also means that 'you will no where find such multitudes of unemployed persons, loiterers, vagabonds and beggars' and that 'the streets are by night polluted with lewd women, or infested by villains, notwithstanding the number of watchmen and the glare of lights.' Mixing with such pollutants is to be avoided. Covent Garden, 'the great square of Venus,' and the Strand are to be shunned.[167] While counseling caution could serve to draw attention to these places, the necessity for self-government was explicitly stated:

> It follows, that those, who are not well acquainted with the town, must be earnestly advised, as they entertain a proper regard for themselves, to keep good hours; . . . to have a perpetual watch and guard upon their passions; and not to suffer themselves to be too much occupied and taken up with the idle vanities and nocturnal amusements of the town.[168]

In its lightly satirical tone Gay's poem is more interesting than these bald instructions. It is a hymn to the seeking out of urban experiences, thrills, and adventures, while at the same time avoiding the dirt and disorder associated with being in public in a city of commerce and exchange. Its opening lines set this out:

> Through winter streets to steer your course aright,
> How to walk clean by day, and safe by night[169]

The poem goes on to warn of avoiding flour from the baker, powder from the barber or the fop, soot and grime from sweeps and dustmen, grease and fat from butchers and chandlers, spurts of mud from passing traffic and loose paving stones, plaster from masons working overhead, the confidence tricks of card sharps, the calls of prostitutes, the dangers of theft, and even the smells of fish and rubbish in Thames Street. All of these are dangers of 'The mingling press,' the perils of a thriving commercial city. While dirt may not have assumed the enormous symbolic importance that it would for the Victorians, it did threaten to blur the boundaries and erase the distinctions based on civility and polished politeness.[170] At the heart of this new urban experience lay the difficulty of being both part of the public and being an autonomous, private individual. In Gay there are two ways in which this problem was resolved. First, through strategies based on self-control. The problem was of being out in the moving, rushing crowd but not being part of it:

> Ever be watchful to maintain the wall;
> For should'st thou quit thy ground, the rushing throng
> Will with impetuous fury drive along;
> All press to gain those honours thou hast lost,
> And rudely shove thee far without the post.[171]

The solution was to construct a particular way of walking appropriate to the city, a way of walking that retained the privacy of the individual while responding to the public context within which it operated:

> Still fix thy eyes intent upon the throng,
> And as the passes open, wind along.[172]

The second resolution was through the public strategies of urban improvement with which this chapter has been concerned. The following lines echo the image presented on the title page (Figure 6):

> To pave thy realm, and smooth the broken ways,
> Earth from her womb a flinty tribute pays;
> For thee, the sturdy paver thumps the ground,
> Whilst ev'ry stroke his lab'ring lungs resound;
> For thee the scavinger bids kennels glide
> Within their bounds, and heaps of dirt subside.[173]

These changes produced a built environment that gave the city to these walkers. In this case the walker is not engaged in the spectacle of an aristocratic or bourgeois promenade, or in the narcissistic practices of the *flâneur*.[174] It is a relationship to the city that involves a less formalised engagement with public space characterised by an intense sense of the individualised experience of the city and a feeling of being in, if not wholly part of, the crowd. The thrills and novel experiences of the 'surprising metropolis' are important, but so too are the knowledges and

practices—including paving—which render that controllable and allow
these privatised individuals to claim a public sphere that was, in all its
order and civility, appropriate to them.

CONCLUSIONS

This chapter has attempted to understand the philosophical, political
and literary contexts of the newly paved, lit and cleansed London
streets, and in doing so to situate them within an understanding of the
particular nature of their modernity. By interpreting them through the
frame provided by accounts of the public sphere I have argued that
these streets were, in various ways, part of the geography of a modern
public of private individuals. It is this that serves to illuminate Lord Tyrconnel's understanding of the disorder of the built environment in
terms of political authority, politeness, self-control and commerce with
which I started. In each of the contexts that I have discussed—the political philosophies of Shaftesbury, Mandeville and Hume; the politics of
paving Westminster; and a small selection of textual representations of
the city—I have used Habermas's notion of the 'bourgeois public
sphere' as a matter of 'private people come together as a public.'[175] Understanding this 'coming together' as problematic in each context has
shaped the discussion of the ways in which that public was constituted,
the spaces which that involved, and the forms of governance upon
which they depended.

   Working through the philosophical positions formulated by
Shaftesbury, Mandeville and Hume, it was argued that each attempted
to define the relationship between 'public' and 'private' in different
ways, and that it was David Hume whose 'commercial humanism' offered a way of reconciling public and private interests. This was to be
achieved only through a recognition of the governance of private interests—through the state, self-control and the civilising influence of a
gendered and polite sociability—to serve the public. These forms of
governance, and Hume's imaginary urban geography of the civilised
and contemporary city that would be the site for the formation of this
public, connects this political philosophy to Tyrconnel's understanding
of order, governance and cleanliness in a commercial world. However,
actually creating these polite and orderly spaces was a problematic matter. Taking up the understandings of public and private within the debates over the paving of Westminster showed how these improvements
were understood—by men like John Spranger and John Gwynn—

within a desire to create the appropriate urban geography for a commercial and civilised nation. Doing so meant attempting, once again, to find ways of refiguring and recombining public and private interests. The subsequent conflicts over how private householders were to relate to wider authorities in order to transform the streets in a particular direction show quite how difficult this making of a public sphere was as contested versions of 'public' and 'private' came into conflict. Finally, I have also tried to show how the new urban spaces that were constructed—the improved streets—were connected in a literary context with specific urban figures, particular sorts of pedestrian. Doing so once again replays the difficulties of constructing a public made of private individuals and stresses the forms of 'governance'—of self and society—on which that had to be built.

Overall, therefore, I have tried to show that making sense of the modernity of the newly paved and lit streets of the capital in terms of the constitution of a public sphere does not mean simply mapping out that public sphere in space. Instead it means considering those spaces in terms of the tensions involved in the constitution of a public of private individuals. The attempts to manage and resolve these tensions through various forms of governance shaped relations in public, and the spaces in which these relations were constituted, in ways which were both real and imagined. It is these tensions that come to light in different ways in political philosophy, pavement politics, literary representations, and, of course, in Lord Tyrconnel's conjoint concerns over dirt and over 'government,' 'delicacy,' 'civility and politeness,' and 'wealth, commerce, and plenty.' This account cannot, however, exhaust the signs in the street. The improved streetscape with its newly open and attractive shopfronts was also a vital part of the processes of commodification that linked politeness to new forms of consumption.[176] That these processes, and their connections to the dangerous smoothness of the newly paved streets, provoked satirists to condemnations of paving projects in the name of luxury and effeminacy leads down the road toward the commodified spectacles and spaces of Vauxhall Gardens.[177]

CHAPTER FOUR

~⫘

The Pleasure Garden

INTRODUCTION: LEARNING FROM VAUXHALL

In the summer of 1773 Henry Bate—an Essex parson, the editor of *The Morning Post,* and a man with a love of boxing and self-publicity—visited Vauxhall Gardens on the south side of the River Thames. His group included Mrs Elizabeth Hartley, an actress renowned for her beauty who had recently made her first appearance at Covent Garden, and her husband.[1] During the evening Mrs Hartley became distressed when a group of fashionable young men, later identified as Captain Croftes, Thomas Lyttelton and George Robert Fitzgerald, wouldn't stop staring at her. Lyttelton was the son of a well-respected politician who had been a staunch opponent of Robert Walpole. He was a product of Eton, Oxford and the grand tour, and, in contrast to his father, was well known for his loose and prodigal lifestyle.[2] Fitzgerald had been born into a well-connected Irish Protestant family and had been educated at Eton. He was a soldier, a gambler and a duellist who had fought for his honour twenty-five times by the mid-1770s, earning himself the nickname 'Fighting Fitzgerald.' He carried a limp from a duel in Paris and a cracked skull from being shot in the head in Galway. He was a quarrelsome and dangerous man who was eventually hanged for arranging the cold-blooded murder of an Irish neighbour.[3] Collectively, these men were known as 'the Macaronis' in the extensive newspaper debate and gossip that the incident provoked (see Figure 7).[4]

To protect Mrs Hartley, Bate moved to a position that blocked the men's view. He then stared and made faces at them. They stared and

Figure 7 The Maccaroni Sacrifice, 1773. Reproduced by permission of the British Library.

grimaced back. When his party got up to leave, Bate traded insults with Captain Croftes. Later that evening Bate and Croftes encountered each other at the far end of the pleasure garden and resumed their exchange of insults. Fitzgerald's arrival on the scene prompted a heated argument on the rights and wrongs of men looking at women and another flurry of insults. Fitzgerald lambasted the incompatibility of Bate's profession and his love of boxing. Bate ridiculed Fitzgerald's clothing and his appearance: 'The dress, hat and feather,—miniature picture [of himself], pendant at his snow-white bosom, and a variety of other delicate appendages to this *man of fashion*.'[5] A crowd gathered, but the battle was postponed. At two o'clock that morning Bate and Croftes met at a coffeehouse and arranged to duel in Richmond Park. As they prepared to leave, Fitzgerald arrived to tell Bate that there was a gentleman outside, a Captain Miles, who wanted to box him then and there. Bate was unwilling to fight but eventually made things up with Croftes and fought Captain Miles in the front dining room of the Spread Eagle Tavern. Bate beat Miles easily. Strangely, the supposed captain turned out to be Fitzgerald's footman and not a gentleman at all.

I want to use this incident to open up the wider cultural landscape of the pleasure gardens by interpreting Vauxhall and its 'Affray' as part of a 'modern' culture of commodity consumption.[6] This requires interpretation of several parts of the battle between Bate and the Macaronis. First, the sources of the conflict: Why was it so problematic for these men to look at Mrs Hartley? Second, the nature of the insults: Why was 'Macaroni' a term of abuse, and what were the meanings it carried which made sense of miniature portraits, feathered hats and Herculean clubs? Finally, the ways the conflict was 'resolved': What understandings (or misunderstandings) of masculinity and virtue can be attached to a footman dressed as a gentleman fighting a parson? In answering these questions, I will argue that *where* the incident happened is a key to understanding its meaning, and that the connections and tensions that structure the 'Affray'—between masculinity, illusion, commodification and commercialisation—were also the ones that structured and troubled the meanings of Vauxhall Gardens.

Vauxhall was a key site in the geography of eighteenth-century cultural production.[7] The weakness of court and church in late-seventeenth- and early-eighteenth-century England opened a space for new forms of culture and new locations for its production and consumption.[8] Inevitably, these new cultural forms shaped and were shaped by the contexts in which they appeared. Thus, David Solkin reads Vauxhall's importance as the first place where new artistic genres were displayed in public on any scale as part of the production of a new public sphere. Here, in the eyes of its proponents, refined and polite pleasures succeeded in defining new forms of sociability and 'legitimising the elegant pleasures enabled by commercial wealth.' The key process was the separation of these polite enjoyments from the vulgarity of the sensual entertainments of the fair. Solkin reconstructs a history of the progressive cleaning up of the pleasure garden into a place where the repressed carnivalesque could return, but only as pictures of children's games and rural frolics.[9] There were, however, other tensions. What was produced at such sites was produced for the market. Vauxhall's cultural geography was part of the eighteenth century's 'consumer revolution.'[10] Newly commodified pleasures were sold to a broader public than ever before, and the periodic revitalisations and transformations of the market were increasingly driven by the wider, deeper and more rapid changes in fashion that, in this period, was itself transformed from something that was 'expensive, exclusive and Paris-based' to something that was 'cheap, popular and London-based.'[11] What was consumed was consumed in part because it was fashionable and for sale.

It is this link between commodification and fashion that renders Vauxhall a space of modernity.[12] As part of a modern culture of consumption, Vauxhall Gardens was built on an excitement over novelty and surprise that give it a place among those dream worlds of capitalist consumption where identities are created and transformed through an open-ended process of desire and experimentation.[13] The pleasure gardens were key sites for questioning and switching identities within the welter of new experiences brought about by consuming pleasures within novel circuits of commodities. They were places for 'intrigue, "play" and experimenting with social roles.'[14] Yet these pleasures were, at the same time, dangerous. Commodification and desire were always haunted by the vices of avarice and sexual transgression; class and gender identities were threatened by the illicit commerce of luxury and the masquerade; and the stability of appearances was threatened by the fantasies and illusions attendant on commodity consumption.[15] The argument that I want to pursue here is that these pleasures and dangers, which defined this culture of consumption, should be understood in terms of relationships between commodification, sexuality and visual illusion. In doing so I want to show how the processes of commodification characteristic of capitalist modernity are both interpreted through other social and cultural relations—between men and women, and between 'reality' and 'representation'—and are part of the reinterpretations of those relations. Since part of my argument is that a key to these interpretations and reinterpretations is Vauxhall Gardens, it is first necessary to outline its geography in some detail.

A TOUR OF VAUXHALL GARDENS IN THE 1750s

There had been a pleasure garden south of the river at Vauxhall since the 1660s. Set back from the Thames among the fields, it was on the very edge of the city, and most accessible by boat from the stairs at Whitehall or Westminster (see Figure 1). People went to stroll among the trees, to eat, to drink and to listen to wandering musicians, and it had something of a reputation as a place for sexual misadventure.[16] But it was transformed by Jonathan Tyers, who took over the lease in 1728. He landscaped the gardens, replanted them, constructed new buildings, planned new artistic and musical entertainments, and reopened Vauxhall in 1732 with an outdoor masquerade, a *Ridotto al Fresco*. Under Tyers, Vauxhall became London's most popular and fashionable summer evening resort, and it soon bred imitations elsewhere in London, in Dublin, and in Paris.[17]

Figure 8 shows Vauxhall around 1751. The entrance was from the road. Visitors paid an entrance fee of one shilling, left their servants in what was described as a 'coop,' and stepped out into the gardens.[18] The twelve acres were geometrically ordered into a series of tree-lined gravel walks. The entrance was at one end of the 900-foot-long Grand Walk. At the other end was a statue of Aurora and a ha-ha designed to both enclose the gardens and to open up 'a View into the adjacent Meads; where Haycocks, and Haymakers sporting, during the mowing Season, add a Beauty to the Landskip.'[19] Three other walks ran parallel to this one. On the far right was the Druid's Walk, Lovers' Walk, or Dark Walk. Here the trees formed 'a delightful verdant canopy' and a home for songbirds.[20] The gothic obelisk which terminated this walk later replaced the statue of Aurora at the end of the Grand Walk. The next walk contained a series of triumphal arches that framed the view of a building painted to represent the Temple of Neptune. On the far left was what was known as 'the rural downs.' This turf walk contained a statue of Milton and, for a while, the 'musical bushes': three shrub-covered openings from which music emanated.[21] There were also two 600-foot-long cross-walks. One ended with a life-size picture of an alcove with three niches for Flora and her genii; the other ended with a large painted backdrop of the ruins of Palmyra.[22]

At the centre of the gardens stood Tyers's first new development, 'The Grove.' This included an elevated stage for the orchestra, from which music was played at intervals during the evening when the weather was fine. Behind this stood the Prince of Wales's Pavilion which boasted a Doric portico, red curtains, glass chandeliers, and, in its lavishly decorated salon, a series of paintings by Francis Hayman of scenes from Shakespeare.[23] Outside, the Grove was filled with tables illuminated by some of the fifteen hundred glass lamps that lit the gardens.[24] Off to the left was the Rotunda where the orchestra played when the weather was bad. This was a circular building, seventy feet in diameter. Its mosaic-painted walls were punctuated with sixteen sash windows, each surmounted with the Prince of Wales's feathers. Under each window was a bust of a famous person. Interspersing the windows

Figure 8 A General Prospect of Vauxhall Gardens, 1751. Reproduced by permission of the British Museum.

were sixteen mirrors and from the ceiling hung a grand chandelier. The way out to the gardens was through a classical-style salon. Its roof was decorated with paintings of gods and its walls were adorned with picture frames.[25] These were originally designed to hold paintings of the royal family but, by the mid–1760s, they were filled with large canvasses celebrating British military victories. These buildings were collectively described as 'the TEMPLE of Pleasure.'[26]

The salon exited through a gothic temple into a semicircular colonnade that ended where the Grand Walk met the first cross walk. Here another temple housed an animated picture of a water mill which was shown at certain times each night. Within the colonnade were a series of 'supper boxes' containing tables and chairs where the company could eat, drink and admire the view. Each box was decorated with a painting. Most were by Francis Hayman and were light scenes of children's games, rustic pursuits and literary themes, although some were of British naval victories.[27] This curve of supper boxes was mirrored on the other side of the gardens by another less elaborate set, each of which also held a painting. This colonnade framed Louis François Roubiliac's statue of Handel.

Vauxhall Gardens was a hybrid and cosmopolitan space. It was an eclectic and pleasureable modern combination of simulated versions of the classical, the gothic and the exotic, as well as elements of the contemporary European and imperial cultures of which Britain was a part. Within this space men and women walked and talked, ate and drank, listened when the music played, or gazed at the paintings. It was a place for taking polite pleasures, yet this did not preclude a frisson of sexual danger. Vauxhall remained a site for flirtation and assignation: 'Gentlemen who come alone are open to the overtures of any amiable companion, and Ladies who venture without a masculine guide, are not, generally speaking, averse to the company of a polite protector.'[28] That Vauxhall's walks and shades were heavy with sexual tensions cannot be separated from the fact that the space within which they were played out was one that was constructed through commodification and commercialisation. Vauxhall gardens's culture of consumption connected sex and money as both pleasure and danger.

COMMODIFICATION, COMMERCIALISATION AND LUXURY

Vauxhall was a landscape of commodified consumption. Jonathan Tyers's transformation of the gardens involved a substantial injection of capital and a commercialisation of leisure.[29] He was one of 'the new capitalists of cultural enterprise,' an 'entrepreneur of entertainment' who aimed at accumulation through titillation, at commercial success through hedonistic consumption.[30] In order to capture and, in part, to create an expanding middle-class market, he had Vauxhall remodeled and lit with a costly new lighting system. He employed artists, theatrical designers and architects to transform the space into somewhere new, a novelty that he could sell.[31] He reshaped the production of musical entertainment so that formality and spectacle replaced impromptu and mobile music-making. Music became commodified and under the control of the management.[32] In doing all this, Tyers was operating in direct competition with other attractions. This was particularly pertinent after 1742 when Ranelagh opened in Chelsea and Tyers had to improve what he offered in order to compete.[33] He made several major additions in the 1740s (including most of the buildings outside the Grove), and continued to change the entertainments offered throughout the period, selling them as new and fashionable additions.[34] Thus, 'S. Toupee' reported 'an honest old mechanick' as saying 'that [Vauxhall] is said to be so much improved since he was a young man, that he was resolved to see what new-fangled notions they had got now-a-days, to exceed what were in fashion then.'[35]

The commercialisation and commodification of Vauxhall spread beyond its walls, and beyond the pocket and purse of Jonathan Tyers. John Lockman was paid to write promotional puffs for Tyers as well as songs for the gardens. These were turned to account by selling them alongside prints of Vauxhall views.[36] A roaring trade was done. One set of engravings of a selection of Hayman's Vauxhall paintings ran to three editions and became some of the best known images in England.[37] Fans were sold with pictures of Vauxhall on them; songs were sold by virtue of having been sung there; a parodic *Spring Garden Journal* was produced and sold; and masquerade warehouses profited by hiring out costumes for balls.[38] Mr Hart, a music and dancing master from the Strand, set up 'Marble Hall' near Vauxhall as a place where gentlemen and ladies, having first been taught in privacy—partnered only by chairs and members of Mr Hart's family—could dance by private subscription.[39] Mrs Cornelys, known for her masquerades, set up her 'White House' near Vauxhall in 1778. It had a colonnaded garden, supper rooms, a music room and a library, and sought 'to provide a place of entertainment for the polite world during the summer and spring months, where none are to be admitted but subscribers, who must be people of rank and fortune.' She promised that '[t]he contiguity of the place to Vauxhall Gardens gives them an opportunity of mixing with *everybody*, or retiring amongst *themselves,* according to their fancy.'[40] Such endeavours drove up the land prices around Vauxhall and Tyers himself was accused by pamphleteers of profiteering and of buying up land to frustrate his rivals' plans.[41]

Within Vauxhall the main commodities were food and drink. Their sale was highly organised. Numbered waiters were responsible for particular tables, prices were fixed up around the gardens to prevent customers from being overcharged, and the flows of food, drink and money were carefully regulated to prevent the staff from defrauding the management.[42] 'Toupee' claimed in 1739 that this meant that 'Five hundred separate suppers are served in an instant,' and by 1750 Lockman was claiming that this was an '*Order*' so 'exact' that three or four thousand people could be served at the same time.[43]

This commercialisation of culture was not unproblematic. The high cost of food and drink at Vauxhall was a constant topic in commentaries on it.[44] In these satires food became money as its price rose, and it was clear that it was there for pleasure not sustenance. In one example a father complained about the cost while his wife and daughters either spent freely or dreamed of spending his money. When eating, '[t]he old gentleman, at every bit he put into his mouth, amused himself with saying: "There goes two-pence—there goes three-pence—there goes a groat."'[45] Another apocryphal story tells that a carver applying for a job cutting ham at Vauxhall was reported to have said to Tyers, 'Why, if you mean *thin,* sir . . . I'll be shot if I don't cut it so that every single ham will cover all your garden walks like a red and white carpet.'[46] As Tim Breen has pointed out in a different context, '[b]ehind every transaction hovered the spectre of luxury,' and, in posing the distinction between eating to live or eating for pleasure, food had a central place in definitions of the luxurious.[47] Indeed, discussions of Vauxhall's pleasures were always part of the debate over the morality of consumption that revolved around the idea of luxury.

Christopher Berry has argued that there was a sea-change in understandings of luxury between a 'classical'—Greek, Roman and medieval—view that it was dangerous and destructive, and a 'modern' view, beginning in late-seventeenth-century northern Europe, that luxury was vital to the prosperity and liberty of commercial societies. The debate over luxury was a debate over the nature of morality, society, economy and politics in a commercial world. It was part of the debate between Shaftesbury, Mandeville and Hume discussed in Chapter 3. As a result, there were many conflicting discourses of luxury in eighteenth-century London: the notions of the ancients that 'foreign' luxury corrupts, depraves and weakens; Mandeville's ideas that public virtue and prosperity could be built upon private luxurious consumption; and the increasingly sophisticated arguments of David Hume and Adam Smith that the polite, refined and moderate consumption of luxuries was crucial to social and political well-being.[48]

As a new site for the production and consumption of pleasure, Vauxhall was part of this debate. Following David Solkin, I want to illustrate what is at issue here by considering two essays, published anonymously by Henry Fielding in the early 1740s, that end with descriptions of Vauxhall and Ranelagh.[49] Fielding, writing in the guise of a foreign visitor to London, claimed that his 'admiration and respect' for this 'mighty nation' had been overturned by what he had seen of the venality of the English:

> That Money is the universal Idol of all Ranks and Degrees of People; being look'd upon as omnipotent. Like Charity, covering a multitude of Sins; like Fame, bestowing a good Report; like Authority, commanding Respect and Veneration; like Nobility, exacting Place and Precedency; and, like Virtue, attoning for all Defects, both of Body and Mind.
>
> That Patriotism and Public Spirit are held but as beautiful Phantoms, set up to facilitate only the Designs of the Great, and amuse and deceive the Vulgar: That none but Boys and Fools are to be found among their real Worshippers; and even they in the End find out the Cheat, and continue to profess only to be reimbursed as Hypocrites, what they lost as Devotees.
>
> That Self both is, and ought to be uppermost in all our Actions: That to have a generous, benevolent Spirit is to be a Sheep among Men; to be fleeced first and then devoured.[50]

Fielding presents a society in which all morality is dictated by monetary value, and argues that this pursuit of narrowly defined private interests offers little hope for public virtue.[51] In his second essay the analysis is extended to connect the love of money to the love of pleasure:

> Every Thing here is venal; Money is esteem'd an Equivalent for all Things; and this Lust of Lucre is founded on an inordinate Love of Pleasure: The Pleasure of the Sense? Those of the Mind being esteem'd scarce worth coveting, much less purchasing.[52]

He damns the English for their selfish pleasure-seeking—'All are the Children of Luxury, and all must have their Appetites flatter'd as well as fed'—and sets out to analyse these pleasures. In doing so he presents an account of the desires of the English that roots them in eating and drinking, and he provides a class-based interpretation of 'Places of Resort' that ascends from the lowest dives, through beer houses and theatres, to Ranelagh and Vauxhall. Here the tone changes from the general condemnation of 'Eating, Drinking, Smoaking, or making Love to the Ladies of Pleasure . . . the old social, sensual, unpolish'd frolic Turn of the *English*.' The pleasure gardens are presented via an eyewitness account, and the delights to be found are predominantly visual (or aural) rather than the pleasures of the belly (or lower). There is also no straightforward condemnation of them as places of luxury. Ranelagh is an 'enchanted Palace' that, 'at the first Glance,' made him 'dumb with Surprise and Astonishment' at the architecture, decoration and lighting.[53] It was a place where 'Pleasure seem'd to beckon her wanton Followers.' This, however, was not to last: 'Satiety follow'd: In five Minutes I was familiar with the whole and every Part, in the 5 next Indifference took Place, in 5 more my Eyes grew dazzled, my Head grew giddy, and all Night I dreamt of *Vanity Fair*.'

Vauxhall gets a better review. He is 'captivated' by its beauty, and he describes the Grove as 'delightful' and the Pavilion as 'noble' and 'elegant.' As a whole, Vauxhall Gardens 'rival Paradise itself' but, bearing in mind his earlier strictures, there is a sting in the tail:

> I must avow, I found my whole Soul, as it were, dissolv'd in Pleasure; not only you, but even *Paris* itself was forgot—My whole Discourse, while there was a Rhapsody of Joy and Wonder. Assure yourself such an Assemblage of Beauties never, but in the Dreams of the Poets, ever met before—and I scarce yet believe the bewitching Scene was real—
>
> See here the Taste of *Britain*! And reason like a Philosopher and a Politician upon the Consequences!—I add no more, but am now awake, and very sincerely, *Yours etc*[54]

David Solkin argues that in these passages Fielding, albeit awkwardly, exempts the polite diversions of Ranelagh and Vauxhall from the moral condemnation he directs against the pleasures of the lower orders. Fielding rehabilitates luxury through refined consumption and, like Lockman, provides for the production of Vauxhall as 'a space for the manufacture and display of a polite social identity—everything, ostensibly, that the traditional fair was not.'[55] However, the dangers of the fair's grotesque bodies are not the only ones at stake here. While Fielding may help to absolve Vauxhall of that charge, there are other elements to his critique. Fielding does not deny that Vauxhall and Ranelagh are places of pleasure, but that also makes them places of danger. These dangers lie in the powers of illusion. Fielding carefully differentiates between the bewitching enchantments of a world of dreams and illusions, and what should be thought about the love of money and pleasure when the philosopher or politician is 'awake.' These commodified pleasures hide their 'real' social relations and, as for Karl Marx, commodification becomes 'a visual problem in perception.'[56] These luxuries and their link to lucre are constructed through a discourse on the commodification of pleasure that presents Vauxhall as the haunt of illusions and mysterious enchantments; the site of misperceptions and dreams; and the place of the pleasures and dangers of the dissolution of the self. This concentration on the dreamlike state of consumption effectively foreshadows recent reevaluations of eighteenth-century consumption that seek to understand it as the creation of new identities through a 'peculiar, daydream-like fusion of the pleasures of fantasy and reality.'[57]

Fielding's 'critique' is, however, still an ambiguous one. The depiction of Vauxhall as an enchanted dream world, or a bewitching place of illusion, was also part of the puffery used to sell it. John Lockman argued for the necessity of pleasurable consumption since to 'possess, like the *Dutch,* a mighty Magazine of all things useful and curious, for which ev'ry part of the Globe has been ransack'd and not enjoy them; could convey (one would think) no other Satisfaction than that grovelling one which a miser feels.'[58] In doing so he depicted Homer and Virgil singing of Vauxhall Gardens that 'The whole is a delicious Dream!,' and he speculated on what a refined person taken there in their sleep and then awoken might say:

> Where am I? O what Wonders rise?
> What Scenes are these that glitter round.
> Some Vision, sure, must bless my Eyes;
> Or this must be inchanted Ground!
> . . . .
> So fondly ev'ry Sense is charm'd
> O whither shall I turn my Eye!
> Each roving Faculty alarm'd,
> In sweet Amaze enrapt I lie.[59]

This early-modern consumer wonderland, like the department stores, shopping malls and theme parks that followed it, provoked both desire and concern. Its spaces could be either magical or shallow depending upon the author.[60] As John Brewer has argued, it was a part of a culture of consumption whose dreams, illusions and attractions were driven by luxury, social emulation, human appetites, and desires. This meant that the refined pleasures that Vauxhall purveyed were always 'heavily compromised by but dependent upon two forces that undercut its impartiality, namely pecuniary gain—acquisitiveness—and sexual passion.'[61] In this sense Fielding's description of a world of illusion is part of an exploration of the relationship between the love of money and the love of pleasure that suggests that acquisitiveness could never be expelled from the gardens. The rest of this chapter will investigate the relationships between sexuality and commodification, and the anxieties over masculinity and femininity that they staged (and which formed a crucial part of the debates over luxury). Through my discussion of these relationships I want to show that both sexuality and commodification were often understood through invoking the mystifying veils of visual illusion. The first arena for this investigation is Tyers's opening *Ridotto al Fresco;* the second, and much more extensive, arena charts the rise and fall of the Macaronis.

DREAMING OF SEX AND MONEY
AT THE *RIDOTTO AL FRESCO*

The early history of Tyers's Vauxhall is entwined with the history of the carnivalesque. At Vauxhall, as earlier at the London masquerades of the 1720s, the carnival's themes of indulging sensual, bodily pleasures; playing with identities; and mixing and inverting high and low were commodified and made part of the pleasures of polite society.[62] As Brewer suggests, this play of sexual adventure and pecuniary gain—exemplified in the figure of the prostitute, and characteristic of culture as a commodity—was both the underpinning of Vauxhall's success and a persistent threat to its claims to refinement.[63] This is well illustrated in two engravings from the early 1740s (Figure 9 and Figure 10). Both are based upon an engraving by George Bickham Jr. from a picture by Hubert François Gravelot.[64] The engravings combine words and images, and juxtapose the denizens of the Grove to a more crudely drawn group. David Solkin has identified this group as consisting of Vauxhall's gatekeeper, Jonathan Tyers, John Lockman, Dawson the glassmaker (who sold Tyers the lamps that lit the gardens), one of Tyers's 'chaplains' (a moral guardian employed to ensure that the pleasures taken were refined ones), and Robert Walpole. In each engraving polite postures were satirically undercut by the desires upon which Vauxhall depended.

The words that the characters speak mix sexual and pecuniary desire. In the Grove 'all we see are the young men and women of London, unchaperoned and apparently at liberty to pursue their desires,' while as Figure 9 shows, the high prices of food and drink adorn the trees and all who can pay are admitted.[65] The verses below each of the images also shape their meaning. For the engraving in Figure 9 the dominant theme is money: Vauxhall is the place where 'you can't but spend your Brassee.' For the engraving in Figure 10 the dominant theme is sexual desire: Vauxhall is 'wanton in Delights,' a plan where 'all is Mirth & Harmony & Love.' Vauxhall Gardens are built on the desires for both sex and money which, in turn, pull against their politeness and the refined pleasures they offer.

These tensions were evident at the *Ridotto al Fresco* with which Tyers opened Vauxhall Gardens on 7 June 1732. For a guinea each visitor entered an open-air masquerade. Masked balls were already a popular and notorious entertainment that had been profitably commercialised by 'Count' John James Heidegger.[66] They had also been vilified by critics for their immorality. Their pleasures and dangers lay in the ways in which the masking of identities fragmented unitary notions of the self, leveled hierarchies of class and gender, and gave vent—particularly for women—to 'frenetic sexual solicitation' in 'a unique realm of sexual freedom.' Masquerades were a space where fantasies of difference presented 'a collective leap out of the everyday.' They were playful places of deception and illusion where participants quite literally could not believe their eyes.[67] It was these problems of perception that had prompted Henry Fielding, in his *The Masquerade* of 1728, to stress the moral coding of dreaming and awakening when he wrote that 'Waking, all your adventures seem / An idle, trifling, feverish dream.'[68]

In the light of these critiques *The Universal Spectator and Weekly Journal* mocked Tyers's pretensions to refinement, and sought to drive a wedge between polite pleasures and the sexual license of the proposed *Ridotto.* They invented Sir John Meretrix, a magistrate, to address Diana, the goddess of chastity and the directress of the Midnight Academy at Vauxhall:

> No Mortal but a Goddess . . . cou'd have struck out a plan so new, so noble, and so useful, as that of the *Ridotto al'Fresco;* which the generality of Mortals are such Buzzards as to suppose a meer *Masquerade;* and by the Words *al'Fresco* imagine there will be much Frisking in it. But, silly creatures! How will they stare when they find, that under the delicious Disguise of a *Masquerade in the cool Shades,* your real and genuine Design is, to

Figure 9 Spring Gardens, Vauxhall, 1741. Reproduced by permission of the Duchy of Cornwall Office.

Figure 10 Vaux Hall, c. 1741. Reproduced by permission of the Duchy of Cornwall Office.

> instruct both Sexes in *good Letters, good Manners, Writing, Needlework,* and a *nameless et Cetera.*

They satirised the supposed civilising influence of the *Ridotto*'s classical allusions and poked fun at its elevated intentions, seeking to reveal Tyers's true, and venal, purposes beneath. As Meretrix stated, turning education into titillation, 'Your Resolution to appoint the *Teacher* or *instructor* of a different Sex from the *Scholar . . .* is a very happy one.'[69] Similarly, *Applebee's Journal* envisioned the animals of the garden, displaced by the *Ridotto*'s revellers, discoursing on sexual solicitation and its attendant deceptions; it described an 'Orange Wench' dressed as an 'Arcadian Shepherdess' and mistaken for a 'Dutchess'; and a countess dressed as a ballad seller 'Snapt up' by a 'Gaoler, in the habit of a Persian Monarch.'

As the cuckoo and the serpent agreed, there would be many cuckolds made that night by snakes in the grass.[70] Each of these critiques depended for its force upon the frisson of sexual danger that the *Ridotto* also exploited. But some commentators were far less ready to condemn these pleasures. For example, Theophilus Cibber's reworking of *The Harlot's Progress* took Moll Hackabout through her seduction and downfall and into the Bridewell. However, just as the women were about to start their penal work they were whisked off to a *Ridotto al Fresco* at Vauxhall by Harlequin, Scaramouch, Pierrot and Mezetin. The play ended with a 'grand Comic Ballard' at the gardens and only the most ambiguous of moral messages.[71]

Elsewhere sexual pleasure was connected, via illusion, to the world of money. *The Weekly Register* condemned the *Ridotto* in the name of luxury. It was a 'bewitching Kind of Entertainment, so much a novelty in these Parts, [which] took its Rise in *Italy*, where Sloth and Luxury had banished Bravery and Virtue, and from thence has tainted all the polite Nations of *Europe*.' Its full critique operated through a dream sequence:

> I was induc'd to make one of the gay Number at *Spring-Gardens*, and my Heart was weak enough to be captured with so new a Representation of Pleasure. Towards the Morning I retir'd to Bed with my Mind still intent on the Night's Entertainment, so that even my Dreams continued the Scene in the following Manner.

Led by '*Curiousity* herself' around a 'magnificent' and 'enchanting' version of Vauxhall Gardens, he enters 'The Palace of Pleasure.' Here the Goddess of Pleasure promises her followers continual joy in any of four delights—love, wine, ambition and money—which are represented by buildings visible at the ends of the 'adjoining Vistas.' He, 'as much inclin'd to the soft invitation as any,' cannot choose, but finds himself guided by 'a grave, sober, lovely Matron': Virtue. The Houses of love, wine and ambition all present magnificent spectacles of amorous, bibulous and sumptuous pleasures and pleasure-seekers. The dazzled dreamer longs 'to mingle with them,' but each time Virtue takes him behind the spectacle to see its other side. Behind the House of Love is 'Jealousy, Revenge, Disease and Want'; behind the House of Wine are 'the dying Drunkard,' 'the enervated Reveller' and 'the prodigal Spendthrift'; and behind the House of Ambition he 'saw the Assassin's Dagger, the envenom'd Present, the Engines of Death and Infamy, and all the Tools of Oppression.' The last temple is that of money:

My Guide for the last Time led me thro' a horrid, lonely Passage, into a large Hall full of Cobwebs and Dust, where, by a dim Light thro' a paint-ed Window, we discover'd a wrinkled, hoary old Man sitting on an im-mense Heap of Riches, and counting it over with a look of Suspicion and Fear. This was the God *Plutus,* attended by a number of Votaries with the lowest Protestations, but even while they worshipp'd they cheated their God. The Evils of *Avarice* put on no Gloss. Doubt and Fear are the Covetous Man's Companions, Oppression and Dishonesty his Slaves, and Ignominy and Curses his Reward. Yet I could hardly resist the Tempta-tion; but *Virtue* reclaim'd me once more to herself, and having again bid me *beware,* left me in the midst of the visionary Scene to make the Appli-cation of her Precepts.[72]

What is striking about this use of Vauxhall as a moral allegory is that it starts with lust and ends with the love of money, connecting the two in its critique of pleasure and desire. The same connection was made in *Applebee's Journal* where the Devil was presented as originating the *Ridotto al Fresco* when he disguised himself as a serpent to seduce Eve in the Garden of Eden. His votaries were said to be 'The *Miser, Stockjobber, Extortioner,* [and] *Pawnbroker,*' all of whom profit from pre-tence and illusion.[73] Also, by presenting this moral vision through the device of a dream retold, the *Weekly Register* not only distances the cri-tique from the reality of Tyers's *Ridotto,* but also presents its pleasures as ultimately illusory while admitting the power of their seductions for those not fully 'awake' to virtue.[74] These ways in which the discussions of the *Ridotto* connect concerns around sexuality to questions of com-modification and commercialisation through the play of spectacle and illusion also structure the world of the Macaronis.

THE TRUE ORTHODOX TREAD UPON FAIRY GROUND: LOCATING THE MACARONI

From the middle of the 1760s the term 'Macaroni' designated a particu-lar sort of fashionable man. The term had originated with a group of rich, young associates of Almack's Club and the court who, it was said, having returned from European grand tours enamoured of continental style, had set up, as an in-joke, the Macaroni Club. Horace Walpole re-ferred to it as 'composed of all the travelled young men who wear long curls and spying glasses.' Both hair and vision were enduring parts of Macaronidom, as was the implicit rejection of the robust anglophilia of roast beef.[75] From being an amusement for a small coterie, the term be-

came, via the popular periodicals and, in particular, the prints of
Matthew and Mary Darly, the primary vehicle for satire in the years
1772 and 1773. From 1771 the Darlies produced an extensive series of
prints that in presenting a vast variety of Macaroni images—including
'The Clerical Macaroni,' 'The Noviciate of a Macaroni' (Figure 11),
'The Bath Macaroni,' and 'A Mungo Macaroni' (Figure 12)—satirised
both social types and specific individuals.[76] For example, Joseph Banks
appeared as the 'Fly-Catching Macaroni'; Charles Fox was 'The Original Macaroni'; and his brother Stephen was 'The Sleepy Macaroni.'
Elsewhere, William Dodd, the Chaplain of the Magdalen Hospital who
was hanged for forgery, was described as 'The Macaroni Parson.'[77] The
prints were, as Dorothy George notes, 'a guide to the celebrities of the
day.'[78] While there are doubts about how deep and wide the audience
for political prints was, and how effective the shop window could be for
popularising visual satires, Macaroni images do seem to have a privi-
leged relationship to this form of publicity. Of 'the small body of [sur-
viving] prints depicting the print-shop window and its spectators,' two
are of Macaroni subjects.[79] *The London Magazine,* aware of the tides of
fashion, noted that 'As it is now at its height, our print-shops are filled
with *Maccaronies* of a variety of kinds,' and the fact that Macaronis were
'affixed in every print shop' prompted the publication of even more
Macaroni material.[80] This knowledge was not confined to London.
Robert Hitchcock's play *The Macaroni* (1773) was performed in York;
The Town and Country Magazine, which vigorously attacked Macaroni
fashions, was read by both urban merchants and country gentry; and it
even went transatlantic as Yankee-Doodle-Dandy put a feather in his
cap and called it 'Macaroni.'[81]

Although they were widespread, and different audiences must have
had different interpretations of these Macaronis, the satires did have a
particular edge to them. Valerie Steele has identified them as political
attacks by a rising urban middle class on the young nobles of St James's,
and on Charles Fox in particular.[82] They were attacks that questioned
the legitimacy of an aristocratic political system and, at the same time,
operated in the economic realm as critiques of a particular mode of
consumption that linked luxury and effeminate masculinity to a lack of
patriotism, and therefore to a failure of cultural and political leadership.
However, tracing out the contours of this critique also reveals a series of
ambivalences. These attacks on pleasure, luxury and fashion were themselves commodities enmeshed in the processes of consumption. Macaroni dress was not really so different from what everyone 'fashionable'
was wearing. In the periodicals that decried them, Macaroni satires, like

Figure 11 The Noviciate of a Macaroni. *Ranelagh*, 1772. Reproduced by permission of the British Museum.

other attacks on luxury, 'nestled uneasily amidst . . . accounts of the latest dresses, nosegays, coiffeurs, and cuisine.'[83] Here, as elsewhere, commodity culture provoked both fear and fascination, laughter mixed with disgust.[84]

Macaronis were defined from the outset in terms of what they consumed, and particularly what they wore. While being a Macaroni was still a matter of elite play Frederick St. John, second Viscount Bolingbroke, wrote to George Selwyn, the politician and wit, then in Paris.

Figure 12   A Mungo Macaroni. Reproduced by permission of the British Museum.

He informed him that 'I do most heartily lament with you that my brother has turned his thoughts to intrigue, dress, and all the personal accomplishments of the most refined Macaroni.'[85] Yet any serious concern was not without desire. He later sought to transform himself:

> As Lord B much admires the taste and elegance of Colonel [John] St. John's [his younger brother] Parisian clothes, he wishes Mr Selwyn would order Le Duc to make him a suit of plain velvet. By plain, is meant with-

out gold and silver; as to the colours, pattern, and design of it, he relies upon Mr Selwyn's taste. A small pattern seems to be the reigning taste amongst the Macaronis at Almack's, and is, therefore what Lord B chooses. . . . As to the smallness of the sleeves, and the length of the waist, Lord B desires them to be outré, that he may exceed any Macaronis now about town, and become the object of their envy.'[86]

Dressing as a Macaroni was a matter of masculine fashion and display, a competitive and European world of men turning themselves into spectacles to impress other men. In the newly fashion-conscious eighteenth century these styles soon spread. *The Town and Country Magazine* told its readers that 'The infection at St. James's was soon caught in the city, and we have now Macaronies of every denomination, from the colonel of the Train'd Bands down to the errand boy.'[87] As it spread, Bolingbroke's self-conscious humour turned to satire. The Darly prints worked by simply dressing up people like Banks and Fox as Macaronis. The clothes carried the satirical meanings. In this process the Macaroni followed the path described by Neil McKendrick for eighteenth-century fashion in general. It went from being something that was 'expensive, exclusive and Paris-based' to being something 'cheap, popular and London-based.' To go further, like the dolls that carried new fashions to England and which McKendrick took as his way into explaining the 'consumer revolution,' Macaronis went from being something life-size, extravagantly decked-out and at court to being something small, made of paper and widely distributed.[88]

The satires that appeared in the periodical press depended upon characterising the Macaroni as an entirely modern figure, a man driven by the dictates of fashion's novelties: 'In short he must be a *museum* of everything that has not yet been imagined or worn before the year 1772.'[89] They then satirised this figure through exhaustive descriptions of dress that set out the commodities that made a Macaroni in attentive detail. Here is one from *The Macaroni Jester*:

> His Coat is very short, and long waisted, with a Fly flap cut, leaving only Pocket-Room enough for a Handkerchief and Snuff-Box. The Sleeves are very low on the Arm, and Button close around the Wrist. It is made so scanty over the Breast as only to meet by Means of two Pairs of Hooks and Eyes, the uppermost of which is contrived to pass through a small Eyelet-Hole made in the Bosom of the Shirt, so that the Frill hangs in Sight. His Waistcoat is out of all Taste if not made remarkably short indeed; and edged with a Point d'Espagne, of a different Colour from the Coat; with Pockets just large enough to hold a Bit of sealing Wax . . . His

Breeches must be made of French Black Soy, with Buttons about as large as the Head of a Blanket Pin:- they must come up close under the Midriff, be large enough for the A——— of a Dutchman; and hang in a most loose and slovenly Manner. He must wear white, or speckled Silk Stockings; Shoes buckled almost down to the Toe, and just enough behind to get his Heel in. His Hair must be full of Powder and Pomatum, and the Curls pasted close above the ear. The Bag of his Wig or Hair must be as broad at least, as a large Trencher; and his Hat must be very small, and sharpened before like the Bow of a Thames Wherry, the better to make its Way through Wind and Water. The Fob of the Breeches must contain a Watch with a long Gold Chain loaded with Trinkets and Baubles; but it is not necessary that the Pockets should be loaded with any Money. A long Sword, or a *Couteau de Chasse,* must be tucked on the left Hip, and a Cane, with a rich Tassel, must dangle from his right Hand. He must have a large Ring on his little Finger. . . . Thus equipped, he is fit for the Park or the Playhouse, and all the World will allow that he *cuts a Figure—A-la-mode de Macaroni.*[90]

This figure also needs to be placed within the history of a changing relationship between men and clothes that now located them within the streets of a commercial city and nation rather than among the ornate displays of the Renaissance court.[91] *The Macaroni Jester* performs this contextualisation and draws out its moral implications, eliding as it does so its own position in the world of fashionable commodification:

Walking in the Streets of London is the true orthodox Tread upon Fairy Ground—You have the Spells of Pick-pockets, the enchantments of Beauty, the Incantations of Pleasure, and the Lures of Vice, around you. You may have Intoxication in a Tavern—Love in an Alley—Musick in the Market-place—Coffee in every street—and Ox-cheek and Oysters in every Cellar. . . . London is the grand Mart of the World. . . . It is more religious and more profligate—more rich and more admired than all the Cities of the World for its modern Exellencies. . . . A man who has money, may have at once every delicate, every dainty, and every ornamental Beauty of the four Quarters of the World. Asia, Europe, Africa, and America, are cultivated and ransacked to indulge the Inhabitants in every luxury; and when this Island shall be conquored and depopulated, how will the rising World wonder at the luxurious Lives which English Peasants led, when they are informed, that their common Drink was composed of a Plant which grew in China, drawn with hot Water, and mixed with the Juice of the West India Sugar-cane made into a hard Consistence; and that Liquor was called *Tea!*
    It is this luxury, that will prove the ruin of this island.[92]

Placing the Macaroni on the shopping streets means that he was understood within the international chains of commodities that made London itself a dangerous place through the ways in which its endless varieties of consumption brought together the produce of the world. Within the discourse on luxury the taking up of tropical staples like coffee, tea and sugar by the labouring classes became a key site for denunciations of new consumer habits, and for the delineation of class-based models of masculinity and femininity.[93] The Macaroni, like the ruinous tea tables of these luxurious 'Peasants,' brought together luxuries from far-flung places and, in the transgression of boundaries that the hybrid forms of hot sweet tea and commodified masculinity represented, threatened Britain's decline.

These denunciations of the Macaroni's luxurious consumption were also part of a new discourse on luxury in the late eighteenth century. Instead of simply denouncing the poor, the popular periodicals increasingly attacked 'the indolent or wasteful rich' for their extravagant and 'excessively fashionable' lifestyles. From the 1770s this new emphasis upon fashion debated the relationship between property and conduct by contrasting the excessive luxury of the rich with 'a clear middle class morality' obsessed with respectability and proper appearances.[94] The Macaroni was, therefore, 'distinguished by carrying to the most ridiculous excess, dissipation, softness of manners, and modish novelty of dress.'[95] Through the ways in which these fashionable excesses transgressed the boundaries of sober respectability the Macaroni became a monstrosity.[96] In turn, these '[s]tudies of the outlandish and the grotesque would reaffirm the rules of polite behaviour and present object lessons in the observance of correct taste.'[97] In the global welter of commodities that shaped Macaroni hybridity these satires also served to map out the boundaries of an Englishness that international commodity circulation threatened to dissolve.

Marcourt, the first Macaroni character on stage, appeared in George Colman's (1770) comedy *Man and Wife*.[98] The play is set in Stratford-upon-Avon against the background of David Garrick's Shakespeare Jubilee of 1769. Like that piece of commercialised bardolatry, it staged a confrontation between England and the Continent. Garrick's three days of processions, music, transparencies, fireworks and balls succeeded in constructing a new 'national cultural heritage' that monumentalised Shakespeare as England's poet, and set the actor-manager up as his living representative.[99] Its high point was Garrick's carefully staged reading of a dedicatory ode and the discussion afterward. Garrick had set this up as a confrontation between himself and the actor Tom

King, who was dressed as 'a fashionable Frenchified fop' and spoke for a fictional anti-Shakespearean 'Anti-Goth Society' in words written for him by Garrick.[100] Englishness was being forged against its 'others,' and Colman's play can be understood as a similar use of the theatre as a 'bulwark of national manners, language, morality, virtue and spirit.'[101] It dramatised the confrontation for the hand of the wealthy Charlotte Cross between Marcourt's fancy, aristocratic and foreign manners—favoured by Charlotte's mother, a woman whose devotion to fashionable consumption is driven by social emulation—and Kitchen's robust, heavy-eating Englishness, which smacked of the squirearchy and was favoured by Charlotte's father. Kitchen sums up this confrontation of national and class-based consumption identities when he says that 'modern Italy is no more to be compared to Old England than a sirloin of beef to a spoonful of macaroni.'[102] During the play Marcourt is ridiculed for his snobbery, his gambling, the attention he pays to his hair, his diet—'nothing but froth, and whipt-sillabub'—and, most of all, the clothes that he lovingly wears and describes.[103] His successor, Jack Epicene in Hitchcock's *The Macaroni,* is similarly lambasted for having his clothes sent from Venice so he does not have to wear anything made in England, and for preferring Italian singers to English entertainers.[104] As his hairdresser says, he is 'So gentilesse, von wou'd swear dere was not von drop of de English blood in you.'[105] That Marcourt's refinements are contrasted to Kitchen's rough and ready Englishness does not mean that the latter is simply valued. His lack of manners and refinements are as vilified as Marcourt's excesses and, after the confusions of a masquerade scene, Charlotte marries Frankly who combines both Englishness and refinement without excess. He has successfully managed to play one off against the other to his own advantage.

The question of marriage is a vital one in that it engages one of the Macaroni's key characteristics: effeminacy. They were, at best, 'a thing of the neuter gender.'[106] Jack Epicene's name testifies to that, as do the popular periodicals' satires:

> Is it a man? 'Tis hard to say—
> A woman then?—A moment pray—
> So doubtful is the thing, that no man
> Can say if 'tis man or woman:
> Unknown as yet by sex or feature,
> It moves—a mere amphibious creature.[107]

This is a matter of being excessively fashionable since a Macaroni 'renders his sex dubious by the extravagence of his appearance.'[108] It also structures his relationships to women. In Hitchcock's play, Lord Promise's libertine masculinity is contrasted with that of the Macaroni. Promise is devoted to ruining women and, although he is reformed in the end, he ridicules Epicene's 'degenerate exotic effeminacy' and 'the cold, unanimated, unworthy ideas, you always entertain'd of these master-pieces of nature.'[109] Macaronis were represented as either not interested in women or actively disliking them.[110]

The connection that is forged here between a 'degraded' masculinity and the effects of 'foreign' luxuries has a lineage that can be traced back at least as far as Plato.[111] However, its appearance here in the specific context of commodified fashion and the forging of national identity meant that Macaroni effeminacy was understood as having serious consequences. The Macaronis threatened an overturning of the gender order. *The Macaroni Jester* predicted that if they prevailed for fifty years 'the *women* will become the best men,' and it provided spoof news stories of women highway robbers, preachers and duellists; of rumours that the Duchess of Cumberland was to be made lord chancellor; and of a man becoming dangerously ill after being frightened by a mouse.[112] A gender revolt was threatened that would make real the Macaronis' refusal to mark gender boundaries. *The London Magazine* had women saying 'let the more effeminate sex wear the petty-coat, we will hence-forward dispense with our charter, we will wear breeches.'[113] A report on a masquerade also portrayed the women who were dressed as men as just as manly, but more charming and admirable, than 'the ridiculous *Billy Whiffles* of the present age.'[114] Macaroni effeminacy was also understood as rendering a proud martial nation unsafe. As Jack Epicene says, 'I . . . have an aversion to a sword out of its scabbard, much more to its being lodg'd in my body.'[115] While their refinements made them less dangerous on the streets of London than the Bloods, Bucks, Mohocks and Roaring Blades of previous generations, their delicacy as soldiers rendered them contemptible.[116] In 1771 *The Town and Country Magazine* pointed out that the young noblemen in the days of Agincourt and Poitiers 'were as vigorous as they were brave . . . but modern refinements have unnerved us, every corner of the globe is ransacked for the destruction of our health.'[117] A year later this accusation was directed at the Macaronis when it was asked, 'Whither are the manly vigour and athletic appearance of our forefathers flown? Can these be their legitimate heirs? Surely no; a race of effeminate, self-admiring, emaciated fribbles can never have descended in a direct line from the heroes of Poitiers and Agincourt.'[118] In more poetic vein *The Matrimonial Magazine* described 'One of the modern mysteries of St James's' as follows:

Our modern monkey of manhood, is by name a soldier; but never felt any ball, but a wash ball; nor ever smelt any powder, but hair-powder; who never saw any service but that of the table and the toilet; who never had any wounds but from minikin pins and Cupid's darts; who never marched further than the gay parade.[119]

To attack the Macaronis was to attack an aristocratic form of government through notions of luxurious consumption and the effeminate masculinity associated with it. Through the codes of cultural nationalism and the polemical debates over luxury, they were presented as unpatriotic, undemocratic and un-English. As such, the discussions of Macaroni masculinity were part of the process of defining both nation and commerce in an age of empire and global trade.[120] Vauxhall Gardens was also part of that process although the images on show were rather different.

IMPERIAL VAUXHALL

As well as being a locus of the hybrid culture of luxurious consumption, Vauxhall Gardens was a site for the performance of modes of masculinity that connected military heroism, Britishness and empire. As Mollie Sands, writing about Ranelagh, pointed out long ago, the pleasure gardens 'and the new age were born together. It was to be an age of imperial expansion and European commitments, and the topic of war—whether on the Continent, in India, in Canada or in America, at sea or on land—was never to be long absent from the promenaders.'[121] Vauxhall always played upon a carefully contrived note of chauvinism. It was part of the spectacle. The gardens were a place for the patriotic and imperial displays that were part of the complex politics of nation and empire in the eighteenth century. For example, Vauxhall's association with Frederick, the Prince of Wales, as ground landlord and occasional visitor (he was at the opening *Ridotto*) was a matter of patriotic celebration and display that tied the gardens (and Tyers) into the politics of the Whig opposition organised around Leicester House.[122] This connection was also signaled in the celebration at Vauxhall of the taking of Porto Bello in 1739 by the opposition hero Admiral Vernon. This consisted of the exhibition of four maritime scenes by Peter Monamy including one of Vernon's triumph 'with Six Men of War only' which 'drew the whole town to Vauxhall Gardens.'[123] However, Vauxhall's location as part of the spectacle of imperial expansion was most evident in the context of the Seven Years War, when victories in India and the Americas were enthusiastically received across the country.[124] At Vauxhall imperial warfare was celebrated in song and on canvas.

Vauxhall and Ranelagh are credited with being the nurseries of English song. These forms of nationalised cultural production were constructed against 'foreign' entertainments in both form and content. Their 'literary and dramatic' form was contrasted to the 'vocal gymnastics' of French or Italian styles.[125] A nationalist and imperial content was also made clear in many of the songs written for Vauxhall during the Seven Years War. For example, John Lockman, Tyers's publicist, composed 'Cape Breton and Cherburg' (1758) which compared General Amherst's Canadian war with Edward III's war in France to the tune of 'God Save Our Noble King.' Amherst was also praised in Lockman's (1760) 'A Song on the Taking of Montreal.'[126] In addition, the songwriter was the secretary of the Society of the Free British Fishery which, as Bob Harris has argued, 'encapsulated the essence of the politics of empire in the early 1750s.'[127] In that capacity he wrote the ballads 'Britannia's Gold Mine; or the Herring Fishery for ever' (1750) and 'Flourish the Herring-Fishery' which were sung at Vauxhall, as well as pamphlets entitled 'The Vast Importance of the Herring Fishery &c. to These Kingdoms' and 'The Shetland Herring and Peruvian Gold Mine, A Fable.'[128] The connections between Vauxhall, song and empire may have been particularly strong in the 1750s and 1760s, but while the 1770s and 1780s were less triumphalist, and there was less to sing about, old victories were still rehearsed in songs like 'The Englishman's Wish' and 'The Valiant Sailors,' and new ones were heralded wherever possible. For example, 'On Admiral Rodney' and 'The Dutch Defeated' celebrated the admiral's controversial capture of the small Caribbean island of St Eustatius in 1781.[129] More generally, 'The New Naval Ode for 1780' and 'The Wooden Walls of England' still set out in words and music notions of the legitimacy of British imperial power that repeated many of those earlier themes.[130]

In terms of the visual arts, Vauxhall holds a special place within imperial culture. In the 1740s Hayman's paintings of Shakespearean scenes exhibited in the Prince of Wales's Pavilion had begun to forge some of the meanings of Englishness that Garrick would later render as explicit performance.[131] It was, however, the decoration of the Grand Salon in the 1760s that constructed Vauxhall as an imperial space. The walls that were to have been hung with portraits of the royal family were then adorned with enormous canvasses by Hayman of themes from the Seven Years War.[132] There were two allegories—*The Triumph of Britannia* (1762) and *Britannia Distributing Laurels* (c. 1764)—and two history paintings—*The Humanity of General Amherst* (1760) and *Lord Clive Receiving the Homage of the Nabob* (c. 1761–1762). The first allegory represented medallions of George III and seven admirals being carried through the waves by nereids alongside Britannia on Neptune's chariot. The other featured leading generals in Roman costume.

The two histories are rather more interesting. The first presented the aftermath of Amherst's taking of the last French stronghold in Canada, and showed the uniformed general 'surrounded by a considerable number of miserable French' fearful of the vengeance of the victors (Figure 13).[133] He stands, however, leaning forward, hands outstretched, giving mercy and charity to these supplicant and defeated civilians. This posture is mirrored in the second picture (Figure 14) where Lord Clive, 'with a most pleasing expression of modest triumph in his looks,' also extends his mercy to the defeated 'Meer Jaffer.'[134] They were, Solkin argues, the beginning of a new, and potentially disruptive, genre of 'serious history-painting' that depicted real, contemporary events and appealed to, and were seen by, a large, nonelite audience.[135] They were pictures that addressed and constituted a new public, and they did so in a particular way. Both paintings foregrounded the sympathetic sensibilities of the imperial hero: Clive in his noble acceptance of the nabob's surrender, Amherst in his charitable actions. Doing so elided the material realities of imperial warfare. For Solkin, the painting of Clive 'is a marvellous piece of eighteenth-century imperialist propaganda: a brutal seizure of power, for the benefit of the East India Company and its shareholders, is described in terms that transmute a violent conquest into a demonstration of the victor's sensitivities.'[136] Indeed, the attention given to shaping the meanings of imperial war in this way would have been particularly pertinent in these cases. British attempts to differentiate their mode of imperialism from that of the French had valorised naval power and the capture and defence of trade routes rather then the holding of territory as colonies.[137] Throughout the eighteenth century the army carried connotations of absolutist tyranny, while the navy was seen as the bulwark of 'English' liberties.[138] Admirals, therefore, made rather better national and imperial heroes than generals who, without the language of mercy, could be dangerous symbols of power and conquest incompatible with British notions of an 'Empire of Trade.'[139] Through these carefully constructed images an imperial public was constituted. By addressing them as 'bound together by a common national [and imperial] interest, and by the "natural" ties of sympathy, [Hayman] offered the victors of a commercial war, and of a commercial system in general, the pleasurable confirmation of their virtuous character.'[140]

It is, however, also clear that the constitution of this public, and the making of a moralised and sentimentalised version of empire as what bound them together, depended upon the spectacle of a particular form of masculinity. Clive and Amherst were presented as admirable men— even if they were not admirals. In doing so the genre of history paint- ing, considered to be the most public and masculine genre, was trans- formed toward modern and popular subjects, opening it up to the dis- cussion of versions of masculinity that characterised eighteenth-century artistic representation more generally.[141] Chloe Chard, in her account of eighteenth-century commentaries on classical sculpture, argues that a strong distinction was drawn between the 'craggy' masculinity of the club-carrying *Farnese Hercules* and the effeminacy of Michaelangelo's *David*. Neither was seen as the ideal. What was valued was the way that the *Borghese Gladiator* seemed to combine both strength and sensitivity into another form of masculinity.[142] This was repeated in the way that the mode of masculinity through which Hayman represented Clive and Amherst combined both power—exhibited in the signs and history of imperial victory—and sympathy—in the reported actions and bodily gestures of mercy. Making this sort of spectacle of masculinity was part of the context for the attacks on the Macaronis. The masculine and im- perial heroics of Clive and Amherst can be juxtaposed to the effeminate and unpatriotic luxuriousness of Macaroni masculinity.[143] Indeed, this can be read as part of the history that Kathleen Wilson reconstructs of the ways in which a broad mercantile interest deployed a popular impe- rialism as part of a critique of aristocratic government—including charges of effeminacy and luxury—and its nonexpansionist foreign pol- icy. However, Wilson's argument that it was simply an 'aggressive mas- culinity' that was valued at the heart of this imperial project needs to be questioned.[144] These representations of Clive and Amherst suggest that there was more variety in imperial masculinities. Different versions would be appropriate to different contexts. As I have argued above, gen- erals and admirals had different symbolic connotations and tensions that had to be attended to. Also, London's role as the imperial capital would have shaped its relationship to empire in different ways to that of provincial ports or manufacturing towns, which might be expected to be more bellicose. Finally, the publics and the spectacles of the popular theatres that Wilson concentrates on would have been different from

Figure 13 *The Humanity of General Amherst.* Francis Hayman (1760) oil on canvas 27 7/8 × 36 in. The Beaverbrook Foundation. The Beaverbrook Art Gallery Fredericton, N.B., Canada.

146

Figure 14 Modello for *Lord Clive Receiving the Homage of the Nabob,* Francis Hayman, c. 1761–1762. Reproduced by courtesy of the National Portrait Gallery, London.

those of Vauxhall, demanding different representations of imperial victory. Each of these factors would have shaped the forms and spectacles of imperial masculinity exhibited at different sites.[145]

This consideration of different versions of masculinity also raises the question of the contested relations between men, and between men and women, that lay at the heart of the conflict between Bate and the Macaronis. The precise point of conflict between them was over the rights and wrongs of looking at women, and the use of that to differentiate the Macaronis from other sorts of men. In order to explain why looking at Elizabeth Hartley was so problematic, I want to explore the ways in which Macaronis and actresses were thought about in terms of vision and, more broadly, to situate them all within the culture of vision and illusion in and around Vauxhall Gardens.

GAZING UPON MADAM HARTLEY

As it was later retold, probably erroneously, the cause of the conflict between Bate and the Macaronis was when 'Fitzgerald, evidently for the purpose of reckless insult, put up his glass and peered into the lady's face.'[146] Bate certainly reported that Fitzgerald had asked him 'Whether any man had not a right to look at a fine woman?,' and that he had replied, 'Most certainly, and that I despised the man that did not look at a fine woman; However, I begged leave to observe, that there were two distinct ways of looking at her—with *admiration,* and with *unauthorized contempt:*—that the conduct I censured was strongly of the latter kind.'[147] Looking was both differentiated and problematic when it came to interactions between men and women. As the author of a poem entitled 'The Macaroniad,' published in *The Whitehall Evening Post,* had it:

> . . . Many ills doth him environ,
> Who madly meddles with a siren;
> And such *Fitzgiggio's* case was partly,
> For gazing upon Madam *Hartley:*
> To Gaze!—Or not to gaze! In Fun
> Fops, fools, and fiddlers are Undone.[148]

In part the conflict was due to the Macaronis' relationship to the visual. *The London Magazine* argued that they were devoted to the refined and distanced pleasures of the eye rather than the grosser pleasures of the belly:

> The eye is the paunch of *a virtuoso Maccaroni,* as the stomach of the glutton. The *devouring Maccaroni* does not derive the appellation from an immoderate indulgence in animal food; the idea would be too coarse and sensual; nor is it intended to convey a carniverous or vinibibous meaning.[149]

This hungry gaze was a problematic one. It was dangerously self-regarding and was interpreted as creating men who wanted to be looked at by women but only pretended that they enjoyed looking back. Yet it was also a gaze that was used to terrorise women. Macaronis were said to go to church only 'to ogle the Women, and put the Parson out of Countenance.'[150] *The Macaroni Magazine* warned that 'If you see him at the theatre, he will scarcely wink without his opera-glass, which he will thrust into a lady's face, and then simper, and be "pruddigishly entertenn'd" with her confusion.'[151] Fitzgerald's reported action was certainly the act of a Macaroni.

The object of the gaze was also problematic. Elsewhere Mrs Hartley was someone to look at and, in her case, the theatre's 'roaringly successful commodification of female sexuality' was certainly a matter of what she looked like, or the illusion that she presented on stage, rather than how she sounded.[152] For some the publicity of her performing life rendered her the legitimate object of the Macaronis' gaze, and an illegitimate candidate for Bate's protection. As 'Veritas' said in *The Morning Chronicle,* '[F]or what, Sir, can we style a party at *Vauxhall,* an intimate acquaintance with a lady in a public character, and a display of knight-errantry in her defence, but an offering to the shrine of Pleasure.'[153] Yet this equation of public women and illicit desire was countered by 'Censor':

> The plain meaning of it is, that a woman in a *Public Situation* is so far from being entitled to any decency or good manners from others, (be her private conduct ever so prudent or commendable) that it becomes her to submit without complaining to whatever wanton outrageous behaviour our young Rakes (particularly those of quality) shall think proper to bestow on her;—so that whenever a set of such *worthies* have a mind for a frolick, they have nothing to do but to seek out an *Actress;* and whether at Vauxhall, Ranelagh, or other public place, attack her by impudent ogling, staring, and every other species of nameless audacity, till they have hunted her from the community.[154]

Here, public reputation depended upon private morality, and to defend Mrs Hartley from the Macaronis' gaze can be read as a defence of the ideology of domesticity that strained to contain the contradictory figure that the actress presented as a woman in public. Thus, Mrs Hartley was a problem of vision. The eighteenth century may have seen the emergence of the modern ocular and sexual ideology of the male spectator and the female spectacle, but this was never fixed, even from the beginning.[155] Mrs Hartley may not have actively resisted the Macaroni gaze, but constructing her as a spectacle in Vauxhall Gardens rather than at the theatre, in a space between domesticity and publicity, was problematic enough to reveal a sexual politics of the gaze that was part of a complex culture of vision.[156] This means taking seriously Parson Bate's insistence that there were different ways of looking, and situating Vauxhall Gardens within them.

VISION IN VAUXHALL

The rich visual culture of the eighteenth century can be investigated by starting with the Panopticon. This was a machine for vision that created ways of looking. It constructed subjects and objects of vision and structured the gazes that ran between them in paradigmatic ways. It can also be read as a sign of the modernity of vision. There was, however, more than one Panopticon, and it is not Bentham's utilitarian model prison with which I want to start, but Pinchbeck's Panopticon.[157] This 'well-known and celebrated Panopticon,' created in the early 1740s, was a 'triangular musical machine, which for its vast variety of moving figures, etc. is allowed to be one of the first pieces of mechanism in Europe.' One side showed a country fair with musicians and blacksmiths moving in time; the second showed a ship-carpenter's yard—with artificers and ships moving to music; the third was a 'beautiful landskip'—with a moving river, mill and hunters. The box played a variety of tunes and simulated birdsong.[158] The Panopticon was a spectacle to be looked at and wondered at as it created a series of visual illusions. It was exhibited at Christopher Pinchbeck Jr.'s repository in Cockspur Street along with other useful and curious things that had been made by the clockmaker with the 'entrepreneurial eye' and, having attracted an array of spectators, it was raffled off.[159]

The Panopticon takes its place among the shows of London. Christopher Pinchbeck Sr. had been exhibiting near-life-size automated figures at fairs since 1734, and moving pictures had been on show in the capital since 1709.[160] Vauxhall Gardens was part of this visual culture. This is seen most directly in the exhibition of the 'Tin Cascade,' 'a very natural representation of a water-mill, with the miller's house, and a fine cascade, all illuminated with concealed lights. . . . It is the representation of a storm, in which the trees are furiously agitated, and the thatch of a cottage blown down. A church, and a bridge of one arch, through which rolls a rapid stream, are the principal objects in the scene; and over this bridge sometimes passes a waggon and horses, and sometimes a party of soldiers &c.'[161] This 'very curious piece of machinery' was said to 'have a very pleasant effect both on the eye and the ear of the spectator,' and serves to introduce Vauxhall's other visual pleasures.[162]

Vauxhall Gardens was made of spectacles. The walks were vistas that framed views with trees and buildings. There were the paintings and pictures in all their variety; statues of Aurora, Handel and Milton; fashionably decorated rooms; the illuminated moon, sun and stars on the gothic temples; the painted backdrops and alcoves that terminated the cross-walks; and, if one looked out of the gardens, the contrasting views of the country and the city. In many ways, it was visual rather than musical or alimentary pleasures that predominated, and these pleasures were staged for the spectators. Tyers's transformations had used devices from the baroque theatre, the elaborate lighting heightened the effects, and John Lockman's publicity concentrated on guiding his readers' vision.[163] He instructed them on how to view the composition and arrangement of the buildings, on where to stand so that 'the whole may appear to him a magical Scene,' and on ways of looking at the gardens so as to continually see them anew.[164] As Lockman concluded, 'In short, when the Night is warm and serene; the Gardens fill'd with fine Company, and different Parts of them are illuminated, the Imagination cannot frame a more enchanting Spectacle.'[165]

The audience itself was very much part of this spectacle. Lockman said of the Grove that 'Here the Splendour is so great, as well as in the *Temple of Pleasure,* that the juvenile Part of both Sexes may enjoy their darling Passion:—the seeing others, and being seen by them.'[166] Everyone was on stage, and if these forms of observation of others can be understood as techniques for disciplining refinement in the public sphere, they were also sexually charged.[167] It was the pleasures of looking at others that were stressed, particularly of men looking at women. For example, 'Toupee' suggested that men might cast their eyes over the women in the supper boxes while pretending to examine the pictures.[168] However, there was assumed to be pleasure in being looked at as well as in looking.[169] As an intersection of these gazes the spectator became intensely self-conscious and self-regarding. Again Vauxhall presented this act of looking as a pleasurable one. Lockman encouraged his readers to stand in the Rotunda of the 'Temple of Pleasure' surrounded by mirrors where, 'In all these glasses the spectator, when standing under the balls of the Grand *Chandelier,* might see himself reflected at once, to his pleasing wonder.'[170] Here the solitary, self-observing subject is involved in the consumption of 'his' own self-image, and in the construction of identity through the pleasures of visibility.[171] Vauxhall, like the Magdalen Hospital, presented a spectacle of self-regarding subjectivity that manipulated solitude for personal transformation. Unlike the Magdalen Hospital, however, it constituted this transformation through the pleasures of consumption rather than the constraints of discipline (see Chapter 2).

Finally, Vauxhall's visual pleasures were the pleasures of illusion.[172] The separate triumphal arches were meant to be viewed so 'that the whole has the Appearance of a noble *Edifice*.' The moving picture and the painted backdrops that terminated the cross-walks were pleasing visual tricks. The gardens and the elements within them were arranged so that they would 'sometimes deceive the Eye very agreeably.'[173] More generally, the appeal of Vauxhall was to the imagination. Its architects manipulated the visual to create an aura of 'enchantment,' a blurring of the real and the represented, of fantasy and reality, in the name of pleasure.[174] Visitors could be led to these pleasures through Lockman's positioning of their gaze: 'A Spectator, who, in the Night, should stand at that *Obelisk,* and look down the *Garden,* would perceive at the Extremity of this View, a glimmering Light, (that in the opposite *Alcove*) which might image to him an *Anchoret's* Cave; for instance, that of the imaginary *Robinson Crusoe*.'[175] In a world where the Enlightenment's clarity of vision structured many gazes, these illusions were pleasurable diversions. When it was said in 1755 that the paintings were 'damaged last season by the fingering of those curious Connoisseurs, who could not be satisfied without *feeling* whether the figures were alive,' the implied appeal was to the enchantments of the visual imagination rather than to fact.[176]

All of this can be summed up by the obelisk. From the 1760s it was to be seen on entering Vauxhall framed by buildings and trees at the end of the Grand Walk's long vista. Closer inspection would, however, have revealed it to be, like most Vauxhall spectacles, painted canvas and boards and not stone at all. It was modern not ancient, and it had been made for money. Alongside Hayman's paintings of chained slaves it bore the legend "Spectator fastidiosus sibi molestus," the arrogant (or fastidious) spectator troubles (or vexes) himself. This mild rebuke, which certainly signals the difference between Bentham's Panopticon and Pinchbeck's, reminded the spectators of their active part in the maintenance of the fictions required to establish the pleasure of the illusion and, at the same time, made the spectator aware of his or her position as a spectator. It turned their gazes back upon themselves once more.[177] As Peter de Bolla has argued, also using the example of this obelisk, what is made visual at Vauxhall is visuality, the act of looking itself.[178]

These visual pleasures were, however, troubled ones when the connections between masculinity, commodification and illusion came into view. The Macaronis serve to demonstrate these tensions. They created problems by turning men's bodies into the wrong sorts of spectacles. They disrupted the heterosexual structuring of gazes expected of Vauxhall flirtations by 'aim[ing] only to be looked at and admired' by both men and women and by 'drawing up their *brazen artillery* to attack a *woman,* and *stare* her out of countenance.'[179] They also created themselves as spectacles of commodities rather than, for example, as spectacles of heroic and sympathetic imperial masculinity. Like actors 'who make spectacles of themselves for a living,' and like the fops who were accused of luxury and effeminacy earlier in the century, the Macaronis 'muddy the distinction between sexual object and sexual subject, spectacle and spectator, commodity and consumer.'[180] As *The Macaroni Jester* more succinctly put it, 'manhood is a thing unbought.'[181]

The Macaroni spectacles were illusions just as Vauxhall's were, but they were problematic rather than pleasurable deceptions. It became a problem that there was nothing behind the spectacle's painted boards. Macaronis were described as 'Puffs of Wind,' 'hollow Animals,' or a '*perfect nothingness.*'[182] Fitzgerald was described as 'A thing so meagre and so thin, / So full of *emptiness*—and sin.'[183] They were represented as nothing but their modish clothes. This was part of a critique of fashion as an empty illusion, but it also ran deeper than that.[184] As Barbara Maria Stafford argues:

> What was new to the eighteenth-century experience—as codes of polite behaviour spread to broader and lower strata of society—was the frightening possibility that nothing stood behind decorum. No gold standard guaranteed inflated or deflated currency; no original preexisted the copy; no durable skeleton shored up the frail anatomy. Fashion, masquerade, theater, cross-dressing emphasised the total disagreement between seeming and being, the deliberately fabricated incongruity between exterior and interior.[185]

Or, as on attack on the Macaronis had it, 'For shame, for shame, shake off this apish whim / and be without as you should be within.'[186] Macaronis were dangerous fakes whose world of refined appearances and ambiguous spectacles threatened to undermine gender and class boundaries, and the systems of credit and value that depended upon them. Vauxhall's pleasures had always been about 'experimenting with social roles,' and this had always had the frisson of a dangerous pleasure.[187] However, Fitzgerald's dressing up of his manservant as the fictitious Captain Miles in order to fight Parson Bate was an act of class crossdressing that provoked outrage at the erosion of boundaries that it rep-

resented.[188] The disruption caused by these transgressions was only partially restored by Bate's rather late decoding of the fraud's visual signs,
that 'His most amazingly confused address, the manner in which his
friends treated him, and his new awkward vestments, all conspired to
convince us he was a *made-up gentleman* for the business.'[189] The concern arose because 'social "transvestism"' was a crucial part of the extensive and fragile networks of credit upon which England's economy depended in the eighteenth century.[190] Credit depended upon reputation
which, in turn, depended upon self-presentation within the market-
place and, more importantly, within tight and sociable networks of similarly placed traders.[191] These performances, like the discourses of public credit, involved a simulation of solidity, respectability and gentility in
the interests of stability. Those seeking credit sought to create a spectacle of gentility, often one that crossed class boundaries, which *would*
provide the otherwise absent gold standard.[192] In the credit crisis of the
1770s the Macaronis threatened to show that the modern self was an illusion made of commodities and fantasies with no real, knowable sub-
stance.[193] Because their illusions were ones of masculinity, class and
commodification, they threatened to erode boundaries and destroy realities that others sought to protect.

Lastly, the pleasures of Vauxhall's self-regarding spectator become,
with the Macaronis, an illegitimate narcissism. This, as reflected in
Fitzgerald's miniature portrait of himself, was a key part of the charges
of effeminacy:

> When *Britain* calls her valiant sons to arms,
> Their milky souls no martial ardour warms,
> For all their *courage* lodges in the heel,
> And *fear's* the only passion they can feel;
> Save that, in which they every hour employ,
> (Narcissus-like)—*the self-admiring joy.*
> haste—seize the *dear insipids*—bravely dare
> To wage with Folly and with fashion war.[194]

The pleasures of self-observation threatened military defeat and imperial decline. They also threatened decline through a failure to marry and
reproduce. The Macaroni 'loves nobody but himself; and by nobody, except himself; is he beloved.'[195] He prefers the pleasures of the mirror to
those of marriage:

> Like fair Narcissus, in yourselves you see,
> Of all that's charming the epitome,

> And like him too, you pine, you sink, you die,
> To all that's manly underneath the sky.[196]

The fact that gardens like Vauxhall were 'sites of self-celebration, of self-observation, even of self-creation' meant that in France they destabilised the theatre of monarchy and posed new radical possibilities.[197] In England, as well as presenting new pleasures and new possibilities, they also posed the dangers of the fluidity and privatisation of identities rooted in fashion and commodification. In all these ways the Macaronis can be read as a destabilisation of the idealised relations between commodification, masculinity and vision. It was not that they overturned the refined and polite pleasures that Vauxhall presented—the pleasures of commercialised leisure, the pleasures of looking at men, the pleasures of illusion—they simply pushed them into excess, thereby revealing the tensions and contradictions upon which Vauxhall Gardens was built.

CONCLUSIONS

The 'Vauxhall Affray' was a matter of the differentiation and contestation of masculinities within a culture of commodified consumption exemplified by Vauxhall Gardens. In the press representations of it a Macaroni masculinity built around conspicuous consumption and display confronted a bourgeois masculinity defending plain dress and a patriarchal domestic respectability. They contested the right to look at Mrs Hartley: the right to define the male gaze within a complex field of visual pleasures and dangers.[198] In this confrontation various signs and symbols were made meaningful and deployed as Bate had Croftes, Lyttelton and Fitzgerald burnt outside the Temple of Virtue (Figure 7). Parson Bate's Herculean club, a symbol of a rugged, moralising masculinity, was counterposed to Fitzgerald's miniature portrait, a symbol of an effeminate and foreign self-love. The Macaroni's feathered hats—symbols of private, venal and luxurious consumption—were juxtaposed to Bate's quill pen, a symbol of the power of a supposedly virtuous public sphere. This was a conflict over what it meant to be a 'gentleman' at a time and place where the term was in danger of losing its meaning as the behaviours and dress codes through which it has been previously defined—and which shored up fragile credit networks—were so readily simulated.[199] This brought with it an anxiety over masculinity and class as an illusion or spectacle which, as I have shown, structured the Vauxhall Affray. The Macaronis transgressed the boundaries of masculine decorum and virtue both by cross-dressing a servant as a gentleman and by exhibiting themselves as hybridised commodity spectacles. Doing so threatened to reveal the construction of masculinity and gentility as illusions dependent upon commodity consumption, venality and sexual desire. This would have undermined the careful balance between refined pleasures and excessive, hedonistic luxury on which Vauxhall Gardens depended. It would also have threatened the equally careful construction of nation and empire as a matter of justified conquest and judicious mercy that was displayed at Vauxhall as an acceptable spectacle of English masculinity. In this way the 'Affray' can be seen as part of the process—one continually underway within Vauxhall Gardens—whereby relationships between men and women, between masculinity and femininity, were ways of interpreting new forms of commodification, and were also interpreted through ideas around the commodity as well.

While this dichotomous version of the conflict reveals a lot, it also serves to conceal the complexities of the identities of the participants. The 'Affray' was not solely a straightforward conflict between an effeminate Macaroni masculinity embodied by Fitzgerald and a robust, patriarchal and public masculinity embodied by Bate. Henry Bate is better understood as a confusion of categories: the pugilistic parson. His profession and his wielding of the Herculean club were seen as combining the incompatible:

> [W]e surely cannot be at a loss to determine that the Parson behaved well, as a *bruiser* and defender of the fair, but ill as a *parson* and lecturer of others; as parsons, like cobblers, should not go beyond their *last* or text; . . . it is therefore hoped that this will be a lesson to all parsons to stick to their texts, and not to ramble again to public places, not even with gods or goddesses either of the stage, pit, or gallery.[200]

The 'Macaronis' were also more complicated. Croftes, Fitzgerald and Lyttelton were all military men, and while Bate might have argued that 'they fight with scented quil pop-guns, loaded with *bleu mange*,'[201] Fitzgerald could present himself very differently:

> As to *good* qualities, some I have perhaps though few in number. This, however, I can say for myself, no man can impeach my courage in the field, my honour on the turf, or my credit at the Royal Exchange. If it appears *singular* that I have not plunged into the gallantries of the present times, let it be remembered on the other hand, that I am a married man, and that I prefer the domestic happiness of the amiable partner of my life,

and our little offspring, to all the mummery and perfidy of private fashionable intrigues.[202]

Here he was both heroic (according to an aristocratic model) and sensitive rather than a young spark of fashion. Indeed, these categories and their confusions help us to understand Vauxhall's culture of commodity consumption as a matter of mixed and multiple identities. The processes of commodification, commercialisation and fashion within which I have located Vauxhall's modernity and its Macaronis were ones that transformed and problematised the question of identity. They made it into something fluid, mutable and difficult to determine. Commodified pleasure and its new hybrid identities were part of a world of illusion that brought both the enchantments of Vauxhall Gardens and the fear of a hollow luxurious excess. Commodification both played up the difficult relationship between 'reality' and 'representation' and was understood through it. One way in which these tensions were played out was through the debate over the rights and wrongs of looking at Mrs Hartley. Another way in which the new world of commodities shaped identities and power, linking consumption in London with warfare overseas, was through the state's arrangements for taxing production. There, as the next chapter shows, rational spaces and bureaucratic identities were created in an attempt to dispel all possibility of illusion.

CHAPTER FIVE

Excise Geographies

INTRODUCTION: THE CAPACITIES OF THE MODERN STATE

The fortunes of the English (and then British) imperial state from the late seventeenth century onward depended upon the accurate assessment of two capacities: the capacity of the state to wage war and the capacity of the cask (see Figure 15). The first was a matter of population, production, trade and military strength assessed via the protocols of political arithmetic, a new mathematical accounting of power. The second depended upon the mathematics of gauging, ullaging and inching, which understood casks as regular geometrical figures whose volumes could be accurately measured.

The historical geography of modernity that I want to reconstruct in this chapter involves the connections between these two capacities: the warfare state and the barrel. In one sense this is quite unproblematic. It is now a commonplace to argue that states wage war with each other for imperial hegemony. To do so, they raise taxes, including taxes on commodities in casks. Through these processes 'modern' states are constructed.[1] More specifically, John Brewer has argued that the period from 1688 to 1783 saw the development of the 'fiscal–military state.'[2] While domestic economic and social regulation within the British state was characterised by 'a uniquely decentralised political system' of local and landed power, it was highly effective, centralised, and—at least in part—bureaucratised in terms of its capacity to raise taxes and to fight wars.[3] The state's imperial ambitions were made manifest in an increas-

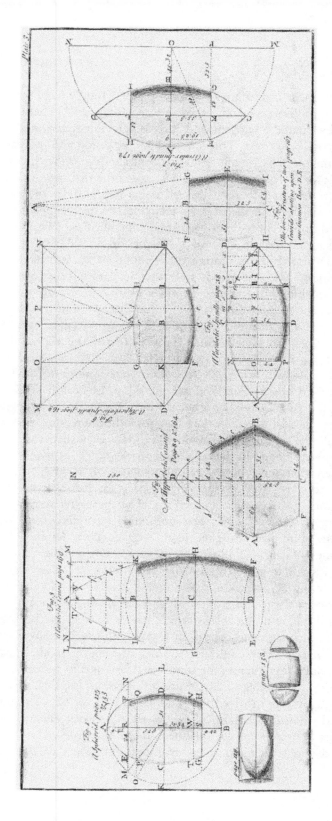

ing involvement in warfare, fought on an increasingly large scale by increasingly professional and expensive armed forces.[4] These were financed by taxing a buoyant and increasingly integrated, if essentially
preindustrial, economy.[5] This required an expansion and reorganisation
of government departments and their centralisation under the Treasury
Board.[6] It also involved the establishment, for the first time, of a national debt (as opposed to the personal debts incurred by the monarch)
based on the new forms of long-term borrowing needed to finance
huge, and more short-term, wartime expenditures.[7] This debt bal-
looned from nothing in 1689 to £245 million in 1783.[8] Such a 'financial revolution' required, among other things, large, stable and reliable
tax revenues.[9] These demands were met in part through a long-term
process that shifted the balance of power over taxation from the personal estate of the monarch to control by Parliament.[10] They were also met
through excise taxation—taxes levied on the producers of certain commodities, especially beer—which 'proved [to be] the key to the fiscal
cupboard.'[11] After 1714 excises provided over 40% of a total revenue
that had increased from £3.64 million per annum for the period
1689–1697 to over £12 million per annum in the period 1775–1783.[12]
In short, the beer barrel's volume and the state's military strength were
connected in that it was excises that paid the increasing costs of the
state's military ventures and serviced the debt they incurred. The two
capacities were linked in the 'fiscal–military state.'

In another sense, however, this connection is problematic. The
problem concerns the production of space. In part this involves the
'production' of the mathematicised spaces of the barrel and the nation-
state. First, I want to argue that both only existed within forms of
knowledge appropriate to particular contexts. They are the 'imagined
geographies' of 'calculable spaces' produced under specific conditions.[13]
Second, I want to problematise the production of other spaces, and
ways of acting across space, that connect the barrel and the imperial
state. Between the gauging of a cask and the waging of a campaign was
the administrative framework—which I refer to here as 'the Excise'—
put in place to assess and collect these taxes. This was a complex system
that had to be attentive to the surveillance of even the smallest spaces, to
ensuring uniformity across the state's territory, and to maximising revenue without losing legitimacy. Putting this system in place, adjusting it,
and maintaining it, involved the production of a set of roles and practices, and, inseparable from them, a set of spaces characteristic of
modernity. These were the planned, rationally ordered, hierarchical,
routinised and scrutinised roles, practices and spaces of the modern

state. By emphasising the construction, or production, of this geography, I want to stress the contingency of the political and administrative forms that, where they were operated successfully, made possible and guaranteed the connections between the commodity and military might. The state's modernity was a contingent construction whose development was fought for and negotiated from a variety of positions.

This chapter is, therefore, concerned with the modernity of the geographies of excise taxation. The argument requires some initial attention to what that modernity might consist of and some caution as to how far such interpretations can be taken. Assessments of the modernity of the Excise have generally rested on the degree to which it fits Weberian models of bureaucracy and the state. Perhaps unsurprisingly, while acknowledging the 'radical departure' that the Excise represented, the distance between 'ideal type' and empirical reality has also been stressed. However, following John Brewer's argument that the 'English Excise more closely approximated to Max Weber's idea of bureaucracy than any other government agency in eighteenth-century Europe,' it is possible to consider *processes* of bureaucratisation, differentiation or monopolisation rather than expecting their full realisation.[14] Modernity is always partial. In addition, the modernity of the Excise should not be limited to strict Weberian formulations. The modernity of the state is also a matter of the connections between time–space distanciation, rationality, mediated action, planning and ordering, and the consciousness of the contingency of the self that Pocock argues first becomes evident in its modern form with William III's military and financial innovations.[15] These can be come at through Weber, or through reformulations of Weber, but also in other ways that stress the particular geography of the modern state: well-defined boundaries policed by warfare; an internal territory that is closely administered via mechanisms of routinised surveillance that connect authorities at different scales; and the capacity to organise space, time, knowledge, and both human and non-human resources for unprecedented levels of action at a distance.[16]

Even given this expanded notion of modernity, it is important to stress the limitations on such interpretations of the Excise. Although it was more efficient and rationally organised than other branches of the state, it was not uniformly efficient and rational. Moreover, while personal connections were subordinated to a concern for professionalism, employment within the Excise still remained part of the patronage system.[17] This does not mean that it was simply the most modern part of a modernising state apparatus, or necessarily the most important.[18] It must be seen as one branch of government within a complex 'patchwork' of institutions and practices that mixed the innovative and the long-standing.[19] For example, excises were raised alongside first the assessment and then the land tax. These forms of direct taxation were important throughout the period and changed their 'administrative repertoire[s]' very little. They were collected through established county elites and local officeholders rather than via a professionalised administration. Their success relied upon knitting together central and local government on conventional lines rather than on modernising state structures or attempting to make accurate and systematic evaluations of wealth.[20] Yet the success of the state relied upon this combination of the land tax and excises. If the land tax offered legitimacy and incorporation through local (under)assessment and (under)collection, it could do so partly because of the revenue cushion provided by the excises. In turn, part of the basis on which excises could be increased was the continuing ideological, and financial, importance of the land tax.[21] The state's uneven modernity helped to raise revenue while maintaining legitimacy.

While I am more than willing to admit the seventeenth- and eighteenth-century state's uneven modernity, I maintain that the geography of the Excise is worth investigating. It provides a setting within which the administrative spaces, roles and procedures characteristic of the modern state can be investigated as they were constructed. By doing so, the contingent and uncertain making of modernity can be revealed beneath what is otherwise too easily taken for granted.[22] The construction of the spaces of excise taxation—mathematicised barrels, numerical nation-states, and the administrative networks that stretch between them—reveals the production of modernity. Reconstructing this historical geography involves four investigations into the production of space. First, I examine the political arithmetic of Charles Davenant to show how it figured an 'imagined geography' of the nation-state that was used to make claims for increasing excise taxation within the debates over political power in the 1690s. Second, I will move back to the 1680s to examine Davenant's role in the shaping of the Restoration excise system. My purpose is to show how the production and reproduction of a national, rational and bureaucratised administrative 'network' of practices, powers and spaces was achieved and how it aimed to guarantee the accurate, uniform, efficient and legitimate operation of the Excise. Third, because this 'network' depended upon the officers who staffed it, excisemen who became 'symbol[s] of a new form of government,'[23] I will discuss their role. Examining these officers' lives brings to light some of the ambivalences that lay beneath the smooth running of Davenant's administrative machine. Fourth, these three discussions also involve a historical geography of London quite different from those presented in the preceding chapters of this book, but no less bound up with the city's modernity. This is London as a capital, an administrative centre of power and knowledge, through which and around which the state's networks gradually formed, themes that are explored in more detail in the next chapter. As such, the geography of London's implication in the development of the fiscal–military state can be explored by going beyond the boundaries of the city. However, London's own internal spaces were also reshaped in subtle ways by the often invisible geography of the Excise. The final section of this chapter returns to the capital to examine the nature of the eighteenth-century state's administrative spaces, roles and procedures at their most developed. Together these discussions map out key contours of the historical geography of the Excise.

CHARLES DAVENANT'S POLITICAL ARITHMETIC

Charles Davenant, eldest son of the poet William Davenant, was born in London in 1656. He entered Balliol College in 1671 but did not graduate. He was a playwright, theatre owner, and lawyer, the MP for St Ives, and an excise commissioner from 1678 until 1689. He then published a series of political writings, including works of political arithmetic. In 1705 he was appointed inspector general of imports and exports. He died in office in 1714.[24]

Davenant's essays were part of the boom in the production of political arithmetic in the late seventeenth century associated particularly with William Petty, whom Davenant both emulated and criticised, and Gregory King, whom he probably supplied with data.[25] This form of knowledge was, as Davenant put it, 'the art of reasoning by figures upon things relating to government.'[26] It attempted, via mathematical calculation, to assess states' populations, occupations, wealth, balance of trade and military power. It sought to make mathematics an instrument of the state, and argued that any worthy statesman must have 'a computing head.'[27]

Number—or 'number, weight and measure,' as Petty had it—was part of a moralised, modernising and rationalising ethos that saw 'numerical calculation' as 'a powerful solvent of custom, superstition and prejudice.'[28] It offered a powerful tool for state power, providing it with knowledges that could be legitimised as objective and rational, above party and faction, and superior to those of the 'projectors,' 'flatterers,' 'admirers' and 'dependants' who surrounded the powerful.[29] Number was also crucial to the geography that political arithmetic figured. Arithmetic was, as Keith Tribe notes, 'the only means available for conceiving the nation as a whole.'[30] Political arithmetic conjured a nation-state space in a world of competing nation-states, and these political entities gave the discourse its unity and organising principles.[31] States' capacities could be judged because these spaces were bounded. For example, the key idea of a 'balance of trade,' the area where Davenant made his main contribution to economic doctrine, depended upon understanding the importance of trade as commodities crossing these boundaries and a system of spatial accounting that tallied flows and weighed them against each other via a universal numerical metric: money.[32] The modernity of political arithmetic lay not just in its 'passion to order and systematise as well as to measure and calculate,' but also in its imagining of the political geography of the nation-state and the nation-state system.[33]

This imagined geography enabled Davenant to undertake comparative studies of the major northern European powers in mathematical terms in order to assess their military capacity:

> If it could be clearly stated what the real wealth and stock of a kingdom is, and if it can be known by what degrees it grows rich in times of peace, and by what steps it becomes poor at other seasons, some opinion might be formed, and a judgement made, how long, and upon what foot, a war might be carried on with safety to the public.[34]

He compared English, French and Dutch state finances, and these states' ability to wage war, arguing that managing 'the affairs of war and peace' required 'reasoning by figures upon things.'[35]

This reasoning meant understanding how a state's political economy was composed of interlocking parts—taxes, regions, or branches of trade or manufacture—that could be rationally assessed, evaluated and adjusted as a way toward ordering the whole. As Davenant put it, 'To object against the motion of one wheel, without knowing and seeing how the whole engine moves, is to no manner of purpose.'[36] These relationships were understood in terms of circulation; indeed Davenant often used body metaphors to stress the unity of the parts and the importance of flows of money and goods.[37] For example, he argued that without government action to encourage the circulation of silver, there would be 'a total stagnation in this nerval juice, a dead palsy would forthwith seize the body politic.'[38] He sought a total numerical picture of this whole, of 'all the public revenues' and 'the product and manufactures of every county and place.'[39] Yet this was not the revelation of a preexisting economic order through mathematics. It was a political ordering of economic forces by arithmetic that understood them as part of the polity and operated in the interests of the sovereign or statesman.[40]

The political arithmetic of the 1690s was, therefore, an attempt to use number to make intelligible and controllable, through an imagined geography (and anatomy) of boundaries and circulation, the workings of a 'political oeconomy.' This knowledge was, however, specific to its immediate political context. Peter Buck argues that Petty's political arithmetic (written in the 1680s) was very much a creature of the Restoration. Although it was based upon the Hobbesian foundations of understanding politics via geometry (and reconstructing them both in the process), there was less of Hobbes's concern—prompted by the English Civil War—to establish the very basis for political authority. Petty's aim was to supplement, enhance and facilitate the power of the king by increasing 'administrative efficiency' rather than by securing the theoretical foundations of monarchical rule.[41] A greater contrast is with the period after 1750 when political arithmetic was uncoupled from the state and used by men like Richard Price to make local and nonlanded claims for political legitimacy that attacked the extension of state authority and offered a very different connection between space, knowledge and power.[42] In turn, Davenant must be read in terms of the 1690s. His essays on taxation from 1695 and 1698 were written as contributions to the debates over how to provide the unprecedented levels of revenue needed to finance William III's wars and, intimately connected to that, Parliament's concern to limit the financial independence of the monarchy and preserve the 1688 political settlement. His arguments for excise taxation, seen as the form most likely to pose this threat, can be understood in the light of political arithmetic's evaluation of productive taxation and concerns over constitutional guarantees.

The huge demand for revenue in the 1690s prompted a wide variety of proposals for new taxes—on shoes, woollen cloth, rooms, graven images, horses, servants, postage, and so on—and new forms of government borrowing.[43] Taxation also played a central role in political arithmetic.[44] The data that Davenant used to compare states was produced for and by taxation. Taxes were also the key means of intervention in circulation, and provided a basis for assessing the contributions of various branches of trade or manufacture. Thus, Davenant's (1695) 'Essay on

Ways and Means' aimed to assess how a reorganisation of taxation could be the basis for an English victory in the war against France. For him, 'the whole art of war is in a manner reduced to money,' and, he argued, 'Whenever this war ceases, it will not be for want of mutual hatred in the opposite parties, nor for want of men to fight the quarrel, but that side must first give out where money is first failing.'[45] His 'Discourses on the Publick Revenues and on the Trade of England' (1698) were written in peacetime, and argued that a reorganisation of taxation would enable England to pay off its debts before France, and therefore 'be in the best condition to preserve its empire and dominion.'[46]

How to tax was based on principles and priorities derived from political arithmetic. This involved computing where value came from, what particular taxes could be expected to yield, and their impact on the system as a whole. Tax yields could, it was argued, be computed from knowledge of the size of the population, of 'the present capabilities and condition of the kingdom; of the current cash, and even of the disposition of the people to pay the duty. The nature of the commodity likewise to be charged must be considered, whether it be the proper object of a duty, and not easily concealed and conveyed away, and whether its collection is to be ascertained by high or easy penalties; and whether it is to be come at by a few or many officers.'[47] The key principle was to tax 'without hurting trade, land and the manufactures,' the sources of wealth and political stability.[48] Following this principle, Davenant focused his attention on excises. He argued that they could tap the two-thirds of the population unaffected by land taxes and customs and make them pay up:

> So that usurers, lawyers, tradesmen and retailers, with all that troop that maintain themselves by our vice and luxury, and who make the easiest and most certain gain and profit in the commonwealth, contribute little to its support; all which, by excises, would be brought to bear their proportion of the common burthen.[49]

Excises would 'let land breathe a little' and spare the merchant. They also promised high revenues, a way of getting London to pay in proportion to its size, and the 'equality' of an indirect tax that would 'lie equally upon the whole' by taxing those who chose to consume.[50] All of these benefits depended upon the excises being properly set. For example, Davenant calculated that a tax on beer was better than one on malt since the former 'lies with less weight upon individuals, because such a variety of individuals help to bear the burthen; and the force of the stream is not so great, for it having taken such a long and crooked circuit.' '[T]he hop merchant, the cooper, the collier, and all trades that have relation to the commodity' would all pay their part. More generally, 'All excises should be laid as remotely from land as possible; it is true they yield less when so put, because the first maker is best come at; but when the last manufacturer or vender is charged, they lie with most equality upon the whole body of the people, and come not upon land in so direct a manner.'[51] It was, therefore, in accordance with the principles of his political arithmetic that Davenant argued in 1695 that well-set 'Excises seem the most proper Ways and Means to support the government in a long war, because they would lie equally upon the whole, and produce great sums, proportionable to the great wants of the public.'[52] Similarly, in 1698, he suggested that, along with a wider range of other measures, excises were the best way to pay off the public debt. Their certain and regular payments offered the best security.[53]

However, arguing to increase excise taxation in the 1690s could not simply be a matter of mathematical demonstration. It was also an issue of constitutional politics. Excise taxation was favoured by the executive because of its potentially high yield and, as argued by Davenant, because its spread across a large number of people made it relatively painless to any particular interest.[54] Parliament opposed it on the grounds that it would dangerously inflate executive power.[55] The high yields and 'ease' of excises made them hard to revoke and likely to be extended. Their extension threatened to remove the power of Parliament to grant taxes. Moreover, collecting these taxes from thousands of small producers scattered across the country meant, in the words of an opponent, the need 'to keep up a standing army to gather it.'[56] These officers, answerable to the executive, dependent upon it for work, and independent of 'the configurations of class, locality and kinship that structured English politics,' would threaten domestic privacy and be able to influence elections.[57] John Brewer succinctly sets out the case:

> A single excise presaged a general one; a general one promised fiscal independence to the crown; fiscal independence to the crown threatened the revolutionary settlement; excises therefore threatened the Glorious Revolution.[58]

Since the 1688 settlement 'gave Parliament control of the purse,' Parliament sought to 'Do what is necessary to carry on the Warr but [to] do nothing which may destroy the Constitution.'[59] MPs consequently refused, or at least limited, the introduction of excises. Proposals for a 'general excise'—on all commodities—that were supported by King William's government failed at the committee stage in 1689 and in the whole Parliament in 1690.[60] Only restricted excises on specific commodities were granted after extensive debate. Parliament preferred forms of taxation, the assessment and the land tax, whose administration was tied to local and landed structures of status and prestige.[61] That the years from 1688 to 1714 was the only period when direct taxation was predominant was the result of a parliamentary strategy to limit the growth of the fiscal–military state and the power of the executive without denying William III the finances necessary to wage war on an enormous scale.[62]

Davenant supported a general excise, but having been involved in drafting the failed proposal in 1689 he was well aware of the need to shape his arguments to meet those of the parliamentary opposition. Indeed, the importance of his work is that he argued for excise taxation at least partially from within this framework, trying to weigh the need to 'supply the war' against 'the safety of our constitution.'[63] In doing so, he stressed the importance of virtue in public life; argued that 'The rights of the people are safe so long as we preserve parliaments' made up of vigilant land owners; and suggested that no tax was so 'easy' that it would not prompt the debate and opposition that Parliament provided. He also emphasised the dangers of taxes on land that were so heavy that they would put an indebted landed gentry into the pocket of the king or of usurious money men. He saw the need for the government to demonstrate that 'the Liberties of the people are the chiefest view . . . in a matter that appears so nice and new as a home excise.'[64] In part, this meant preserving the rights of domestic privacy by exacting excises from 'public dealers' rather than from private families. It also meant imposing legal restrictions and selection criteria that would mean that excise officers were 'persons without interest or authority' unable to influence the political process.[65] A key problem, however, was the number of officers that an effective excise on a range of commodities needed:

> [S]uch a revenue in this wide country cannot be gathered and so ascertained, as the government may depend upon it for subsistence, but by a multitude of officers, peradventure dangerous to liberty.[66]

His way round this problem was to suggest that increasing excise revenues, particularly in peacetime, was less a matter of imposing new taxes or of making large increases in the numbers of officers required to collect them, than of 'a good management of the existing duties,' and the extension of these methods to any future ones.[67] It was the way that excises were managed that would limit the numbers of officers and help to resolve the conundrum of adequate supply and the preservation of liberty.

Accordingly, he applied the tools of political arithmetic to excise administration and calculated how much of the increase in the period from 1684 to 1689 was due to improvements in management rather than to growing population and wealth. He also compared the revenues for the periods 1684–1689 and 1690–1696 in order to argue that a one-third decline was caused 'by changing the former methods and course of management' established in the earlier period.[68] He set these methods out as follows. The commissioners from 1683–1689 had appointed able, efficient and salaried officers on merit at all levels until 'they had got together 1200 gaugers, active and skilful; and such a set of men, as perhaps no prince had ever a better employed in his revenue.' They had sought national uniformity of best practice, so that 'they settled one uniform method throughout the whole kingdom; taking that form for a pattern, which had been made use of with most success in the best managed collections.' They established effective surveillance over all areas by appointing a graded cadre of supervisors. They instituted cost–benefit procedures for administrative change, only making alter-ations 'upon a full conviction, that such encrease of expense would turn to the king's account.' In their own activities they sought to be 'steady,' 'constant,' 'impartial' and 'uncorrupt,' 'managing the revenue with the same care, affection, and frugality, as the father of a family would use in the ordering of his own affairs.'[69]

Arguing for a return to the management style of the 1680s was, of course, a matter of personal interest for Davenant. He had been one of the commissioners whose management skills he celebrated, but he had not been reappointed after 1689 because he was unable to provide the king with the substantial loan required from the new commission.[70] His essay was both a demonstration of his skills and an argument for the primacy of the branch of the revenue that he knew best. It was a plea for a position, as were many of his other writings, but this self-interest is not the only context for his work.[71] As has been shown, Davenant used the principles of his political arithmetic to argue that it was the way that excises were managed that would limit the numbers of officers and help to resolve the conundrum of ensuring both an adequate supply of rev-enue and the preservation of liberty. By investigating his role in the management of the Excise in the 1680s, I want to argue that his active engagement in the shaping of excise administration sought, through the production of accurate knowledges somewhat different from those of political arithmetic, an efficient tax-gathering machine that would also raise sufficient revenue without losing legitimacy. This was where he learned about the principles of management, and it was where his efforts provided the administrative basis for what was to come.

SHAPING THE EXCISE, 1683–1689

Excises were first raised in 1643 by both Parliament and Charles I to finance a civil war that had made direct taxation problematic for both sides. Initial, occasionally riotous, opposition against the imposition of government tax collectors on localities led to alterations in duties and administrative procedures which, ironically, meant that what had been considered a 'revolutionary' tax could be continued at the Restoration to meet Charles II's pressing financial needs.[72] From 1660 to 1688 the executive and the legislature came into conflict over granting excises, with Parliament keeping close control over what it saw as the fiscal basis for absolutist rule. In an attempt to increase efficiency, the excises were leased by county to tax farmers from 1662. This arrangement also promised 'large credit advances in the form of an advance payment of part of the rent,' a guaranteed rental income, and a way to pass on the costs of administration 'at a time when the existing machinery of collection threatened to swallow up the bulk of the proceeds.'[73] The leases were, in part, granted to groups from the local gentry who were recommended by the magistrates. Here the government sought local support and legitimacy rather than simply maximising the income from the highest bidders. However, since the highest rent collections were leased to groups of London merchants, each round of new leases meant that by 1670 virtually the whole country was in the hands of the London financier Sir William Bucknall and his associates. Since this concentration had also brought increases in administrative efficiency, although at the cost of renewed friction between excise officers and county justices, the Excise was leased as a single farm from 1673. This involved tighter government controls over the 'running cash' (how rapidly collected revenues should be delivered to the Exchequer) and the 'overplus' (the amount of revenue raised over and above the rent). The controls were further tightened in 1680 when a system of 'management' was instituted whereby excise 'farmers,' now more like government agents than independent contractors, ran it in return for a fixed sum to pay the administrative costs and one shilling in the pound of the overplus. This,

however, prompted a decline in efficiency. In the face of the substantial-
ly reduced advantages from making a large overplus, the 'managers' dramatically weakened the local administration in order to secure a larger
proportion of the fixed sum. Combined with the disaffection of the
county justices, and the financial crisis of the early 1680s, this led to the
return of the Excise to direct collection in 1683 and the restructuring
of its administration.

The importance of the period from 1683 to 1689 for the subsequent history of taxation and the state has been stressed by historians of
the Excise. Edward Hughes argued in 1934 'that the outstanding
changes in the public finance of William III's reign were directly condi-
tioned by a revolution in fiscal policy, notably the abandonment in the
system of farming in the principal branches of the king's revenues
which took place in the reign of Charles II.'[74] C. D. Chandaman also
situated the modernisation of public finance in the Restoration and
recognised the fiscal and administrative contribution of the direct collection of excise taxation after 1683.[75] Even historians who emphasise
the financial revolution of the 1690s have signaled the importance of
the 1680s, with John Brewer arguing that 'Post-revolutionary finance
was built on a pre-revolutionary model' since 'the administrative foundations of the eighteenth-century tax system had been firmly laid' by
1688.[76] Finally, Michael Braddick, who has made the case that significant features of the fiscal–military state were formed in the 1640s, notes
that the period after 1670 was notable for increases in revenue from institutional reorganisation and that, as a result, 'James II's successor inherited a remarkably efficient excise administration marked by considerable
professionalism.'[77] Davenant's case continues to be made.[78] The irony is
that it was James II's attempts to ensure financial independence—and
perhaps absolutism—based on a royal bureaucracy that not only
prompted the Glorious Revolution but hastened the modernity of the
state via a transformation of excise administration.

In the summer of 1683 the excise commissioners inherited a national system of spatial administration and the personnel who ran it,
some of whom would have seen several different central authorities
come and go.[79] England and Wales were divided into 886 'districts' or
'divisions,' consisting of rural 'rides' and urban 'walks.'[80] In 1684 the average ride in Kent was 38 miles long and the average walk was 6 miles
long.[81] Each division was assessed by an individual officer. They were
grouped into thirty-six 'collections,' each about the size of a county although not contiguous with them, and overseen by one or two supervisors.[82] These officers and supervisors were answerable to the collectors

who gathered the taxes in the collections. The volume of business that had to be dealt with was prodigious. By 1685 the Excise was charging 784 common brewers for over 1.8 million barrels of strong beer and over 1.1 million barrels of small beer. It also charged 45,655 victuallers for over 2.7 million barrels of strong beer and over .9 million barrels of small beer. It assessed and charged excises for over 6.5 million barrels of beer in total.[83] In order to do this effectively the commissioners had to reassert central control over the country localities and reorganise the way in which the work of the Excise was done.[84] Davenant emphasised one part of their new administrative arrangements:

> . . . as a check above all, (and which was indeed the life of their whole af-
> fair) the Commissioners themselves made frequent circuits around the
> kingdom, viewing every particular officer in his respective division; with-
> out which, the inferior officers would have run into sloth, and the superi-
> or into corruption.
>   And in these circuits, they could observe who were remiss, who
> diligent, who deserved advancement; who wanted removing; and here
> they suited each man's district to his capacity; and if their officers were
> corrupt, here they got true information of their proceedings.[85]

It is the record of Davenant's own circuits that I want to use to show the remaking of excise administration between 1683 and 1689 toward the 'perfect management' that both the Excise and Treasury Boards sought.[86]

Figure 16 shows what can be reconstructed of Davenant's main horseback journeys around south and west England, and into Wales, between 1683 and 1689. Since there are substantial periods of time, especially after 1685, that cannot be accounted for, he presumably made other journeys for which no record survives.[87] We can also only assume that the other commissioners covered the rest of the country in similar ways and with similar diligence. Each of the journeys mapped here followed a more or less circular path, if at times a rather tortuous one, out from and back toward London. These movements served to tie the localities to the centre, and together they covered most of the region, with some places being visited more than once. On each circuit he would generally visit a different division, and sometimes several divisions, every day, only spending more time in the larger towns or ports which had more officers and from which he could visit nearby divisions. In each place he noted how it was organised in order to make alterations on the spot or after his return to London.

At the heart of excise administration and, like Davenant's political arithmetic, a way of maximising revenue without endangering political legitimacy, was the accurate gauging of casks. Accuracy allowed excise officers to ensure that they could, where necessary, assess and charge everything that was due to the king, but not a drop less and not a penny more. This sought legitimacy for the Excise at the point of contact between the producers and the excisemen by countering the fear that the officers could wield extensive and arbitrary powers, a suspicion that had bedeviled the Excise in its early years.[88] Accuracy could guarantee the Excise, but how could accuracy itself be guaranteed?[89] In part, this hap-

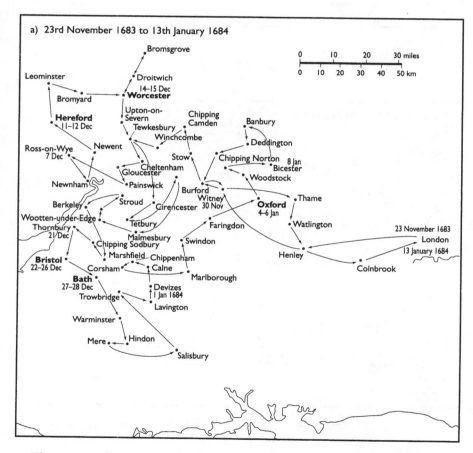

Figure 16 a–e Charles Davenant's Travels, November 1683 to September 1685. *(Continued on next page)*

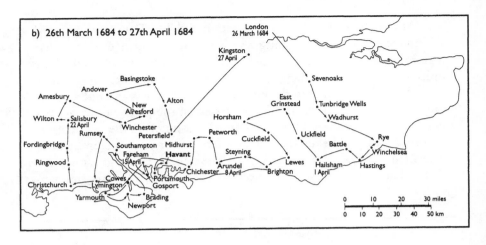

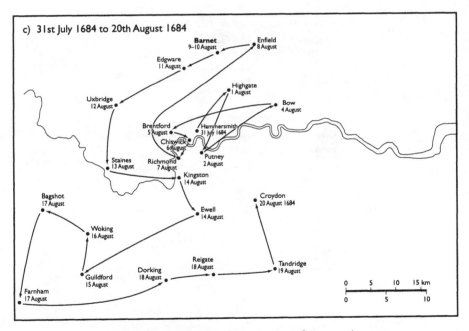

Figure 16 *(continued; continues on facing page)*

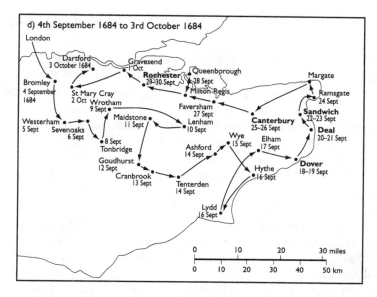

d) 4th September 1684 to 3rd October 1684

London

Dartford
3 October 1684

Gravesend
1 Oct

Queenborough

Margate

Bromley
4 September
1684

St Mary Cray
2 Oct

Rochester
29–30 Sept

28 Sept
Milton Regis

Ramsgate
24 Sept

Wrotham
9 Sept

Sandwich
22–23 Sept

Westerham
5 Sept

Sevenoaks
6 Sept

Maidstone
11 Sept

Faversham
27 Sept

Canterbury
25–26 Sept

Deal
20–21 Sept

8 Sept
Tonbridge

Lenham
10 Sept

Wye
15 Sept

Elham
17 Sept

Goudhurst
12 Sept

Ashford
14 Sept

Dover
18–19 Sept

Cranbrook
13 Sept

Tenterden
14 Sept

Hythe
16 Sept

Lydd
16 Sept

0	10	20	30 miles
0	10	20	30	40	50 km

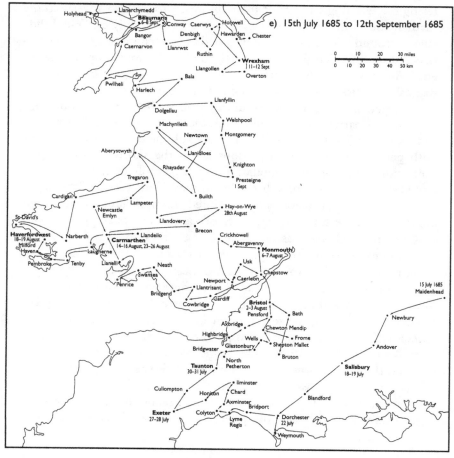

e) 15th July 1685 to 12th September 1685

Holyhead

Llanerchymedd

Beaumaris
6–8 Sept

Conway

Caerwys

Holywell

Bangor

Denbigh

Hawarden

Chester

Caernarvon

Llanrwst

Ruthin

Wrexham
11–12 Sept

Pwllheli

Bala

Llangollen

Overton

Harlech

Llanfyllin

Dolgellau

Machynlleth

Welshpool

Newtown

Montgomery

Aberystwyth

Llanidloes

Rhayader

Knighton

Tregaron

Presteigne
1 Sept

Cardigan

Lampeter

Builth

St David's

Newcastle
Emlyn

Hay-on-Wye
28th August

Haverfordwest
18–19 August
Milford
Haven

Narberth

Llandeilo

Llandovery

Brecon

Crickhowell

Carmarthen
14–16 August, 23–26 August

Llanelli

Neath

Abergavenny

Monmouth
6–7 August

Laugharne

Usk

Pembroke

Tenby

Swansea

Newport

Caerleon

Chepstow

15 July 1685
Maidenhead

Penrice

Bridgend

Llantrisant

Cardiff

Cowbridge

Bristol
2–3 August
Pensford

Bath

Newbury

Axbridge

Chewton Mendip

Highbridge

Wells

Frome

Andover

Bridgwater

Glastonbury

Shepton Mallet

Taunton
30–31 July

North
Petherton

Bruton

Salisbury
18–19 July

Cullompton

Ilminster

Chard

Honiton

Axminster

Bridport

Blandford

Exeter
27–28 July

Colyton

Lyme
Regis

Dorchester
22 July

Weymouth

0	10	20	30 miles
0	10	20	30	40	50 km

pened through the skillful deployment of the first four rules of mathematics.[90] There was, however, no agreement on the best method, and so a variety of subtly different forms of gauging were set out in a number of books from the 1670s onward. Each of them claimed to offer increased clarity through attention to practicalities or more comprehensive coverage via detailed accounts of mathematical principles.[91] Since mathematics was not widely taught in schools, these instruction manuals, written both by excise officers and by those who wrote more generally on mathematical subjects, found a market among excisemen and, to enhance their appeal, often included not only instruction in gauging but also guidance on the practicalities, routines and legal complexities of the excise officer's craft.[92] Each book, therefore, provided some portable expertise that officers could deploy in their divisions. They also served to advertise 'things useful in the Excise,' attaching themselves to particular retailers of ledgers, county maps, printed forms, and acts of Parliament, as well as offering the teaching services of their authors.[93] Many also advertised the mathematical instruments—gauging rods and differently calibrated slide rules—around which they had developed their versions of gauging practice and upon which their commercial and professional hopes depended.[94] Again, these instruments condensed and made portable a mathematical expertise beyond that of the individual officer.

In fact, there was not much in the basic mathematics behind gauging that was particularly new, although there were many different ways to tackle the same problems.[95] While any volume could be worked out with pen and paper, the innovations lay in the shortcuts. In general, these either consisted of computations with specially designed and calibrated slide rules from some basic dimensions of the cask and the depth of liquid in it, or calculations from printed tables of figures that related depth to volume for different sorts of cask.[96] For example, Richard Collins's method was based on 'reducing' casks to cylinders, either through simple arithmetical operations or via a table, and then using another table to calculate the volume from measurements of the cylinder's diameter and the depth. He claimed that 'there are no cask or Brewing Vessels that you will meet withall, but they may be Gauged by the following Tables by any person, though he be a stranger to the Art of *Arithmetic*.'[97] Unsurprisingly, it was precisely this absence of the mathematical arts that condemned tables in the eyes of supporters of the slide rule and the pen.[98] However, despite their differences, all of the methods depended upon assuming that the casks were formed of regular, geometrical shapes. For example, Charles Leadbetter later dealt with casks assumed to be parts of spheres, paraboloids, hyperboloids and cones (Figure 15). This was, of course, an impossible assumption of regularity, but it was a necessary one if gaugers were to claim the legitimacy that number gave, often to several decimal places.[99] They all, therefore, relied upon conjuring an imaginary calculable space—an idealised container made of mathematical lines—that abstracted the cask and its commodities from the artisanal circuits of wood and beer within which they also existed and within which other skills and practices, often legitimated by custom rather than by mathematical reasoning, governed their usage.[100] By doing so casks and mathematics were made to answer the purposes of the Excise and the ends of accuracy. As Keith Thomas says, '[T]he concern for exact measurement operated within a limited sphere.'[101]

However, having this knowledge in books was not enough, even if those books were in the hands of the officers. A national system of accurate gauging depended upon nationally agreed units of measurement, or at least units agreed for determining excises. While these were fixed in the capital, and in many cases had been fixed by legislation for some time, they had to be made available elsewhere and in ways that maintained their standardisation.[102] The brass measures in London's Guildhall had to be accurately replicated everywhere else. Thus, the excise officer of Newport on the Isle of Wight requested that Davenant supply him with 'a seal gallon which may serve upon any dispute in other places.'[103] In this way agreed-upon measures—and the national system of accuracy that they contained—might be made available in local places, at least within the circuits of the Excise.

Alongside these standard measures accuracy also had to be guaranteed by the precision of the measurements of volumes and calculations of charges made out in the field, rather than those laid down in books on gauging. Ensuring accuracy here was, in part, dependent upon the calibre and training of the officers employed at the lowest level, those whom Davenant called 'the wheels upon which the whole engine moves.'[104] His task was to identify the officers whose skills were inadequate and either instruct them, reassign them or dismiss them.[105] He checked their gauging and their mathematics.[106] He noted those who undermeasured or could not divide, and those who could not gauge at all.[107] He was interested in the skills the officers showed rather than who they had been recommended by.[108] He also sought to detect, by taking gauges himself and checking them against the officers' records, those who made 'false surveys' or engaged in 'chamber practice.'[109] In part this was a matter of each man's mathematical training, but it was also a question of technique. Davenant fought a running battle for the use of the 'semicircular rule' against Thomas Everard's 'sliding rule' on the grounds of precision.[110] He also suspected Richard Collins's tables, or 'book,' of inaccuracy, substituting for the artistry of mathematics and encouraging chamber practice.[111] He thus sought to spread what he considered to be best practice in the interests of a uniform geography of accuracy and precision.[112] He also sought to standardise the officers' bookkeeping techniques, which were hindered by Everard's continual introduction of new methods and helped by the examination of all officers' books at the Excise Board in London.[113] Only with accurate and standardised measurement and bookkeeping could anyone rely on the officers' gauges or charges.[114]

For these precise and standard techniques deployed by skillful officers to be effective in the production of accuracy, the unpredictability of the environment within which they operated had to be tamed. The gaugers had to know the dimensions of all the brewing vessels each brewer used in order to be able to take the few quick measurements that would give them the volumes of liquid that they contained. Gauging each vessel every time would have been time-consuming and costly. In order to ensure the comprehensive, accurate and legitimate recording of these dimensions, Davenant called for a centralised and regularly updated system of recording:

> To order all the supervisors throughout England forthwith to gage all the vessells in their respective districts & to send up an accompt of their gages to the office [of the excise commissioners in London]. A register to be kept of this & the Superv^{ers} to be charged once in every six settings, to gage anew every vessell &c. This method may prevent frauds and save the King a great deal.[115]

Davenant sought a guarantee of accuracy via the centralisation of knowledge and through hierarchical administrative injunctions over its collection and precision. In doing so, he was trying to counter the fraudulent alteration of vessels and the inaccuracies introduced by frequent changes due to breakages and, more importantly, from the brewers' practice of swapping vessels with each other.[116] Such exchanges could not be prosecuted as fraud, although they certainly were employed with the hope of getting away with some unexcised drink or, at least, 'to puzzle the officers.'[117] They had to be dealt with through the management of accurate knowledge.

The main purpose of collating these measurements, and one of the key aims of Davenant's travels and the new commission, was to facilitate a nationwide alteration in the point of the brewing process where amounts were gauged and brewers charged.[118] Understanding these changes requires knowing a little about how beer is brewed. Every separate brewing is called a 'guile.' To start it, malt is coarsely ground and mixed with hot water (known as 'liquor') in the mash tun; the strength of the beer is mainly dependent on the proportion of malt to water (or 'length'). The liquid (called 'worts') is drawn off into a copper vat and boiled with hops for flavour. Yeast is added to the strained liquid after it has been cooled in large shallow vessels called 'backs.' It is then fermented in the working tun (or guile tun). The yeast is removed as the beer is 'cleansed' into barrels.[119] The change that was sought was from measuring the stock—the end product in its casks—to gauging the 'worts' during the brewing process, and as near the beginning as possible.[120] Davenant sought to enforce this change on the grounds that it increased the accuracy of the measurement and therefore boosted the revenue.[121] It also prevented frauds from going undetected. For example, in Hereford brewers would siphon some of the guile off before putting the rest into the tuns. It never got into the casks that were measured. On the Isle of Wight casks were spirited away to nearby ships before they could be assessed.[122] So the earlier the gauge could be taken, the less chance brewers had to split the guiles. Where all their vessels had been measured, gauges could be taken at any stage in the brewing process. If all was done properly—if the gauges were accurate and the brewers honest—measurements taken at different stages of the same guile should, with some allowance for heat expansion, all coincide.[123]

There were objections of course. The producers argued that no account was taken of spillage and waste, and that the allowances for heat expansion were unfair.[124] Some brewers managed to dictate where the gauge should be taken to their advantage.[125] The excise commissioners had to answer concerned letters and Davenant had to face, or avoid, angry victuallers in Cirencester, Tetbury, Malmsbury, Northleach and Stroud.[126] He also had to investigate reports that some excise officers objected 'by conscience' to people being 'oppressed by being charged in the worts.'[127] The argument of the excise commissioners was simply that 'there can bee noe difference between Gageing by the Cask or by the ffat if what is Gaged in the ffat bee all putt into the Cask.'[128] Davenant's reasoning was similar:

> The people of . . . [Tetbury] came to me likewise in a body complaining of the great oppression they suffer by being taken in the worts. . . . A great reason of all this clamour is that the cask have been hitherto under

gaged & now they think they pay God knows how much more than they
ought to pay. Many casks formerly gaged at 56 now new gaged hold 64
we suffer by the former management. They paid before lesse than they
ought to have paid and now think themselves injured to pay their due.[129]

They were paying what they legitimately should, and would be asked
for nothing more than that. However, winning such local battles was a
matter of negotiation as well as accuracy. Davenant was, along with the
rest of the excise establishment, aware of the need to ensure that the key
local officials, the justices of the peace, were on the side of the Excise.[130] Their support would guarantee the conditions for accurate assessment by upholding the legitimacy of such changes and enforcing
excise law. In Tetbury he convinced the JPs 'of the lawfulness and necessity of it,' and elsewhere he sought to discover which magistrates
might cause trouble, which were 'very kind to the Excise,' which might
be buttered up, and which might be brought on side via judicious use of
the patronage system.[131] Indeed, in this way informal social contact and
patronage might serve the administrative goals of accuracy and uniformity.[132]

    Magistrates and their courts had to be carefully managed. In excise
cases a national system was judged in the preeminent theatre of local
power. National claims would not carry the day there unless they had
local support and allowed the magistrates a certain freedom of action,
although censure from London could also be used sparingly. There was
no absolute certainty that the magistrates would act against the brewers
and in the interest of the revenue.[133] The necessary manoeuvring is apparent in the pursuit of another aim of Davenant and the new commission: ensuring that as much drink as possible was charged as ale rather
than as beer.[134] Traditionally, ale was unhopped, heavier and sweeter
than beer. However, by the late seventeenth century the main difference
was that the capacity of a beer barrel was set at 36 gallons, an ale barrel
at 32 gallons. Under the same duty per barrel the latter paid more excise.[135] Thus, the fact that Salisbury's brewers made a drink that was
dealt with as beer but would have been treated as ale in any other part
of the country became a problem for Davenant as brewers in other
places noted that 'if people will stand it out with us we doe not charge
them ale.'[136] Bringing them to heel in the courts meant ensuring,
through negotiation and threats, that the balance of the JPs would support the Excise.[137] Also, in order to ensure that the best case was made,
William Burridge, 'a Brisk & experienced Blade,' was the officer chosen
to give evidence—supported by his well-kept books and experience of

a similar case in Plymouth—rather than Woodward, who 'humms & ha's so that I think him not proper.'[138] Decisions on what was ale and what was beer were more a matter of the demands of the revenue, efficient officers and well-conducted court cases than matters of fact.[139] In turn, uniformity was a matter of local negotiations.[140] Careful awareness of the geography of power within the state was necessary to change beer into ale, and to shift the gauging point from the stock to the worts.

Charging from gauges in the worts also necessitated increased accuracy elsewhere. It meant that 'stocking'—keeping running tables of the stocks held by brewers—had to be more carefully done to uncover fraudulent concealments and 'mixing' without making false accusations or losing revenue that should have been collected.[141] Officers had to know that what could be seen in the numerical record was a fraud and not a clerical error.[142] Again, there was a best practice to be spread called, appropriately enough, 'the method.'[143] The aim was to accurately and continuously track each productive process in tabular form, noting the volumes and strengths in each successive vessel, and to keep a running record from which charges could be cast. In his circuits Davenant aimed to discover those officers whose books were 'not in the right method' and to teach it to them.[144] What was called 'methodising' aimed at uniformity both within collections and nationally. As he said of Kent, 'almost every offic[r] in this county has a different method. I have given em all one method and ordered them to keep to it.'[145] More generally, he argued 'there should be one method of keeping bookes[,] all stock books differ of each county I have seen.'[146] Achieving this uniformity meant reconciling both brewers and officers to the technique and removing at least one county supervisor 'who is not a Friend to the method.'[147] It could also be achieved by moving officers. Christopher Banson, who had devised the method in Wales, had moved a series of officers into other collections to introduce it.[148] Davenant continued this practice, and sought to extend it:

> To send of those that attend at the Board 3 into every Welch Collection. &3 into every Northern and some likewise into Yorkshire & other parts that are well mannaged there to walk and be instructed. Then whoever of the Commissioners that Rides these counties let him take an accompt how all the present officers in these places are qualified & what kind of business every one has. By this means we can supply counties not well mannaged thus. Draw from the best businesses those that you want[,] supply those vacant places with experienced officers that are in lesser

businesses & into those Lesser Concerns put in the new Officers that wait
for employ besides to have in every County one or 2 to stand candidate
upon the Negligence of any Officer.[149]

This strategy aimed to produce both a uniform geography of accuracy
and to enable gauging to be done everywhere 'in the worts.' But it required constant surveillance. The danger was that if officers had failed
to charge in the worts, they would be unwilling to charge the stock and
then whole brewings would be lost to cover their failure.[150] Its success,
like so much of the restructuring of the excise collection, depended
upon a finely graded and territorially organised hierarchy of superviso-
ry officers.[151]

Beyond the method, moving officers between divisions and collections was a fundamental part of adjusting excise administration, and
Davenant would order such 'removes' after consultation locally and with
London.[152] Incompetent officers were replaced; some officers' requests
for removes were granted; and in places where there were 'several il
Customes introduced which [the incumbent officer] is a shamed to alter,' Davenant would assign a new officer who had no such local obligations and could enforce national policy.[153] All these changes were part
of the way in which the excise commissioners dealt with the localities.
Their attempts to ensure accuracy, uniformity and steady revenue meant
being responsive to local specificity without compromising what had to
be a national system. Being locally responsive meant that every walk or
ride had to be under adequate surveillance by its officer to prevent
brewers from producing unexcised drink.[154] Gaugers had to know how
much beer was likely to be made each week, each month, and in each
brewing, and when the brewing usually started.[155] Davenant tried to
ensure such knowledge by getting officers to survey, gauge and stock
more frequently, but all districts were not equal and neither were their
officers.[156] Davenant faced a variegated and changing topography of
potential taxation revenue that depended upon the size of the divisions
and the numbers, types and locations of brewing premises within them.
These differences also dictated differences in the skills required to make
them productive. Some districts responded best to diligence and appli-
cation, while others required the full expression of the gauger's artistry.
Davenant sought to match officers to areas by matching capability, demands and revenue potential.[157] As one of his principles simply stated,
'Bad officers to be removed to Smaller districts.'[158]

He also adjusted the size and shape of districts. He catalogued each
walk or ride he visited to show the places it covered, the distances be-

tween them, and the number of premises to be surveyed. Judging each one in the context of the collection as a whole, he could recommend a new geography. This might involve decreasing the size of a ride to compensate for an increased number of premises, equalising the work between rides, or introducing a new ride and adjusting the others accordingly. Each change was justified on the basis of tabulations of the revenues of each ride in relation to its collection and the country as a whole, which helped in ascertaining whether the increased revenue would be greater than the costs of implementation. Within this context, Davenant might also recommend that some producers—often those in locations that made them difficult to visit—'compound' to pay a regular fixed sum rather than being visited and gauged. Such discretion was possible within the overall framework of regulation and revenue maximisation, and if it threatened corruption or tax avoidance it might, in certain cases, be what was necessary to ensure a regular flow of revenue.[159] In general, therefore, this new geography involved the reductions in size that made adequate surveillance possible, shifted the advantage from the brewer to the gauger, and allowed the other changes— stocking and charging by the 'method,' gauging in the worts, and charging ale—to be put in place. Accuracy and revenue levels depended, therefore, not only on the technique of the gauger and his instruments, and on keeping him under surveillance, but on the geography of the administrative divisions within which he worked.

This responsiveness to local conditions was, however, undertaken in a pursuit of national priorities that was also evident in the management of corruption, disputes, appointments, promotions, and officers' responsibilities.[160] This is particularly clear in those removes designed to avoid the Excise becoming locally compromised, including those where new officers were brought in to stamp out customary practices. Another of Davenant's principles was for 'Removes to be made where officers have been long.'[161] They were moved from places where they had debts or, in their supervisors' or Davenant's eyes, too much local familiarity, particularly with brewers and victuallers, which could compromise their objectivity and lead them into corruption.[162] Excise officers were to be national officers who worked locally. This positioning was produced through the removes that served to guarantee their objectivity, accuracy and fidelity to the Excise rather than to any locality.

Davenant's circuits—and the work he performed through them— constructed, adjusted and carefully maintained a network of people (gaugers, supervisors, collectors, magistrates, brewers), instruments (seal measures, casks, tuns, the semicircular rule), and documents (running stock books, brewers' ledgers, scribbled calculations, legal decisions, and his own diaries) that could only operate in and through a set of carefully calibrated spaces that ranged in scale from the barrel to the nation-state, and that sought to guarantee the production of accuracy, political legitimacy and the taxation revenues necessary to wage war.[163] It was a network that centred on London and covered the whole country. It did so even more after Davenant had acted out the series of orders, stan-dardisations, consultations and negotiations that defined the centre's role, and had ridden the journeys that, along with the flows of money, the checking of ledgers and the making of appointments, tied the local-ities to the centre. In part, it was through his efforts that London's role as an administrative capital was reshaped through new forms of power and knowledge. Indeed, without his work the network that was constructed might have fallen apart as it started to do in the early 1690s. That it was this 'modern' territorial state apparatus 'which was indeed the life of their whole affair' is well illustrated by an event that occurred toward the end of Davenant's work as an excise commissioner and which refers back to the national standardisation of measurements where my ac-count began.[164]

The mathematician and excise gauger John Ward reported that a Dr Wybard had calculated that the sealed wine gallon measure at the Guildhall—the standardised unit for wine, brandies, spirits, strong wa-ters and cider—was not the 231 cubic inches that it was supposed by law to contain, but only 224 cubic inches. To check this, an experiment was conducted by two excise officers on 25 May 1688 at London's Guildhall in front of the lord mayor, the excise commissioners (proba-bly including Davenant), the astronomers John Flamsteed and Edmond Halley, and 'several other ingenious gentlemen.' They poured liquid from a specially designed brass parallelepipedon with a volume of 224 cubic inches into the standard wine gallon. It was filled to the top. However, as Ward notes, 'for *several Reasons* it was at that Time thought convenient to continue the former supposed content of 231 *Cubic Inch-es* to be the *Wine Gallon.*'[165] What was important was not the icon that sat sealed in the Guildhall, supposedly guaranteeing the national unifor-mity of accurate measurement, but the figure that was deployed in countless acts of measurement and calculation, and that was in circula-tion within a complex national network made up of mutually depen-dent guarantees of accuracy, efficiency and legitimacy. It was not simply the centre that was important but its relation to the network.

There is, however, a danger of idealising the efficiency of the Ex-cise in the 1680s. It was undoubtedly effective in raising revenue but the machinelike qualities of its administration need to be disrupted. There were undoubtedly many frauds that went undetected. The evidence that survives shows how hard it was to discover many of the brewers' tricks.[166] They only became a problem, however, if revenue levels were insufficient or if the legitimacy of the system was threatened. Thus in their regular conversations among the vats and casks, there was a form of 'negotiation,' although rarely explicit, between the excise officers and the brewers over enforcement and compliance that determined the efficiency of excise collection, and which existed alongside the explicit negotiations over taxation conducted through the courts. It is also necessary to bear in mind the amount of work required by Davenant and others to make the system run smoothly. When that was not forthcoming the system faltered as it had done under the system of 'management' between 1680 and 1683, and as it was to again in the 1690s. Finally, little has been said here about those whom Davenant called 'the wheels upon which the whole engine moves': the excisemen themselves.[167] So far they have been assumed to be a relatively unproblematic part of that 'engine'—if differentiated in skills, diligence and believability—and that is generally the way in which Davenant saw them. However, examining them through other sources reveals the ambivalences of their position.

INTERPRETING *THE EXCISE MAN*

So far I have presented the gaugers in their divisions through the training that Davenant sought to give them, the work they had to undertake, and the removes that they had to endure. As such they were intimately connected with the instruments, writings, spaces and other officers that made up the Excise, and their diligence was a crucial guarantee of accuracy. In this section I want to look at them in more detail to examine how those requirements affected their lives, but also to argue that this involved them in an active and creative process of self-fashioning that both shaped their selves to the modern state as a vital part of its effective operation and, through laughter, distanced them from it. I want to reveal the production of the exciseman, and his ambivalences, alongside, and as part of, my accounts of the production of the Excise's geography and of accuracy. To do so, I will concentrate on one text, Ezekial Polstead's *The Excise Man,* published in 1697.[168]

Ezekial Polstead was gauging in Abergavenny Town in September 1685 when Charles Davenant visited and described him as 'a brisk officer.' He had probably been recommended to the position by his kinsman Sir Denny Ashburnham, another excise commissioner. He later served as an officer in Monmouth, and by Christmas 1690 he was gauging in Cardiff and was promoted to being supervisor of the Wales east division. He was still a supervisor in Wales in 1696.[169] He was, it seems, a successful officer with career experience behind him when he dedicated his book to the excise commissioners, and described it as 'a brief and lame Account of the *Excellencies of our Excise-Men* in the *knowledge of the Arts, Men and Laws;* together with the many *Advantages,* as well as *Pleasures,* that naturally result from that Employment.'[170] This was, however, neither a simple celebration of the Excise, nor a political critique.[171] It was an affectionate and sometimes critical account written from within the world of the Excise which, I want to argue, can be interpreted as representing the ways in which excisemen's identities were fashioned and lived.

Polstead shows how the gauger's job shaped his life and gave it meaning. He presented the job as hard work: the constant battle against retailers who saw it as no crime to cheat the revenue; the need to strive because of the uncertainty of preferment and promotion; and the struggle when young to ensure that enough was earned to provide financial security for old age.[172] The 'Excise Man' is defined by his job and how vigilantly he does it:

> [H]e embraces every Opportunity, and lets not anything miss him for want of Circumspection and care. He is watchful to an Excess; and if he sleep, it is as the Naturalists observe of the Hare, i.e. with his Eyes open; for he always considers, that Foxes when sleeping have nothing fall into their mouths.[173]

The job also imposed other requirements. Polstead warned against immoderate drinking and gambling on the grounds that they 'wholly discompose him for the Duty of the subsequent day,' and that they undermine the capacity for 'Self-government.'[174] Gambling was also decried on moral grounds as a 'Loss of Time and Money' that promotes the 'Bestial Part' through 'Great engagements of the Passions.'[175] Within the Excise, where what was at stake was the state's wealth and legitimacy, each officer's conduct had to guarantee that security and legitimacy. As a result, each exciseman lived with the continual threat of being discharged and the continual injunction to make sure that 'his *Life* and *Actions* are all *white* and *innocent.*'[176] Excisemen had to make themselves, and in a specific mould.

These pressures are clear in Polstead's reflections on what it meant to be a salaried and professional officer in a centralised state bureaucracy. This, he argued, imposed a dual requirement of fidelity to the king and dutiful and conscientious performance of duty. Indeed, doing the job well became the sign of fidelity. In turn, the salary meant that his time was not his own: 'he is paid for it, and consequently becomes accomptable.'[177] In depicting the implications of being situated within a large and complex state bureaucracy, Polstead did not simply endorse it. He was well aware that such hierarchies, particularly those in which promotion depended upon the will of those at the top, created competition, frustration and resentment lower down.[178] The way he wrote of 'our Excise-Man' was to present him as a paragon of virtue. His satirical intent is, I think, clear:

> And as our *Excise-Man* is wholly satisfied in relation to the Government in general, so has he full Contentment under his present Circumstances in particular; and thankfully embraces whatever his Superiors suppose necessary for him. And indeed there is a necessity in a Man of Prudence for it; for though wee'l allow *Merit* ought, yet is it altogether impossible it should always meet *Preferment*. . . . [O]ur *Excise-Man* never thinks of Advancement 'till his *Commissioners* do, and receives it then with an *Ex Mero Motu;* and if they should, his chiefest Ambition is to climb up to their good Opinion, on which only he values himself. So that he is not intoxicated with that ambitious Madness, as to covet that which he is no way capable of performing.[179]

Polstead's imaginary exciseman had no dreams of future grandeur, no envy for any who succeed before him, and no covetousness of what others have, even when promotions did not seem to be a matter of 'Endeavour or Merit.'[180] By depicting this ideal, Polstead marked the gap between it and the actual situation. He showed that this was how excisemen had to present themselves no matter how they really felt about colleagues and superiors.

The Excise Man represented this bureaucratic role as an identity shaped by being a professional state official, but also by the bureaucratic hierarchy and its vicissitudes. Excisemen had a social status that was based on knowledge and employment, rather than on the personal or family wealth that would allow other sorts of position to be bought.[181] While patronage and seniority were still important, their jobs meant that they were in a distinctly ambiguous social position, defining them-

selves on new criteria, and concerned about their possible rise or fall.
Polstead's commentary on how the 'Excise Man' selects his 'company' is
full of these tensions, and full of the problems of self-creation:

> [H]is choice is ever for the best: For he knows, that as the Profane can
> only assist him in his Damnation, so the Poor can never help him at all;
> and he concludes, that as either of them are to be avoided, so is also the
> Company of Fools, who can be no way serviceable towards the improve-
> ment of his Intellectuals, which he presumes to be the design'd Origin of
> Society. And although his Place may inevitably cast him amongst them,
> yet he is ever upon his Guard . . . and indeed there seems a necessity of
> his being well arm'd, to clear himself of the Greatest part of the World's
> Composition; and it is his whole study to make himself a Separatist here-
> in, for he knows in relation to the first [his inferiors], that Contamination
> is an infallible Incident, since the defil'd Fly that feeds on dung, has ever
> its correspondent Colour. To the second [his equals] he is satisfied against
> ordinary Company, since the meanness of the Commodity makes it for
> every Bodies money. And in respect to the last [his superiors], he con-
> cludes, that as it is no advancement of his Qualifications, so must it of ne-
> cessity immerge those he was happy in before, Scandal and Infamy being
> its inseparate Attendant.[182]

In terms of the sources of his status and his search for upward mobility, he was a man out of place. He might succeed in being able 'to
avoid the Censure of being imagin'd of the Dunghill straine,' and in in-
gratiating himself with superiors who promise advancement, yet his
gentility was always in the hands of his employers: 'He is (it is true) a
Gentlemen by his Place . . . and he knows very well that one Post may
destroy that.'[183] As Polstead notes, he must be humble and servile both
to secure favour for himself and because that is 'his Duty.' In addition, he
had to exercise 'Discretion and Caution' in his dealings with the local
'Gentlemen' in case familiarity led to negligence or corruption.[184] In
short, the exciseman was caught between the informal obligations of
class-based sociability and the formal obligations of bureaucratic fidelity.

The self-making of the exciseman was, therefore, a process of
shaping himself to fit, more or less, the requirements of the state. It was,
however, also the case that the job offered a range of resources for a
more positive set of identifications and common meanings that forged
its officers into a "tribe."[185] In the series of jokes with which he ended
his book Polstead included the question: 'Whether he can *Err*, that ever
walks by *Rule*?' By punning on law, morality and geometry (via the

slide rule), he revealed a network of connections around mathematical proficiency that were crucial to the exciseman's identity.[186] Their world was a mathematical one:

> *Geometry* must him confess
> The *Center* of each Happiness;
> For as their *Patron,* Him alone
> The *Mathematicks* wait upon.[187]

It was mathematics that set them apart. Their status was based on specialised knowledges and was maintained through intellectual boundary drawing. Assessments of the difficulty of these knowledges were crucial in establishing their cultural capital: 'Could every ignorant Rustick attain to a perfect knowledge in the Mathematicks, its Excellency would be converted into contempt.'[188] Indeed, in an attempt to further confirm the impermeability of 'The Excise Man's' otherwise shaky status, Polstead suggested that the books by 'Eminent *Gaugers'*—he cites William Hunt and Thomas Everard—tell only what is obvious, and that the real key to success is 'natural inclination' and the sort of practical activity only learned through long experience.[189] Indeed, excisemen might be made of mathematics. In a flight of fancy Polstead imagines a divine correspondence between men's bodies and geometry that serves to sanction those who 'rule':

[T]here might be something *ab initio* particularly respecting him; For as some compare his Head to the Round Heavens, his Eyes to the Sun and Moon, his Hairs to the Trees and Grass; his Flesh to the Earth; his Veins to the Rivers; and his Bones to the precious Gems, Metals and Minerals, which are the Riches of the Earth; so some have been led to imagine, that his body was not made in all the *Geometrical Proportions* that are or can be thought of, but as a *Demonstration* of the *Excellency* of our *Excise-Man,* who should make the greatest use of them.

For all Numbers and Proportions of Measure, whether Inches, Cubits, Feet, etc. are deriv'd from the Members and Dimensions of Him, some few of which may not be impertinently subjoin'd.

First then, let us see how a *Circle* was thought of; for let but the hands fall somewhat stradling a little with the Legs, the Extremes of the Fingers, Head and Toes, make as exact a Circle as you are capable of making with your Unerring Compasses, where you may, if you please, make the *Navel* the *Center.*

Again, *A Geometrical Square is a Superficial Figure made up of four equal Sides or Angles:* Now for a demonstration of this Figure from Man's Body, it is but stretching out your Hands as far and directly upon a Plane as possible from each side, the Body being exactly upright, and the Feet clos'd together.

Lastly, *A Triangle is a Figure containing three Sides:* Now if the Body be plac'd directly upright, and a line drawn from each extended hand, to the Feet enclos'd, it makes an exact Triangle.[190]

Mathematics, it seems, was not only 'an essentially masculine affair' in terms of who got to teach and learn it, it was also a source of social prestige and moralised self-discipline that could be used to imagine a professional masculinity that was made meaningful, valuable, regular, rational, timeless and natural through its correspondence with geometrical order.[191]

If the 'Excise Man' was geometrical, he was also mobile. He had to survey his division every day, while supervisors and collectors traveled even further. He was also subject to being removed from one district to another and, in a national system, promotion could mean relocation—as it did for Polstead himself. These arduous journeys in all weathers are represented in *The Excise Man* as an advantage, a pleasure, although again Polstead's satirical intent would have been clear to his readers. For him, instead of the European grand tour where young aristocrats only learned to throw away money and time, excisemen gained a valuable knowledge of England and Wales. Moreover, the exciseman's constant circuits meant that he knew his division so intimately that 'he must be the most competent Judge of making a *Geographical Description* of every Road, that instead of Miles, can tell you the very Steps: and the most exact *Historiographer* when nothing worthy of *Remark* can miss his *Observation*.'[192] Polstead wrote of the pleasures of being paid to take a series of long, healthy and beautiful country walks, enabling geographical, historical and nature study as well as contemplation and reflection. Where these rural pleasures failed, there were the sociable pleasures of the city that his mobile existence also afforded him.[193]

Geographical mobility was the exciseman's lived experience. Polstead justified the bureaucratic imperative of mobility by rendering it virtuous in a litany that set stasis against motion: standing lakes are never clean and wholesome, while moving streams carry away contagion; fixed trees bear worse fruit than transplanted ones; the most bewitching perfumes come from rubbing and chafing; fixed stars are less beautiful than moving ones. As he finally puts it:

> My Country is where're my *Bread* I get,
> Not where I was *Bred,* but where I have *Meat:*

> Where I am *known* not *Christen'd;* there I dwell
> (And no where else) wherever I do well.[194]

In order to guarantee the effectivity and legitimacy of the state's taxation system, the exciseman had to be mobile. He had to live a separate life, remaining aloof from and free of the taint of local connections and their potential for corruption.[195] Accordingly, Polstead depicted the local scene as one of venality and self-interest. People seek to curry favour with the 'Excise Man' via flattery, gifts and invitations in the hope that the ties of intimacy will override the claims of national authority.[196] He had to avoid monetary debts that could both undermine his neutrality and encourage embezzlement. He had to resist entanglement in all these local corrupting bonds in favour of retaining the legitimacy of, and his position within, a national administrative system whose sets of connections and responsibilities operated at scales larger than the locality.[197] These imperatives fashioned his life. Polstead points to the characteristically nonlavish lifestyle of the 'Excise Man': 'A prudent Frugality' and the avoidance of those 'gilded Fopperies, which terminate in a Gaol.'[198] His life was characterised by an avoidance of excess since any hint of corruption could result in removal or dismissal. His intimate social relations were also shaped by these concerns. As Polstead has it, 'he is even shy of *Familiarity:* For though *Humanity* obliges him to a common Respect, yet *Prudence* denies an *Intimacy.*'[199] Polstead's own removal from Abergavenny Town to Monmouth for 'having got too much acquaintance' in his walk may well have prompted these reflections.[200]

Avoiding local connections was a matter of maintaining the claims of autonomy, rationality, objectivity and, therefore, legitimacy against both a venal, local corrupting of the national uniformity of the Excise and the claims of excessive state intervention raised by its opponents. These rational, bureaucratic practices had to be lived out and performed in public by the exciseman. This meant a careful modulation of language and feeling, a process of self-fashioning. If in relation to his own promotion prospects he was to have no 'wild and irrational Inclinations,' then the dual and combined requirements of respectability and rationality also counseled moderation in his dealings with others.[201] As a national officer acting locally, he found condensed within the routine and everyday actions of gauging and charging that he had to perform the much wider political forces that asserted and denied the grounds of legitimacy on which the Excise was based. He was required to manage these within the face-to-face social relations of excise taxation. In a remarkable passage Polstead set out these requirements in ways that con-

nect rationality, authority, the management of passions, the control of
language, and the classed and gendered identities that such self-control
implied:

> He is not to be biass'd by his excited Passions, nor hector'd by Affronts
> and Clamor. He considers the Loser, claims the priviledge of *Speaking,*
> but not of *Prating.* He allows their asking Questions moderately, but not
> making Solutions Scandalously: Such Persons ever calling all things into
> question, but are not capable of approving any thing; which Considera-
> tion leads him to the remembrance of the Adage, That he that will allow
> himself to be a *Sheep,* must allow himself to be eaten by *Wolves.*
>   I would not be here mistaken, as if our *Excise-Man* should be guilty
> of opprobrious and railing Terms, generally predominant, No; But he ei-
> ther moderately convinces them with the severest Scrutinies of Reason,
> or (to those not susceptible of such) answers them with *Silence.* He knows
> such language becomes only *Billingsgate,* and not any there, but the *weaker
> Sex,* He concludes it very much beneath a Man (much more an *Excise-
> Man*) to be guilty of such scandalous Actions, so extravagantly contradic-
> tory to those common Rules of Civility, he is so strictly charg'd, as well as
> desires to be observant of.[202]

The 'Excise Man' could only offer reason or silence.[203] These limited
and strictly modulated options arose from the imperatives of maintaining an appropriately masculine and respectable identity—defined
against the Billingsgate fishwife, but also against a modish, courtly civility—which, in turn, sprang from the need to maintain the ability to
make rational decisions and legitimate judgments.[204] The 'Excise Man'
had to find resolutions that were neither unfair to the state or to the
taxpayer. This *'reading of Men,'* as Polstead terms it, had to be worked so
'that he does not *ignorantly impose on* others, and that he is not *impertinently impos'd on* himself.'[205] In his behaviour and language the exciseman lived out, and tried to find local resolutions for, the central paradox
of the fiscal–military state: the need to raise unprecedented levels of
taxation through an expanded central state apparatus while preserving
the rights of liberty and private property, and therefore the state's legitimacy.[206] If part of the solution was the production of accuracy, another
connected part was the precise and careful self-regulation of the exciseman. Any loose talk had to be replaced with reason or silence, and emotion by moderation.

The exciseman was defined by the nature of his position as a
salaried bureaucrat in the fiscal–military state and by the active process
of self-fashioning that this required. Polstead's account was, in part, a

guide to and celebration of the ways in which excisemen were meant
to be. He celebrated the fact that 'by admitting none but the *robust and
sensible*' they take only the best of men. He also celebrated their life of
moderation, rationality and order. Happiness was, for them, 'a perfect
Mediocrity' or, more geographically, 'That as East and West upon the
Globe are divided only by a Mathematical Point, so happiness and Misery with all Extremes are still contiguous, a Mean was ever held the
safest.'[207] As such, the 'mean' was not only the stuff of gauging mathematics but a set of cultural qualities. Again Polstead punned:

> Whether if a *Mean* be the most *desirable in all our Actions,* he is not *extreme-
> ly qualified,* that is conversant therein continually?[208]

Working for the government was, therefore, a matter of 'Self-government.'

However, it is also clear in the satirical tone of Polstead's book that
there was no perfect match between regulated selves and bureaucratic
demands.[209] The gap between Polstead's imaginary 'Excise Man' and his
thousands of real counterparts left room for laughter. This, however, was
not the Rabelaisian laughter that, using the abusive idiom of 'billingsgate,' 'builds its own world versus the official world, its own church versus the official church, its own state versus the official state,' and, in doing so, cracked the carapace of medieval seriousness and ushered in the
Renaissance.[210] This was a laughter that operated *within* the 'official
state.' Its parodies did not turn the world upside down but revealed the
small gaps and fissures in the structures of modernity that allowed their
inhabitants to maintain 'some remnants of individual elbow room'
while operating within them.[211] This laughter is marked as modern in
another way. J.G.A. Pocock has argued that the new combination in the
1690s of a standing army, a national debt, and indirect taxation undermined classical notions of self-hood based on the armed and landed citizen and replaced them with a world 'of the circulation of signs acting
at a distance' within which the value of property and personality could
fluctuate as public confidence fluctuated. This new world of debt, fictional wealth and uncertain futures 'rendered both property and public,
and consequently the self, altogether contingent, subjective and historical.' Pocock claims that the subsequent 'awareness of the self's contingency, and the contingency of the forms among which it lives' and the
protests against it are 'an early, perhaps the first modernism.'[212] The
same can be claimed for Polstead. In showing the self as contingent
upon the structures and spaces of the modern bureaucratic state, Pol-

stead displayed this modernism. In showing the work of self-creation undertaken by the excisemen, and the comedy of the gaps between what should be and what was, his laughter was modern too.

THE EXCISE IN EIGHTEENTH-CENTURY LONDON

By the early eighteenth century parliamentary restrictions on excise taxation and the unwillingness to undertake long-term borrowing to finance increasingly expensive imperial wars provoked a 'fiscal crisis whose resolution guaranteed both permanent debts and perpetual taxes.'[213] Excises were laid on an increased range of commodities, including candles, soap, hides, glass, coffee, tea and chocolate. Their administration, while retaining the basic forms of organisation forged in the 1680s, was extended and elaborated. This section discusses the production of space (and time) within the Excise at its most developed, in London after 1750. Here, moving from looking at the city as the centre of a network of regulation to seeing how it was itself regulated, there is the marking out of a bureaucratised geography in and among the streets of the capital. While this process was often invisible, traced most clearly in the movements of excisemen carrying ledgers and slide rules from one brewery or chocolate dealer to another or in the dimensions of a vessel inscribed in an official record, it represents a reconfiguration of both the state and the geography that it deployed in the eighteenth-century city.

The capital was the most heavily regulated part of the country, and increasingly so. In the late seventeenth century London officers made up around 9% of all excise 'field officers,' but by the late eighteenth century the figure was around 18%.[214] By 1763 there were 684 field officers in London. They were divided up to cover the excised commodities: 156 dealing with beer; 113 with the distilled spirits; 121 with candles and soap; and 65 with coffee, tea and chocolate.[215] The productivity of excises in London was both cause and consequence of this level of regulation, which is detailed in the printed instructions issued to officers by the excise commissioners.[216] These periodically gathered together the orders and letters by which policy was directed and changed.[217] As well as setting out the routine procedures for 'the country' and the capital, these instructions, alongside books of excise regulations and advice, also showed how frauds might be perpetrated and detected.[218] Clearly, these instructions offer an idealised vision of excise administration since there would have been a gap between what they contained and what was actually done. Alongside the dangers of bureaucratic stagnation and corruption, governments seeking to alter excise arrangements had to be responsive to political pressure from outside Parliament, as was particularly clear in the Excise Crisis of 1733. The Excise was not shaped by its administrative rationale alone.[219] It is, however, this idealised vision that interests me here in that it offers another imaginary geography, a modern dream of rationally planned order and control.

The largest branch of the Excise in London was the brewery, and its taxation received special attention.[220] In 1750 there were 165 common brewers in London who brewed 979,542 barrels of strong beer and 544,059 barrels of small beer that year.[221] London's geographically concentrated market made it the only place where large breweries could develop. This, along with the suitability of porter for mass production, enabled a 'revolution' in its brewing industry in the decades after 1720. As a result, the big breweries became some of the largest industrial concerns in the capital, responsible for an increasing share of beer production, and run by politically powerful figures.[222] Effectively taxing the London brewers and, to a slightly lesser extent, the producers of other excised commodities involved the production and control of spaces and times that were rational, planned, hierarchical, routinised and under regular and seamless surveillance. These were the bureaucratised spaces and times of modern state administration.

To tax the brewers London was divided, by 1750, into ten divisions with associated outwalks, including Hackney, Islington and Knightsbridge. Three of these divisions had three officers, the rest had six officers but were each divided into two parts. Each division had a surveyor (or 'supervisor') who, with his assistant, was to keep everything under inspection. Each division had, near its centre, 'a common Chamber' where the division's books were kept and where each officer's shift, or 'course,' started and ended. From Monday to Friday these shifts were six hours long and started at midnight, 6:00 A.M., noon, and 6:00 P.M. To cover both day and night, while continually rotating the times at which particular officers surveyed, they worked six hours on followed by twelve hours off. In every six-hour course the brewery officers were to gauge all their premises at least twice. They also had to survey the victuallers' stocks at least three times a week. Supervisors had to tour the whole division at least once a day checking officers and their books, recommending removes, taking independent gauges, and ensuring that all absences were covered. They also had to survey the brewers and maltsters in the outwalks once or twice a week and stock all the victuallers once a month. Officers had to be punctual, or risk dismissal, and were prohibited from going off duty until they were relieved, even if this meant surveying the walk again. To facilitate this process, the surveyors, single men, and lodgers had to live in the division. The rest were required to live nearby. Saturdays were spent with the surveyor at the chamber examining and comparing all the gauges on each guile, working out the charges, and entering them in the ledger while the assistants surveyed the brewers. On Sundays one officer had responsibility for the division.[223] Each of the other branches of the Excise also had its own spatial organisation and temporal routines. Although they shared many of the general requirements set out above, their precise shape depended upon the scale, geography and temporality of the trade they dealt with.

For the brewery, the aim was to ensure that every guile was identified, recorded and charged by type (ale, strong beer or small beer), and quantity of drink. This depended upon rendering the spaces of the brewing process visible and known. Brewers were required by law to 'enter' (or declare) all the buildings and rooms that they used for brewing. Each officer was required to 'make himself acquainted with all the Store-houses belonging to every Brew-house in his walk.'[224] Each place was then marked with white lead and written down. Any changes had to be reported to the Excise Office, shown to an officer, and reported to the surveyor, or the officer would be dismissed. Officers then had a right of entry to all these places—as long as they made the proper request, showed their commission, and were accompanied by a constable at night—and the right to take gauges, break down doors and dig up ground to pursue frauds.[225] In these ways the Excise opened private spaces to state surveillance and regulation. The significance of all this was signaled in the requirement that officers be both civil to those whose premises they entered and well aware of the limits of their powers.

This surveillance of spaces operated at a smaller scale too. Brewers had to 'enter' all their utensils (backs, coppers and tuns) and were not permitted to change, move or alter any without informing the Excise Office (this was also the case for other commodities). These were gauged by two officers, marked for identification and written down. Copies of these details went to the brewer, the chamber, each officer and the Excise Office. These 'Decade' or 'Inch' books had to be dated, regularly checked, and updated when necessary.[226] In addition, for each utensil a 'dipping place' where the liquid in it would be measured had to be defined by the surveyor and marked.[227] This was to be used by all officers and regularly checked and amended by the surveyor.

The aim of all this was to ensure that every gauge could be compared with certainty, so that different gaugers could contribute to the assessment of the charges. Further sets of regulations secured this. Gaugers were all to work to the same degree of precision. They were to use their own regularly inspected instruments, not rules and measures supplied by the brewers. All gaugers were to be trained to the same standard and certified. The surveyor was 'also to satisfy himself that he is a likely man to make a good Officer, that he writes a good hand, and understands the four first Rules of vulgar and decimal Arithmetic, that he is brisk and healthy, that he is of a sober life and conversation, of a good family, of the communion of the Church of England, well affected to the Government, not encumbered with debt, nor a larger family than a wife and two children.'[228] Fidelity was further secured with an oath of office. Finally, each gauge was to be taken independently of other gaugers and of the influence of the brewer. No measurements were to be lent to other officers and no money borrowed from the brewers. With all this in place, gauges could be compared, charges could confidently be made from the highest gauge, and frauds could be detected. Again, the other branches had similar requirements.

Tracking production and charging the full excise duty was also a matter of shaping the timing of surveillance to that of the brewing process and vice versa. It was important to ensure that officers were present at the key times when liquid was moved between vessels and mixing or concealments might occur. For example, officers were assigned to cleansings via a series of 'sealed notes' issued at the chamber.[229] They also had to ensure that they turned up when the brewers were not expecting them.[230] In general, the gap between visits to brewers was not to exceed four hours and, for the other commodities, the timing of each production process and its potential frauds shaped the timing of surveillance in different ways. In turn, the temporality of production was influenced by the Excise Office. Producers had to inform them when production would start each time and when deliveries were being made.[231] Distillers were only permitted to operate at certain times. Finally, a more complete surveillance was possible. Where a brewer was particularly suspected the surveyor was to 'attend a Guile of Drink of the said Brewers, from the Beginning to the End, and use [his] utmost Diligence to discover in what Part, or how the Brewer commits any Fraud.'[232]

All of this was captured in a web of writing or, more accurately, in the specific notations that enabled the concise tabular representation of brewhouse utensils, brewing processes, stocks and officers' movements. For each branch of the Excise the proper mode of bookkeeping was prescribed which allowed the production process to be tracked at every stage. All brewery officers and surveyors had to enter every gauge they took in a minute book (or diary) 'in bold and strong, not little Figures' before they left the brewhouse, and leave a record of it for the brewer in case of disputes.[233] These were also to be posted in the ledger at the end of the course and signed. All of the records had to tally, and they all had to combine to be an unimpeachable record. Officers were to fill them in so that they could not subsequently be altered. They were forbidden to use loose sheets, to erase, to scribble out, or to cut out any part of the book. Any error had to be identified and accounted for, at the risk of dismissal. These records were also scrutinised by the central authorities in order to ascertain both the state of the revenue and its officers. Every Tuesday each brewery surveyor had to send a range of documents to the examiners at the Excise Office: the voucher of charges and a report on the revenue that week; his minute book; his officers' minute books and reports on each officer; the ledger from the chamber; and answers to any queries made on the previous week's submission. Perhaps the Excise's most minute controls over space—which were also controls over time, goods and money—were the injunctions surrounding permits for transporting coffee, tea and chocolate. These had to be issued by the Excise Office for all consignments. They specified where the goods were going from and to, their volume, and how long delivery should take. Precision and the prevention of fraud were to be ensured by regulations concerning their writing that required that 'the last Word expressing the Quantity be writ so close to the beginning of the next that no Syllable may be put between. Let all Spaces between words be filled up with Dashes, so that no Room be left to put in a Word or Syllable.'[234] It is unsurprising that the generic officer's name that appeared on the Excise's printed forms was 'William Careful.'[235]

Together these practices of spacing, timing and writing shaped the spaces of the city, albeit in ways only visible within the movements of officers, the timings of brewings, and in the pages of ledgers. They remapped London according to a set of routinised, rationalised, planned, scrutinised and hierarchical forms of space, time and knowledge that were fundamental to generating excise revenue and, more generally, were the very basis of the bureaucratic forms and administrative powers of the modern state.

CONCLUSIONS

This chapter has attempted to demonstrate the ways in which the production of space was crucial to the modern state and, most importantly,
to highlight the active and problematic construction of modernity.
More particularly, this has meant showing how specific forms of space,
shaped in various ways by the geometries of mathematical reasoning,
underpinned, perhaps even made, the eighteenth-century fiscal–military
state. This has involved understanding how an imagined geography of
the nation-state and its boundaries ordered the numerical procedures of
political arithmetic in ways that enabled the long-term planning of
warfare and the taxation revenues on which it depended. It also involved revealing the contextual nature of such rational knowledges and
their embeddedness within the politics of state formation. Contextualising Charles Davenant in this way allowed the basis for his emphasis on
'good management'—a set of bureaucratised administrative procedures—to be understood in terms of the dual concerns of revenue raising and protecting constitutional freedoms. Davenant's modernity lies
both in his deployment of political arithmetic and in his faith in the
benefits of a rationally ordered, planned and territorially complete bureaucracy, even if setting it out for his readers was a plea for patronage.
Looking at these principles and practices in action within the restructuring of excise taxation in the 1680s highlighted what was at stake in
constructing an administrative framework that could operate effectively
across the state's territory. This needed to be able to produce increasing
amounts of revenue and to safeguard political legitimacy at the same
time. Doing so, I have argued, meant guaranteeing the accuracy and
precision of the system of gauging and charging. This was done within
a network of people, papers, practices and instruments that was able to
effectively operate across space only through the careful production of
other spaces, knowledges, objects and people. The modernity of excise
administration resides in this carefully calibrated and slowly extended
network—the spaces between the barrel and the nation-state—and the
powers it mobilised. It also resides in responses to it. Looking more
closely at what it meant to be an exciseman means seeing how a new
form of subjectivity was formed by the exigencies and geographies of
state administration. These bureaucrats did not simply appear when
called: their formation was an active process. It involved shaping an
identity to the structure of the fiscal–military state, but it also meant retaining a sense of the laughability of the structures of modernity and,

one of the keys to modernism, the need to maintain individuality within those structures. Finally, I have brought this back to London in order
to demonstrate the spaces of the Excise at its most developed, a rationalised and routinised web of paths, points and divisions that covered
the city and, although mostly invisible, marked its modernity as part of
the geography of the modern state. Indeed, the foundations of these
spaces were laid in Davenant's political arithmetic, the reshaping of the
Excise in the 1680s, and the making of excisemen.

In all of this it is the *production* of these spaces, and therefore the
production of the powers of the modern state, that is important. Each
instance—Davenant's construction of arguments and administrative
networks, Polstead's representation of the 'Excise Man's' constructed
identity, the excise commissioners' construction of London's bureaucratised geography—reveals the specificity and contingency of these spaces
and powers. Although the Excise was only one part of an eighteenth-
century state that cannot readily be called 'modern,' an attention to its
geographies helps in understanding the construction of modernity and
aims to reveal the partiality (and perhaps the laughability) of what is so
often treated as a monolithic and irreversible historical transformation.
As a 'network' that stretched across space and time and, in doing so, produced them in new forms, the Excise enabled the mobilisation of unprecedented resources and powers. The anxieties that such mediated action at a distance provoked was not simply a matter of state power. The
hopes and fears associated with the control and deployment of knowledge over space structured other areas of life. The next chapter explores
another example.

CHAPTER SIX

The Universal Register Office

INTRODUCTION: TIME, SPACE AND MODERNITY

The economic and political transformations of the eighteenth century reshaped space and time in London and beyond. They brought with them an increasingly integrated national economy and polity, and bound it into a trading and territorial empire that stretched across the globe. Londoners' lives and futures became more intimately tied to other places, both near and far, and for better and worse. In turn, those places increasingly felt the influence of London. Central to these transformations were new ways of gathering, organising and using information. This was the case when moving people and news, when governing, when fighting wars, and when making money. In this chapter I want to explore those transformations in space, time and information and the hopes and anxieties that they brought with them. This is done primarily through interpreting contending representations of the uses and abuses of information in what Henry and Sir John Fielding called their 'Universal Register Office.' However, before discussing their plans in more detail I want to provide a backdrop to their scheme by setting out in some detail the ways in which the entwined geographies of locality, city, nation, empire and globe were being reshaped along with and through the management and politics of information.

There may have been no eighteenth-century 'transport revolution,' but the turnpike trusts and the stagecoaches wrought between them an integration of the road transport network that bound places together, as well as increases in the speed of travel that brought those

places closer to each other.[1] The turnpiking of roads was 'a vital element in the process that saw the remnants of traditional society cleared
away and replaced by the logic of the market,' as the upkeep of the
highways ceased to be a communal institution and became one based
on the cash payment of tolls at the newly erected gates. During the
'turnpike mania' between 1750 and 1772 over 15,000 miles of road
were covered by some five hundred turnpike trusts. Indeed, 52% of the
total mileage constructed between 1696 and 1836 was authorised in the
twenty years between 1750 and 1770.[2] By midcentury the turnpiking
of the busy routes to London, and of those in the Severn and Wye val-
leys and the West Riding, had produced 'a fairly comprehensive system
of turnpiked main roads as well as important provincial networks.' This
structure was 'considerably elaborated' by 1772, reducing the degree to
which it centred on the capital.[3] This also reduced road transport
charges, increased the speed and volume of passenger transport, and di-
minished its seasonal differentiation. The turnpike network's integration
of the economy increasingly brought local prices into line with national patterns and promoted local production for wider markets.[4] Along
these roads moved goods, people and information. New tastes and fashions from London found their way to provincial towns and the countryside, while orders and commodities, travelers and migrants moved
along them too.[5]

It was the stagecoaches, especially the 'flying coaches' of the 1750s
and 1760s, that meant that the extension and improvement of the road
network was met by an increase in the speed of passenger travel and in
the variety of destinations and routes. Thanks to their improved design
and regular horse changes, 'a new age of speed had dawned,' even if that
speed was only an average of eight miles per hour.[6] Places were brought
closer together. Between 1750 and 1850 the speeds possible between
major towns increased fivefold, in train with an equally dramatic increase in the frequency of services. Places were also better integrated.
Before the 1760s the coaching network had centred on London. Over
eight hundred coach services left there each week for the provincial
towns in 1715.[7] The second half of the century saw the development
of interregional links and a radical improvement in coaching sched-
ules.[8] All the services ran to timetables that became increasingly accurate and coordinated, thereby providing the information necessary to
enable transportation over long distances. With the turnpikes and the
stagecoaches 'the roads now served national rather than predominantly
local purposes.'[9]

Many of these routes also served the Post Office as it carried various forms of information—official and unofficial—to an ever increasing clientele. Initially the mail moved along the six post roads out of London, but thanks to Ralph Allen's development of the cross-posts it increasingly operated through 'a thickening web of routes' that provided a 'remarkable expansion' of the network and the frequency of service.[10] By 1756 there were daily services, except on Sundays, along the roads west to Exeter, Plymouth and Truro; to Bristol; to Swansea via Gloucester; and to Carmarthen and Pembroke via Hereford. The Holyhead post road also had a daily service, with a branch to Shrewsbury and boat services to Ireland and back every day but Sunday. Going north there was a daily service via Warrington to Lancaster, and the Great North Road carried mail every weekday. Carlisle was served by the road that took the daily mails to Edinburgh, and routes ran to Sheffield via Nottingham and to Derby through Northampton. Other daily posts went south and southeast from London to the coast, and east to Norwich and Yarmouth. Finally, a cross-road from Exeter to Chester had been extended in 1755 to serve Manchester and Liverpool. Further extensions and increases in speed and punctuality followed the introduction of the mail coach in 1784. All in all, a national service was provided to distribute information, if at increasing cost.[11]

The Post Office was also 'the centre of imperial communications,' crucial to sending and receiving intelligence and instructions, particularly in times of war.[12] A fortnightly service to La Coruña from Falmouth had started in 1689, to be replaced during the War of the Spanish Succession by a weekly service to Lisbon. The first attempt to run a regular service to the Americas was made by Edmund Dummer in 1702. He was contracted to run monthly sailings from Falmouth which would serve Jamaica, Barbados, Antigua, Montserrat, Nevis and St Kitts on a 'definite schedule.'[13] After heavy losses to privateers the service was discontinued in 1711. Communication was irregular until 1755 when two London merchants, John Sargent and Richard Stratton, were contracted to run two voyages a year to the West Indies, and four other franchises were established to serve Helvoetsluys, Leghorn, Lisbon and New York. The government's need to keep the services running during the Seven Years War made substantial profits for the contractors and imposed severe costs on the Exchequer. They did, however, establish regular lines of official communication across the Atlantic.[14]

The eighteenth-century Post Office was also used to political ends as 'a propaganda and intelligence organ, serving as the government's mouthpiece, eyes and ears.'[15] In the first half of the century, particularly under Walpole, the government organised the production of several newspapers and a huge range of pamphlets, and had tens of thousands of them distributed by post, and then by customs officers and excisemen, to the coffee houses and taverns of provincial towns.[16] The state also used the Post Office to transmit, collect and create intelligence. It carried messages, gathered reports from its officers in the country on local affairs and, through the Deciphering Branch and the Secret Department, detained, opened and copied correspondence for domestic and foreign political purposes.[17] However, the relationship between governing an imperial power and the control of information is not exhausted by propaganda and the cloak-and-dagger world of the secret services. The state was increasingly involved in more routine forms of information collection, collation and use. As the previous chapter has shown, the eighteenth-century English state was, at least when it came to the Excise, coordinating a national administrative system which relied upon precise information being channeled along carefully defined pathways between London and the rest of the country. To effectively govern across nation and empire required detailed and accurate information which had to be sifted, sorted, filed and copied so that it could be made useful to clerks, ministers and Parliament. This information was increasingly made available in statistical form, enabling the computations and comparisons necessary to assess, evaluate and change policy.[18] Government was a matter of access to and control over information, and so was politics. Increasingly, interest groups representing branches of trade or manufacture, regions, towns or colonies sought to influence parliamentary policy decisions—particularly on taxation—by offering specialist information, or by using and contesting government figures. In part this 'politics of information' was about the availability of official data as new lines were drawn between a bureaucratic state and civil society.[19] Yet it was also a matter, particularly after the Excise Crisis of 1733, of appeals made by private interests to the adjudication of state policies by 'the sense of the people.'[20] The processes of evoking, involving and informing this wider public were played out in print and, most influentially, in the pages of metropolitan and provincial newspapers.

The contestation of this politics of information through newsprint was both cause and effect of the expansion of newspaper publishing as part of a much wider 'print culture' whose development reshaped the social production and use of information in the eighteenth century.[21] The press grew considerably after the Licensing Act lapsed in 1695.[22] Although circulation figures are hard to assess, some indication can be given. In 1704 some 44,000 copies of various newspapers were sold in London each week. The top three papers each had circulations of over

9,000. By 1713 there were around 2.4 million stamped newpapers produced annually, and by 1776 Lord North claimed that 12.23 million
newspapers were sold every year. In 1760 London had four dailies and
five or six triweeklies; by 1783 there were nine dailies and ten bi- or triweeklies. Similarly, the number of provincial papers grew from twenty-
five in 1735 to thirty-five in 1760 (although one hundred thirty had
been started since 1700), and to fifty by 1782. The more successful ones
had circulations of around 2,000. Distribution in London was through
subscriptions, street-hawkers, and the numerous coffeehouses. Provincial newspapers were distributed through 'regional and national distribution networks' of news-agents and traveling newsmen.[23] For example,
The Sheffield Advertiser had agents in twenty-three towns in 1761. Many
provincial newspapers were delivered to London coffeehouses. Although provincial newspapers were often partially composed of items
from the capital's press, which, in turn, often took news from them,
many London newspapers depended upon a market outside the metropolis. Before 1720 papers such as *Post Man, Post Boy* and *Flying Post*
were 'specifically oriented towards the provinces' and were produced in
London on Tuesdays, Thursdays and Saturdays to catch the evening
posts.[24] Newspapers which were delivered this way were either franked
free by MPs, and sent to their friends and connections, or franked on a
large scale, for profit, by the six clerks of the roads. The extent of this
was such that in the year from 5 April 1764 over a million newspapers
passed through the General Post Office in London. In later years newspaper distribution benefited from the extensions of the postal system
and the increased speeds of the mail coaches.

The expansion of newspaper publishing and distribution reshaped
access to information. The information itself was also shaped in important ways. Newspapers provided particular versions of politics that integrated different localities and social groups into national and imperial
political affairs in different ways.[25] They moulded people's understanding of the relationships between Britain and the rest of the world.
British newspapers were full of 'wars in Europe, America, Africa, and
the East Indies, and the prizes taken in battle,' charting and assessing the
fortunes of Britain's forces, allies and enemies. They were also read for
their reports of 'the comings and goings of merchant ships, often with
lengthy lists of the products of their laden bottoms; prices, stocks, and
bullion values; and advertisements for luxury goods from international
and colonial markets—tea, coffee, chocolate and tobacco; calicoes and
silks; wines, rum and spirits; fruits and seeds; furs, exotic birds and plants,
and ivory.' War and trade, the very stuff of Britain's empire, were daily

paraded in the pages of its newspapers in ways that 'produced an "imagined community" of producers, distributors, and consumers on both sides of the Atlantic, who shared an avid interest in the fate of the "empire of goods" that linked them together in prosperity or adversity.'[26] Newspapers reshaped space as they reported on nation and empire.

Imperial expansion also transformed global geographies. Britain's empire was extended through warfare, and as trade expanded it was protected by military force. From the capture of Jamaica in 1655 to the securing of the North American colonies in 1763, wars had been fought across four continents and the oceans between them, and the British 'empire of the seas' had increased its territorial extent fivefold.[27] Fighting global wars required new levels of coordination and control of military information which meant that Britain had, through permanent naval stations spread across the empire, 'established the basis of a global infrastructure of navel power' by the late eighteenth century.[28] Similar problems of coordination and control faced the merchants who dealt in and created this new geography. As merchant vessels knitted together the East Indies, Scandinavia and the Baltic, the Mediterranean and the transatlantic trade between West Africa, the Caribbean, North America and northwestern Europe, there was a massive expansion of trading routes and an extension of the distances over which trade was conducted. The volume of Britain's trade tripled in the eighteenth century and its centre of gravity shifted west. Around 1700 over 80% of England's exports and re-exports went to Europe, and less than 20% to America, Africa and India. By the 1770s these imperial markets accounted for around 60% of exports. Imports also saw a similarly dramatic shift; in qualitative terms, this meant that Britain's consumer revolution was fed by sugar, tobacco and rum from the Americas and coffee, calico, silk and tea from the Near and Far East.[29] As James Walvin has shown, these products soon became staples among all classes, and the china cup of hot sweet tea or the pipe of tobacco and glass of rum transformed notions of Britishness through their reshaping of the routines, practices and tastes of both domestic femininity and masculine public sociability.[30] The local, national and global were worked together into a new and hybrid modernity.

These local and global economic transformations ultimately depended upon the exploitation of slave labour in the Americas and, therefore, the trading of two million Africans for goods in the eighteenth-century Atlantic triangle.[31] By the 1740s Britain led the world in carrying human cargoes, and in the 1760s, accounted for the lion's share of the 27,200 slaves shipped each year.[32] Populations were reor-

ganised on a global scale, and the social relations of production and reproduction were transformed locally, regionally and nationally across
the world. Racial slavery wrenched millions from the places and times
that they knew and thrust them into the 'ungenteel modernity' of the
Atlantic crossing, the organised mass labour of the plantation, and the
complicity of racism and Enlightenment science.[33] As Paul Gilroy has
argued, it 'marked out blacks as the first truly modern people.'[34]

The slave trade also marked those European merchants who conducted it as moderns. They operated globally, trading cloth from the
East Indies, American tobacco, Dutch knives, and British glassware, toys
and spirits for slaves, using for currency small shells brought from India,
and driven to hard bargains by the discerning consumers of West
Africa.[35] For these merchants, according to the meticulous research of
David Hancock, 'A single act, such as the exchange of East Indian cloth
for West African slaves, required years of preparation and co-ordination
in the markets of India, England, Holland, France, Africa, and the
Americas.'[36] Many of these commodities were moved through London.
Although much of the Atlantic trade had passed to Liverpool and Bristol, London still handled over 60% of the exports of English produce
and manufactures between 1700 and 1770. It was the 'life-pumping
heart' of Britain's trading empire, which depended for its existence and
expansion on other places, and on binding them ever closer together.
London helped join capital, labour, materials and markets across the
globe, creating a network of connections within which the city prospered and its built environment was transformed as docks, quays and
whaves extended along the banks of the Thames downstream from
London Bridge.[37] Or, at least, some people prospered. The Atlantic
merchants, whose shipping, plantation, trading and military provisioning
concerns spanned continents, depended upon London for their success.
They had to keep their ships moving and full of cargo, including the in-
digo, sugar and people from their own plantations and slave depots. To
do so, Hancock argues, they had to be in London—'the center of the
empire' and 'the center of world commerce in the eighteenth century.'
They had to be in London to satisfy their 'omnivorous appetite for information': to keep up with the news; to know what was coming in and
what was going out; who should be hired and who should not; when to
buy and when to sell. They were also in London to collate, control and
use information. Their global operations worked through 'international
networks of suppliers, clients, correspondents, agents, factors, and employers' and depended upon the organisation of communication across
space and time.[38] So, at the heart of the counting houses, at the heart of

empire, were mechanisms that sought to survey, order and control global commercial information:

> [T]he most imposing and revealing piece of furniture in [John] Sargent's house was an object possessed by nearly every trans-Atlantic merchant in London—the Merchant's Bureau—a piece usually placed in the Clerks' Room. The Bureau figured as a concrete representation of the mastery of detail so integral to commercial success. The typically 7' to 9' tall, 5' wide mahogany 'double desk' rose in three stages above the chaos of the surrounding desks and tables: the lower stage, the bottom half, contained sixteen drawers; two doors opening outward revealed the top half, which contained the middle and upper stages, each fitted with shelves, pigeon-holes, and small drawers for ledgers and papers. Prominent among the compartments were six divisions used for filing:
>
> London Dock Accounts
> Customs House Duties
> Contracts
> Remittances
> Average Documents
> Bills of Lading
>
> A double row of horizontal boxes, lettered 'A' to 'Z,' was reserved for correspondence with clients. Order was demanded throughout. . . . The compartmentalized Merchant's Bureau thus gave substantive meaning to the maxim 'a place for everything and everything in its place.'[39]

The extension of imperial commerce was based upon the careful ordering of information in ways that meant that it could be located, retrieved, used and proved. That eighteenth-century trade gradually 'settled into more or less regular channels' based upon a more orderly international market chain was, in part, due to the efforts of intellectual labour by clerks and merchants that brought them the command over information that made them, in Daniel Defoe's words, "master[s] of the geography of the Universe" who might "kno' a thousand times more in doing it than all those illiterate sailors."[40] Yet these global connections were also forged by the blood, sweat and tears of those sailors who carried the goods and protected the routes. There was here another 'politics of information.'

As Peter Linebaugh, Marcus Rediker and Paul Gilroy have shown, there were other geographies of information that lay outside the mercantile channels, but were still organised by its circuits. The flows of

workers, sailors and slaves that created European imperialism and a capitalist world market also forged new conditions for the transatlantic 'circulation of experience within the huge masses of labour that . . . had
[been] set in motion.' The ships on which they traveled, as well as
bringing international commodification, were 'an extraordinary forcing
house of internationalism.'[41] In this way the expanses of the 'Black Atlantic' were traversed not only by slaves but by black activists 'engaged
in various struggles towards emancipation, autonomy, and citizenship.'[42]
These were men and women who were simultaneously inside and outside Western modernity and combined in various ways with other Atlantic 'countercultures.' Their circuits of information, both practical and
political, shaped resistance to commodification, imperialism and incar-
ceration on all sides of the ocean.[43] Within this geography London was
'a centre for the circulation of worldwide experiences' where '[o]ut-
casts, runaways, mariners, castaways, the disinherited and the dispos-
sessed found . . . a place of refuge [and] of news.' It contained a larger
black population than any city outside Africa, as well as many from Ireland, or those just back from the Americas or the East Indies. London's
workers were as 'Atlantic and international' as its merchants and they
too reshaped the city as they worked, danced and rioted.[44]

Each part of these economic and political transformations—transportation, the Post Office, newspapers, government, warfare and commerce—shows institutions, organisations and individuals increasingly
spanning larger expanses of space and time. It is, however, not simply a
matter of extension. Messages, merchants and migrants have always
traveled long distances. What was different in the eighteenth century
was the volume of connections and the ways in which they were being
made routine, organised and carefully integrated through new ways of
collecting, collating, retrieving and using information. Ideally, for those
seeking control, the world was becoming more like the new ency-
clopaedias that described it. The whole was available to view through
carefully organised knowledges, and each part had a well-defined and
easily located place within that whole.[45] That these local, national and
global connections made economies and societies more prone to the
spectacular disruptions that flowed through the networks only increased
the search for order and control.[46] However, each of these new geographies of communication created differences of access and control.
There were those who lived off the beaten track; those who could not
afford the newspapers and the stagecoaches; those left out of the national and international 'publics' figured in the press; and those who suffered
at the hands of, rebelled against or escaped from the combinations of

capital, force and data that reshaped space across the empire. In each
case the geographies of information were at issue.

These transformations of time and space are also crucial to certain
versions of modernity. In Anthony Giddens's account of *The Consequences of Modernity* modern institutions, particularly the 'nation-state'
and 'systematic capitalist production,' operate across space and time in
ways that mean that the pace, scale and scope of change are dramatically extended, and 'the very tissue of spatial experience alters, conjuring
proximity and distance in ways that have few close parallels in prior
ages.'[47] The same can be said of David Harvey's account of capitalist
modernity as a process of 'time–space compression.'[48] Sustaining these
new geographies, for Giddens, is 'the collection and collation of information' and its 'storage and control,' which has meant that '[m]odern societies have been . . . "information societies" since their inception.'[49] To
take one example that ties this theoretical account to the histories outlined above, Giddens argues that the stagecoach's extension of the transportation network and its organisation through increasingly precise
timetables—'a time–space ordering device which is at the heart of
modern organisations'—makes it 'the first modern rapid-transit form of
transportation.'[50] What is stressed throughout Giddens's account is a
new set of social relations 'stretched' across time and space and based on
novel forms of trust. He argues that institutions operating at a distance
through the collection and control of information require new levels of
confidence both in the institutions and in the people who operate
them. The consequences are both far-reaching and close to home, since
'[t]he modes of life brought into being by modernity have swept us
away from *all* traditional types of social order, in quite unprecedented
fashion. . . . [T]hey have served to establish forms of social interconnec-
tion which span the globe [and] . . . they have come to alter some of
the most intimate and personal features of our day-to-day existence.'[51]

One way of understanding the implications of this is through the
discussion in Chapter 4 of masculinity and the globalisation of commodification, where the Macaronis' consumption practices were shown
to dangerously conjure proximity and distance in a global marketplace.
Another would be the connections between the sweetness of sugar and
the violent and wholesale global transformations of society and nature
needed to establish the commercial and military powers necessary to
bring it to so many Western tables and taste buds.[52] However, in this
chapter I want to explore these implications by examining the meanings and interpretations of one of the 'technologies'—much like the
merchant's bureau—that was used to collect, collate and administer in-

formation in order to transform time and space. There are two parts to this interpretation of eighteenth-century information technology. First, there is the thrill of new information and, particularly, of the new ways of organising and using it. This thrill is part of modern dreams of the power of information control to transform the world, what Rosalind Williams describes as 'a shared, powerful cultural assumption that it is the destiny of the West to promote circulation through technological systems building.'[53] Second, this is coupled with a fear of information out of control or in the wrong hands. This is the other side of Giddens's novel forms of trust. There are concerns over who has information, to what ends it is being put, and what power it gives those who hold it over others. The 'information technology' that I want to examine here is what was called the 'Universal Register Office.' First, I will examine it as a utopian scheme for managing commercial information in the pamphlets of Henry Fielding and his half-brother John. Second, I will address a farcical vision of dangerous information in Joseph Reed's play *The Register Office*.

THE UNIVERSAL REGISTER OFFICE

The World Together in One Place

On 19 February 1750, in premises opposite Cecil Street on the Strand, John Fielding and his associates set up what they called the 'Universal Register Office.'[54] It was located on one of London's main shopping streets, just down the road from the New Exchange where commerce and business intelligence met (see Figure 1). Its principles were set out in a pamphlet written primarily by Henry Fielding:

> The Design of which Office is to bring the World, as it were, together into one Place. Here the Buyer and the Seller, the Tutor and the Pupil, the Master, the Scholar and Usher, the Rector and Curate, the Man of Taste and ingenious Artificer, the Virtuoso with Curiosities, the Traveller and a Companion, the Tradesman and the Partner, the Master and Apprentice, or Book-keeper, the Master and the Servant, &c are sure to meet: Here ingenious Persons of all Kinds will meet with those who are ready to employ them, and the Curious will be supplied with every thing which it is in the Power of Art to produce.[55]

Through a series of registers—of property to buy and rent; of investments and investors; of 'Places and Employments . . . Ecclesiatical, Civil,

Military'; apprentices and apprenticeships; of teachers in sciences and arts; of trading partners; of servants of all kinds from butlers to laundry-maids; of goods, first- and secondhand; and of transport services by sea and land—'buyers' and 'sellers' would be put in touch with one anoth-er.[56] Each was to pay between three pence and a shilling to put an item onto the appropriate register or to consult it. The Universal Register Office was an impressive exercise in the collection, collation and re-trieval of information in the service of commerce and profit. It met with initial success, so much so that associated offices were opened in Bishopsgate—on the edge of the City of London—and in Dublin.[57]

In its essentials this was not a novel idea. John Fielding later claimed, perhaps for advertising purposes, that the undertaking was 'en-tirely new to this and every other Kingdom,' but Henry Fielding had cited the influence of an essay of Montaigne's that proposed a similar plan.[58] There were also several seventeenth-century forerunners in both England and France.[59] For example, in 1650 Henry Robinson set out plans for an 'Office of Addresses and Encounters' which may never have been put into practice but which also proposed a scheme that would put people in touch via a central bureau. Again there were to be regis-ters of lands, goods, investments, positions and services. In many ways it offered a parallel vision of economic transformation through the con-trol of information. However, the underlying economic principles of the two schemes were significantly different. Robinson promised that:

> The poore, together with all others, will likewise reape this benefit, by this Office, in that it will much prevent retailing, which is but a higling of Commodities, to a greater quantity and value; whereas, if the Buyer buyes for his use, and to serve his petty Customers onely, and the Seller sels to put himself into money: both the buyer pays less than he should get the same Commodity for, from a Retailer; and the seller also, sels for more than a Retailer would likely give him.[60]

This ordering of the scheme in terms of use values—which if not anticommercial was certainly antiretailing—also explains Robinson's suggestion that the poor could use his office as a weapon to drive up wages and, with full information, could prevent 'rich men . . . more and more undervaluing poore men's paines, and labours.'[61] This, I want to argue, is very different from the 'ideology of circulation' within which the plans for the Universal Register Office unfolded.[62] Here, moral and economic value and progress were understood as created through the extension and promotion of commercial exchange. As Rosalind

Williams puts it, 'Social progress was assumed to depend on [the] construction of connective systems: communication and transportation
grids, layer upon layer of roadways for the circulation of people, goods,
and ideas.'[63] In the founders' view, the more transactions there were, the
better things would get. The vision that guided the Fieldings' project
was of a particular sort of perfect society:

> If any Society ever hath been, or ever can be so regulated, that no Talent
> in any of its Members, which is capable of contributing to the general
> Good, should lie idle and unemployed, nor any of the Wants of its Mem-
> bers which are capable of Relief, should remain unrelieved, that Society
> might be said to have attained its utmost Perfection.[64]

All needs and desires were to be met and all capabilities were to be
employed. Since 'Man is said to be by Nature a social Animal,' 'his' society would be perfect only when it could seamlessly match the supply
and demand that were created as collectivities allowed the 'Opportunity
of exerting all the human Faculties'—a releasing of forces impossible to
the solitary individual—and 'provide[d] for all the wants of which our
Nature is susceptible'—a natural division of labour that meant that each
could 'mutually enjoy the Benefit of the Vast Variety of Talents with
which they have been severally endowed.'[65] Here, productive forces and
divisions of labour were rendered natural through an understanding of
'the Members of the Body Corporate, like those of the Natural Body,
having their several Uses and Qualifications, all jointly contributing to
the Good of the Whole.'[66] This presentation of head and hands working in harmony was a naturalised sociology that recognised social differences while denying that they might be the sources of conflict or
change. It was combined with a harmonious vision of commerce as the
threads or arteries that bound the parts together. This moralised view
allowed Fielding to sidestep the concerns over luxury that attended discussions of commercial societies.[67] It also provided a particular version
of history that reduced it to the overcoming of problems of time and
space, of integration and communication. This view was used to explain
urbanisation and the binding together of nation-states through networks of transportation and commerce:

> Now Society itself alone creates all these Wants, and at the same Time
> alone gives us the Methods of supplying them by the Invention of what
> is called trade or Traffick. And yet as Societies of Men increased into
> great and populous Cities and extended Countries, the Politician found

something still wanting; and this was a Method of communicating the various Wants and Talents of the Members to each other; by which means they might be mutually supplied. Hence the Invention of Fairs, Markets, Exchanges, and all other Publick Meetings for carrying on Traffick and Commerce between Men, in which the common and ordinary Wants of the Society are from Time to Time provided for.[68]

In the promotion of Dublin's Register Office this view could, appropriately enough, be extended to explain the global relationships of commercial empires:

In Order to impel mankind to Society, and to promote the several Systems of Community upon Earth, Providence hath appointed to every one a Number of Wants, which he of himself is not able to supply, and at the same Time, hath furnished him with a Number of Talents, which, being superfluous to himself, are yet necessary for supplying the suitable Wants of others.

This divine Appointment may with Justice be carried further, and applied to particular Nations, as well as particular Men. Each Climate differs from others in its Genius, Capacity, Cultures, Products, and Manufactures; and no one Country can be amply supplied, but by the Contribution of All.[69]

Nature, and the God-given geography of supply and demand, posed the problem. Nature also provided the solution since 'The Beasts that bear our Burdens, the Woods that supply our Ship-wrights, the Rivers, the Seas, the Winds, the Tides, seem as it were impatient to unite into one Body, the several distant Members of Mankind.'[70] In this idealised vision it was natural forces rather than commercial ones that spanned the globe. The world was united, not divided, by commerce.

These idealised sociologies and historical geographies of capitalist modernity reified exchange to a position where its progressive extension could explain everything. They also offered a vision of further progress through ever-increasing exchange. However, the achievement of this vision was seen as blocked by the barriers presented by the nonuniversality of these forms of communication. That they remained inadequate, and society remained imperfect, was a problem of geography:

All these Methods, however, are so far defective, as they fail to be universal; for to the Perfections of a Society it is required, that none of the various Talents of the Members shall remain unknown and unemployed, nor any of their Wants unsupplied. This, as it seems, can only be attained, by providing some Place of universal Resort, where all the Members of the Society may communicate all their mutual Wants and Talents to each other. So that no Person may want what another is capable of supplying him with, provided he is willing and able to pay the Price.

In large and populous Cities, and wide extended Communities, it is most probable that every human Talent is dispersed somewhere or other among the Members; and consequently every Person who stands in Need of that Talent, might supply his Want, if he knew where to find it; but to know this is the Difficulty, and this Difficulty still encreases with the Largeness of the Society.[71]

Or, to put it more dramatically:

In this Place there is an abundance of what is wanting in that, and there again is a Superflux of what here is deficient. But there is no sufficient Knowledge of this, no Medium whereby the grateful Exchange might be effected; the Superfluities therefore perish, and the indigences remain.[72]

The only solution was a universal solution, a Universal Register Office that would, to repeat, 'bring the World . . . together into one Place.' It would connect all 'Talents' and 'Wants,' bring light to 'the buyer and the seller [who] are groping after each other in the dark,' and permit the universal extension of commerce, and the progress, happiness and per-fection which it was thought that would bring.[73]

It must, of course, be allowed that the hyperbole demanded of eighteenth-century advertising means that these claims are not to be taken simply at face value. The Universal Register Office would not change the world. I have, however, tried to show that there was a way of understanding the connections between commerce and society, and, more broadly, between time, space and information, that animated this project and others like it. This version of the 'ideology of circulation' should be taken seriously as an interpretation of, and intervention in, the temporal and spatial transformations of eighteenth-century Lon-don. As with many other 'spaces' detailed in this book, the overblown utopianism of this project can be used to reveal the characteristics of its modernity.

First, the Universal Register Office relied upon the idea that lan-guage could be made transparent. Wants, needs, talents, availabilities and prices could be fully communicated. Exactly what was wanted and ex-actly what was available could find a perfect match and would remain available for matching for much longer where information in a register replaced the face-to-face exchange of the marketplace. To speed up transactions, but also as the very essence of the scheme, the owners asked customers to 'bring a particular Description in Writing of the Person or Thing wanted with them to the Office [to] . . . prevent unnecessary Questions, and make the supplying their Wants easy to themselves and to the Proprietors.'[74] Customers were also encouraged to attend personally the first time they used the Register Office, rather than sending letters or servants, so that they could find out what information was required and how to provide it. Having gained that knowledge, they could then use letters and servants if they wished. The key was in establishing the form of information that would allow the scheme to work. On the one hand, it had to communicate the particularities of what was sought or offered, and John Fielding stressed that 'No description can be too particular.'[75] On the other hand, it had to be fitted to the requirements of the registers so that it could be collated and retrieved alongside other pieces of information that were similarly structured but different in content. It was this shaping of information to fit these dual requirements that allowed perfect communication.

Second, it was based upon a notion of the morality of commerce. As I have already argued, the scheme depended upon an understanding of commerce as morally valuable and progressive. Trade was seen as a good thing in itself, as the 'desirable intercourse and community, of country with country, and man with man.'[76] It was a social glue that, through its extension in the work of the Register Office, supported the 'Dependency, which knits Society together.'[77] The Universal Register Office was also organised to guarantee moral commerce in other ways. Advertisements published by John Fielding and Saunders Welch, who had also invested in the scheme, stressed that it could save innocent newcomers from the country from falling victim to metropolitan sharp practice and deception, and that by carefully matching masters and apprentices it could prevent dissatisfaction and crime.[78] An attention to morality also worked to extend trust in what was potentially an anonymous and dangerous interaction. Each Register Office ensured the public that the proprietors' 'characters for integrity, expedition, secrecy and punctuality, are as universally acknowledged as known,' and that business would 'be executed with the utmost Care, Regularity, and Fidelity, and as much secrecy as shall be desired by the Parties themselves.'[79] The proprietors set themselves off against the counterfeit offices run by disreputable, discharged clerks, and against jobbers only interested in serving themselves.[80] They also reassured their middle-class clients that on visiting the Register Office 'they will find proper rooms for their Accommodations and proper Persons to attend to them.'[81]

This attention to the nuances of class and gender that structured respectability and gentility and shaped the proper relationships of a moralised commerce was also present in the Register Office in other ways. First, there were some transactions that were not included in the Universal Register Office. Henry Robinson's plan in 1650 had included a register of 'Such as desire to dispose of themselves, or friends in Marriage' which showed 'what encounters there are to be had, both of Persons and Portions.'[82] It had also included registers of charities and lost property, and a detection service. The Universal Register Office's exclusion of marriage and charity from its range of services held these transactions outside the realm of commodified exchange. Some forms of exchange, particularly those that linked sex and money, were ruled out of this world of commerce to ensure the moral tone guaranteed by its increasingly strict and idealised distinctions between the tradesman's masculinity and the consumer's femininity. Just as women in business posed problematic questions because their acts of selling transgressed boundaries between the public and the private, so marriages could not be contracted on the open market.[83] Other services, like detection, were the province of other similar schemes (see below). Second, in the hiring of servants the rules of the market that governed the transaction were, in part, moral rules. Employers were informed 'that none will be registered in this Office who give the least suspicious Account of themselves, and who have lived in any disreputable Places,' and that any servant they dismissed would not be registered if the proprietors were informed of their names.[84] For servants, the register was to act as a 'public eye' monitoring and regulating their behaviour.[85] To this end John Fielding published instructions 'To The Faithful, Honest and Industrious' that could be hung in the servants' hall and that stressed the message that maintaining a good character—the account of themselves on which servants would be judged—meant paying careful attention to hierarchy, property, morality and time discipline.[86] Finally, although the Universal Register Office was to be a centre of consumption, the whole tone of its discussion denied the role of pleasure in consuming in favour of stressing the necessity and practicality of exchange. Henry Fielding argued that providing for 'Wants,' even those beyond the level of subsistence, 'is as essential to the Happiness of him who hath them, as it is to a Savage to supply any of those few Necessities with which a State of Nature, as some call it, abounds.'[87] The Universal Register Office aimed at happiness, but it was no palace of luxuries, no Vauxhall Gardens. Commerce was transformed into a moral arena structured by class and gender.

Finally, the Universal Register Office promised the perfectibility of society along the lines defined by its 'ideology of circulation.' Through the collection, collation and retrieval of information, time would be saved as buyers and sellers 'are at once brought together,' and 'Gentlemen and Ladies may in a Minute's Time survey all the Houses and Lodgings which are to be let in several Streets in *London* and *Westminster*, and in a whole Parish or Town in the Country.'[88] In turn, information on transportation would mean that 'all Persons will, as it were, be brought nearer together, for traffick and Communication of every sort, and will acquire greater Power, Wealth, and Satisfaction by being thus united, in a Manner, into one Family.'[89] Doing so would effect the economic integration of 'one great and continued Market of the Nation,' and the Universal Register Office would do the social and political work involved in 'that estimable Scheme of uniting the whole Kingdom into one Body.'[90] Indeed, the image of the body was used to represent this vision of perfection:

> [P]erhaps, this Scheme may carry the Allusion between the Body-natural and the Body-politic, much further than Truth would hitherto admit. Where this *Universal Office* or *Great Mart* in Society, may be answerable to the *Heart,* in the System of the Human Body; which, receiving the Blood from every Part, again dispenses it to all, in such Portions, and of such Qualities as assimilate to the Nature, and supply the demands of each, and by thus suitably corresponding to the Wants of every Member, continues Life, Health and Vigor to the whole Frame.[91]

Within this vision the circulation of information became the key to the future. The Universal Register Office offered the idea that control over information—gathering it from further and further afield, and collating and ordering it in ways that meant that it could be easily located, retrieved and used in the future—would transform society. This vision contained a certain geography. It offered a natural and national market open to the 'Wants' and 'Talents' of all prepared to shape their desires or abilities to the exigencies of the fragments of information on which the Universal Register Office fed. The geography was one of a homogenous space of perfect communication open to all who spoke its language. This space was then criss-crossed with innumerable lines from its centre on the Strand—or Bishopsgate, or Dublin's College Green—to an infinite number of points, as buyers and sellers far distant from each other were connected through its written registers. This was an imagined geography that took part in the process whereby 'in the eighteenth century extended lines replaced the enclosed garden as the dominant image of utopia.'[92] The Universal Register Office's control of information promised a thrilling and dramatic transformation of time and space for all concerned in its exchanges. Yet there was also a politics of information here too. The registers were written in and read from only at a price. While in large part the only differences that mattered in the Universal Register Office were differences of 'Wants' and 'Talents,' I have also shown that there was a careful attention to the codes of class and gender which, in seeking the trust of its customers, shaped the information the Register Office depended upon to certain ends and made it run in particular channels. The Register Office was certainly not there to contract advantageous marriages, to allow the lowering of commodity prices for the poor, or to raise the wages offered for their 'paines, and labours.'[93]

These visions of the potential for the organisation of information to transform control over space and time, and to create powerful resources for reforming and improving the 'Body-politic,' were also evident in schemes that promised increased state power over civil society. Henry Robinson had suggested that his proposed office offered, as '*Arcanum Imperii*,' the opportunity for 'publique magistrates' to 'make thereof such an instrument or engine, both for the securing of themselves, and the happy estating of a nation in peace, plenty, and contention to perpetuity.'[94] More significantly, the Fieldings, acting as Westminster magistrates in the 1750s, made a series of innovations that used the new possibilities that eighteenth-century developments in communications had opened up for the collection, collation and distribution of information in attempts to prevent crime and detect criminals on first a metropolitan and then a national scale.[95] I want to give a brief account of these innovations here in order to show how closely they depended upon the same principles and techniques as those that governed the Universal Register Office.

The Vigorous Circulation of the Civil Power

Henry Fielding transformed the policing of London in the 1750s. From his office in Covent Garden he organised a new system of crime prevention and detection. Central to this was the establishment of his Bow Street office as a place from which the magistrates and a group of constables 'collected together, known to each other, and bound by the Connections of good Fellowship, Friendship, and the Bonds of Society' could operate.[96] Most importantly, it meant making it 'a central bureau of information' that would work 'by bringing all Informations of Fraud and Felony into one Point, keeping a Register of Offenders, making quick pursuits, opening a general Correspondence with all the active Magistrates in the Country, and defraying little Expences of Enquiries, Messengers, and of Pursuits in the first Instance.' In this way, his half-brother argued, 'Escapes are rendered difficult and Discoveries easy.'[97]

Fielding's scheme relied upon opening 'an anonymous correspondence with the Public' to receive information from sources other than criminal informers seeking clemency.[98] He assured the public that the office would be staffed so that 'There is always one or more orderly Men on Duty to enquire into the Truth of Informations,' and that it would provide 'A Register-Clerk to keep an exact Register of all Robberies committed; Descriptions of all Goods lost; the Names and Descriptions of all Persons brought before the said Magistrate who stand accused either of Fraud or Felony, or suspected of either; of the Houses that harbour them and receive their stolen Goods.' The public had to respond with 'exact Descriptions of Persons and Things.'[99] It was only if the magistrates were provided with accurate details of the location and timing of crimes, as well as full descriptions of criminals and stolen goods, that this information could 'be centrally stored, sorted, and cross-referenced for use on real London streets, and also to yield convincing accounts at the Old Bailey.'[100] Just as in the Universal Register Office, the information had to be shaped to fit the purpose. Here the wider purpose was to use carefully compiled and detailed registers to counter the criminals' control over time and space in a city with many dark places and unknown corners.[101] It was a city where they could disappear. It was also a place where they could easily disguise themselves to take advantage of the multitude of transactions between strangers that took place every day. It was a city where a rogue, in order to divert a delivery or snaffle a portmanteau, simply 'plants himself at some convenient Passage, puts his Hat into his Pocket, and sticks a Pen in his Wig to represent a Book-Keeper.' They could also be found playing on the trust necessary in exchanges with strangers by pretending to be merchants, servants and waiters, or sea captains trading to the American plantations. Fielding's Bow Street registers sought to detail their identities and actions, find their hidden places, and still their shape-shifting.[102]

It also extended the power of the magistrates in time and space. Sir John Fielding reported to a House of Commons committee in 1770 that this scheme had allowed offenders to be 'detected several years after the offences are committed.' It took the brief moments of the ancient 'hue and cry,' when offenders might be caught immediately after the act by the watch or the neighborhood's inhabitants, and, through the powers of storage and retrieval that the written registers offered, extended these moments to days, weeks, months or even years. In space it transcended the patchwork of parochial watches that divided London up into a multiplicity of separate territories whose 'frontiers' could be crossed by criminals much more easily than by the parish watchmen who pursued them.[103] It also extended the magistrates' power beyond the capital, for Henry Fielding got 'a Correspondence settled with many of the active Magistrates in the Country, at all Distances, who constantly give Notice . . . when they have committed any desperate Rogue, or Suspicious Man . . . by which Means they are often furnished with Materials to bring such Offenders to Justice.'[104] The adoption of a central office and written registers promised a transformation in authority through the collection and control of information.

This scheme was also a matter of disseminating information in ways that meant that 'print culture' was used to serve the ends of policing. The Fieldings made extensive use of newspaper advertising to pursue prevention and detection. Henry published calls to give information at Bow Street in *The Covent Garden Journal,* which had initially been established to promote the Universal Register Office.[105] He also published details of stolen goods in *The Public Advertiser,* which, as his biographers note, was relaunched on 1 December 1752 'in part to aid Fielding in his war against crime and [also] to provide a continuing vehicle for the Universal Register Office.'[106] Newspaper advertisements were important ways of getting information about crimes circulated rapidly to a relatively large number of people. Later, John Fielding and others also published books and pamphlets that sought to reduce crime. These were accounts of the laws in force in the metropolis and of the sorts of offences to which Londoners were vulnerable. The aim was to counter the effectivity of criminal scams by providing detailed accounts of how they were carried out. Explaining The Kidd, The Drag Lay, The Knuckle, The Jump, The Sneak, The Drop, The Thrust, and The Hoist, or Touching the Rattler, Starring the Glaze, and Flying the Basket—the very terms suggesting an enclosed world with its own private language—would, through the wide circulation of this information, mean that the forewarned were forearmed. Publishing would prevent the passing off of brass as gold or tinsel as silver.[107]

John Fielding, a Westminster magistrate from 1754, extended his half-brother's innovations in many ways. He sought 'the Certainty . . . of speedy Detection' by making the operation of the Bow Street office 'incessant.'[108] He also proposed a plan for a network of magistrates distributed across London who would all 'act upon One uniform Plan,' each keeping registers and transmitting copies of them to the 'Center Office' in Covent Garden to be collated into 'One general Register.'[109] More importantly, he made national what Henry had operated on a metropolitan scale. He extended the use of newspaper advertisements to the provincial press, drawing on his experience of advertising the Universal Register Office outside London, and implemented a 'General Preventative Plan' for the whole country.[110]

Sir John referred to his plan as 'my favourite preventative Machine.'[111] Instituted between 1772 and 1773, it was 'designed to collect, collate and circulate criminal information on a national scale for the first time.'[112] Fielding encouraged magistrates in the counties and boroughs to send him detailed descriptions of fugitives from justice who had escaped from their jurisdictions. In the anticipation that they might be hiding out in London or in other areas of the country where they could go unsuspected and undetected, he collated this information, along with material from the Bow Street registers on crimes committed in the capital, and sent it all back out to the magistrates. It was to be used by them and their constables in the work of detection and prosecution. It was also to be 'stuck up in some conspicuous Part of the Town,' displayed on the church door of every village and in all the principal inns. Again, the descriptions in which Fielding dealt needed to be 'very exact' to be useful for detection on a national scale.[113] Some indication is given in his attempt to compile a national list of offenders from information sent by the gaols of 'the Name of every Prisoner, his Offence, his Age, Place of Nativity, Heighth, Trade, and a short Description of his Person.' To this he added that 'every Addition to their Description must be of singular Use in the Detection of old Offenders.'[114] With careful administration and detailed information, this 'Communication and Intercourse between the Civil Power in the Country and the Metropolis' would, he argued, give the authorities the advantage, since it 'must infallibly detect them, because it cuts off every Prospect of escape.'[115]

Until John succeeded Henry at Bow Street he had been living in the Strand and attending the Universal Register Office every day from nine in the morning until seven at night. His duties as a magistrate meant that he could only be there on Thursdays between midday and two.[116] Yet the Universal Register Office and the Fieldings' work as magistrates were clearly not so far apart. If the Register Office was based on an 'ideology of circulation,' then John Fielding also celebrated 'the vigorous Circulation of the Civil Power' that lay at the heart of the General Preventative Plan.[117] Both were part of 'the densely stored, cross-referenced informational networks that characterize written accounting in the modern metropolis.'[118] They both sought to extend power and influence through the ordering and distribution of information. Both centralised the control of knowledge to allow it to flow further and further from the centre and to enhance action at a distance. They both sought geographies of total coverage. The Register Office had to be universal to succeed, and the General Preventative Plan, at least as an ideal, prompted John Fielding to ask 'What Stratagem can evade this Pursuit, and what Force resist its Power!'[119] In short, they both promised dramatic, thrilling and utopian transformations of time, space and social life—whether primarily concerned with economy or polity—through the collection, collation and distribution of information. This control of knowledge was presented as the promise of modernity in both the Universal Register Office and the General Preventative Plan. It was presented in quite a different way—as farce—in Joseph Reed's play *The Register Office*.[120]

THE REGISTER OFFICE: TRICKS, VILLAINY AND CHICANERY

Joseph Reed was a ropemaker from Stockton whose business proved profitable enough to allow him to indulge his literary aspirations. By 1757 he was a published author and had moved his family and business to London on the back of this success. His first London show was a burlesque tragedy called *Madrigal and Trulletta* produced at Covent Garden by Theophilus Cibber. It was judged to be humorous but overlong. *The Register Office* somewhat revived his reputation. This continued to go up and down. His next venture, a tragedy on the life of Dido 'in the manner of Shakespeare,' was disliked by both David Garrick and Samuel Johnson.[121] On its opening at Drury Lane, Garrick, in a letter to his brother, suggested that it was 'time to leave ye Stage, if such a performance can Stand upon Its legs.'[122] And, after having had the play read to him by Reed, Johnson caustically remarked, 'I never did the man an injury, yet he would read his tragedy to me.'[123] Although Reed claimed that these distinguished critics were in the distinct minority, the reviewers and audiences tended to agree with them rather than with the 'halter-maker,' and *Dido* was performed only three times. This failure was followed by a successful version of Henry Fielding's *Tom Jones* and an adaptation of *Gil Blas,* both of which were performed at Covent Garden. The publication of his various plays, pamphlets, and verses may have given him 'an unwarrantable high opinion of his own literary achievements,' but his adoption of the Register Office as the location for a farce allows a reinterpretation of that institution and of the meanings of the control of information.[124]

Reed's 'very amusing,' 'boisterous and indelicate farce' was completed in 1761; a censored version was first performed at the Theatre Royal in Drury Lane on 23 April; and the full text of the play was published somewhat later.[125] It was frequently performed in the 1760s. Some of the scenes were subsequently rewritten in an attempt to get round the censors, but when it was republished in 1771 again some sections were banned from the stage. In the context of the 1760s its themes were 'topical and apt.'[126] The early success of the Universal Register Office had spawned a host of imitators. The older 'intelligence offices'—which had acted as labour exchanges—quickly changed their names to "register offices" and a rash of new businesses also appeared.[127] The General Register Office opened in Southwark, the New General Register Office in Lincoln's Inn Fields, and the Public Register Office in King Street, Soho. John Fielding complained that these rivals had pirated the plan for the Universal Register Office, warned the public that they could not be trusted, and engaged in a furious 'Paper War' with Philip D'Halluin, the Belgian proprietor of the Public Register Office. Without a protected monopoly, and angered that these 'rival concerns had made the term "Register Office" both commonplace and disreputable,' John Fielding left the business in the same year that Reed's play was first performed.[128]

In part, Reed was simply opportunistic. The Register Office offered a resonant location for a play whose comedy would be derived from the fact that 'this laudable Institution hath been strangely preverted [*sic*], thro' the Villainy and Avarice of some of its managers.'[129] Indeed, in its Prologue Reed argued that farces had no duty to instruct, only to entertain. The play cannot be interpreted as an explicit attack on the Universal Register Office, nor as a thoughtful—let alone political—meditation on the control of information.[130] It was a farce. As such, my interpretation will concern itself with the tensions that this comedy explored and exploited. What was funny about the Register Office? Why did its manipulation of information make for good comedy? How did it depict a world where control over information promised social transformation?

The play opens with a rich widower, Harwood, who has come to

London to find and marry his housemaid Maria. He tells his friend Frankly that she had run away after he had tried to seduce her, and that he had realised that he was wrong to continue to avoid marrying her only because she had no money. To find Maria, but largely for amusement, Harwood and Frankly are hidden by an old schoolfriend, Williams, in the Register Office where he works. They are positioned so that they can see everything that takes place in the office, but they themselves cannot be seen. This puts them in the ideal location to collect and use information. The other person dealing in information is the proprietor, Gulwell. He is only concerned to manipulate what he finds out for his own ends. As Williams says, 'A *Register-Office,* under the Direction of so conscientious a Person as Mr *Gulwell,* instead of a public Good becomes a public Evil.'[131] In the passing in and out of the office of a host of stock eighteenth-century comedy characters we are shown how the Register Office is put to work in the service of avarice and immorality.

Gulwell lies, cheats and swindles those who want to use the office to find places and positions. He advertises an 'imaginary Place' to take a shilling from each of the applicants, and thus seeks to 'swell his Bags, by the Folly or Credulity of Mankind' while thanking 'the Memory of our *witty* founder' for saving him from a life of 'Quill-driving' poverty.[132] Gulwell is paid to fabricate an advertisement for a French 'Hair and Corn-Cutter' who has pretensions to being 'von of de Gens de Qualité' and is seeking a rich wife and an easy job.[133] He takes money for a nonexistent position as housekeeper from Margery Moorpout, 'a Specimen of *Yorkshire* Simplicity' recently arrived from the country. He also bilks a fervently nationalistic but poverty-stricken Scot who claims a 'Family . . . as auncient as ony i' a' *Scotland,*' but who has been reduced to seeking 'ony Station, where Learning is necessary.' Gulwell also aims to profit from Captain Le Brush, 'A spruce Coxcomb of the military Cast!,' and his attempts to purchase a commission; from the poor, illiterate, nonsense-talking Irishman whom he intends to sell into indentured labour in America while telling him he is going 'a little round the Land's-End . . . [to] a very considerable Farm in the West'; and, finally, from Maria, who he calculates will 'make a pretty Penny.'[134]

Those tricked by Gulwell are not tragic victims. Le Brush, for example, wants to get rid of his rich, old wife so that he can marry her young niece. With the exception of Maria, all the victims are set up to be laughed at by the audience either for their nonmetropolitan credulity (Margery and the Irishman) or for their pretensions to 'Iddication' and high birth (the Frenchman, the Scotsman and Le Brush).[135] Gul-

well pricks these pretensions. His only bit of 'plain dealing' concerns
Mrs Slatternella Doggerel, a 'Dramatic Poetess' and author of 'no less
than nine Tragedies, eight Comedies, seven Tragi-comedies, six Farces,
five Operas, four Masques, three Oratorios, two mock Tragedies,
and one Tragi-comi-operatico-magico-farcico-pastoral, dramatic Ro-
mance.' Of these, only 'The Tragedy of Betty Canning' had been performed, and that was by a puppet theatre.[136] Gulwell advises her to
burn her plays and never write again. In return she threatens to pen a
farce called 'The Register Office' to expose his tricks.[137] Yet even with
unsympathetic victims the nature of Gulwell's cheats are clear. The information he deals with is lies or puffery, and is not to be trusted. He is
even prepared to dress blackmail up in respectable language and call it
payment for 'Advice and Secrecy.'[138]

In addition, the connections between 'buyers' and 'sellers,' or between employers and employees, that Gulwell makes through the information gathered and distributed by his Register Office are dangerous
and disreputable ones. All those who want to use his 'registers' do so for
vicious ends. Mrs Snarewell, whose scenes were banned by the censors
in 1761 and 1771, referred to by Gulwell as his 'Sister in Wickedness,' is
a hypocritical hypochondriac, a gin-swilling procuress, and a Methodist
convert who uses the Register Office to find 'fresh faces.'[139] She ensures
that 'among its other Conveniences, the good old Trade of *Pimping* is
carried on with great Success and Decency.'[140] Lady Wrinkle, another
dissolute hypocrite whose scenes were banned by the 1761 censors, is
looking for a handsome, well-built, well-bred manservant to replace
Richard whom she had sacked for the impudence of 'seducing' her. She
needs, Gulwell deduces, someone to fill Dick's place in her 'Family Affairs.'[141] Finally, Lord Brilliant is also seeking a new housekeeper to seduce while he sets up his previous one as a mistress. Gulwell offers him
Maria. In each case, the Register Office and the information provided
by Gulwell is to be used to exploit others. The power that the collection and use of information gives is put to immoral ends.

In short, I want to argue that in rendering the Register Office
problematic, Reed's play reverses the characteristics of the Fieldings'
scheme. First, the play demonstrates that there can be no perfect communication. Instead of being transparent, language becomes opaque.
Much is made of illiteracy and linguistic inability, and much of the
comedy is derived from it. The characters speak in dialects, heavy ac-
cents and slang, devices that Reed explicitly avoided in his *Tom Jones* in
case 'the pronunciation of an uncouth and difficult dialect, should produce an Inattention to the more material business of the drama.'[142] In

The Register Office it is the material business. The different ways of speaking emphasise the differences between the characters. Margery Moorpout claims that 'I knaw nought o Speldering—I'se nea Schollard.' The Frenchman believes that his 'Connaissance in de Langue *Angloise* be not de most *inconsiderable,*' although when it comes to discussing money he cannot speak a word.[143] The Scotsman, as well as speaking dog Latin, pronounces that:

> Ye may ken by my Elocution, A'm a Man o' nae sma' Lair—I was sae weel-leer'd that ilka auld Wife in *Aberdeen* wald turn up the Whites o'her Een, like a Mass *John* at Kirk, an cry, 'Ay! God guide us! What a pauky Chiel is Donald! He's sae ald-gabbit tha a speaks, like a Print Buke.'[144]

This affirmation of the clarity of print only goes to confirm the gap between the printed word and the Scot's own language. Elsewhere, it is this gap that is celebrated by Captain Le Brush for whom language's opacity is the medium of trickery. He claims that 'Logic and Poetry [are] the only two Studies fit for a Gentleman; as the first will teach you to cheat the Devil, and the last to charm—the Ladies.'[145] Instead of a homogenous space of free exchange, Reed's play presents a differentiated patchwork of mutual incomprehension and double-dealing.

Second, in the play's world commerce becomes an immoral arena rather than a moral one. The play presents the commodification of things that should not, according to the Fieldings, be bought and sold. As Gulwell says, 'when we *make* Characters, we must be paid, for them —We have Characters, as Jockies have Pedigrees, from five Shillings to five Guineas.' Writers must sell their consciences to write partisan pamphlets in a 'political Squabble.' The Irishman is sold to the plantations; the women in Mrs Snarewell's brothel are termed 'Commodities'; and virginities are offered for sale at high prices.[146] In general, monetary relations between people are put to immoral ends: selling people, selling sex, gaining financial advantage by means of fraud, religion, violence, deceit, or marriage. This is a depiction of immorality that was avoided by Reed in other contexts.[147] In his defence Gulwell argues that everyone is doing it, and that success is based upon money not merit. For him, 'there is roguery in all the employments under the sun. Every Day's Experience will convince you, that there is no getting through the World, without a necessary Portion of Trick and Chicanery.'[148] He deals with greedy cheats and fraudsters and tries to swindle them before they swindle him. In this context morality gets distorted, and Mrs Snarewell can claim that she has too much 'Sense of Religion' and 'Honour and Conscience' to fob Mr Zorobabel Habbakuk off with a coun-terfeit virgin.[149] In *The Register Office* commerce only brings people to-gether to be cheated. It also explodes the boundaries between what should be commodified and what should not, opening up dangerous exchanges of sex and money.

Finally, these nefarious uses of the Register Office promise a di-vided and conflict-ridden society based on self-interest rather than one made perfect through the circulation and control of information. The ability to collect information about others is used by Gulwell to line his pockets. He also shows Lord Brilliant to a position where he can secret-ly observe Maria and gives him 'Rochester's Poems, and the *Memoirs of a Woman of Pleasure'* to enhance this sexual surveillance.[150] Even Har-wood and Frankly—and, indeed, the play's audience—are observing the swindling of others for their own amusement. Reed's emphasis on the differences between the characters—differences of class, gender, nation and ethnicity—shows them to be structured by exploitation and con-flict in loveless marriages for money, prostitution, and exploitative work. Lady Wrinkle, for example, tells Gulwell that 'With the Mushroom Part of Mankind we can do as we please; treat them with all the Contempt, State, Intolerance, and Superiority, which characterise the Woman of Quality.'[151] This emphasis on the exploitation of difference undermines the notions of utopian progress within the 'ideology of circulation' that were promised by the Universal Register Office. This is summed up by Reed's Scotsman who recounts how he was beaten up on the way to Portsmouth by men who 'wha gar'd me strip frae the muckle Coat o' my Back to my verra Sark; an rubbit me o' a,' ay an mare nor a,' I could ca' my ain—An no content wi' taking my Gudes, they ruggit my Hair; they pou'd me by the Lugs; they brisset and skelpit me to sic a Gree, that the Gore Blude rin into my Breeks, an my Skin was amaist as black as Pick—Nay when I gran'd i' meikle Dool an Agonie, the Fallows leugh at my pitifu' Mains, caw'd me an ill-far'd scabbit Tyke; and bad me be gane into my ain crowdie Country to sell Butter and Brunstane.'[152] In Reed's *The Register Office* there is no homogenous space of commerce and communication opened up by the administration of information. Instead, there is a fractured landscape of incomprehension, jiggery-pok-ery and exploitation by those with power and knowledge.

CONCLUSIONS

Setting *The Register Office* against the Universal Register Office in order to interpret the cultural politics of the uses of information in the eighteenth century is not a matter of understanding Reed's play as a direct critique of the Fieldings' project. Reed admired Henry Fielding and, as I have stressed, was keen to avoid posthumously blackening his name by impugning his invention. However, their different presentations of the manipulation of information, of trust (or lack of it), and of the social relations and imagined geographies of communication in a commercial society have opened a space for interpretation.

In the Universal Register Office the Fieldings and their associates offered a moral geography of the flow of information and exchange, and an ordered vision of a perfect society that was based on communication and commerce that might be extended more and more profitably to more and more people through the efficient collection, collation, retrieval and distribution of information. In contrast, Reed showed how the Register Office produced an immoral and fragmented space of conflict and power within which commerce mixed the previously unmixed, commodified what should not be commodified, and exploded carefully constructed moral boundaries as it extended exploitative economic and sexual relations. In the Fieldings' rhetoric the Universal Register Office operated in the interests of 'society,' bringing to a wide public the benefits provided by the power that comes from the control of information, as well as turning a profit for them. Reed's comedy shows how the same techniques of information manipulation and usage could just as easily become a tool for private, venal interests. The thrilling and dramatic possibilities of an 'information society' heralded by the Universal Register Office is matched by the dangers of the powers it unleashes. If the plan and the play do not map out a coherent politics of information in terms of who was included and excluded from such new technologies, they do reveal something of the hopes and fears that they embodied.

The transformations of time and space promised and effected by the storage and control of information in modern institutions mean that new possibilities and anxieties are woven inseparably together. This was the case for transportation, print culture, government, warfare and trade. Modernity's information revolution was both thrilling and frightening or, as David Harvey has it, 'challenging, exciting, stressful, and sometimes deeply troubling.'[153] The new relationships formed with and through institutions that depended upon access to, and government of, information resources and expertise far beyond that of any individual are not simply governed by blind trust, but by what Giddens calls a 'bargain with modernity' that must be struck by each person and, as he says, 'The nature of the bargain is governed by specific admixtures of deference and scepticism, comfort and fear.'[154] Here the play's ending is instructive. Gulwell's complicity in the conspiracy to defraud Maria of her inheritance is discovered when a letter falls into the wrong hands and information he wants kept secret is divulged. His downfall follows from losing control of the collection and distribution of information. His punishment, at least in the original version, is to give £500 to the Magdalen Hospital for 'the support of *ruin'd* innocence,' to undo a little of the damage he has done.[155] He is also beaten and publicly ducked in the 'Horse-Pool' by the Irishman, the Scotsman and the Frenchman, although not before the rivalries between them also surface.[156] They had all found out his tricks through networks of information based on friendship and informal contact outside the control of the Register Office. Again Gulwell is undone by his loss of control over information. However, despite this happy ending, all is not simply remade as utopian. There remains a distinct ambiguity over the trust that can be vested in a Register Office:

> *Frankly:* So the Adventure of the Register-Office hath turn'd out a lucky Affair?
>
> *Harwood:* Fortunate for me indeed! And were I not convinced of the Service arising to the community, from the institution and proper management of a Register Office, I should be apt to conclude, from the Trick, Villainy, and Chicanery I have seen within this Hour, that none but a Fool or Knave would ever set Foot within its Walls.[157]

CHAPTER SEVEN

Maps of Modernity

Bringing this book to a conclusion is not an easy matter. In part the aim has been to splinter and fragment the notion of modernity by attending to the contextualised historical geographies of some of its disparate spaces. At times these have seemed worlds apart. The geographies described sit somewhat uneasily alongside each other, and the ways of writing their histories have shifted and altered between the chapters. What, for example, have the visual illusions of Vauxhall's pleasure gardens, and an analysis that owes much to recent forms of art history, to do with the rationalised and bureaucratised spaces of excise taxation that invisibly mapped and ordered the city in order to bring the shadowy patterns of fraud to light, and which have been interpreted here with some of the tools of the history of science? Tying all this up neatly, reintegrating the city within a rethought conception of modernity, would be far from convincing and far from the intentions set out in the introduction. Yet bringing these studies together does rely upon the usefulness of 'modernity' as a concept. What is necessary, then, is an assessment of the implications of the theoretical strategies deployed in this book for understanding eighteenth-century London and the wider landscapes of modernity.

    Fracturing modernity and understanding it through the production of its spaces has been a profitable way of working. Various, predominantly theoretical, approaches to modernity—from understandings of modern subjectivity or the emergence of the public sphere to the globalising reach of time–space distanciation—have been used to pose and address questions specific to the eighteenth-century context and to

London in particular. For example: Why was prostitution seen as a problem and how can we understand the proposed solutions? How was the fiscal–military state constructed 'on the ground'? What were the tensions around new forms of commodification and how were they understood? Grounding the interpretations of often aspatially conceived processes of individualisation, the making of public spheres, commodification, bureaucratisation, state formation and the control of information in the spaces and places through which these processes were constituted has allowed me to offer detailed, contextualised readings of their contours and implications that have been attentive to questions of power and difference. In each chapter I have been able to develop particular arguments and draw specific conclusions. In Chapter 2 I argued that taking the Magdalen Hospital as a key site of the discourses and practices that shaped notions of self-reflection and self-control means renewed attention to the gendering of 'modern' versions of subjectivity. Close attention to the imagining, making and representing of streetscapes in Chapter 3 concluded by stressing the forms of order and control—including self-control—upon which the making of a public sphere depended. Moving to the pleasure garden, my reading of the complex landscape of Vauxhall underlined how the tensions that attended commodity consumption clustered around masculinity and the problems of telling between reality and illusion. In turn, Chapter 5 detailed the making of a taxation system to argue for the importance of understanding the various geographies of the modern state—from barrel to empire—and the ways in which that means attending to how the state apparatus—conceived as a network of people, knowledges, powers and material objects—was actively produced. And, finally, in Chapter 6 I worked through the promises and fears surrounding the control of information in order to argue that trust and anxiety were knit together in the experience of time–space distanciation. Each discussion springs, therefore, from understanding these dimensions of modernity through the ways in which they were produced in and through the city's spaces and, in turn, shaped the city.

Among the chapters there are also several common themes or threads that come out of the theoretical discussion of modernity in the introduction, and which together provide a distinctive cartography of eighteenth-century London and a particular map of modernity. In each case attention to the production of closely defined spaces—the solitary cell, the paved street, the pleasure garden, and bureaucratic or information networks—has meant that the partiality and specificity of those spaces has been stressed. In doing so, the various social relations and power relations of modernity have been anchored in their geographies—even if those geographies are ones that spread out way beyond the bounds of the city—in order to highlight these relationships and processes as themselves partial and specific. They not only have a history that marks their beginnings, development and, perhaps, decline, but also a geography that charts their contours, extent and limits. So, to draw out more threads, this has meant detailing the ways in which modernity is seen as full of both excitement and danger by understanding that duality in terms of the particular forms it takes in terms of sexuality and the city, luxurious consumption, and the centralisation and manipulation of information. It also means attending to a whole set of 'modern' gendered identities—including the disciplined penitent, the pedestrian, the Macaroni, the exciseman, and the investigating magistrate—that disperse any notions of 'a modern self' or 'the modern subject' across the multiple spaces of which these disparate figures are constituent parts. Overall, what each chapter contributes to is a concern to elucidate modernity's implication of institutional transformations of space and social relations with new identities. Exploring these intersections allows an understanding of the experience of inhabiting the modern world.

In doing this a map of the city and, indeed, a map of modernity emerges. This map presents a variegated topography, a patchwork of spaces, places and networks, from the confines of the Magdalen's rooms to the connections across space made in the Universal Register Office's transactions. Within this topography the multiple social relations, institutional dimensions and identities of modernity are configured. While I have only managed to shade in a small selection of the geographies that such a map might contain, it is clear that this conceptual cartography usefully counters singular and totalising versions of either modernity or the eighteenth-century city. It does, however, do so at the cost of splitting modernity and the metropolis into seemingly separate and unconnected parts.

One response to this is to return to Figure 1 and relocate the geographies set out here on the map of the city. The Magdalen Hospital (in both its locations) and Vauxhall Gardens in the south took advantage of cheap land and improving transport, as well as the moral and aesthetic codings of country and city, to locate at the urban margins. The paved streets of Westminster and the Universal Register Office were part of a different, West End urbanity that signaled the development of polite public sociability and crowded shopping streets. Finally, the Excise, operating from the government offices of the capital, sought to keep this complex whole under a unified system of control. They can, therefore, be located on the same map, but it is one that depicts a shifting and heterogenous urban space, a city that is growing and becoming more internally differentiated.

Another response is to emphasise the connections linking the 'spaces of modernity' that I have discussed. These offer somewhat different maps. For example, connections can be pursued through individual figures, and often more assiduously than I have done. Henry and John Fielding, in a range of different roles, link designs for a Magdalen Hospital, representations of the city, concerns over luxury, and the grand scheme of the Universal Register Office whose control of information repeats not only their roles as magistrates but many of the practices that also served those concerned with taxation. Jonas Hanway, perhaps unsurprisingly, offered support for John Spranger's paving plan as well as championing the ordering and disciplining of the spaces and bodies of penitent prostitutes. Others who were less well known would, no doubt, have crossed between these spaces and traversed these different geographies. There were certainly prostitutes at Vauxhall, but were there also excisemen?

Connections can also be pursued in other ways. The disruptions and tensions attendant upon commerce and commodification shaped many of the spaces. They lay behind concerns over prostitution in debates about women who not only sold themselves but threatened the commercial strength of the country. They were part of the discourse that political philosophy conducted about the city within the language of private interests and public benefits. As fashion and luxury, within and outside the magical world of Vauxhall, they disrupted notions of masculinity and blurred the boundaries between fantasy and reality. Finally, it was the power of commerce that generated both the Fieldings' attempts at the universal connection of buyers and sellers and the bureaucratic networks that sought to track commodities in order to tax them so that a commercial empire, endangered by more than harlots, might be protected by military strength. This prompts other connections. The forms of rational and rationalising order that sorted the Fieldings' ledgers—whether they were catching criminals or customers—find counterparts in Davenant's suggestions for the registering of brewers' vessels and the to-and-fro of documentation into and out of the Excise Office. They also find echoes in the reports compiled on the Magdalens whose ordered lives, devoid of dirt and disruption, were mirrored in the clean, polite, paved and lit streets of Westminster. Looking for connections can, therefore, find again the workings of rationality and capital that guided so many of the theories of modernity discussed in Chapter 1. However, instead of these becoming the centres around which modernity is composed into a seamless and tidy package, they serve to suggest an overlapping web of connections between a series of differently composed geographies.

This suggests an alternative cartography. It is worth returning again to Henri Lefebvre's image of urban space as it 'emerged in all its diversity . . . with a structure far more reminiscent of flaky *mille-feuille* pastry than of the homogeneous and isotropic space of classical (Euclidean/ Cartesian) mathematics.'[1] There is a sense here of a haphazardly layered topography; not a hierarchy of levels, but a complicated and shifting space of connections and simultaneity. It is an image that offers an understanding of the geography of modernity as something more than a patchwork of spaces and processes, but something less than a singular, linear transformation of space, time and being in a well-defined direction. In attending to the production of space, I have stressed the variety of geographies that are involved: the precise definition of spaces and their boundaries; the imagined geographies of cities, gardens and global processes of imperialism and trade; and the extension of networks across city, nation and world. Together these offer a sense of the historical geography of eighteenth-century London as one of ongoing, if partial, transformation through the spaces that I have dealt with and, of course, others. These changes in geographies, practices, lives and experiences—some more visible than others and some more tangibly felt—should, as I have tried to show, be understood in terms of their connections and the simultaneity of these transformations, as well as stressing the differentiated spaces of the modern metropolis and the different identities that they throw up. It was the same, but differentiated, urban space that was ordered by paving and lighting, criss-crossed by bureaucrats, punctuated with the tight geometries of disciplinary institutions, spun out to connect with other places through commerce and communication, and dotted with magical gardens woven of commodities and illusions.

This map of modernity, poised between integration and fragmentation, offers an understanding of its geographies that accords in many ways with Kathleen Wilson's version of 'the discontinuous and plural nature of the eighteenth-century experience' which she describes as 'marked as closely by slavery as liberty, racial, class and gender exclusions as universality, and fractured and "double" as unitary identities.' Indeed, situating some of these identities and experiences within the discussions of the spaces through which they emerge suggests that her assessment that this 'requires nothing less that a modification of the boundaries by which "modernity" and "postmodernity" are demarcated and understood' might be applied to the questions of space and the city as well as to identity and experience.[2] Eighteenth-century London was marked and shaped by the fragmentation of space, the surveillant eye, the information flows, and the commodified simulations that have also been taken to characterise postmodern urbanity. Yet this city cannot be confidently designated modern, postmodern, or even premodern. The version of modernity's 'project' offered here suggests a differentiated and plural understanding of change that disperses its various transformations across a range of connected sites, scenes and networks. It is also clear that the discussion of the sorts of 'spaces of modernity' that I have tried to identify in the preceding chapters must also address what are perhaps rather more ambiguous spaces. This has been raised in part through my discussion of the modernity of the Excise and its relationships to other parts of the eighteenth-century state, but it can also be served by a final example that blurs the boundary between modernity and 'ancien regime.'

The peace treaty ending the War of the Austrian Succession was signed by Britain, France and Spain at Aix-la-Chapelle in October 1748. It was to be celebrated in London on 27 April 1749 with a spectacular fireworks display close to Buckingham House in Green Park.[3] This display of over ten thousand rockets—six thousand in the final, explosive Girandole—and over twenty-one thousand other fireworks was choreographed by Gaetano Ruggieri and Guiseppi Sarti of Bologna. After the performance of music specially composed by Handel, the illuminations were set off from 'a magnificent Doric temple' designed by the Italian chevalier Servandoni.[4] Topped by a burning sun that shone the words VIVAT REX into the night sky above George II's coat of arms, this building—or 'machine'—was 176 feet high and, including its two flanking pavilions that served as storehouses for the engineers, over 400 feet long. It positively bristled with classical statues of virtues, gods, and goddesses, and with allegorical tableaux carrying Latin inscriptions celebrating the king, the nation and the treaty. The central image showed George II giving Peace to Britannia attended by Plenty, Riches, Fidelity, Trade, Commerce, Liberty, Agriculture and the Arts and Sciences. As such, it was the latest in a line of pyrotechnical and allegorical celebrations of the achievements of royalty that stretched back through celebrations of royal births, coronations and military achievements under James II and Charles II to, at least, a display for Elizabeth I held at Warwick castle in 1572. It might also be linked to the popular incendiary

politics of bonfires and squibs, and to the uneasy intersection of the de-
motic and the official in the celebrations of the Protestant calendar and,
especially, the anti-Catholic revelry of November 5th.[5] The display celebrated a notable victory, it marked the final acceptance by the French
of the Protestant succession, and it did so through the iconography of
monarchy and the ancients.

Yet this display also signals its modernity in various ways. Although
tickets were issued by the Lord Chamberlain's Office, and many were
allocated to members of both Houses of Parliament, it also operated as a
commercialised entertainment. Entry charges for the private viewing
galleries were graded in terms of the quality of the view and the degree
of comfort, and food and wine were to be served to the spectators.
There were also more direct connections to the pleasure gardens. The
spectacle mirrored the much smaller firework displays that were to become established parts of their entertainments. Servandoni's building
was also a wood and canvas construction offering, through comparable
techniques, the same sort of pleasurable illusions as Vauxhall's arches.
Moreover, Handel's music for the display had already been practised at
Vauxhall, reportedly drawing a crowd of 12,000 people, and the 'machine' itself had been a site on polite London's itinerary for the many
weeks of its construction and preparation.[6] The display was also part of
the world of nation-states, warfare and diplomacy. The connections between this official spectacular and the institutions of a state monopoly
of violence can be seen in that the machine was built by the master car-
penter to the Board of Ordnance, and the fireworks were to be ignited
by Charles Frederick Esq, comptroller of His Majesty's Laboratory at
Woolwich.[7]

Its modernity also concerned those who shunned the celebrations.
While what was being fêted in Green Park was presented as a peace
treaty signed in the interests of the global trade upon which British imperial fortunes depended, many were unhappy with the treaty and with
the spectacle. Coffeehouse politicians argued that the deal with France
and Spain was a bad and unstable one, and that it had been signed because of the exhaustion of both sides—especially in terms of the finances needed to wage war—rather than as a real resolution of territorial claims in India and North America.[8] Coming on top of the increases in taxation to fund the war, the expenditures from 'the publick purse'
on a vast conflagration, particularly one organised by foreigners, seemed
like a shameful waste of money that could have been better spent on
building bridges, draining land, mending roads, or even paying off the
national debt. These debates over foreign policy, taxation and improve-

ment were conducted alongside concerns about the 'growing appetite for luxury and prodigality,' and worry that such frivolities would keep the poor from the discipline of work, leading to passion and pleasure overcoming reason and provoking 'a dead stagnation of business, giddiness in every head, frolic in every heart, and all those other symptoms which lead to a state of beggary.'[9] Finally, it was a critique that unfavourably contrasted the Ancients and 'The Moderns'; revealed the illusory display of riches that the 'machine' and the country presented as 'all a painted Sepulcher, / Rotten within, with Outside fair'; and presented the fireworks as a dangerous and seductive 'NOVELTY'—that 'fav'rite passion' which 'runs thro' the Nation'—which blinded the people to the real actions and intentions of their political leaders.[10] Concern over these fireworks was structured by the tensions within the eighteenth-century modernities set out in the preceding chapters.

In the end, after an hour of the display, a stray firework set one of the temple's pavilions alight, burning much of the building to the ground before the fire was extinguished. Servandoni, seeing his creation being destroyed, drew his sword on Charles Frederick, who promptly had him disarmed and arrested. Although the show went on, it was agreed by all that it had not lived up to expectations. My intention is not to somehow to recoup this uneasy icon of state, commerce and spectacle as 'modern,' but to highlight the blurring of the boundaries between an 'ancien regime' of monarchic power and confessional politics and a modern world of national debts, commercial empires, coffee-house conversations, and the seductions of novelty. They exist together in the ambiguous space of Servandoni's 'machine' and the spaces of eighteenth-century London.

This blurring of temporal boundaries and the cartography of modernity that I have outlined above offer a way of mobilising its conceptual power to understand the spaces and places of the past that stands against other alternatives: abandoning the notion altogether, presenting accounts of modernity devoid of context and colour, or wheeling it on unexamined as a final explanatory flourish. Instead, they hold out the possibility and puzzle of examining a complex and interconnected topography of transformations in institutions, experiences and identities in ways that try to engage the changes signaled by the term 'modernity' while maintaining the specificity of the historical geographies of the spaces that they configure. Understanding these 'spaces of modernity,' in eighteenth-century London and elsewhere, is always about traversing the ground that lies between totalisation and difference.

Notes

CHAPTER 1

1. Christopher Hill on Daniel Defoe, quoted in Roy Porter (1990) *English Society in the Eighteenth Century* 2d ed. (Penguin, Harmondsworth, UK) p270.
2. Throughout this book I use the term 'London' to refer to the entire urban area; I specify 'the City of London' where necessary.
3. See, e.g., Rita Felski (1995) *The Gender of Modernity* (Harvard University Press, Cambridge, MA); Paul Gilroy (1993) *The Black Atlantic: Modernity and Double Consciousness* (Verso, London); and Allan Pred (1995) *ReCognizing European Modernities: A Montage of the Present* (Routledge, London).
4. The term is used in Griselda Pollock (1988) *Vision and Difference: Femininity, Feminism and the Histories of Art* (Routledge, London) Chapter 3: 'Modernity and the spaces of femininity.'
5. Bryan S. Turner (ed.) (1990a) *Theories of Modernity and Postmodernity* (Sage, London).
6. Henri Lefebvre (1995) *Introduction to Modernity: Twelve Preludes, September 1959–May 1961* (Verso, London) p184.
7. For the 'iron cage,' see Max Weber (1976, orig. 1904–1905) *The Protestant Ethic and the Spirit of Capitalism* (Allen & Unwin, London). For melting solids, see Karl Marx and Friedrich Engels (1971, orig. 1848) *The Communist Manifesto* (Penguin, Harmondsworth, UK), and Marshall Berman (1983) *All That Is Solid Melts Into Air: The Experience of Modernity* (Verso, London).
8. Peter Osborne (1995) *The Politics of Time: Modernity and Avant-Garde* (Verso, London) p29.
9. Charles Whitney (1986) *Francis Bacon and Modernity* (Yale University Press, New Haven, CT) p8, and Osborne, *The Politics of Time,* x. See also

Reinhart Koselleck (1981) 'Modernity and the planes of historicity,' *Economy and Society* 10 pp166–183.

10. Philibert Secretan (1984) 'Elements for a theory of modernity,' *Diogenes* 126 p74.
11. Osborne, *The Politics of Time*, p17.
12. Gilroy, *The Black Atlantic*, p49; see also p197.
13. John A. Hall and I. C. Jarvie (eds.) (1992) *Transition to Modernity: Essays on Power, Wealth and Belief* (Cambridge University Press, Cambridge), p4, presents Ernest Gellner's discussion of historical change in these terms.
14. Jessica Benjamin, quoted in Barbara L. Marshall (1994) *Engendering Modernity: Feminism, Social Theory and Social Change* (Polity Press, Cambridge, UK) p15.
15. Bryan S. Turner (1990b) 'Periodization and politics in the postmodern,' in Bryan S. Turner (ed.) *Theories of Modernity and Postmodernity* (Sage, London) pp6–7.
16. Tilo Schabert (1983) 'Modernity and history,' *Diogenes* 123 pp116–117. See also Whitney, *Francis Bacon and Modernity*, and the discussion in Stephen Toulmin (1992) *Cosmopolis: The Hidden Agenda of Modernity* (Chicago University Press, Chicago).
17. Weber, *The Protestant Ethic and the Spirit of Capitalism*, p26, and Ian Burkitt (1992) 'Beyond the "iron cage": Anthony Giddens on modernity and the self,' *History of the Human Sciences* 5 pp71–79.
18. Zygmunt Bauman (1991) *Modernity and Ambivalence* (Polity Press, Cambridge, UK) p68.
19. See Peter Wagner (1994) *A Sociology of Modernity: Liberty and Discipline* (Routledge, London) p158.
20. Zygmunt Bauman (1989) *Modernity and the Holocaust* (Polity Press, Cambridge, UK) x, xiii, and p15, and Bauman, *Modernity and Ambivalence*, p267.
21. Bauman, *Modernity and the Holocaust*, p13. See also Wagner, *A Sociology of Modernity*, p118.
22. Bauman, *Modernity and Ambivalence*, p255.
23. Theodor Adorno and Max Horkheimer (1979, orig. 1944) *Dialectic of Enlightenment* (Verso, London). See also Nicholas J. Rengger (1995) *Political Theory, Modernity and Postmodernity: Beyond Enlightenment and Critique* (Basil Blackwell, Oxford, UK).
24. E.g., Jürgen Habermas (1987) *The Philosophical Discourse of Modernity: Twelve Lectures* (Polity Press, Cambridge, UK). See also Diane Coole (1992) 'Modernity and its other(s),' *History of the Human Sciences* 5 pp81–91.
25. Berman, *All That Is Solid Melts Into Air*, p15. See also Perry Anderson (1984) 'Modernity and revolution,' *New Left Review* 144 pp96–113.
26. Allan Pred and Michael J. Watts (1992) *Reworking Modernity: Capitalisms and Symbolic Discontent* (Rutgers University Press, New Brunswick, NJ) p12, and David Harvey (1989) *The Condition of Postmodernity* (Basil Blackwell, Oxford, UK).

27. Berman, *All That Is Solid Melts Into Air,* p15.
28. Gilroy, *The Black Atlantic,* pp46–49, and Derek Gregory (1994) *Geographical Imaginations* (Basil Blackwell, Oxford, UK) p293.
29. See Ellen Meiksins Wood (1991) *The Pristine Culture of Capitalism: A Historical Essay on Old Regimes and Modern States* (Verso, London), and also see Derek Gregory's criticisms of Edward Soja, in Gregory, *Geographical Imaginations,* p308.
30. Pred and Watts, *Reworking Modernity,* xiv–xvi.
31. Elizabeth Wilson (1987) *Adorned in Dreams: Fashion and Modernity* (University of California Press, Berkeley and Los Angeles) and Harvey, *The Condition of Postmodernity,* p216.
32. Turner, 'Periodization and politics,' p1. For a confident statement, see Ferenc Fehér (1990) *The French Revolution and the Birth of Modernity* (University of California Press, Berkeley and Los Angeles).
33. Bruno Latour (1993) *We Have Never Been Modern* (Harvester Wheatsheaf, Hemel Hempstead, UK), p12, and Barry Smart (1990) 'Modernity, postmodernity and the present,' in Bryan S. Turner (ed.) *Theories of Modernity and Postmodernity* (Sage, London) pp14–30.
34. Toulmin, *Cosmopolis,* p5.
35. Gregory, *Geographical Imaginations,* p339.
36. Bauman, *Modernity and Ambivalence,* pp3–4.
37. Felski, *The Gender of Modernity,* p7 and p8. See also Paul Rabinow (1989) *French Modern: Norms and Forms of the Social Environment* (MIT Press, Cambridge, MA) p8.
38. Latour, *We Have Never Been Modern,* p41 and p72.
39. Felski, *The Gender of Modernity,* p12.
40. See Bruno Latour (1987) *Science in Action: How to Follow Scientists and Engineers through Society* (Open University Press, Milton Keynes, UK).
41. Latour, *We Have Never Been Modern,* p124; see also p48.
42. Latour, *We Have Never Been Modern,* p108.
43. Anthony Giddens (1990) *The Consequences of Modernity* (Polity Press, Cambridge, UK) p1 and p3.
44. Giddens, *The Consequences of Modernity,* p6.
45. Giddens, *The Consequences of Modernity,* p12 and p174.
46. Burkitt, 'Beyond the "Iron Cage," ' p75.
47. Giddens, *The Consequences of Modernity,* p139; see also Bauman, *Modernity and Ambivalence,* pp11–12.
48. Gilroy, *The Black Atlantic,* p30; see also p172.
49. Roger Friedland and Deirdre Boden (eds.) (1994) *NowHere: Space, Time and Modernity* (University of California Press, Berkeley and Los Angeles) p2.
50. Marshall, *Engendering Modernity,* p7.
51. See, e.g., Irving Velody (1992) 'Rationality deferred: An introduction to the politics of modernity,' *History of the Human Sciences* 5 p1; Lynn Hunt (ed.) (1993) *The Invention of Pornography: Obscenity and the Origins of Modernity* (Zone Books, New York); Allan Pred (1990) *Lost Words and*

Lost Worlds: Modernity and the Language of Everyday Life in Late Nineteenth-Century Stockholm (Cambridge University Press, Cambridge) xiii–xiv; Pred, *ReCognizing European Modernities*, pp14–15; Turner, 'Periodization and politics,' p6; and Berman, *All That Is Solid Melts Into Air*, p16.

52. Felski, *The Gender of Modernity*, p9.
53. S. N. Eisenstadt (ed.) (1987) *Patterns of Modernity. Vol. I: The West* (Francis Pinter, London) vii; Berman, *All That Is Solid Melts into Air;* and Mark Elvin (1986) 'A working definition of "modernity"?,' *Past and Present* 113 pp209–213.
54. Felski, *The Gender of Modernity*, p9.
55. Osborne, *The Politics of Time*, p5.
56. Berman, *All That Is Solid Melts Into Air*, p85.
57. Wilson, *Adorned in Dreams*, p63. See also the discussion of modernity as both 'structure' and 'mood' in Rengger, *Political Theory, Modernity and Postmodernity*.
58. Rengger, quoting Richard Bernstein, *Political Theory, Modernity and Postmodernity*, p43.
59. Pred and Watts, *Reworking Modernity*, xv.
60. Cf Toulmin, *Cosmopolis*, with Wagner, *A Sociology of Modernity*, and Giddens, *The Consequences of Modernity*.
61. Toulmin, *Cosmopolis*, x.
62. Toulmin, *Cosmopolis*, p42 and p34.
63. Toulmin, *Cosmopolis*, p62, p70, p104 and p128.
64. This is also apparent in the ways in which Michel Foucault 'historicizes reason'; see Deborah Cook (1990) 'Remapping modernity,' *British Journal of Aesthetics* 30 p38.
65. Gilroy, *The Black Atlantic*, p46.
66. Gilroy, *The Black Atlantic*, p39, and Gert Oostindie (ed.) (1995) *Fifty Years Later: Antislavery, Capitalism and Modernity in the Dutch Orbit* (KITLV Press, Leiden).
67. Marshall, *Engendering Modernity*.
68. Felski, *The Gender of Modernity*, p21 and p7.
69. Felski, *The Gender of Modernity*, p9.
70. Marshall, *Engendering Modernity*, p160.
71. Gilroy, *The Black Atlantic*, p16, and Felski, *The Gender of Modernity*, pp211–212.
72. Gilroy, *The Black Atlantic*, p29 and p4, draws on Peter Linebaugh (1982) 'All the Atlantic mountains shook,' *Labour/Le Travailleur* 10 pp87–121, and on Marcus Rediker (1987) *Between the Devil and the Deep Blue Sea: Merchant Seamen, Pirates and the Anglo-American Maritime World, 1700–1750* (Cambridge University Press, Cambridge).
73. Pollock, *Vision and Difference*, p70, p72 and p84.
74. Jenny Ryan (1994) 'Women, modernity and the city,' *Theory, Culture and Society* 11 p38 and p40. On 'the *flâneur*,' see Janet Wolff (1985) 'The invisible *flâneuse*: Women and the literature of modernity,' *Theory, Culture and Society* 2 pp37–46, and Elizabeth Wilson (1992) 'The invisible flâneur,' *New Left Review* 191 pp90–110.

75. Friedland and Boden, *NowHere,* and Osborne, *The Politics of Time,* pp15–16.
76. Berman, *All That Is Solid Melts Into Air,* p68, and Marshall Berman (1984) 'The signs in the street: A response to Perry Anderson,' *New Left Review* 144 p122.
77. Wagner, in *A Sociology of Modernity,* argues that '[a] general characteristic of modernity seems to be the wide social and spatial extension of its institutions' (p26). He is also concerned with the formation of boundaries and their role in forms of ordering.
78. Giddens, *The Consequences of Modernity,* p140.
79. Anthony Giddens (1985) *The Nation-State and Violence* (Polity Press, Cambridge, UK) pp48–49.
80. Giddens, *The Nation-State and Violence,* p57.
81. Bauman, *Modernity and Ambivalence,* p183.
82. Bauman, *Modernity and the Holocaust,* p34, p192 and p194.
83. Bauman, *Modernity and Ambivalence,* p3.
84. Gregory, *Geographical Imaginations,* p293.
85. Eisenstadt, *Patterns of Modernity,* viii.
86. Wagner, *A Sociology of Modernity,* and Pred, *ReCognizing European Modernities.*
87. Pred and Watts, *Reworking Modernity,* p18 and p107. See also Pred, *Lost Words and Lost Worlds.*
88. Osborne, *The Politics of Time,* p34; see also p13 and p21.
89. For alternative views, see, e.g., Pyrs Gruffudd (1994) 'Back to the land: Historiography, rurality and the nation in interwar Wales,' *Transactions of the Institute of British Geographers* 19 pp61–77; Stephen J. Daniels (1996) 'On the road with Humphrey Repton,' *Journal of Garden History* 16 pp170–191; and Gilroy, *The Black Atlantic,* p45, who 'argue[s] for the inversion of the relationship between margin and centre as it has appeared within the master discourses of the master race.'
90. Friedland and Boden, *NowHere,* p32.
91. Henri Lefebvre (1991) *The Production of Space* (Basil Blackwell, Oxford, UK) p53 and p317.
92. Lefebvre, *The Production of Space,* p86.
93. Lieven de Cauter (1993) 'The panoramic ecstasy: On world exhibitions and the disintegration of experience,' *Theory, Culture and Society* 10 pp1–23, and Gregory, *Geographical Imaginations.*
94. See, e.g., R. C. Harris (1991) 'Power, modernity, and historical geography,' *Annals of the Association of American Geographers* 81 pp671–683; Derek Gregory (1991) 'Interventions in the historical geography of modernity: Social theory, spatiality and the politics of representation,' *Geografiska Annaler* 73B pp17–44; Philip Howell (1993) 'Public space and the public sphere: Political theory and the historical geography of modernity,' *Environment and Planning D: Society and Space* 11 pp303–322; Richard Dennis (1994) 'Interpreting the apartment house: Modernity and metropolitanism in Toronto, 1900–1930,' *Journal of Historical Geography* 20 pp305–322; Nicholas Blomley (1994) *Law, Space, and the Geographies of*

Power (The Guilford Press, New York) Chapter 3: 'Legal territories and the "Golden Metewand" of the law'; and Pred, *ReCognizing European Modernities.*

95. Berman, *All That Is Solid Melts Into Air;* Pred, *Lost Words and Lost Worlds;* and Carl E. Schorske (1981) *Fin de Siècle Vienna: Politics and Culture* (Cambridge University Press, Cambridge).

96. See the discussion in Charles W. J. Withers (1996) 'Encyclopaedism, modernism and the classification of knowledge,' *Transactions of the Institute of British Geographers* 21 pp275–298.

97. J. H. Plumb (1983) 'The acceptance of modernity,' in Neil McKendrick, John Brewer and J. H. Plumb (eds.) *The Birth of a Consumer Society: The Commercialisation of Eighteenth-Century England* (Hutchinson, London) p327.

98. David Spadafora (1990) *The Idea of Progress in Eighteenth-Century Britain* (Yale University Press, New Haven, CT) p411, and Robert Mollenauer (ed.) (1965) *Introduction to Modernity: A Symposium on Eighteenth-Century Thought* (University of Texas Press, Austin).

99. Plumb, 'The acceptance of modernity,' p316 and p333.

100. Jonathan C. D. Clark (1985) *English Society, 1688–1832: Ideology, Social Structure and Political Practice during the Ancien Regime* (Cambridge University Press, Cambridge) p42, and Jonathan C. D. Clark (1986) *Revolution and Rebellion: State and Society in England in the Seventeenth and Eighteenth Centuries* (Cambridge University Press, Cambridge) p68. Clark's targets are J. H. Plumb, E. P. Thompson, Eric Hobsbawm, Christopher Hill, and Roy Porter.

101. Jonathan C. D. Clark (1992) 'Reconceptualising eighteenth-century England,' *British Journal for Eighteenth-Century Studies* 15 p136, and Clark, *Revolution and Rebellion,* p3. See also Jonathan C. D. Clark (1984) 'Eighteenth-century social history,' *Historical Journal* 27 pp773–788.

102. Wood, *The Pristine Culture of Capitalism.*

103. Joanna Innes (1987a) 'Jonathan Clark, social history and England's "ancien regime,"' *Past and Present* 115 pp165–200; W. A. Speck (1992) 'The eighteenth century: England's ancien régime?,' *British Journal for Eighteenth-Century Studies* 15 pp131–133; and Roy Porter (1992) 'Georgian Britain: An ancien regime?,' *British Journal for Eighteenth-Century Studies* 15 pp141–144.

104. Peter Mathias (1959) *The Brewing Industry in England, 1700–1830* (Cambridge University Press, Cambridge) xxvii.

105. 'Hegemony' seems to be a useful device that allows Marxists and revisionists alike (even when used ironically) to argue over singular definitions of cultural power. See Clark, *English Society,* pp93–118, and his argument that in the "ancien regime" 'a part came to stand for and maintain its dominance over a diverse whole'; Clark, 'Reconceptualising eighteenth-century England,' p135.

106. Linda Colley (1986) 'The politics of eighteenth-century British history,' *Journal of British Studies* 25 p371.

107. Innes, 'Jonathan Clark,' p177.

108. The quotation is from Jeremy Black (1993) *The Politics of Britain, 1688–1800* (Manchester University Press, Manchester, UK) p24. See Porter, *English Society;* Paul Langford (1989) *A Polite and Commercial People: England, 1727–1783* (Oxford University Press, Oxford); Paul Langford (1991) *Public Life and the Propertied Englishman, 1689–1798* (Clarendon Press, Oxford); and Derek Jarrett (1986) *England in the Age of Hogarth* (Yale University Press, New Haven, CT). Significantly, in terms of high politics, Plumb also argues that '[t]he years before the wars with revolutionary France were the years of England's *ancien regime.*' See J. H. Plumb (1950) *England in the Eighteenth Century* (Penguin, Harmondsworth, UK) p85.

109. Porter, *English Society,* p360. See also Black, *The Politics of Britain,* pp15–18, and Norma Landau (1988–1989) 'Eighteenth-century England: Tales historians tell,' *Eighteenth-Century Studies* 22 pp208–218.

110. Tom Keymer (1995) 'Smollett's Scotlands: Culture, politics and nationhood in *Humphrey Clinker* and Defoe's *Tour,*' *History Workshop Journal* 40 pp118–132; John Money (1993a) 'Teaching in the market-place, or "Caesar adsum jam forte: Pompey aderat": The retailing of knowledge in provincial England during the eighteenth century,' in John Brewer and Roy Porter (eds.) *Consumption and the World of Goods* (Routledge, London) pp335–377; John Money (1993b) 'The Masonic moment; or, Ritual, replica, and credit: John Wilkes, the Macaroni Parson, and the making of the middle-class mind,' *Journal of British Studies* 32 pp358–395; and Porter, 'Georgian Britain,' p142.

111. Lynn Hunt (1994) 'The virtues of disciplinarity,' *Eighteenth-Century Studies* 28 p6. See also Barbara Maria Stafford (1994) 'Redesigning the image of images: A personal view,' *Eighteenth-Century Studies* 28 p15, who argues that '*Dix-huitiémistes* of all stripes need to present alternative scenarios to the reductively pessimistic narrative of the "Age of Reason" as predominantly materialistic, skeptical, and technocratic.'

112. Kathleen Wilson (1995a) 'Citizenship, empire, and modernity in the English provinces, c 1720–1790,' *Eighteenth-Century Studies* 29 p70. See also Kathleen Wilson (1995b) *The Sense of the People: Politics, Culture and Imperialism in England, 1715–1785* (Cambridge University Press, Cambridge), and John Bender (1992) 'A new history of the Enlightenment?,' *Eighteenth-Century Life* 16 pp1–20.

113. Wilson, 'Citizenship, empire, and modernity,' p70.

114. Wilson, 'Citizenship, empire, and modernity,' p71.

115. Wilson, 'Citizenship, empire, and modernity,' p71.

116. Dorinda Outram (1995) *The Enlightenment* (Cambridge University Press, Cambridge) p12.

117. David N. Livingstone and Charles W. J. Withers (eds.) (forthcoming) *Geography and Enlightenment* (Chicago University Press, Chicago); David P. Miller and Peter H. Reill (eds.) (1996) *Visions of Empire: Voyages, Botany, and Representations of Nature* (Cambridge University Press, Cambridge); Michael Bravo (1996) 'The great South Sea caterpillar,' *Journal of Historical Geography* 22 pp484–488; John Gascoigne (1994) *Joseph Banks and the*

English Enlightenment: Useful Knowledge and Polite Culture (Cambridge University Press, Cambridge); Roy Porter and Mikulás Teich (1981) *The Enlightenment in National Context* (Cambridge University Press, Cambridge); and Robert Darnton (1984) *The Great Cat Massacre and Other Episodes in French Cultural History* (Penguin, Harmondsworth, UK).

118. Barbara Maria Stafford (1991) *Body Criticism: Imaging the Unseen in Enlightenment Art and Medicine* (MIT Press, Cambridge, MA) p131.

119. Wilson, 'Citizenship, empire, and modernity,' p71.

120. Porter, 'Georgian Britain,' p142.

121. Wagner, *A Sociology of Modernity,* p4 and p175; Osborne, *The Politics of Time,* p10; Koselleck, 'Modernity and the planes of historicity,' p174; and Friedland and Boden, *NowHere,* p10.

122. Bauman, *Modernity and Ambivalence,* p4 and p7.

123. Pred, *ReCognizing European Modernities,* p19.

124. The following paragraphs are based on Henry B. Wheatley (1914) 'Rocque's plan of London,' *London Topographical Record* IX pp15–28; Hugh Phillips (1952) 'John Rocque's career,' *London Topographical Record* XX pp9–25; Ida Darlington and James Howgego (1964) *Printed Maps of London circa 1553–1850* (George Philip & Son, London); Philippa Glanville (1972) *London in Maps* (Connoisseur, London); and Ralph Hyde (1982) 'The making of John Rocque's map,' in *The A–Z of Georgian London* London Topographical Society Publication 126. (London Topographical Society, London).

125. John Varley (1948) 'John Rocque: Engraver, surveyor, cartographer and map-seller,' *Imago Mundi* 5 p83.

126. John Brewer (1997) *The Pleasures of the Imagination: English Culture in the Eighteenth Century* (Harper Collins, London). See also David H. Solkin (1993) *Painting for Money: The Visual Arts and the Public Sphere in Eighteenth-Century England* (Yale University Press, New Haven, CT).

127. See Brewer, *The Pleasures of the Imagination,* p166, and the comments on subscription in *An Alphabetical Index of the Streets, Squares, Lanes, Alleys, &c. Contained in the Plan of the Cities of London and Westminster, and the Borough of Southwark . . .* (London, 1747).

128. Max Byrd (1978) *London Transformed: Images of the City in the Eighteenth Century* (Yale University Press, New Haven, CT) pp12–13.

129. For other representations of the city in terms of liberty and commerce, see Daniel Defoe (1724–1727) *A Tour thro' the Whole Island of Great Britain* (London); William Maitland (1739) *History of London from Its Foundation by the Romans to the Present Time* (London); and John Noorthouck (1773) *A New History of London* (London). For an interpretation of the changes in some of these depictions of cities, see Rosemary Sweet (1996) 'The production of urban histories in eighteenth-century England,' *Urban History* 23 pp171–188.

130. *An Alphabetical Index,* iv.

131. It must, however, be pointed out that the survey was not entirely mathematically precise, and that there were existing lanes and courts that did not find their way onto the map.

132. Arthur J. Weitzman (1975) 'Eighteenth-century London: Urban paradise or fallen city?,' *Journal of the History of Ideas* 38 pp469–480.

133. Hyde, 'The making of John Rocque's map.'

134. E. A. Wrigley (1967) 'A simple model of London's importance in changing English society and economy, 1650–1750,' *Past and Present* 37 pp44–70.

135. Peter Linebaugh (1991) *The London Hanged: Crime and Civil Society in the Eighteenth Century* (Penguin, Harmondsworth, UK) p69.

136. See, e.g., Catherine Nash (1996) 'Men again: Irish masculinity, nature, and nationhood in the early twentieth century,' *Ecumene* 3 pp427–453.

137. The following paragraphs are based on P. J. Corfield (1982) *The Impact of English Towns, 1700–1800* (Oxford University Press, Oxford); M. Dorothy George (1987, orig. 1925) *London Life in the Eighteenth Century* (Penguin, Harmondsworth, UK); John Summerson (1991, orig. 1945) *Georgian London* (Penguin, Harmondsworth, UK); L. D. Schwarz (1992) *London in the Age of Industrialisation: Entrepreneurs, Labour Force and Living Conditions, 1700–1850* (Cambridge University Press, Cambridge); Peter Earle (1994) *A City Full of People: Men and Women of London, 1650–1750* (Methuen, London); and Roy Porter (1994) *London: A Social History* (Hamish Hamilton, London).

138. Porter, *London,* p93 and p131.

139. Wrigley, 'A simple model of London's importance,' p50.

140. Corfield, *The Impact of English Towns,* p66.

141. Earle, *A City Full of People,* p86.

142. Linebaugh, *The London Hanged.* Schwarz, in *London in the Age of Industrialisation,* argues that the changes were not as systematic or dramatic as Linebaugh presents them.

143. Summerson, *Georgian London,* p26.

144. George, *London Life in the Eighteenth Century,* p15.

145. Porter, *London,* p95.

146. Summerson, *Georgian London,* p21.

147. Porter, *London,* p96.

148. Porter, *London,* p168.

149. John Landers (1993) *Death and the Metropolis: Studies in the Demographic History of London 1670–1830* (Cambridge University Press, Cambridge).

150. George, *London Life in the Eighteenth Century,* p33.

151. James Walvin (1997) *Fruits of Empire: Exotic Produce and British Taste, 1660–1800* (Macmillan, Basingstoke, UK), and Elizabeth Kowaleski-Wallace (1997) *Consuming Subjects: Women, Shopping, and Business in the Eighteenth Century* (Columbia University Press, New York).

CHAPTER 2

1. Peter Wagner (1994) *A Sociology of Modernity: Liberty and Discipline* (Routledge, London) p6 and p45, and Zygmunt Bauman (1991) *Modernity and Ambivalence* (Polity Press, Cambridge, UK) p68. The gendering of the 'modern subject' is one of the concerns of this chapter.

2. David Harvey (1989) *The Condition of Postmodernity* (Basil Blackwell, Oxford, UK) p258; Wagner, *A Sociology of Modernity,* p46; and Terry Castle
   (1986) *Masquerade and Civilization: The Carnivalesque in Eighteenth-Century
   English Culture and Fiction* (Methuen, London) p103—the quotation is
   from Mikhail Bakhtin.
3. See Michel Foucault (1977) *Discipline and Punish: The Birth of the Prison*
   (Allen Lane, London); Michel Foucault (1979) *The History of Sexuality.
   Vol. 1: An Introduction* (Allen Lane, London); Norbert Elias (1978) *The
   Civilizing Process. Vol. 1: The History of Manners.* (Pantheon, New York) and
   Norbert Elias (1982) *The Civilizing Process. Vol. 2: State Formation and
   Civilisation.* (Basil Blackwell, Oxford, UK). On subjectivity and state
   power, see, e.g., Colin Gordon (1987) 'The soul of the citizen: Max We-
   ber and Michel Foucault on rationality and government,' in Scott Lash
   and Sam Whimster (eds.) *Max Weber, Rationality and Modernity* (Allen &
   Unwin, London) pp293–316. Donna Haraway connects politics to science in arguing that as the ' "autonomous" individual' this subject is firmly embedded as a 'non-problematic starting point' in 'western liberal political theory' and science; see Donna Haraway (1989) *Primate Visions:
   Gender, Race, and Nature in the World of Modern Science* (Routledge, London) p405 footnote 38.
4. Marshall Berman (1983) *All That Is Solid Melts Into Air: The Experience of
   Modernity* (Verso, London) p39, p49 and p96.
5. Stephen Toulmin (1990) *Cosmopolis: The Hidden Agenda of Modernity*
   (University of Chicago Press, Chicago) p42. See also Norbert Elias
   (1991) *The Society of Individuals* (Basil Blackwell, Oxford, UK); Wagner, *A
   Sociology of Modernity,* p45; Barbara L. Marshall (1994) *Engendering Modernity: Feminism, Social Theory and Social Change* (Polity Press, Cambridge,
   UK); and Georg Simmel (1971, orig. 1903) 'The metropolis and mental
   life,' in Donald Levine (ed.) *Georg Simmel on Individuality and Social Forms*
   (University of Chicago Press, Chicago) pp324–339.
6. Berman, *All That Is Solid Melts Into Air,* p96, and Colin Campbell (1987)
   The Romantic Ethic and the Spirit of Modern Consumerism (Basil Blackwell,
   Oxford, UK) pp205–206.
7. Bauman, *Modernity and Ambivalence,* p68, and Anthony Giddens (1991)
   Modernity and Self-Identity: Self and Society in the Late Modern Age (Polity
   Press, Cambridge, UK).
8. Bauman, *Modernity and Ambivalence,* p158.
9. Bauman, *Modernity and Ambivalence,* p201. See also Giddens, *Modernity
   and Self-Identity,* p186.
10. For a critique of this, see Paul Gilroy (1993) *The Black Atlantic: Modernity
    and Double Consciousness* (Verso, London).
11. Simmel, 'The metropolis and mental life,' p325.
12. Giddens, *Modernity and Self-Identity.*
13. Such accounts generally connect individualism to a historical narrative
    that explores the development of capitalism from the seventeeth century
    onward. On the culture of 'economic individualism,' see Christopher Hill

(1967) *Reformation to Industrial Revolution: A Social and Economic History of Britain, 1530–1780* (Wiedenfeld and Nicolson, London)—the quotation is from p231; Ian Watt (1969) 'Robinson Crusoe, individualism and the novel,' in Frank H. Ellis (ed.) *Twentieth Century Interpretations of Robinson Crusoe* (Prentice Hall, Englewood Cliffs, NJ) pp39–54; Ellen Meiksins Wood (1991) *The Pristine Culture of Capitalism: A Historical Essay on Old Regimes and Modern States* (Verso, London); and Castle, *Masquerade and Civilization*, p105 and p106. On the economics and politics of 'possessive individualism,' see C. B. Macpherson (1967) *The Political Theory of Possessive Individualism: Hobbes to Locke* (Clarendon Press, Oxford), and the commentary in James Tully (1993a) 'After the Macpherson thesis,' in James Tully (ed.) *An Approach to Political Philosophy: Locke in Contexts* (Cambridge University Press, Cambridge) pp71–96.

14. Lawrence Stone (1977) *The Family, Sex and Marriage in England, 1500–1800* (Wiedenfeld and Nicolson, London), and John R. Gillis (1987) 'Married but not churched: Plebeian sexual relations and marital nonconformity in eighteenth-century Britain,' in Robert P. Maccubbin (ed.) *'Tis Nature's Fault: Unauthorized Sexuality during the Enlightenment* (Cambridge University Press, Cambridge) pp31–42.

15. Campbell, *The Romantic Ethic,* p73 and p70. Castle also argues that the period witnessed 'the intense evocation, at least in fantasy, of the freedom of the individual'; see Terry Castle (1987) 'The culture of travesty: Sexuality and masquerade in eighteenth-century England,' in G. S. Rousseau and Roy Porter (eds.) *Sexual Underworlds of the Enlightenment* (Manchester University Press, Manchester, UK) p174.

16. Jonathan C. D. Clark (1985) *English Society, 1688–1832* (Cambridge University Press, Cambridge) x, p4 and p7.

17. Alan Macfarlane (1978) *The Origins of English Individualism: The Family, Property and Social Transition* (Basil Blackwell, Oxford, UK). Both Clark and Macfarlane see each other as allies in arguing for 'continuity.' See Alan Macfarlane (1987) *The Culture of Capitalism* (Basil Blackwell, Oxford, UK), p221, and Jonathan C. D. Clark (1989) '1688 & all that,' *Encounter* LXXII pp14–17. For a Marxist critique of both positions, see Wood, *The Pristine Culture of Capitalism*.

18. Steve Pile and Nigel Thrift (eds.) (1995) *Mapping the Subject: Geographies of Cultural Transformation* (Routledge, London).

19. John Bender (1987) *Imagining the Penitentiary: Fiction and the Architecture of Mind in Eighteenth-Century England* (University of Chicago Press, Chicago).

20. The term is from Jonas Hanway (1776) *Solitude in Imprisonment* (London). See Bender, *Imagining the Penitentiary,* esp. Chapter 7: 'The aesthetic of isolation as social system.'

21. See, e.g., Miles Ogborn (1995) 'Knowing the individual: Michel Foucault and Norbert Elias on *Las Meninas* and the modern subject,' in Steve Pile and Nigel Thrift (eds.) *Mapping the Subject: Geographies of Cultural Transformation* (Routledge, London) pp57–76; Janet Wolff (1985) 'The invisible

flâneuse: Women and the literature of modernity,' *Theory, Culture and Society* 2 pp37–46; and Elizabeth Wilson (1992) 'The invisible flâneur,' *New Left Review* 191 pp90–110.

22. Nancy Armstrong (1987) *Desire and Domestic Fiction: A Political History of the Novel* (Oxford University Press, Oxford) p8.

23. Armstrong, *Desire and Domestic Fiction,* pp23–24.

24. G. J. Barker-Benfield (1992) *The Culture of Sensibility: Sex and Society in Eighteenth-Century Britain* (University of Chicago Press, Chicago) p100. For a discussion of the role of consumer goods in the creation of a new domestic space, see Carole Shammas (1980) 'The domestic environment in early modern England and America,' *Journal of Social History* 14 pp3–24, and for an earlier sexual politics of the closet, see Alan Stewart (1995) 'The early modern closet discovered,' *Representations* 50 pp76–100.

25. Both Campbell, in *The Romantic Ethic,* p70, and Barker-Benfield, in *The Culture of Sensibility,* stress the centrality of consumption changes to new forms of selfhood. Ian Watt (1957) *The Rise of the Novel: Studies in Defoe, Richardson and Fielding* (Chatto & Windus, London); Bender, *Imagining the Penitentiary;* and Kathryn Shevelow (1989) *Women and Print Culture: The Construction of Femininity in the Early Periodical* (Routledge, London) all emphasise the importance of reading and writing.

26. Armstrong, *Desire and Domestic Fiction,* p24, and Barker-Benfield, *The Culture of Sensibility,* p326.

27. Stanley Nash (1984) 'Prostitution and charity: The Magdalen Hospital, a case study,' *Journal of Social History* 17 p624. Colin Jones (1978) 'Prostitution and the ruling class in eighteenth-century Montpellier,' *History Workshop Journal* 6 pp7–28, argues that similar institutions were being established in France at the same time. Cf. Jacques Rossiaud (1985) 'Prostitution, sex and society in French towns in the fifteenth century,' in Philippe Ariès and André Béjin (eds.) *Western Sexuality: Practice and Precept in Past and Present Times* (Basil Blackwell, Oxford, UK) pp76–94. The aim of the name was to emphasise the notion of repentance that lay at the heart of the new institution. See A. B. [Nathaniel Lardner] (1758) *A Letter to Jonas Hanway Esq; in Which Some Reasons Are Assigned, Why Some Houses for the Reception of Penitent Women, Who Have Been Disorderly in Their Lives, Ought Not to Be Called Magdalen-Houses* (London), and Jonas Hanway (1759) *Thoughts on the Plan for a Magdalen House for Repentant Prostitutes* 2d ed (London).

28. Jonas Hanway (1758a) *A Plan for Establishing a Charity-House, or Charity-Houses, for the Reception of Repenting Prostitutes. To Be Called the Magdalen Charity* (London) xxvi and footnote p35; see also Edward G. O'-Donoghue (1929) *Bridewell Hospital: Palace, Prison, Schools from the Death of Elizabeth to Modern Times* (John Lane, London). Jonas Hanway's (1712—1786) activities are detailed in James Stephen Taylor (1985) *Jonas Hanway, Founder of the Marine Society: Charity and Policy in Eighteenth-Century Britain* (Scolar Press, London).

29. Pieter Spierenburg (1984) 'The sociogenesis of confinement and its de-

velopment in early modern Europe,' in Pieter Spierenburg (ed.) *The Emergence of Carceral Institutions: Prisons, Galleys and Lunatic Asylums, 1550–1900* (Centrum Voor Maatschappij Geschiedenis, Erasmus Universiteit Rotterdam) pp9–77, and Pieter Spierenburg (1991) *The Prison Experience: Disciplinary Institutions and Their Inmates in Early Modern Europe* (Rutgers University Press, New Brunswick, NJ).

30. Thorsten Sellin (1944) *Pioneering in Penology: The Amsterdam Houses of Correction in the Sixteenth and Seventeenth Centuries* (University of Philadelphia Press, Philadelphia), and Simon Schama (1988) *The Embarrassment of Riches: An Interpretation of Dutch Culture in the Golden Age* (Fontana, London).

31. Quoted in Sellin, *Pioneering in Penology,* p95.

32. Hanway, *A Plan for Establishing a Charity-House,* xxii, and Jonas Hanway (1758b) *Thoughts on the Plan for a Magdalen House for Repentant Prostitutes* 1st ed (London) pp33–35.

33. Pieter Spierenburg (1987) 'From Amsterdam to Auburn: An explanation for the rise of the prison in seventeenth-century Holland and nineteenth-century America,' *Journal of Social History* 20 pp439–461, and Joanna Innes (1987b) 'Prisons for the poor: English Bridewells, 1555–1800,' in Francis Snyder and Douglas Hay (eds.) *Labour, Law and Crime: An Historical Perspective* (Tavistock, London) pp42–122.

34. W. A. Speck (1980) 'The harlot's progress in eighteenth-century England,' *British Journal for Eighteenth Century Studies* 3 pp127–139.

35. Nash, 'Prostitution and charity.'

36. Hanway, *Solitude in Imprisonment.* Michael Ignatieff (1978) *A Just Measure of Pain: The Penitentiary in the Industrial Revolution, 1750–1850* (Pantheon Books, New York), p54, argues that Hanway was the first to propose confining prisoners under sentence in solitude. It is worth noting that one of Hanway's early-eighteenth-century predecessors, Thomas Bray, had also written on both solitude and the reformation of prostitutes. See Robin Evans (1982) *The Fabrication of Virtue: English Prison Architecture, 1750–1840* (Cambridge University Press, Cambridge).

37. Any assessment of everyday life in the Magdalen Hospital, and of the accommodations and resistances to its regime by the women who lived within it, is virtually impossible due to the disappearance of the institution's own records.

38. Quoted in Donna T. Andrew (1989) *Philanthropy and Police: London Charity in the Eighteenth Century* (Princeton University Press, Princeton, NJ) footnote 76 p120. For Robert Dingley's involvement, see Jonas Hanway (1758) *Letter V to Robert Dingley* (London), and John H. Appleby (1992) 'Mills, models and Magdalens: The Dingley brothers and the Society of Arts,' *Journal of the Royal Society of Arts* 140 pp267–273. See also *Rambler* no 107, 26 March 1751, pp638–640.

39. John Fielding and Saunders Welch are discussed in Patrick Pringle (1955) *Hue and Cry: The Birth of the British Police* (Museum Press, London).

40. Sarah Lloyd (1996) '"Pleasure's golden Bait": Prostitution, poverty and

the Magdalen Hospital in eighteenth-century London,' *History Workshop Journal* 41 pp50–70, and Markman Ellis (1996) *The Politics of Sensibility: Race, Gender and Commerce in the Sentimental Novel* (Cambridge University Press, Cambridge).

41. Magdalen Hospital (1759) *The Rules, Orders and Regulations, of the Magdalen House, for the Reception of Penitent Prostitutes* 2d ed (London) p6.

42. Hanway, *Thoughts* 1st ed., p5, p23 and pp30–31. Hanway's pamphlet traced ancient, medieval and modern European precedents—including the Amsterdam *Spinhuis*—but also marked his distance from them.

43. Randolph Trumbach (1987a) 'Modern prostitution and gender in *Fanny Hill*: Libertine and domesticated fantasy,' in G. S. Rousseau and Roy Porter (eds.) *Sexual Underworlds of the Enlightenment* (Manchester University Press, Manchester, UK) pp69–85; Randolph Trumbach (1991) 'Sex, gender, and sexual identity in modern culture: Male sodomy and female prostitution in Enlightenment London,' *Journal of the History of Sexuality* 2 pp186–203; and Speck, 'The harlot's progress.' See also the connections made between modernity and sodomy in Randolph Trumbach (1987b) 'Sodomitical subcultures, sodomitical roles, and the gender revolution of the eighteenth century: The present historiography,' in Robert P. Maccubbin (ed.) *'Tis Nature's Fault: Unauthorized Sexuality during the Enlightenment* (Cambridge University Press, Cambridge) pp109–121, and Rector Norton (1992) *Mother Clap's Molly House: The Gay Subculture in London, 1700–1830* (Gay Men's Press, London).

44. Marc Raeff (1975) 'A well-ordered police state and the development of modernity in seventeenth- and eighteenth-century Europe,' *American Historical Review* 80 pp1221–1243; Marc Raeff (1983) *The Well-Ordered Police State: Social and Institutional Change through Law in the Germanies and Russia, 1600–1800* (Yale University Press, New Haven, CT); Gerhard Oestreich (1982) *Neostoicism and the Early Modern State* (Cambridge University Press, Cambridge); and Leon Radzinowicz (1956) *A History of the English Criminal Law and Its Administration from 1750, Vol. 3: Cross-currents in the Movement for the Reform of the Police* (Stevens & Sons, London) pp1–8.

45. G. S. Rousseau and Roy Porter (eds.) (1987) *Sexual Underworlds of the Enlightenment* (Manchester University Press, Manchester, UK) p2, and Roy Porter (1982) 'Mixed feelings: The Enlightenment and sexuality in eighteenth-century Britain,' in Paul-Gabriel Boucé (ed.) *Sexuality in Eighteenth-Century Britain* (Manchester University Press, Manchester, UK) pp1–27. On toleration see Paul-Gabriel Boucé (1980) 'Aspects of sexual tolerance and intolerance in eighteenth-century England,' *British Journal for Eighteenth-Century Studies* 3 pp173–191, and Vern Bullough (1987) 'Prostitution and reform in eighteenth-century England,' in Robert P. Maccubbin (ed.) *'Tis Nature's Fault: Unauthorized Sexuality During the Enlightenment* (Cambridge University Press, Cambridge) pp61–74.

46. Hanway, *Thoughts* 1st ed., p13, p14, and p24.

47. Hanway, *Thoughts* 1st ed., p26.

48. On charity and 'Britishness,' see Ellis, *The Politics of Sensibility*, p15.
49. Andrew, *Philanthropy and Police*, and David Hancock (1995) *Citizens of the World: London Merchants and the Integration of the British Atlantic Community, 1735–1785* (Cambridge University Press, Cambridge) p311.
50. Saunders Welch (1758) *A Proposal to Render Effectual a Plan, to Remove the Nuisance of Common Prostitutes from the Streets of This Metropolis; to Prevent the Innocent from Being Seduced . . .* (London) footnote p13.
51. On empire and the regulation of sexuality, see Ruth Perry (1991) 'Colonising the breast: Sexuality and maternity in eighteenth-century England,' *Journal of the History of Sexuality* 2 pp204–234, and Felicity A. Nussbaum (1995) *Torrid Zones: Maternity, Sexuality, and Empire in Eighteenth-Century English Narratives* (Johns Hopkins University Press, Baltimore).
52. Robert Dingley (1758) *Proposals for Establishing a Public Place of Reception for Penitent Prostitutes, &c* (London) pp4–5.
53. Hanway, *Thoughts* 1st ed., p12.
54. Welch, *A Proposal*, p13.
55. Welch, *A Proposal*, footnote p14.
56. Mr. Marchant (1758) *Observations on Mr Fielding's Plan for a Preservatory and Reformatory* (London) p12.
57. Hanway, *A Plan for Establishing a Charity-House*, p31, and Hanway, *Letter V to Robert Dingley*.
58. John Fielding (1758a) *A Plan for a Preservatory and Reformatory, for the Benefit of Deserted Girls, and Penitent Prostitutes* (London) p10 and p15.
59. J. Massie (1758) *A Plan for the Establishment of Charity-Houses for Exposed or Deserted Women and Girls, and for Penitent Prostitutes* (London).
60. Hanway, *Thoughts* 1st ed., p30; Magdalen Hospital, *Rules, Orders and Regulations,* 2d ed., p7; Dingley, *Proposals,* p5. See also Magdalen Hospital (1758) *The Plan of the Magdalen House for the Reception of Penitent Prostitutes* (London) p21.
61. Michel Foucault (1988) 'The political technology of individuals,' in Luther H. Martin, Huck Gutman, and Patrick H. Hutton (eds.) *Technologies of the Self* (Tavistock, London) p153 and pp155–156.
62. Paul-Gabriel Boucé (1982) 'Some sexual beliefs and myths in eighteenth-century Britain,' in Paul-Gabriel Boucé (ed.) *Sexuality in Eighteenth-Century Britain* (Manchester University Press, Manchester, UK) p299; Andrew, *Philanthropy and Police*, p119; and Ludmilla Jordanova (1987) 'The popularisation of medicine: Tissot on onanism,' *Textual Practice* 1 pp68–79.
63. Magdalen Hospital, *Rules, Orders and Regulations,* 2d ed., pp3–4.
64. Magdalen Hospital, *Rules, Orders and Regulations,* 2d ed., p1.
65. Hanway, *Thoughts* 1st ed., p26. The connections between the pronatalism of these forms of social policy and people's sexual practice form the basis of Tim Hitchcock (1997) *English Sexualities, 1700–1800* (Macmillan, Basingstoke, UK).
66. Nussbaum, *Torrid Zones*, p2.
67. Welch, *A Proposal*, p57, and John Fielding (1758b) *An Account of the Ori-*

gin and Effects of a Police Set on Foot by His Grace the Duke of Newcastle in the Year 1753, upon a Plan Presented to His Grace by the Late Henry Fielding (London).

68. Nicholas Rogers (1991) 'Policing the poor in eighteenth-century London: The vagrancy laws and their administration,' *Histoire Sociale/Social History* XXIV pp127–147. Hanway certainly saw this disorder as a matter of 'idleness' (Hanway, *Thoughts* 1st ed., pp49–51) and a lack of 'discipline, and obedience . . . among the *common* people' (Hanway, *Thoughts* 1st ed., p45), but he also attacked the idle rich (Hanway, *Letter V to Robert Dingley,* p8) for their 'many refinements in vice' (Hanway, *A Plan for Establishing a Charity-House,* viii). See also *A Congratulatory Epistle from a Reformed Rake, to John F—g, Esq; Upon the New Scheme of Reclaiming Prostitutes* (London, 1758).

69. Anthony Henderson (1992) *Female Prostitution in London, 1730–1830* unpublished PhD thesis, University of London, p252 and p196. He also shows the impact on the geography of prostitution of the more effective policing of the City of London, particularly in relation to bawdyhouses.

70. Welch, *A Proposal,* p7. See also Magdalen Hospital, *The Plan,* p4, and Hanway, *Thoughts,* 1st ed., p42.

71. Welch, *A Proposal,* p15 and p17, and Hanway, *Thoughts,* 1st ed., p42.

72. Jonas Hanway (1775) *The Defects of Police, the Cause of Immorality* (London) p61. Welch, in *A Proposal,* pp4–5, also argued that prostitution was caused by overeducation, imitation and vanity, the products of the erosion of class boundaries.

73. The term is from Nussbaum, *Torrid Zones,* Chapter 4.

74. Welch, *A Proposal,* p19 and footnote p18. Also see the discussion of Welch in Elizabeth Kowaleski-Wallace (1997) *Consuming Subjects: Women, Shopping and Business in the Eighteenth Century* (Columbia University Press, New York).

75. Fielding, *A Plan for a Preservatory and Reformatory,* p41, and Welch, *A Proposal,* p57 and p15.

76. Welch, *A Proposal,* and Hanway, *A Plan for Establishing a Charity-House,* footnote p35. These concerns and Hanway's suggestion that ineffectiveness may also have been increased by the bribery of petty officers (see Hanway, *Thoughts,* 1st ed., p42) seem to be confirmed by Henderson, *Female Prostitution in London.*

77. Welch, *A Proposal,* p67. These ideas are in a letter of 1753 that he published in 1758 with his Magdalen pamphlet.

78. Hanway, *A Plan for Establishing a Charity-House,* xxxvii; Magdalen Hospital, *Rules, Orders and Regulations,* 2d ed., p6; Hanway, *Thoughts,* 1st ed., p40; and Jonas Hanway (1761) *Reflections, Essays and Meditations on Life and Religion* (London) Vol. II pp19–20.

79. Hanway, *Thoughts,* 1st ed., p40.

80. Hanway, *Thoughts,* 1st ed., pp41–42.

81. Lloyd, '"Pleasure's golden Bait"'; Ellis, *The Politics of Sensibility;* and Hitchcock, *English Sexualities.*

82. Wolff, 'The invisible *flâneuse*,' p41. She makes the point in relation to Baudelaire.
83. For examples, see Hanway, *A Plan for Establishing a Charity-House*, xxxii; Welch, *A Proposal*, pp4–5; Marchant, *Observations*; and Magdalen Hospital (1770) *An Account of the Rise, Progress and Present State of the Magdalen Hospital* 4th ed (London). Interpretations are provided by Speck, 'The harlot's progress'; Lloyd, ' "Pleasure's golden Bait" '; and Ellis, *The Politics of Sensibility*.
84. *The Histories of Some of the Penitents in the Magdalen House, as Supposed to Be Related by Themselves* (London, 1760), and William Dodd (ed.) (n.d.) *The Magdalen; or, History of the First Penitent* (London) which presents the same story as the first in *The Histories* with elements of the other stories interspersed.
85. Speck, 'The harlot's progress.'
86. Lady Barbara was the daughter of the first Earl of Halifax; Scott was the sister of Mrs Elizabeth Montagu, the bluestocking. The two lived together in what Elizabeth Montagu described as a 'convent,' devoting themselves to writing and charitable works, much like the women in Scott's novel *Millenium Hall* (London, 1762). See also T. C. Duncan Eaves and Ben D. Kimpel (1971) *Samuel Richardson: A Biography* (Clarendon Press, Oxford), p462, and Ellis, *The Politics of Sensibility*. I owe these references to Judith Hawley.
87. Barker-Benfield, *The Culture of Sensibility*, p64, and J. V. Price (1982) 'Patterns of sexual behaviour in some eighteenth-century novels,' in Paul-Gabriel Boucé (ed.) *Sexuality in Eighteenth-Century Britain* (Manchester University Press, Manchester, UK) pp159–175.
88. *The Histories of Some of the Penitents*, Vol. I xx.
89. *The Histories of Some of the Penitents*, Vol. I xxiii and xxi.
90. Dodd, *The Magdalen*, xiii.
91. Bender, *Imagining the Penitentiary*, and Ellis, *The Politics of Sensibility*.
92. Price, 'Patterns of sexual behaviour,' p171.
93. Bender, *Imagining the Penitentiary*, p165.
94. Bender, *Imagining the Penitentiary*, footnote 2 p253 and p177, and Watt, *The Rise of the Novel*, p35.
95. *The Histories of Some of the Penitents*, Vol. I, p98.
96. Bender, *Imagining the Penitentiary*, p115.
97. Dodd, *The Magdalen*, pp77–78.
98. With regard to 'vanity,' see *The Histories of Some of the Penitents*, Vol. I, p54 and p139.
99. *The Histories of Some of the Penitents*, Vol. I, vi.
100. Ellis, *The Politics of Sensibility*, p184.
101. Castle, *Masquerade and Civilization*, p116, quoting from Tony Tanner (1979) *Adultery and the Novel: Contract and Transgression* (Johns Hopkins University Press, Baltimore). Defoe also argues that 'there cannot be the same Life, the same Brightness and Beauty in relating the penitent Part, as is in the criminal Part . . .'; see Daniel Defoe (1722) *The Fortunes and Mis-*

fortunes of the Famous Moll Flanders 3d ed. (London). In relation to *The Histories of Some of the Penitents,* it is worth noting both Lady Barbara Montagu's approval of the 'pious fraud' that would be played on those who bought them expecting a rather racier read (See Eaves and Kimpel, *Samuel Richardson,* p463), and Horace Walpole who visited the Magdalen Hospital in 1760 and had to restrain himself from cracking inappropriate jokes about animal fertility, although he could not resist them in a letter to George Montagu (28 January 1760); see W. S. Lewis (ed.) *Horace Walpole's Correspondence* (Yale University Press, New Haven, CT) Vol. IX, pp271–275.

102. Barker-Benfield, *The Culture of Sensibility,* p344.

103. Ellis, *The Politics of Sensibility,* p160, and Lloyd, ' "Pleasure's golden Bait." ' For examples, see *The Histories of Some of the Penitents,* Vol. I, xv; Hanway, *Thoughts,* 1st ed., p15 and p43; Dingley, *Proposals,* pp3–4; and Marchant, *Observations,* pp1–2.

104. *The Histories of Some of the Penitents,* Vol. II, p248. This echoes Dingley's conviction that these women act 'not of choice, but through fatal necessity'; see Dingley, *Proposals,* p4. See also Massie, *A Plan,* and Magdalen Hospital, *Rules, Orders and Regulations,* 2d ed., p5.

105. *The Histories of Some of the Penitents,* Vol. I p103 and Chapter XXI.

106. *The Histories of Some of the Penitents,* Vol. II p24.

107. *The Histories of Some of the Penitents,* Vol. II p21.

108. *The Histories of Some of the Penitents,* Vol. II p163 and p164.

109. The same confusion of choice and compulsion, guilt and innocence is present in the chaos of causes of prostitution named in the pamphlet literature: necessity, vanity, want of education, not knowing one's place, seduction, a mind abandoned to debauchery, and so on. Indeed, Sarah Lloyd argues that the Magdalen Hospital's appeal was based upon contradictory and ambivalent understandings of the power of 'passion'; see Lloyd, ' "Pleasure's golden Bait." '

110. Ronald Paulson (1975) *Emblem and Expression: Meaning in English Art of the Eighteenth Century* (Thames & Hudson, London) p40.

111. Anthony Giddens (1990) *The Consequences of Modernity* (Polity Press, Cambridge, UK). In the first story the sense that character can be made and unmade through experience is clear: 'I had been bred up in religious principles, but at that age they could not be deeply grounded, nor so fixed as to stand against the temptations of the world, into which I was now thrown'; *The Histories of Some of the Penitents,* Vol. I, p10. More generally, Zygmunt Bauman quotes Nicholas Luhmann's identification of "the causes of . . . ego-centrism and individualism—in the ever-increasing differentiation, complexity and hence opacity of interactive networks"; see Bauman, *Modernity and Ambivalence,* p201.

112. Hanway, *A Plan for Establishing a Charity-House,* p22; Magdalen Hospital, *The Plan,* p17; and Herbert F. B. Compston (1917) *The Magdalen Hospital: The Story of a Great Charity* (SPCK, London) p199.

113. Hanway, *Reflections*, Vol. II, Letter 15: 'On Repentance.' Elizabeth Wilson argues that 'what distinguishes great city life from rural existence is that we constantly brush against strangers; we observe bits of the "stories" men and women carry with them, but never learn their conclusions; life ceases to form itself into epic or narrative, becoming instead a short story, dreamlike, insubstantial or ambiguous'; see Wilson, 'The invisible flâneur,' p107. John Bender, in *Imagining the Penitentiary*, has, of course, argued that certain forms of fiction and penitentiary spaces are intimately connected.

114. *The Histories of Some of the Penitents*, Vol. I, p133. See also Magdalen Hospital, *Rules, Orders and Regulations*, 2d ed., p4.

115. *The Histories of Some of the Penitents*, Vol. I, p30.

116. *The Histories of Some of the Penitents*, Vol. I, p36.

117. *The Histories of Some of the Penitents*, Vol. II, p144.

118. The challenges these characters offer are seen as out-of-the-ordinary. As one of the women says, 'The world is so obliging, or so indolent, it seldom disputes our title to what we seem confident we are in possession of'; *The Histories of Some of the Penitents*, Vol. I, p140.

119. Ellis, *The Politics of Sensibility*, p183, argues that these stories are all defences of orthodox marriages based on romantic love. This may be broadened to a notion of 'loving family values.' See Magdalen Hospital, *Rise, Progress and Present State*, 4th ed., pp37–38, which relates an 'Authentic narrative' within which 'the early impressions of parental tenderness' helped 'to awaken reflection and to shew her herself.'

120. *The Histories of Some of the Penitents*, Vol. I, pp13–14, p41, and p48.

121. *The Histories of Some of the Penitents*, Vol. II, p38 and pp91–92.

122. Magdalen Hospital, *The Plan*, p5. This account of the regime of the hospital is primarily based upon Magdalen Hospital, *The Plan*; Magdalen Hospital, *Rules, Orders and Regulations*, 2d ed.; and Magdalen Hospital, *Rise, Progress and Present State*, 4th ed. Material is also drawn from the pamphlets already cited.

123. Hanway, *A Plan for Establishing a Charity-House*, p2.

124. 9 Geo. III cap 31 (1769) *An Act for the Establishing and Well Governing a Hospital for the Reception, Maintenance, and Employment, of Penitent Prostitutes*. The house was said to be too small and 'in a very ruinous condition' (p911) and in 1770 Sir John Fielding told Parliament that Goodman's Fields was the location of 'brothels and irregular taverns ... many of which are remarkably infamous'; *The Parliamentary History of England from the Earliest Period to the Year 1803*, ed. William Cobbett (London, 1813) Vol. XVI, pp938–939.

125. Andrew, *Philanthropy and Police*, p49, and Hanway, *A Plan for Establishing a Charity-House*, p3.

126. For some of the problems with this, see Hancock, *Citizens of the World*, p312.

127. Hanway, *Thoughts* 1st ed., p57.

128. The building is described in Compston, *The Magdalen Hospital*, p60, and

in *A Brief Description of the Cities of London and Westminster, the Public Buildings, Palaces, Gardens, Squares, &c. With an Alphabetical List of All the Streets, Squares, Courts, Lanes, and Alleys, &c. within the Bills of Mortality* (London, 1776) p128.

129. Massie, *A Plan*, p40.
130. Magdalen Hospital, *The Plan*, p14.
131. Dingley, *Proposals*, p15, and Magdalen Hospital, *The Plan*, p19.
132. Magdalen Hospital, *The Plan*, pp14–15.
133. This is in marked contrast to the permeable boundaries of the unreformed prisons described by Bender, in *Imagining the Penitentiary*, and Evans, in *The Fabrication of Virtue*.
134. Evans, *The Fabrication of Virtue*, p56, remarks on the novelty and significance of specifically designed penal institutions at this time.
135. The complexities of the chapel as a public space are explored in Lloyd, ' "Pleasure's golden Bait." '
136. Hanway, *A Plan for Establishing a Charity-House*, p20.
137. Massie, *A Plan*, p35. See also Hanway, *A Plan for Establishing a Charity-House*, footnote p19. Jeremy Bentham argued that prisoners should be divided into classes on the basis of their susceptibility to punishment and that "circumstances" such as "sex, age, rank, race, climate, government, education, religious profession" could be used as indicators of this; quoted in Bender, *Imagining the Penitentiary*, p38.
138. Hanway, *Thoughts*, 1st ed., p26, p32, and p47; and Hanway, *A Plan for Establishing a Charity-House*, x.
139. Hanway, *Thoughts*, 1st ed., pp26–27.
140. Hanway, *Thoughts*, 1st ed., p9. Ignatieff, *A Just Measure of Pain*, p71, and Bender, *Imagining the Penitentiary*, p29, disagree on the extent to which religious ideas of 'conscience' and 'the soul' were assimilable to Lockeian ones of 'understanding' and 'the mind.' On the evidence of Jonas Hanway's writings, it appears that even if they weren't wholly assimilable they could be worked together in usable ways.
141. Hanway, *Thoughts*, 1st ed., p20, and James Tully (1993b) 'Governing conduct: Locke on the reform of thought and behaviour,' in James Tully (ed.) *An Approach to Political Philosophy: Locke in Contexts* (Cambridge University Press, Cambridge) p223.
142. Hanway, *Reflections*, Vol. II, p65.
143. Hanway, *A Plan for Establishing a Charity-House*, p2 and p17.
144. Hanway, *Reflections*, Vol. II, p332. He also planned to hang dietaries in the hospital; see Hanway, *A Plan for Establishing a Charity-House*, p23.
145. Hanway, *A Plan for Establishing a Charity-House*, p23, and Dingley, *Proposals*. On Hanway's own diet, see Betsy Rodgers (1949) *The Cloak of Charity: Studies in Eighteenth-Century Philanthropy* (Methuen, London) p46. He was, in addition, well known for his views on the dangers of tea; see Jonas Hanway (1756) *An Essay on Tea: Considered as Pernicious to Health; Obstructing Industry; and Impoverishing the Nation . . .* (London).

146. Magdalen Hospital, *The Plan,* p. 18. On leaving. each woman would get the money she had earned, and an additional monetary reward dependent on 'virtue.'

147. Hanway, *Letter V to Robert Dingley,* p24; Hanway, *Thoughts,* 1st ed., p51; and Hanway, *Reflections,* Vol. II, p334.

148. Magdalen Hospital, *Rise, Progress and Present State,* 4th ed., p208.

149. Jordanova, 'The popularisation of medicine,' p77.

150. Hanway, *A Plan for Establishing a Charity-House,* p23; Magdalen Hospital, *The Plan,* p17; and Magdalen Hospital (1776) *An Account of the Rise, Progress and Present State of the Magdalen Hospital,* 5th ed. (London) p323.

151. Magdalen Hospital, *Rise, Progress and Present State,* 5th ed., p314 and p317.

152. Hanway, *A Plan for Establishing a Charity-House,* p35 and p37.

153. Magdalen Hospital, *The Plan,* p16, and Dingley, *Proposals,* p13.

154. Hanway, *Reflections,* Vol. II, p425.

155. Hanway, *Reflections,* Vol. I, p26.

156. Hanway, *Thoughts,* 1st ed., p10 and p28; Massie, *A Plan,* pp32–33; Fielding, *A Plan for a Preservatory and Reformatory,* p18; and Hanway, *Reflections,* Vol. II, pp328–329 and p419.

157. Hanway, *Reflections,* Vol. II, p337.

158. Magdalen Hospital, *Rise, Progress and Present State,* 4th ed., p222.

159. Magdalen Hospital, *Rise, Progress and Present State,* 4th ed., p216.

160. Hanway, *Reflections,* Vol. II, p429.

161. Such an unmediated relationship between God and the individual was characteristic of Protestantism. See Campbell, *The Romantic Ethic;* Hill, *Reformation to Industrial Revolution;* and Barker-Benfield, *The Culture of Sensibility,* p83.

162. Hanway, *Reflections,* Vol. II, p337. Note also that there were punishments for swearing, telling lies, and spreading malicious stories; see Hanway, *A Plan for Establishing a Charity-House,* p36.

163. Hanway, *Reflections,* Vol. II, p349.

164. Magdalen Hospital, *Rules, Orders and Regulations,* 2d ed., p6.

165. The same basic picture appears in Magdalen Hospital (1769) *The Rules, Orders and Regulations, of the Magdalen House, for the Reception of Penitent Prostitutes* 4th ed. (London), and in Magdalen Hospital, *Rise, Progress and Present State,* 4th ed. and 5th ed., but without the woman at the base of the tree. It was perhaps too much to suggest in its official literature that such behaviour was possible within the walls of the institution.

166. Hanway, *Reflections,* Vol. II, p349 and p421. On eighteenth-century meanings of kneeling, see Barker-Benfield, *The Culture of Sensibility,* p295.

167. Evans, *The Fabrication of Virtue,* p71, is wrong to suggest that this was the case.

168. Hanway, *A Plan for Establishing a Charity-House,* footnote p21.

169. Magdalen Hospital, *The Plan,* p16 and pp19–20; Hanway, *A Plan for Establishing a Charity-House,* p22 and p36. That this was for solitary reflec-

tion rather than for a group is supported by Dingley's proposal of a small apartment 'for each of the most serious, and best-behaved'; see Dingley, *Proposals,* p14.

170. Bender, *Imagining the Penitentiary,* p44, and Ignatieff, *A Just Measure of Pain,* p54.

171. *The Histories of Some of the Penitents,* Vol. I, xiii.

172. Hanway, *The Defects of Police,* pp52–55 and p65; Hanway, *Solitude in Imprisonment,* pp31–32; and Jonas Hanway (1781) *Distributive Justice and Mercy* (London) pp174–175.

173. *The Histories of Some of the Penitents,* Vol. I, xiii–xiv and p127; Dodd, *The Magdalen,* pp77–78, who was brought to repentance within the institution. See also Hanway, *Thoughts,* 1st ed., p29.

174. Hanway, *Solitude in Imprisonment,* pp98–99.

175. Hanway, *Reflections,* Vol. II, pp328–329.

176. Hanway, *A Plan for Establishing a Charity-House,* p5, and Hanway, *Reflections,* Vol. II, p295. He goes on to say that 'the *higher* classes, from *false* reasoning, and many of the *lower* from no reasoning at all, are apt to go into *strange excesses.*'

177. Hanway, *A Plan for Establishing a Charity-House,* x; Hanway, *Thoughts,* 1st ed., p37; and Hanway, *Reflections,* Vol. I, p27 and Vol. II, p291.

178. Hanway, *Thoughts,* 1st ed., p18, and Hanway, *Reflections,* Vol. II, pp415–416.

179. Hanway, *Reflections,* Vol. II, p416; Hanway, *A Plan for Establishing a Charity-House,* p34; and Hanway, *Thoughts,* 1st ed., p10.

180. Barker-Benfield, *The Culture of Sensibility,* and Claudia L. Johnson (1995) *Equivocal Beings: Politics, Gender, and Sentimentality in the 1790s. Wollstonecraft, Radcliffe, Burney, Austen* (University of Chicago Press, Chicago). Wollstonecraft is quoted in Kowaleski-Wallace, *Consuming Subjects,* p139.

181. Hanway, *Thoughts,* 1st ed., p17.

182. Hanway, *Reflections,* Vol. II, p307.

183. Hanway, *Reflections,* Vol. II, p307 and Marchant, *Observations,* p9.

184. Hanway, *Thoughts,* 1st ed., p14.

185. Massie, *A Plan,* p23.

186. Fielding, *A Plan for a Preservatory and Reformatory,* p23, and Magdalen Hospital, *Rise, Progress and Present State,* 4th ed., p20.

187. Hanway, *Thoughts,* 1st ed., p30.

188. Hanway, *Reflections,* Vol. II, p415.

189. Hanway, *Thoughts,* 1st ed., p28.

190. Lloyd, ' "Pleasure's golden Bait," ' p53 and p63.

191. Magdalen Hospital, *Rules, Orders and Regulations,* 2d ed., p8.

192. See, e.g., Ignatieff, *A Just Measure of Pain;* Foucault, *Discipline and Punish;* and Dario Melossi and Massimo Pavarini (1981) *The Prison and the Factory: Origins of the Penitentiary System* (Macmillan, Basingstoke, UK).

193. Ignatieff, *A Just Measure of Pain.*

194. *Dictionary of National Biography* Vol. VIII, p1197, and Taylor, *Jonas Hanway.*

CHAPTER 3

1. Quoted in Sir Walter Besant (1902) *London in the Eighteenth Century* (Adam & Charles Black, London) p91.
2. Eric L. Jones and Malcolm E. Falkus (1990) 'Urban improvement and the English economy in the seventeenth and eighteenth centuries,' in Peter Borsay (ed.) *The Eighteenth-Century Town: A Reader in English Urban History, 1688–1820* (Longman, London) pp116–158 [originally published in 1979], and Peter Borsay (1989) *The English Urban Renaissance: Culture and Society in the Provincial Town, 1660–1770* (Clarendon Press, Oxford).
3. Penelope J. Corfield (1990) 'Walking the streets: The urban odyssey in eighteenth-century England,' *Journal of Urban History* 16 p150. Corfield is specifically referring to the paving stones that are my key concern here. Similarly, Malcolm E. Falkus (1976) 'Lighting in the dark ages of English economic history: Town streets before the Industrial Revolution,' in D. C. Coleman and A. H. John (eds.) *Trade and Economy in Pre-Industrial England: Essays Presented to F. J. Fisher* (Wiedenfeld and Nicolson, London) pp248–73, argues that '[t]he development of artificial lighting provides one of the major divisions between modern and pre-modern towns' (p248).
4. Jürgen Habermas (1989) *The Structural Transformation of the Public Sphere: An Inquiry into a Category of Bourgeois Society* (Polity Press, Cambridge, UK). [originally published in German in 1962]. For a variety of critical perspectives, see Craig Calhoun (ed.) (1992) *Habermas and the Public Sphere* (MIT Press, Cambridge, MA).
5. Philip Howell (1993) 'Public space and the public sphere: Political theory and the historical geography of modernity,' *Environment and Planning D: Society and Space* 11 pp303–322. See also John Keane (1988) 'Despotism and democracy: The origins and development of the distinction between civil society and the state, 1750–1850,' in John Keane (ed.) *Civil Society and the State* (Verso, London) pp35–71. On the usefulness of Habermas to studies of the eighteenth century, see Dena Goodman (1995) 'Introduction: The public and the nation,' *Eighteenth-Century Studies* 29 pp1–4, and Roy Porter (1997) 'The new eighteenth-century social history,' in Jeremy Black (ed.) *Culture and Society in Britain, 1660–1800* (Manchester University Press, Manchester, UK) pp29–50.
6. Habermas, *The Structural Transformation of the Public Sphere*, p27.
7. Habermas, *The Structural Transformation of the Public Sphere*. See also Jürgen Habermas (1985) 'Modernity—An incomplete project,' in Hal Foster (ed.) *Postmodern Culture* (Pluto Press, London) pp3–15, and Jürgen Habermas (1987) *The Philosophical Discourse of Modernity: Twelve Lectures* (Polity Press, Cambridge, UK) Lecture 12: 'The normative content of modernity,' pp336–367.
8. A similar history is presented in Reinhart Koselleck (1988, orig. 1959) *Critique and Crisis: Enlightenment and the Pathogenesis of Modern Society* (Berg, Oxford, UK).

9. Habermas, *The Structural Transformation of the Public Sphere*, pp14–26.
10. Jürgen Habermas (1984a) *The Theory of Communicative Action, Vol. I: Reason and the Rationalisation of Society* (Heinemann, London), and Jürgen Habermas (1984b) *The Theory of Communicative Action. Vol. 2: Lifeworld and System: A Critique of Functionalist Reason* (Polity Press, Cambridge, UK).
11. Habermas does not ignore these issues (see Habermas, *The Structural Transformation of the Public Sphere*, p56), but their implications are explored in much greater depth in Joan B. Landes (1988) *Women and the Public Sphere in the Age of the French Revolution* (Cornell University Press, Ithaca, NY); E. J. Clery (1991) 'Women, publicity and the coffee-house myth,' *Women: A Cultural Review* 2 pp168–177; Mary P. Ryan (1992) 'Gender and public access: Women's politics in nineteenth-century America,' in Craig Calhoun (ed.) *Habermas and the Public Sphere* (MIT Press, Cambridge, MA); Dena Goodman (1992) 'Public sphere and private life: Toward a synthesis of current historiographical approaches to the old regime,' *History and Theory* 31 pp1–20; Lawrence E. Klein (1993) 'Gender, conversation and the public sphere in early eighteenth-century England,' in Judith Still and Michael Worton (eds.) *Textuality and Sexuality: Reading Theories and Practices* (Manchester University Press, Manchester, UK) pp100–115; and Lawrence E. Klein (1995a) 'Gender and the public/private distinction in the eighteenth century: Some questions about evidence and analytical procedure,' *Eighteenth-Century Studies* 29 pp97–109.
12. Habermas, *The Structural Transformation of the Public Sphere*, p30.
13. Habermas, *The Structural Transformation of the Public Sphere*, p51.
14. Habermas, *The Structural Transformation of the Public Sphere*, p30 and p49. See also Anthony J. La Vopa (1992) 'Conceiving a public: Ideas and society in eighteenth-century Europe,' *Journal of Modern History* 64 pp79–116.
15. Goodman, 'Public sphere and private life,' and Klein, 'Gender and the public/private distinction.'
16. Nancy Fraser (1992) 'Rethinking the public sphere: A contribution to the critique of actually existing democracy,' in Craig Calhoun (ed.) *Habermas and the Public Sphere* (MIT Press, Cambridge, MA) pp109–142, and Goodman, 'Public sphere and private life.'
17. Klein, 'Gender and the public/private distinction'; Howell, 'Public space and the public sphere'; and Derek Gregory (1989) 'The crisis of modernity? Human geography and critical social theory,' in Richard Peet and Nigel Thrift (eds.) *New Models in Geography: The Political Economy Perspective.* (Unwin Hyman, London) Vol. II, pp348–385.
18. Clery, 'Women, publicity and the coffee-house myth,' and Peter Stallybrass and Allon White (1986) *The Politics and Poetics of Transgression* (Methuen, London) p82.
19. For the street theatre of eighteenth-century politics, see George Rudé (1959) 'The London "mob" of the eighteenth century,' *Historical Journal* 2 pp1–18; Nicholas Rogers (1978) 'Popular protest in early Hanoverian London,' *Past and Present* 79 pp70–100; John Stevenson (1979) *Popular*

Disturbances in England (Longman, London); and Robert B. Shoemaker (1987) 'The London "mob" in the early eighteenth century,' *Journal of British Studies* 26 pp273–304.

20. Habermas, *The Structural Transformation of the Public Sphere*, p158.
21. Richard Sennett (1974) *The Fall of Public Man* (Cambridge University Press, Cambridge) p17, p84 and p264. See also David Scobey (1992) 'Anatomy of the promenade: the politics of bourgeois sociability in nineteenth-century New York,' *Social History* 17 pp203–227.
22. Klein, 'Gender and the public/private distinction'; G. J. Barker-Benfield (1992) *The Culture of Sensibility: Sex and Society in Eighteenth-Century Britain* (University of Chicago Press, Chicago); and David H. Solkin (1993) *Painting for Money: The Visual Arts and the Public Sphere in Eighteenth-Century England* (Yale University Press, New Haven, CT). For a useful parallel discussion that interprets the resurfacing of turnpike roads in terms of political identities within the public sphere of a commercial society, see Greg Laugero (1995) 'Infrastructures of enlightenment: Road-making, the public sphere, and the emergence of literature,' *Eighteenth-Century Studies* 29 pp45–67.
23. Barker-Benfield, *The Culture of Sensibility*, p105. This ran counter to the ideas of John Locke who had designed the programme for Shaftesbury's early education.
24. Anthony Ashley Cooper, 3d Earl of Shaftesbury (1711) *Characteristics of Men, Manners, Opinions, Times* (London) Vol. II, p77.
25. Shaftesbury, *Characteristics*, Vol. II, p23, p176 and p80.
26. Barker-Benfield, *The Culture of Sensibility*, p105, and Shaftesbury, *Characteristics*, Vol. II, p139, p98 and pp101–102.
27. Shaftesbury, *Characteristics*, Vol. II, p163, p166 and p171.
28. Shaftesbury, *Characteristics*, Vol. I, pp115–116. This is from Shaftesbury's essay '*Sensus Communis:* An essay on the freedom of wit and humour.'
29. Shaftesbury, *Characteristics*, Vol. II, p63.
30. Shaftesbury, *Characteristics*, Vol. II, p118 and pp139–140.
31. Shaftesbury, *Characteristics*, Vol. II, p155 and p161.
32. Shaftesbury, *Characteristics*, Vol. II, p101.
33. Shaftesbury, *Characteristics*, Vol. II, p137.
34. Shaftesbury, *Characteristics*, Vol. I, p111.
35. J.G.A. Pocock (1975) *The Machiavellian Moment: Florentine Political Thought and the Atlantic Republican Tradition* (Princeton University Press, Princeton, NJ).
36. Stephen Copley (1992) 'The fine arts in eighteenth-century polite culture,' in John Barrell (ed.) *Painting and the Politics of Culture: New Essays on British Art, 1700–1850* (Oxford University Press, Oxford) pp16–17, and J.G.A. Pocock (1985) *Virtue, Commerce, and History: Essays on Political Thought and History, Chiefly in the Eighteenth Century* (Cambridge University Press, Cambridge) p50.
37. John Barrell (1992) 'Introduction,' in John Barrell (ed.) *Painting and the Politics of Culture: New Essays on British Art, 1700–1850* (Oxford University Press, Oxford) p7.

38. David H. Solkin (1992) 'ReWrighting Shaftesbury: The air pump and the limits of commercial humanism,' in John Barrell (ed.) *Painting and the Politics of Culture: New Essays on British Art 1700–1850* (Oxford University Press, Oxford) p84; quote from Shaftesbury on p85. See also Solkin, *Painting for Money,* p7.

39. Solkin, *Painting for Money,* p22 and p25.

40. Klein, 'Gender, conversation and the public sphere,' p109, and Lawrence E. Klein (1989) 'Liberty, manners and politeness in early eighteenth-century England,' *Historical Journal* 32 p586. See also Barker-Benfield, *The Culture of Sensibility,* p110.

41. Lawrence E. Klein (1984–1985) 'The Third Earl of Shaftesbury and the progress of politeness,' *Eighteenth-Century Studies* 18 p213 and Solkin, *Painting for Money,* p4.

42. Shaftesbury, *Characteristics,* Vol. I, p75.

43. Klein, 'Liberty, manners and politeness,' p602.

44. Shaftesbury, *Characteristics,* Vol. II, pp133–134.

45. Klein, 'Shaftesbury and the progress of politeness,' p211. Shaftesbury's choice of Athens is significant. It is a sign of the Whiggish connection being forged between 'virtue and refinement' rather than the Spartan or classical Roman 'virtuous simplicity' of the country ideology that is most identified with civic republicanism. See Solkin, *Painting for Money,* p25, and Lawrence E. Klein (1994) *Shaftesbury and the Culture of Politeness: Moral Discourse and Cultural Politics in Early Eighteenth-Century England* (Cambridge University Press, Cambridge).

46. Klein, 'Shaftesbury and the progress of politeness,' p211.

47. Jack Prostko (1989) ' "Natural conversation set in view": Shaftesbury and moral speech,' *Eighteenth-Century Studies* 23 p58 and footnote 26 p53, and Klein, *Shaftesbury and the Culture of Politeness,* p206.

48. Mandeville first published a poem entitled *The Grumbling Hive* (1705), a Whig tract in defence of the Duke of Marlborough; see Francis McKee (1988) 'Early criticism of *The Grumbling Hive,*' *Notes and Queries* 35 pp176–177. This formed the basis for the 1714 first edition of *The Fable of the Bees; or, Private Vices Publick Benefits* (London) the ideas for which were honed in a print debate with Richard Steele; see M. M. Goldsmith (1976) 'Public virtue and private vices: Bernard Mandeville and English political ideologies in the early eighteenth century,' *Eighteenth-Century Studies* 9 pp477–510. However, it was the second edition in 1723 that stirred the most controversy. Mandeville even had to defend himself against a grand jury charge that he had created a plan 'to debauch the nation'; see Barker-Benfield, *The Culture of Sensibility,* p123.

49. E. J. Hundert (1995) 'Bernard Mandeville and the Enlightenment's maxims of modernity,' *Journal of the History of Ideas* 56 p591, and Barker-Benfield, *The Culture of Sensibility,* xxxii.

50. Anne Mette Hjort (1991) 'Mandeville's ambivalent modernity,' *Modern Language Notes* 106 p954, and Mandeville, *The Fable of the Bees,* p138.

51. Mandeville, *The Fable of the Bees,* no pagination.

52. Mandeville, *The Fable of the Bees*, p19.
53. Mandeville, *The Fable of the Bees*, p8.
54. Mandeville, *The Fable of the Bees*, p81.
55. Mandeville, *The Fable of the Bees*, p34; see also pp24–31 and p86. On Mandeville's economics, see Salim Rashid (1985) 'Mandeville's *Fable*: Laissez-faire or libertinism?,' *Eighteenth-Century Studies* 18 pp313–330.
56. E.g., on meat eating, see Mandeville, *The Fable of the Bees*, pp148–149.
57. Mandeville, *The Fable of the Bees*, no pagination.
58. Solkin, *Painting for Money*, p78.
59. David Hume (1758) *Essays and Treatises on Several Subjects* (London) p29, p56 and p163. In particular, see Hume's essay 'Of Luxury.' See Chapter 4 for a fuller discussion of the debate over luxury.
60. Hume, *Essays*, p38.
61. Solkin, *Painting for Money*, and Barker-Benfield, *The Culture of Sensibility*, p133.
62. Hume, *Essays*, p12. See esp. Part I, Essay IV: 'That Politics May Be Reduced to a Science'; Essay V: 'Of the First Principles of Government'; Essay XV: 'Of Civil Liberty'; and Essay XXIV: 'Of National Characters'; and Part II, Essay XIV: 'Idea of a Perfect Commonwealth.'
63. Hume, *Essays*, p111; see also p16.
64. Hume, *Essays*, p31 and p259.
65. Hume, *Essays*, p17.
66. Hume, *Essays*, pp91–92 and p52.
67. Hume, *Essays*, p82 and p83.
68. Hume, *Essays*, p112.
69. Goodman, 'Public sphere and private life'; Landes, *Women and the Public Sphere*; and Klein, 'Gender, conversation and the public sphere.'
70. Hume, *Essays*, p27.
71. Kathleen Wilson (1995a) 'Citizenship, empire, and modernity in the English provinces, c. 1720–1790,' *Eighteenth-Century Studies* 29 pp69–96, and Stephen J. Daniels (1993) 'The country and the city,' *Journal of Historical Geography* 19 p456.
72. Hume, *Essays*, p112 and p125. See David Miller (1981) *Philosophy and Ideology in Hume's Political Thought* (Clarendon Press, Oxford), and Felicity Nussbaum (1990) 'The politics of difference,' *Eighteenth-Century Studies* 23 p378.
73. Hume, *Essays*, p154, and Christopher J. Berry (1994) *The Idea of Luxury: A Conceptual and Historical Investigation* (Cambridge University Press, Cambridge) pp142–152.
74. Pocock, *Virtue, Commerce, and History*, p250.
75. Hume, *Essays*, p159.
76. Wolfgang Schivelbusch (1988) *Disenchanted Night: The Industrialisation of Light in the Nineteenth Century* (Berg, Oxford, UK) p85. The lighting of Paris had to wait until 1667.
77. Sir Charles Whitworth (1771) *Observations on the New Westminster Paving Act* (London) p47. For a precise chronology and reactions to the new

paving, including praise from the political economist James Steuart, see Sidney Webb and Beatrice Webb (1922) *English Local Government: Statutory Authorities for Special Purposes* (Longmans, Green and Co., London) pp276–287.

78. John Pugh (1787) *Remarkable Occurrences in the Life of Jonas Hanway* (London) p139.

79. Jones and Falkus, 'Urban improvement,' and Falkus, 'Lighting in the dark ages of English economic history.' Traditionally the job of scavengers would also have been filled by the householders in rotation.

80. 13 &14 Car. II cap 2 [1662]. On the politics of this legislation, see Mark Jenner (1995) 'The politics of London air: John Evelyn's *Fumifugium* and the Restoration,' *Historical Journal* 38 pp535–551.

81. 13 &14 Car. II cap 2 [1662].

82. Schivelbusch, *Disenchanted Night*, p82. Until the seventeenth century there were also legal prohibitions on being out in the city at night; see Falkus, 'Lighting in the dark ages of English economic history.'

83. 2 William and Mary session 2 cap 8 [1690].

84. 2 Geo. II cap 11 [1728].

85. *A Bill for Paving, Cleansing, Enlightening and Keeping in Repair the Street Called Pall Mall . . . Read 22nd May 1751* pp1–2.

86. *Reasons for the Petition for Better Paving, Cleansing and Lighting the Streets of Westminster* (London, 1753).

87. John Spranger (1754) *A Proposal or Plan for an Act of Parliament for the Better Paving, Cleansing and Lighting of the Streets, Lanes, Courts and Alleys, and Other Open Passages, and for the Removal of Nuisances, as well within the Several Parishes of the City and Liberty of Westminster . . .* (London); a slightly amended second edition was published in 1756.

88. For other arguments that the improvement commissions represent significantly new forms of urban politics, see Webb and Webb, *English Local Government*; J. H. Plumb (1950) *England in the Eighteenth Century* (Penguin, Harmondsworth, UK); Jones and Falkus, 'Urban improvement'; and Peter Borsay (1990) 'Introduction,' in Peter Borsay (ed.) *The Eighteenth-Century Town: A Reader in English Urban History, 1688–1820* (Longman, London) pp1–38.

89. Spranger, *A Proposal*, no pagination.

90. All quotes are from Spranger, *A Proposal*, no pagination.

91. Spranger, *A Proposal*, no pagination.

92. Spranger, *A Proposal*, no pagination.

93. Spranger, *A Proposal*, p2.

94. He noted that 'as no rate is to be made for Paving, no Person can complain of a Grievance or Injury, when he is compellable to repair no more, than concerns himself, nor more than at present by Law he is obliged'; Spranger, *A Proposal*, 2d ed., footnote p3 and footnote p12.

95. Spranger, *A Proposal*, pp3–4.

96. Spranger, *A Proposal*, 2d ed., p4.

97. Falkus, 'Lighting in the dark ages of English economic history.'

98. Spranger, *A Proposal*, pp9–10.

99. Spranger, *A Proposal*, 2d ed., footnote p18.

100. Jonas Hanway (1754) *A Letter to Mr John Spranger, On His Excellent Proposal for Paving, Cleansing and Lighting the Streets of Westminster* (London) pp21–22, p4, p6, p10 and p50.

101. *Journals of the House of Commons* XXIX [1762], p233. See also Whitworth, *Observations*, p9.

102. 2 Geo. III cap 21 [1762].

103. M. Dorothy George (1987, orig. 1925) *London Life in the Eighteenth Century* (Penguin, Harmondsworth, UK) p107.

104. The act did not cover those London squares that already had similar, if more local, acts in force, e.g., St James's Square, Lincoln's Inn Fields, and Golden Square. See Henry W. Lawrence (1993) 'The greening of the squares of London: Transformation of urban landscapes and ideals,' *Annals of the Association of American Geographers* 83 pp90–118.

105. A Member of Parliament (1769?) *An Explanation of the Proposed Scheme for Better Paving, Repairing, Cleaning and Lighting the Squares, Streets and Lanes of the City and Liberty of Westminster* . . . (London). To qualify to be a commissioner men had to have property worth £300 per annum or a personal estate of £10,000. This was the highest level set in the country and provoked resentment among the tradesmen who helped govern the Westminster parishes. See Paul Langford (1991) *Public Life and the Propertied Englishman, 1689–1798* (Clarendon Press, Oxford) p235.

106. Langford, *Public Life and the Propertied Englishman*, pp453–454.

107. 2 Geo. III cap 21 [1762]. The more general point is made by Philippe Ariès who argues that '[t]he "social space" liberated by the rise of the state and the decline of communal forms of sociability was occupied by the individual, who established himself—in the state's shadow, as it were—in a variety of settings'; quoted in Goodman, 'Public sphere and private life,' p9.

108. Rates for urban improvements have a much longer history, but the extent to which they were raised and their alteration of the responsibilities for the urban environment is most dramatic after 1762. See Jones and Falkus, 'Urban improvement,' and Falkus, 'Lighting in the dark ages of English economic history.'

109. 4 Geo. III cap 39 [1764) and 9 Geo. III cap 13 [1769].

110. 5 Geo. III cap 50 [1765].

111. Charles Walcot (1763) *Considerations for the More Speedy and Effectual Execution of the Act, for Paving, Cleansing, and Lighting the City and Liberty of Westminster, and for Removing Annoyances Therein* (London) p7. Walcot also rather optimistically suggested that people were wholly reconciled to the new rate after a year.

112. Walcot, *Considerations*; 5 Geo. III cap 13 [1765]; and *Queries against the Intended Daily Toll for Paving the Streets of Westminster* (London, 1766?).

113. Zachery Zeal (1764?) *A Seasonable Alarm to the City of London, on the Present Important Crisis, Shewing by Most Convincing Arguments, That the New*

Method of Paving the Streets with Scotch Pebbles and the Pulling Down of the Signs, Must Be Both Equally Pernicious to the Health and Morals of the People of England (London). This used paving as a vehicle to satirise the prevalence of Scots in public positions within England.

114. *Dictionary of National Biography* (Hereafter *DNB*).

115. John Gwynn (1766) *London and Westminster Improved* (London) iii–vi. See also his earlier proposal for an academy for painting, sculpture and architecture which again was to improve the public realm: John Gwynn (1749) *An Essay on Design: Including Proposals for Erecting a Public Academy . . . for Educating the British Youth in Drawing* (London).

116. Gwynn, *London and Westminster Improved*, vii and xiv–xv.

117. Gwynn, *London and Westminster Improved*, p1.

118. Gwynn, *London and Westminster Improved*, p3, p7, p8, p10 and p4. As he said, '[N]othing seems to have been considered but the interest of a few tasteless builders' (p5).

119. Gwynn, *London and Westminster Improved*, pp17–18. Fittingly, in 1771 John Gwynn was appointed surveyor to the new board of commissioners under the Oxford Paving Act; see *DNB*.

120. Gwynn, *London and Westminster Improved*, p6.

121. Gwynn, *London and Westminster Improved*, pp6–7.

122. Gwynn, *London and Westminster Improved*, p130, also referred to the paving as 'the best scheme that ever was thought of for the improvement of any city' (p132).

123. Gwynn, *London and Westminster Improved*, p20.

124. On the power of the Westminster vestries, see George, *London Life in the Eighteenth Century*, and Langford, *Public Life and the Propertied Englishman*.

125. *Observations on the Bill for Paving, Cleansing, Lighting and Regulating the Squares, &c. within the City and Liberty of Westminster . . .* (London, 1767) p1 and p3; *The Paving of Westminster Was Originally Begun upon Public Money . . .* (London, 1769); *Considerations on the New Paving Bill* (London, 1769); and *Observations upon the Considerations on the New Paving Bill* (London, 1769) pp1–2.

126. *Observations upon the Considerations on the New Paving Bill*, p2.

127. *Considerations on the New Paving Bill*, p3.

128. Langford, *Public Life and the Propertied Englishman*, p454.

129. 11 Geo. III cap 22 (1771). The rate had to be less than 1s in the pound for a street and 1s 3d for a square. The commission were empowered to collect the rate only if the committee failed to do so. See Whitworth, *Observations*.

130. Webb and Webb, *English Local Government*, p287, and Langford, *Public Life and the Propertied Englishman*, pp454–455.

131. John Gay (1716) *Trivia; or, The Art of Walking the Streets of London* (London). It is the second edition, also of 1716, that is referred to below. 'Trivia' was the Roman goddess of roadways. See Corfield, 'Walking the streets.'

132. Corfield, 'Walking the streets,' p136, quoting Pat Rogers (1974) *The Augustan Vision* (Wiedenfeld and Nicolson, London) p220.

133. All references below are to the fourth edition: Ned Ward (1709) *The London Spy Compleat in Eighteen Parts* (London), reprinted in Paul Hyland (ed.) (1993) '*The London Spy': Ned Ward's Classic Account of Underworld Life in Eighteenth-Century London* (Colleagues Press, East Lansing, MI).

134. *A Brief Description of the Cities of London and Westminster, the Public Buildings, Palaces, Gardens, Squares, &c. With an Alphabetical List of All the Streets, Squares, Courts, Lanes, and Alleys, &c. within the Bills of Mortality* (London, 1776).

135. Paul Hyland (1993) 'Introduction,' in Paul Hyland (ed.) (1993) '*The London Spy': Ned Ward's Classic Account of Underworld Life in Eighteenth-Century London* (Colleagues Press, East Lansing, MI) xviii.

136. *DNB*.

137. Ward, *The London Spy*, p292.

138. Hyland, 'Introduction,' xiii and xiv.

139. Ward, *The London Spy*, p281.

140. Ward, *The London Spy*, pp10–11 and p34.

141. Ward, *The London Spy*, p180.

142. Hyland, 'Introduction,' xvii.

143. Ward, *The London Spy*, p225, p59 and p61. Even that 'metropolitan maypole,' The Monument, was supposedly built by cheating the poor orphans of their money (pp50–51).

144. See Ward, *The London Spy*, pp69–70, pp168–169 and pp118–119.

145. Gay, *Trivia*, p15.

146. Rogers, *The Augustan Vision*.

147. Gay, *Trivia*, p42.

148. Corfield, 'Walking the streets,' p154, and Paul Langford (1989) *A Polite and Commercial People: England, 1727–1783* (Oxford University Press, Oxford) p425.

149. Gay, *Trivia*, p22.

150. Ward, *The London Spy*, p281.

151. *Brief Description of . . . London and Westminster*, p161, iii and xii.

152. *Brief Description of . . . London and Westminster*, pp14–15, vii and viii.

153. *Brief Description of . . . London and Westminster*, p161 and viii.

154. Spranger, *A Proposal*, no pagination.

155. See Michel De Certeau (1984) *The Practice of Everyday Life* (University of California Press, Berkeley and Los Angeles) Chapter 7: 'Walking in the city,' for an interpretation of the politics of such a transparent view of the city.

156. *Brief Description of . . . London and Westminster*, ix.

157. Corfield, 'Walking the streets,' p132.

158. Ward, *The London Spy*, pp221–225 and p182.

159. See, e.g., Ward, *The London Spy*, pp136–137, p162, p183 and p189, and Elizabeth Bennett Kubek (1995) 'Women's participation in the urban culture of early modern London: Images from fiction,' in Ann Bermingham and John Brewer (eds.) *The Consumption of Culture, 1600–1800: Image, Object, Text* (Routledge, London) pp440–454.

160. Gay, *Trivia*, pp17–18.

161. Gay, *Trivia*, p4, p6, p30 and p36.
162. *Brief Description of . . . London and Westminster*, xiv and xxv.
163. *Brief Description of . . . London and Westminster*, xxiv.
164. Ward, *The London Spy*, p132 and p188.
165. Ward, *The London Spy*, p299.
166. Ward, *The London Spy*, p56, p67, p101, p103 and pp221–225.
167. *Brief Description of . . . London and Westminster*, xxii and xxviii.
168. *Brief Description of . . . London and Westminster*, xxxi.
169. Gay, *Trivia*, p1.
170. Gay, *Trivia*, p16, and Stallybrass and White, *The Politics and Poetics of Transgression*.
171. Gay, *Trivia*, p47.
172. Gay, *Trivia*, p38. See also the discussion of nineteenth-century Paris in Marshall Berman (1983) *All That Is Solid Melts Into Air: The Experience of Modernity* (Verso, London) p159, where 'the archetypal modern man . . . is a pedestrian thrown into the maelstrom of modern traffic.'
173. Gay, *Trivia*, p2.
174. Scobey, 'Anatomy of the promenade,' and Keith Tester (1994) *The Flâneur* (Routledge, London).
175. Habermas, *The Structural Transformation of the Public Sphere*, p27.
176. Paul D. Glennie and Nigel J. Thrift (1992) 'Modernity, urbanism and modern consumption,' *Environment and Planning D: Society and Space* 10 pp423–443.
177. Zeal, *A Seasonable Alarm*.

CHAPTER 4

1. For Bate and Hartley, see *Dictionary of National Biography* (hereafter *DNB*).
2. Thomas Lyttelton is primarily remembered for the foretelling of his death by a spectral visitation. This became one of the most celebrated and retold ghost stories of the subsequent century; see *DNB* and Terry Castle (1995) *The Female Thermometer: Eighteenth-Century Culture and the Invention of the Uncanny* (Oxford University Press, Oxford) p169.
3. For Fitzgerald, see Mary MacCarthy (1930) *Fighting Fitzgerald and Other Papers* (Martin Secker, London). See also *The Trials of George Robert Fitzgerald, Esq; and Timothy Brecknock . . .* (Dublin, 1786); *The Life of George Robert Fitzgerald, Esq* (London, 1786); and *Authentic Memoirs of George Robert Fitzgerald, Esq; With a Full Account of His Trial and Execution for the Murder of Patrick Randall McDonnell, Esq* (London, 1786).
4. Figure 7 is taken from the frontispiece of *The Vauxhall Affray; or, The Macaronies Defeated: Being a Compilation of All the Letters, Squibs etc. on Both Sides of That Dispute* 2d ed. (London, 1773). This collected all the correspondence and commentary on the 'Affray' in the press and resold it to an eager public.

5. *The Vauxhall Affray,* p14.

6. For other interpretations of this incident, see Kristina Straub (1992) *Sexual Suspects: Eighteenth-Century Players and Sexual Ideology* (Princeton University Press, Princeton, NJ) pp16–22, and Peter de Bolla (1996) 'The visibility of visuality,' in Teresa Brennan and Martin Jay (eds.) *Vision in Context: Historical and Contemporary Perspective on Sight* (Routledge, London) pp63–81. For similar incidents, see the newspaper cuttings for 20 May 1751 [f181], 9 June 1759 [f215], and 9 May 1769 [ff243–244], in *A Collection of Tickets, Bills of Performance, Pamphlets, Ms. Notes, Engravings and Extracts and Cuttings from Books and Periodicals Relating to Vauxhall Gardens. Originally Made by Jacob Henry Burn,* which is in the British Library [hereafter referred to as Burn Collection].

7. Roy Porter (1996) 'Material pleasures in the consumer society,' in Roy Porter and Mary Mulvey Roberts (eds.) *Pleasure in the Eighteenth Century* (Macmillan, Basingstoke, UK) pp19–35.

8. John Brewer (1995) '"The most polite age and the most vicious": Attitudes towards culture as a commodity, 1660–1800,' in Ann Bermingham and John Brewer (eds.) *The Consumption of Culture, 1600–1800: Image, Object, Text* (Routledge, London) pp341–361.

9. David H. Solkin (1993) *Painting for Money: The Visual Arts and the Public Sphere in Eighteenth-Century England* (Yale University Press, New Haven, CT). The quotation is from p106. Solkin interprets Vauxhall through the lens provided by Peter Stallybrass and Allon White (1986) *The Politics and Poetics of Transgression* (Methuen, London).

10. The notion of an eighteenth-century 'consumer revolution' is developed in Neil McKendrick, John Brewer and J. H. Plumb (eds.) (1983) *The Birth of a Consumer Society: The Commercialisation of Eighteenth-Century England* (Hutchinson, London). More recent collections have broadened the interpretations of eighteenth-century cultures of consumption; see John Brewer and Roy Porter (eds.) (1993) *Consumption and the World of Goods* (Routledge, London), and Ann Bermingham and John Brewer (eds.) *The Consumption of Culture, 1600–1800: Image, Object, Text* (Routledge, London).

11. Neil McKendrick (1983) 'The consumer revolution of eighteenth-century England,' in Neil McKendrick, John Brewer and J. H. Plumb (eds.) *The Birth of a Consumer Society: The Commercialisation of Eighteenth-Century England* (Hutchinson, London) p43.

12. Elizabeth Wilson (1987) *Adorned in Dreams: Fashion and Modernity* (University of California Press, Berkeley and Los Angeles). Lieven de Cauter (1993) 'The panoramic ecstatsy: On world exhibitions and the disintegration of experience,' *Theory, Culture and Society* 10 pp1–23, describes 'the shock of the new' as 'one of the crucial modern sensations' (p10) and argues that it is 'mostly experienced as pleasure, the pleasure of fashion and shopping, the fascination and fetishism emanating from commodity [*sic*]' (p19).

13. On novelty, see Neil McKendrick (1983) 'Introduction,' in Neil McK-

endrick, John Brewer and J. H. Plumb (eds.) *The Birth of a Consumer Society: The Commercialisation of Eighteenth-Century England* (Hutchinson, London) p2; J. H. Plumb (1983) 'The acceptance of modernity,' in Neil McKendrick, John Brewer and J. H. Plumb (eds.) *The Birth of a Consumer Society: The Commercialisation of Eighteenth-Century England* (Hutchinson, London); and Terry Lovell (1995) 'Subjective powers? Consumption, the reading public and domestic women in early-eighteenth-century England,' in Ann Bermingham and John Brewer (eds.) *The Consumption of Culture, 1600–1800: Image, Object, Text* (Routledge, London) p25. On identities, see Wilson, *Adorned in Dreams,* and Paul D. Glennie and Nigel J. Thrift (1996) 'Consumers, identities and consumption spaces in early-modern England,' *Environment and Planning A* 28 pp25–45.

14. John Dixon Hunt (1985) *Vauxhall and London's Garden Theatres* (Chadwyck Healey, Cambridge, UK) p17.

15. Brewer, '"The most polite age and the most vicious"'; John Brewer (1997) *The Pleasures of the Imagination: English Culture in the Eighteenth Century* (Harper Collins, London); James Raven (1992) *Judging New Wealth: Popular Publishing and Responses to Commerce in England, 1750–1800* (Clarendon Press, Oxford); Terry Castle (1986) *Masquerade and Civilization: The Carnivalesque in Eighteenth-Century English Culture and Fiction* (Methuen, London); and John-Christophe Agnew (1993) 'Coming up for air: Consumer culture in historical perspective,' in John Brewer and Roy Porter (eds.) *Consumption and the World of Goods* (Routledge, London) pp19–39.

16. See *The Spectator* 383, 20 May 1712.

17. Vauxhall Gardens were open from May to August and were visited by around a thousand people every night; see James Edwards (1789) *Description of Southwark, Lambeth, Newington, &c* (London) p23. There was, however, an audience of 12,000 for Handel's rehearsal of the fireworks music in 1749, according to *The Gentleman's Magazine* XIX, April 1749, p185. On the imitations, see *Vaux-Hall: A Poem* (Dublin, 1750), and John Goodman (1992) '"Altar against altar": The Colisée, Vauxhall utopianism and symbolic politics in Paris (1769–77),' *Art History* 15 pp434–469.

18. S. Toupee (1739a) 'An evening at Vaux-Hall,' *The Scots Magazine* 1 p324.

19. [John Lockman] (1752) *A Sketch of the Spring-Gardens, Vaux-Hall, in a Letter to a Noble Lord* p2.

20. *A Description of Vaux-Hall Gardens. Being a Proper Companion and Guide for All Who Visit That Place* (London, 1762) pp40–41.

21. *Description of Vaux-Hall Gardens,* p44. Unfortunately, they were badly affected by damp and had to be removed.

22. Palmyra's ruins would have been known to many of the visitors from the illustrations in Robert Wood (1753) *Ruins of Palmyra, Otherwise Tedmor, in the Desart* (London). See Richard D. Altick (1978) *The Shows of London: A Panoramic History of Exhibitions* (Belknap Press of Harvard University Press, Cambridge, MA) p95.

23. Frederick, the Prince of Wales, was Vauxhall Gardens' ground landlord and an occasional visitor.

24. John Noorthouck (1773) *A New History of London* (London) p693.

25. [Lockman], *Sketch of the Spring-Gardens,* p10.

26. [Lockman], *Sketch of the Spring-Gardens,* p12.

27. These paintings are listed in the *Description of Vaux-Hall Gardens* and discussed in Solkin, *Painting for Money,* and in Lawrence Gowing (1953) 'Hogarth, Hayman, and the Vauxhall decorations,' *Burlington Magazine* 95 pp4–19.

28. Toupee, 'An evening at Vaux-Hall,' 1 p364. Brewer, ' "The most polite age and the most vicious," ' p347, quotes Casanova as describing Vauxhall as a 'rural brothel.' See also *The Connoisseur* 85, September 1754, pp106–107 where the 'female thermometer' finds amorous activity in Vauxhall Gardens.

29. Tyers valued his holdings in the Gardens at £40,000 by the mid–1760s; see Burn Collection, September 1766, f237.

30. Brewer, ' "The most polite age and the most vicious," ' p347, and Altick, *The Shows of London,* p94.

31. Brian Allen (1983) 'The landscape,' in T. J. Edelstein (ed.) *Vauxhall Gardens* (Yale Center for British Art, Yale University Press, New Haven, CT) pp17–24.

32. Solkin, *Painting for Money.*

33. Mollie Sands (1946) *Invitation to Ranelagh, 1742–1803* (John Westhouse, London) and Warwick W. Wroth (1896) *The London Pleasure Gardens of the Eighteenth Century* (Macmillan, London).

34. The changes included a new triumphal arch (see *The Gentleman's Magazine* 43, May 1773, p251), extensive refurbishment, and 'modernised' decorations, including a 130-foot circumference 'Grand Temple' (see *The Universal Magazine* 78, June 1786, p329) and a 'Moving Temple' with 'Illuminated Vertical Columns in Motion' (see Burn Collection, 7 June 1792, f328).

35. Toupee, 'An evening at Vaux-Hall,' 1 p324.

36. Engravings of Canaletto's four views of Vauxhall Gardens were sold by booksellers for a shilling each along with, for sixpence, Lockman's *Sketch of the Spring-Gardens*. See newspaper cutting from April 1752 in Duchy of Cornwall Archives, Print Collection, Folder 28: *A Collection of Newspaper Cuttings and Other Papers Relating to the History of the New Spring Gardens, Popularly Known as Vauxhall,* Item 22.

37. David Coke (1984) 'Vauxhall Gardens,' in M. Snodin (ed.) *Rococo: Art and Design in Hogarth's England,* Victoria and Albert Museum Exhibition Catalogue, pp74–98.

38. An engraving of 'the Vauxhall fan' is in Duchy of Cornwall Archives, Folder 4: *Vauxhall,* along with a newspaper cutting (29 July 1739) advertising another version. *The Ladies Complete Pocket Book for 1758* was sold for 1 shilling and advertised as containing 'The favourite new songs sung last summer at Ranelagh, Vauxhall and Marylebone'; see newspaper cut-

ting from November 1757 in Burn Collection, f209. See also newspaper cuttings from July 1751 (songs), November 1752 (journal) and May 1792 (masquerade warehouses) Burn Collection, f182, f187 and f325, respectively.

39. Newspaper cuttings from 1756, Burn Collection, f204.
40. Newspaper cutting from July 1777, Burn Collection, f259.
41. Newspaper cutting from August 1777, Burn Collection, f261, and *The Evening Lessons. Being the First and Second Chapters of the Book of Entertainments* (London, 1742).
42. S. Toupee (1739b) 'An evening at Vauxhall,' *The Scots Magazine* 12 p409. See also the list of prices in *Description of Vaux-Hall Gardens*.
43. Toupee, 'An evening at Vauxhall,' 12 p409, and [Lockman], *Sketch of the Spring-Gardens*, p24.
44. See *The Evening Lessons*, p6; the 'cartoons' by Cruikshank and Collings in Duchy of Cornwall Archives, Folder 5: *Cartoons and Caricatures of Vauxhall;* and *A Second Holiday for John Gilpin; or, A Voyage to Vauxhall . . .* (London, 1785). It is even mentioned in the *DNB* entry for Jonathan Tyers.
45. *The Connoisseur* 68, 15 May 1755, pp254–255.
46. Newspaper cutting from 1797 in Vauxhall Gardens Archive, Minet Library, Borough of Lambeth. *Bound Vol. 5 (1785–1835)*, f53.
47. Timothy H. Breen (1993) 'The meanings of things: Interpreting the consumer economy in the eighteenth century,' in John Brewer and Roy Porter (eds.) *Consumption and the World of Goods* (Routledge, London), p254, and Christopher J. Berry (1994) *The Idea of Luxury: A Conceptual and Historical Investigation* (Cambridge University Press, Cambridge).
48. Berry, *The Idea of Luxury*, and John Sekora (1977) *Luxury: The Concept in Western Thought, Eden to Smollett* (Johns Hopkins University Press, Baltimore).
49. 'A Letter from an Ingenious Foreigner Now at London, to His Friend at Paris, Translated from the French from the Champion, June 24, No. 407,' reprinted in *The Gentleman's Magazine* 12, 1742, pp314–315, and 'Of the Luxury of the English; and a Description of Ranelagh Gardens and Vaux-hall, in a Letter from a Foreigner to His Friend at Paris. From The Champion August 5 No. 424,' reprinted in *The Gentleman's Magazine* 12, 1742, pp418–420. In attributing both these essays to Henry Fielding and reading them together, David Solkin has been able to correct the 'basic misreadings' of their descriptions of Vauxhall and Ranelagh as 'unequivocally positive' provided by previous historians of the Gardens; see Solkin, *Painting for Money*, footnote 24 p286. The descriptions were, however, also (mis)read as 'puffs' for Vauxhall in the eighteenth century; see *The Evening Lessons*, p9.
50. *The Gentleman's Magazine* 12, 1742, pp314–315.
51. Fielding argues that there *are* men with 'excellent Heads' and 'honest hearts,' but that the conditions under which they have to act are not favourable: see *The Gentleman's Magazine* 12, 1742, p315.
52. *The Gentleman's Magazine* 12, 1742, p418.

53. *The Gentleman's Magazine* 12, 1742, p419.

54. *The Gentleman's Magazine* 12, 1742, p420.

55. Solkin, *Painting for Money*, p120, argues that Lockman's insistence that the scene that the Gardens present is 'of the most rational, elegant, and innocent kind' ([Lockman], *Sketch of the Spring-Gardens*, p28) is much less ambiguous than Fielding's depiction of the Gardens.

56. Ann Bermingham (1995) 'Introduction. The consumption of culture: Image, object, text,' in Ann Bermingham and John Brewer (eds.) *The Consumption of Culture, 1600–1800: Image, Object, Text* (Routledge, London) p8.

57. Agnew, 'Coming up for air,' p25, and Colin Campbell (1987) *The Romantic Ethic and the Spirit of Modern Consumerism* (Basil Blackwell, Oxford, UK).

58. [Lockman], *Sketch of the Spring-Gardens*, p30.

59. [Lockman], *Sketch of the Spring-Gardens*, p24 and p16. See also *The Gentleman's Magazine* 13, August 1743, p439.

60. Robert D. Sack (1992) *Place, Modernity, and the Consumer's World: A Relational Framework for Geographical Analysis* (Johns Hopkins University Press, Baltimore) p169, and Rosalind H. Williams (1982) *Dream Worlds: Mass Consumption in Late Nineteenth-Century France* (University of California Press, Berkeley and Los Angeles).

61. Brewer, '"The most polite age and the most vicious,"' p345.

62. Castle, *Masquerade and Civilization,* and Solkin, *Painting for Money*.

63. Brewer, '"The most polite age and the most vicious."' On prostitution in the gardens, see *The Gentleman's Magazine* 2, June 1732, p820.

64. Figure 9 can actually be attributed to Bickham. See Solkin, *Painting for Money*, who likens these images to the carnivalesque themes of 'Hercules Mac-Sturdy Esq' (1737) *A Trip to Vauxhall; or, A General Satyr on the Times* (London).

65. Solkin, *Painting for Money*, p127.

66. Castle, *Masquerade and Civilization*. A register of books published in 1732 lists 'The Lady's Delight' which contained 'Ridotto al Fresco. A Poem. Describing the Growth of a Tree in the Famous Spring-Gardens at Vauxhall, under the Care of That Ingenious Botanist Dr. H———gg—r,' in *The Gentleman's Magazine* 2, June 1732, p11.

67. Castle, *Masquerade and Civilization*, p31, p44, p74 and p24.

68. [Henry Fielding] 'Lemuel Gulliver' (1728) *The Masquerade. A Poem Inscribed to C———t H———d———g—r* (London) p9.

69. *The Universal Spectator and Weekly Journal* 191, 3 June 1732, p1.

70. *Applebee's Journal,* 10 June 1732, reprinted in *The Gentleman's Magazine* 2, June 1732, p797.

71. Theophilus Cibber (1733) *The Harlot's Progress; or, The Ridotto Al' Fresco: A Grotesque Pantomime Entertainment* (London). See also *Grub Street Journal* 128, 15 June 1732.

72. *Weekly Register,* 2 and 17 June 1732, reprinted in *The Gentleman's Magazine* 2, June 1732, pp802–803 and p812.

73. *Applebee's Journal,* 24 June 1732, reprinted in *The Gentleman's Magazine* 2, June 1732, p812.

74. Tyers's *Ridotto* was attended by around four hundred people (including the Prince of Wales), among whom men outnumbered women ten to one. Only two-thirds of the crowd were masked and not in very dramatic costumes; see *The Gentleman's Magazine* 2, June 1732, p823.

75. Horace Walpole to Lord Hertford, 6 February 1764, in W. S. Lewis (ed.) *Horace Walpole's Correspondence* (Yale University Press, New Haven, CT) Vol. 38, p306. On the Macaroni Club and the Beef-Steak Club, see *The London Magazine* 41, 1772, p193, and Paul Langford (1989) *A Polite and Commercial People: England, 1727–1783* (Oxford University Press, Oxford) p576.

76. M. Dorothy George (1935) *Catalogue of Political and Personal Satires Preserved in the Department of Prints and Drawings in the British Museum, Vol. V: 1771–1783* (Trustees of the British Museum, London), Print Nos. 4997, 4993, 5013 and 5030. The Mungo Macaroni is probably a caricature of Julius Soubise, a well-known black fop. See also Diana Donald (1996) *The Age of Caricature: Satirical Prints in the Age of George III* (Yale University Press, New Haven, CT).

77. The image of Banks [BM 4695] is examined in John Gascoigne (1994) *Joseph Banks and the English Enlightenment: Useful Knowledge and Polite Culture* (Cambridge University Press, Cambridge). The Foxes [Nos. 5010 and 4648] are examined in Valerie Steele (1985) 'The social and political significance of Macaroni fashion,' *Costume* 19 pp94–109. For Dodd, see Gerald Howson (1973) *The Macaroni Parson: A Life of the Unfortunate Dr Dodd* (Hutchinson, London).

78. George, *Catalogue of Political and Personal Satires,* xxix.

79. Eirwen E. C. Nicolson (1996) 'Consumers and spectators: The public of the political print in eighteenth-century England,' *History* 81 p16. The prints are 'The Macaroni Printshop' (1772) [BM 4701] and 'Miss Macaroni and Her Gallant at a Print Shop' (1773) [BM 5220]. See also Roy Porter (1988) 'Seeing the past,' *Past and Present* 118 pp186–205.

80. *The London Magazine* 41, 1772, p193 and 'Ferdinand Twigem' (1773) *The Macaroni. A Satire* (London) no pagination.

81. Robert Hitchcock (1773) *The Macaroni: A Comedy* (York, UK), and James Raven (1995) 'Defending conduct and property: The London press and the luxury debate,' in John Brewer and Susan Staves (eds.) *Early Modern Conceptions of Property* (Routledge, London) pp301–319. For America, see Steele, 'Macaroni fashion,' and Breen, 'The meanings of things,' who quotes a report from the 1772 *Philadelphia Packet* of 'young gentlemen in their Macaroni coats, hats and shoes' (p256).

82. Steele, 'Macaroni fashion.' See also *The Town and Country Magazine* 3, 1771, p598.

83. Raven, 'Defending conduct and property,' p311.

84. Lovell, 'Subjective powers?'

85. John H. Jesse (1843) *George Selwyn and His Contemporaries* (Richard Bentley, London) p44. This undated letter is from c. 1766.

86. Jesse, *George Selwyn*, p113. This undated letter is from c. 1766.
87. *The Town and Country Magazine* IV, 1772, p243. As a fashion it was expected to disappear quickly; see *The London Magazine* 41, 1772, p193.
88. McKendrick, 'The consumer revolution,' p43.
89. *The London Magazine* 41, 1772, p194.
90. *The Macaroni Jester, and Pantheon of Wit; Containing All That Has Lately Transpired in the Regions of Politeness, Whim and Novelty* (London, 1773?) p6. See also *The Town and Country Magazine* IV, 1772, p243, and *The London Magazine* 41, 1772, p195.
91. Susan Staves (1982) 'A few kind words for the fop,' *Studies in English Literature, 1500–1900* 22 pp413–428.
92. *Macaroni Jester*, pp26–27. On the idea that 'modern refinements have unnerved us, every corner of the globe is ransacked for the destruction of our health,' see *The Town and Country Magazine* III, 1771, p598, and Roy Porter's discussion of George Cheyne's use of this argument in 1733, in Porter (1993) 'Consumption: disease of the consumer society?,' in John Brewer and Roy Porter (eds.) *Consumption and the World of Goods* (Routledge, London) pp58–81.
93. James Walvin (1997) *Fruits of Empire: Exotic Produce and British Taste, 1660–1800* (Macmillan, Basingstoke, UK), and Elizabeth Kowaleski-Wallace (1997) *Consuming Subjects: Women, Shopping, and Business in the Eighteenth Century* (Columbia University Press, New York).
94. Raven, *Judging New Wealth*, p169, p175 and p181.
95. *The London Magazine* 41, 1772, p193.
96. The *Macaroni Jester*'s frontispiece has a Macaroni emerging from a gigantic egg. Elsewhere he was 'amphibious'; see *The Macaroni, Scavoir Vivre, and Theatrical Magazine,* March 1774, p241. On monsters and the eighteenth-century 'fearful disdain of mixtures,' see Barbara Maria Stafford (1991) *Body Criticism: Imaging the Unseen in Enlightenment Art and Medicine* (MIT Press, Cambridge, MA) p211.
97. Raven, 'Defending conduct and property,' p309.
98. George Colman (1770) *Man and Wife: Or, The Shakespeare Jubilee. A Comedy, of Three Acts* (London).
99. George Winchester Stone Jr and George M. Kahrl (1979) *David Garrick: A Critical Biography* (University of Southern Illinois Press, Carbondale) p577, and Jonathan Bate (1989) *Shakespearean Constitutions: Politics, Theatre, Criticism, 1730–1830* (Clarendon Press, Oxford) p20.
100. Stone and Kahrl, *David Garrick*, p579. The reference Garrick is making is to the Anti-Gallican Society that was responsible for riots in theatres against 'foreign' entertainments; see Kathleen Wilson (1995b) *The Sense of the People: Politics, Culture and Imperialism in England, 1715–1785* (Cambridge University Press, Cambridge) pp190–192.
101. Kathleen Wilson (1995c) 'The good, the bad, and the impotent: Imperialism and the politics of identity in Georgian England,' in Ann Bermingham and John Brewer (eds.) *The Consumption of Culture, 1600–1800: Image, Object, Text* (Routledge, London) p243. Linda Colley (1992) *Britons: Forging the Nation, 1707–1837* (Yale University Press, New Haven, CT)

argues for the formation, against the French, of a *British* identity in this period. While this is true, 'irreducible tensions between nation and empire' meant the continual negotiation of *Englishness;* see Wilson, *The Sense of the People,* p174. It is this that comes out so strongly in the discussions of the Macaronis.

102. Colman, *Man and Wife,* p17. For a sketch of Kitchen's character, see *The Connoisseur* Vol. 3, 87, September 1755, pp117–124.

103. For gaming and the aristocracy, see Steele, 'Macaroni fashion,' and Jonathan C. D. Clark (1985) *English Society, 1688–1832* (Cambridge University Press, Cambridge) pp106–109. On diet and dress, see Colman, *Man and Wife,* p17 and p13.

104. Hitchcock, *The Macaroni.*

105. Hitchcock, *The Macaroni,* p1. See also Michèle Cohen (1996) *Fashioning Masculinity: National Identity and Language in the Eighteenth Century* (Routledge, London).

106. *The Oxford Magazine* IV, June 1770, p228.

107. *The Macaroni, Scavoir Vivre, and Theatrical Magazine,* March 1774, p241. See also *The Macaroni, Scavoir Vivre, and Theatrical Magazine,* December 1773, p89, and *The London Magazine* 41, 1772, p194.

108. *The Town and Country Magazine* IV, 1772, p243.

109. Hitchcock, *The Macaroni,* p70 and p69.

110. 'Twigem,' *The Macaroni,* p5 and p16; *Macaroni Jester,* p50; and Colman, *Man and Wife,* p13.

111. Berry, *The Idea of Luxury,* pp66–67.

112. *Macaroni Jester,* pp7–8.

113. *The London Magazine* 41, 1772, p194. On eighteenth-century cross-dressing, see Castle, *The Female Thermometer,* Chapter 5.

114. *The Town and Country Magazine* IV, 1772, p237.

115. Hitchcock, *The Macaroni,* p47.

116. *The London Magazine* 41, 1772, p193. On the 'Mohocks' and others, see Daniel Statt (1995) 'The case of the Mohocks: Rake violence in Augustan London,' *Social History* 20 pp179–199, and G. J. Barker-Benfield (1992) *The Culture of Sensibility: Sex and Society in Eighteenth-Century Britain* (University of Chicago Press, Chicago).

117. *The Town and Country Magazine* III, 1771, p598.

118. *The Town and Country Magazine* IV, 1772, p243. See also Hitchcock, *The Macaroni,* p70, and 'Twigem,' *The Macaroni,* p10.

119. *The Matrimonial Magazine; or, Monthly Anecdotes of Love and Marriage, for the Court, the City and the Country* 1, February 1775, p59.

120. Steele, 'Macaroni fashion,' and Wilson, 'The good, the bad, and the impotent.'

121. Sands, *Invitation to Ranelagh,* p35.

122. T. J. Edelstein (1983) 'The paintings,' in T. J. Edelstein (ed.) *Vauxhall Gardens* (Yale Center for British Art, Yale University Press, New Haven, CT) pp25–35. Frederick's death was mourned at Vauxhall; see Christopher Smart (1751) *A Solemn Dirge, Sacred to the Memory of His Royal Highness*

Frederick Prince of Wales. As It Was Sung by Mr Lowe, Miss Burchell, and Others, at Vaux-Hall (London).

123. G. Callender quoted in Alan Russett (1994) 'Peter Monamy's marine paintings for Vauxhall Gardens,' *The Mariner's Mirror* 80 p80. On the politics of Admiral Vernon's victory, see Kathleen Wilson (1988) 'Empire, trade and popular politics in mid-Hanoverian Britain: The case of Admiral Vernon,' *Past and Present* 121 pp74–109, and Gerald Jordan and Nicholas Rogers (1989) 'Admirals as heroes: Patriotism and liberty in mid-Hanoverian England,' *Journal of British Studies* 28 pp201–224.

124. Wilson, 'The good, the bad, and the impotent,' and Bob Harris (1996) '"American idols": Empire, war and the middling ranks in mid-eighteenth-century Britain,' *Past and Present* 150 pp111–141.

125. Sands, *Invitation to Ranelagh*, p27.

126. Newspaper cuttings from September 1758 and September 1760 in Burn Collection, f211 and f217. See also Thomas Arne's 'British Fair,' in Burn Collection, September 1765, f235.

127. Harris, '"American idols,"' p131. While the Fishery had strong opposition connections and had Frederick, Prince of Wales, as a patron, it was never narrowly partisan.

128. *DNB.* John Lockman (1750) *The Vast Importance of the Herring Fishery &c to These Kingdoms . . . in three Letters Addressed to a Member of Parliament* (London), and (1751) *The Shetland Herring and Peruvian Gold Mine: A Fable* (London).

129. See *The Frisky Songster* (London, no date) p5; *The First Part of the Rural Lovers Delight . . .* (London, no date) p28; and *The Songster's Magazine* (London, no date) p7 and p8.

130. Burn Collection, f271 and f275.

131. *Description of Vaux-Hall Gardens,* pp15–17. Solkin, *Painting for Money,* and Gowing, 'Hogarth, Hayman, and the Vauxhall decorations,' discuss Vauxhall's role in the making of a national 'school' of painting.

132. Each was approximately 12 feet by 18 feet. The discussion of them here draws on the excellent analysis in Solkin, *Painting for Money.*

133. *Description of Vaux-Hall Gardens,* p24.

134. *Description of Vaux-Hall Gardens,* no pagination.

135. Solkin, *Painting for Money,* p190. See also Charles Mitchell (1944) 'Benjamin West's "Death of General Wolfe" and the popular history piece,' *Journal of the Warburg and Courtauld Institutes* 7 pp20–33, who discusses the appeal of these paintings to 'ordinary Englishmen' (p27).

136. Solkin, *Painting for Money,* p195.

137. Harris, '"American idols."'

138. John Brewer (1989) *The Sinews of Power: War, Money and the English State, 1688–1783* (Unwin Hyman, London).

139. The painting of Amherst carried the legend 'Power Exerted, Conquest Obtained, Mercy Shewn! MDCCLX,' *Description of Vaux-Hall Gardens,* p26. See also Wilson, 'Empire, trade and popular politics,' and Jordan and Rogers, 'Admirals as heroes.'

140. Solkin, *Painting for Money,* p199.
141. Artistic representation was one of the few sites for an open discussion of masculinity. See Gill Perry and Michael Rossington (eds.) (1994) *Femininity and Masculinity in Eighteenth-Century Art and Culture* (Manchester University Press, Manchester, UK).
142. Chloe Chard (1994) 'Effeminacy, pleasure and the classical body,' in Gill Perry and Michael Rossington (eds.) *Femininity and Masculinity in Eighteenth-Century Art and Culture* (Manchester University Press, Manchester, UK) pp142–181.
143. The most renowned of these images, Benjamin West's picture of the death of General Wolfe, was shown to great acclaim at the Royal Academy in 1771, just as the Darlies were beginning to produce their Macaroni images. See Mitchell, 'Benjamin West's "Death of General Wolfe." '
144. Kathleen Wilson (1994) 'Empire of virtue: The imperial project and Hanoverian culture c. 1720–1785,' in Lawrence Stone (ed.) *An Imperial State at War: Britain from 1689 to 1815* (Routledge, London) p156, and Wilson, 'The good, the bad, and the impotent.'
145. On the problems of the representation of imperial violence in the metropole, see Maaja A. Stewart (1996) 'Inexhaustible generosity: The fictions of eighteenth-century British imperialism in Richard Cumberland's *The West Indian,' The Eighteenth-Century: Theory and Interpretation* 37 pp42–55.
146. *The Life and Times of George Robert Fitzgerald, Commonly Called Fighting Fitzgerald* (Dublin, 1852) p68.
147. *The Vauxhall Affray,* p13.
148. *The Vauxhall Affray,* no pagination.
149. *The London Magazine* 41, 1772, p194.
150. *Macaroni Jester,* p51.
151. *The Macaroni, Scavoir Vivre, and Theatrical Magazine,* March 1774, p242. On other men at Vauxhall staring at women with their spyglasses, see *The Connoisseur* 68, 15 May 1755, p258.
152. Straub, *Sexual Suspects,* p101, and Cheryl Wanko (1994) 'The eighteenth-century actress and the construction of gender: Lavinia Fenton and Charlotte Charke,' *Eighteenth-Century Life* 18 pp75–90. On Elizabeth Hartley, see Philip H. Highfall Jr (1980) 'Performers and performing,' in Robert D. Hume (ed.) *The London Theatre World, 1660–1800* (University of Southern Illinois Press, Carbondale) p170.
153. *The Vauxhall Affray,* p54.
154. *The Vauxhall Affray,* p112.
155. Straub, *Sexual Suspects.* For an example of the presentation of actresses as more than simply spectacles for male pleasure, see Christina H. Kiaer (1993) 'Professional femininity in Hogarth's *Strolling Actresses Dressing in a Barn,' Art History* 16 pp239–265.
156. Peter de Bolla (1995) 'The visibility of visuality: Vauxhall Gardens and the siting of the viewer,' in Stephen Melville and Bill Readings (eds.) *Vision and Textuality* (Macmillan, Basingstoke, UK) pp282–295 situates Vauxhall within carefully differentiated cultures of visuality.

157. On Bentham's Panopticon, see Jeremy Bentham (1791) *Panopticon; or, The Inspection House* (London); Michel Foucault (1977) *Discipline and Punish: The Birth of the Prison* (Allen Lane, London) pp195–228; and Janet Semple (1993) *Bentham's Prison: A Study of the Panopticon Penitentiary* (Clarendon Press, Oxford).

158. See *Remarkable Characters; Exhibitions; Fireworks in the Green Park, 1749,* Fillinham Collection Vol. 5, in the British Library, and Altick, *The Shows of London,* p60. Christopher Pinchbeck Jr followed his father, the inventor of the false gold that bears his name, into the clockmaking and exhibiting trades. He also had two other brothers: John kept the Dwarf's Tavern in Chelsea, while Edward was a West Smithfield pawnbroker.

159. Plumb, 'The acceptance of modernity,' p284.

160. Altick, *The Shows of London.*

161. Edwards, *Description,* p20.

162. Walter Harrison (1775) *A New and Universal History, Description and Survey of the Cities of London and Westminster . . .* (London) p513.

163. Allen, 'The landscape,' p17; Hunt, *Vauxhall,* p13; and Solkin, *Painting for Money,* pp133–134.

164. [Lockman], *Sketch of the Spring-Gardens,* p7, p12 and p17. See also *The Gentleman's Magazine* 8, August 1743, p439, and *Description of Vaux-Hall Gardens,* pp39–40.

165. [Lockman], *Sketch of the Spring-Gardens,* p15.

166. [Lockman], *Sketch of the Spring-Gardens,* p13.

167. For the disciplining gaze, see Scott Paul Gordon (1995) 'Voyeuristic dreams: Mr Spectator and the power of the spectacle,' *The Eighteenth Century: Theory and Interpretation* 36 pp3–23. 'The Visiter,' *The British Magazine* I, September 1746, pp256–259, threatened to tell tales of public misbehaviour to keep people in line, and a newspaper cutting from 1738 in Vauxhall Gardens Archive, Minet Library, Borough of Lambeth. *Press Cuttings 1732–1823* reports on a 'masculine' woman at Vauxhall and notes that 'the Company, out of Respect to themselves, had the Pleasure to stare her and her Attendants out of the Gardens.'

168. Toupee, 'An evening at Vaux-Hall,' 1 p363, and *Description of Vaux-Hall Gardens,* p49.

169. Toupee, 'An evening at Vaux-Hall,' 1 p323, and de Bolla, 'The visibility of visuality' (1995).

170. [Lockman], *Sketch of the Spring-Gardens,* p10.

171. Bermingham, 'Introduction,' p2, and de Bolla, 'The visibility of visuality' (1995).

172. Hunt, *Vauxhall,* p20, describes 'an ambience of make-believe and play.' For the wider culture of illusion, see Stafford, *Body Criticism,* p362.

173. [Lockman], *Sketch of the Spring-Gardens,* p7 and p19.

174. *Description of Vaux-Hall Gardens,* p48: On 'a moon light night there is something more peculiarly pleasing, which so strongly affects the imagination, that it almost instills an idea of inchantment.'

175. [Lockman], *Sketch of the Spring-Gardens,* p5.

176. *The Connoisseur* I, May 1755, p404. Lockman also has Colin, a bucolic

swain, mistaking the statue of Handel for a living musician; see [Lockman], *Sketch of the Spring-Gardens,* pp8–9.

177. *Description of Vaux-Hall Gardens,* pp6–7.
178. de Bolla, 'The visibility of visuality' (1995).
179. *The Vauxhall Affray,* p100 and p65. On the problems of men looking at sculptures of men, see Chard, 'Effeminacy, pleasure and the classical body.'
180. Straub, *Sexual Suspects,* p10 and p57.
181. *Macaroni Jester,* p108.
182. *Macaroni Jester,* p14 and p108.
183. *The Vauxhall Affray,* no pagination.
184. *Fashion: A Poem* (Bath, 1775) p7
185. Stafford, *Body Criticism,* p86.
186. 'Twigem,' *The Macaroni,* p11.
187. Hunt, *Vauxhall,* p17.
188. *The Vauxhall Affray,* p67 and p75. On class cross-dressing, see Breen, 'The meanings of things,' and, for the nineteenth century, Anne McClintock (1995) *Imperial Leather: Race, Gender and Sexuality in the Colonial Contest* (Routledge, London).
189. *The Vauxhall Affray,* p24.
190. Lawrence E. Klein (1995b) 'Politeness for plebes: Consumption and social identity in early eighteenth-century England,' in Ann Bermingham and John Brewer (eds.) *The Consumption of Culture, 1600–1800: Image, Object, Text* (Routledge, London) p374.
191. John Brewer (1983) 'Commercialisation and politics,' in Neil McKendrick, John Brewer and J. H. Plumb (eds.) *The Birth of a Consumer Society: The Commercialisation of Eighteenth-Century England* (Hutchinson, London) pp197–262, and Barker-Benfield, *The Culture of Sensibility,* pp37–103.
192. See Sandra Sherman (1995) 'Credit, simulation, and the ideology of contract in the early eighteenth century,' *Eighteenth-Century Life* 19 pp86–102, and Klein, 'Politeness for plebes.'
193. John Money (1993b) 'The Masonic moment; or, Ritual, replica, and credit: John Wilkes, the Macaroni Parson, and the making of the middle-class mind,' *Journal of British Studies* 32 pp358–395 discusses the importance of the 1770s crisis, the way in which the hanging of William Dodd (the Magdalen Hospital's 'Macaroni Parson') for fraud crystalised concern over patronage and credit, and the role of the Masons in making new credit networks on their 'pasteboard stage' (p392). There is perhaps more to say about Dodd's Macaroni image and his fate.
194. Hitchcock, *The Macaroni,* no pagination.
195. *The Macaroni, Scavoir Vivre, and Theatrical Magazine,* March 1774, p242.
196. 'Twigem,' *The Macaroni,* p15. See also Hitchcock, *The Macaroni,* p5, and *Macaroni Jester,* p51.
197. Goodman, ' "Altar against altar," ' p439.
198. Straub, *Sexual Suspects,* p17.
199. Klein, 'Politeness for plebes.'

200. *The Vauxhall Affray,* p82 and p97.
201. *The Vauxhall Affray,* p50.
202. *The Matrimonial Magazine* 1, April 1775, p187.

CHAPTER 5

1. Michael Mann (1980) 'State and society, 1130–1815: An analysis of English state finances,' in Maurice Zeitlin (ed.) *Political Power and Social Theory: A Research Annual* (JAI Press, Greenwich, CT) pp165–208; Charles Tilly (ed.) (1975) *The Formation of National States in Western Europe* (Princeton University Press, Princeton, NJ); and Charles Tilly (1990) *Coercion, Capital and European States, A.D. 990–1990* (Basil Blackwell, Oxford, UK).
2. John Brewer (1989) *The Sinews of Power: War, Money and the English State, 1688–1783* (Unwin Hyman, London).
3. Lawrence Stone (1994) 'Introduction,' in Lawrence Stone (ed.) *An Imperial State at War: Britain from 1689 to 1815* (Routledge, London) p5.
4. Michael Duffy (ed.) (1980) *The Military Revolution and the State, 1500–1800,* Exeter Studies in History 1 (University of Exeter Press, Exeter, UK).
5. E. A. Wrigley (1994) 'Society and the economy in the eighteenth century,' in Lawrence Stone (ed.) *An Imperial State at War: Britain from 1689 to 1815* (Routledge, London) pp72–95, and Patrick K. O'Brien and Philip A. Hunt (1993) 'The rise of a fiscal state in England, 1485–1815,' *Historical Research* 66 pp129–176.
6. Brewer, *The Sinews of Power.*
7. P. G. M. Dickson (1967) *The Financial Revolution in England: A Study in the Development of Public Credit* (Macmillan, London).
8. Michael J. Braddick (1996a) *The Nerves of State: Taxation and the Financing of the English State, 1558–1714* (Manchester University Press, Manchester, UK) p33; Brewer, *The Sinews of Power,* p114; and Philip Harding and Peter Mandler (1993) 'From "fiscal–military" state to laissez-faire state, 1760–1850,' *Journal of British Studies* 32 pp44–70.
9. Edward Hughes (1934) *Studies in Administration and Finance, 1558–1825, with Special Reference to the History of Salt Taxation in England* (Manchester University Press, Manchester, UK) p167.
10. Michael J. Braddick (1994) *Parliamentary Taxation in Seventeenth-Century England: Local Administration and Response,* Royal Historical Society Studies in History 70 (Boydell Press, Woodbridge, UK) and Braddick, *The Nerves of State,* p10.
11. Hughes, *Studies in Administration and Finance,* p118.
12. Brewer, *The Sinews of Power,* p89.
13. Peter Miller (1992) 'Accounting and objectivity: The invention of calculating selves and calculable spaces,' *Annals of Scholarship* 9 pp61–86.
14. Brewer, *The Sinews of Power,* p68, and Max Weber (1967) 'Bureaucracy,' in

H. H. Gerth and C. Wright Mills (eds.) *From Max Weber: Essays in Sociology* (Routledge and Kegan Paul, London) pp196–198. See Braddick, *Parliamentary Taxation,* p126 and p223; Braddick, *The Nerves of State,* pp100–101; Michael J. Braddick (1996b) 'The early modern English state and the question of differentiation, from 1550 to 1700,' *Comparative Studies in Society and History* 38 p110; Brewer, *The Sinews of Power,* p24 and p64; John Brewer (1994) 'The eighteenth-century British state: Contexts and issues,' in Lawrence Stone (ed.) *An Imperial State at War: Britain from 1689 to 1815* (Routledge, London) pp52–71; Thomas Ertman (1994) 'The sinews of power and European state-building theory,' in Lawrence Stone (ed.) *An Imperial State at War: Britain from 1689 to 1815* (Routledge, London) p36; Gerald E. Aylmer (1980) 'From office-holding to civil service: The genesis of modern bureaucracy,' *Transactions of the Royal Historical Society* 5th series 30 pp91–108; and Wolfgang J. Mommsen (1980) ' "Toward the iron cage of future serfdom"? On the methodological status of Max Weber's ideal-typical concept of bureaucratisation,' *Transactions of the Royal Historical Society* 5th series 30 pp157–181.

15. J. G. A. Pocock (1987) 'Modernity and anti-modernity in the anglophone political tradition,' in S. N. Eisenstadt (ed.) *Patterns of Modernity, Vol. 1: The West* (Frances Pinter, London) pp44–59.

16. Anthony Giddens (1985) *The Nation-State and Violence* (Polity Press, Cambridge, UK); Michael Mann (1984) 'The autonomous power of the state: Its origins, mechanisms and results,' *Archives Européenes de Sociologie* 25 pp185–213; Christopher Dandeker (1990) *Surveillance, Power and Modernity: Bureaucracy and Discipline from 1700 to the Present Day* (Polity Press, Cambridge, UK); Zygmunt Bauman (1991) *Modernity and Ambivalence* (Polity Press, Cambridge, UK) and Bruno Latour (1987) *Science in Action: How to Follow Scientists and Engineers through Society* (Open University Press, Milton Keynes, UK).

17. Aylmer, 'From office-holding to civil service'; Colin Brooks (1987) 'Interest, patronage and professionalism: John, 1st Baron Ashburnham, Hastings and the revenue services,' *Southern History* 9 pp51–70, and Brewer, *The Sinews of Power,* p75. On the increasing formalisation and standardisation of county and parish government, see Joanna Innes (1994) 'The domestic face of the military–fiscal state: Government and society in eighteenth-century Britain,' in Lawrence Stone (ed.) *An Imperial State at War: Britain from 1689 to 1815* (Routledge, London) pp96–127, and Joan R. Kent (1995) 'The centre and the localities: State formation and parish government in England, circa 1640–1740,' *Historical Journal* 38 pp363–404.

18. Although it was used as a model for reforming other branches of government; see Hughes, *Studies in Administration and Finance,* p172, and John Torrance (1978) 'Social class and bureaucratic innovation: The Commissioners for Examining the Public Accounts, 1780–1787,' *Past and Present* 78 pp56–81.

19. Aylmer, 'From office-holding to civil service,' p106.

20. Braddick, *The Nerves of State*, p97, and Braddick, *Parliamentary Taxation*.
21. Colin Brooks (1974) 'Public finance and political stability: The administration of the land tax, 1688–1720,' *Historical Journal* 17 pp281–300, and J. V. Beckett (1985) 'Land tax or excise: The levying of taxation in seventeenth- and eighteenth-century England,' *English Historical Review* 100 p301.
22. Braddick, *The Nerves of State*, p187.
23. Brewer, *The Sinews of Power*, p114.
24. D. Waddell (1958–1959) 'Charles Davenant (1656–1714)—A biographical sketch,' *Economic History Review* 2d series 11 pp279–288, and *Dictionary of National Biography*.
25. Peter Buck (1977) 'Seventeenth-century political arithmetic: Civil strife and vital statistics,' *Isis* 68 pp67–84; Brewer, *The Sinews of Power*, p83; and Paul F. Lazarfeld (1961) 'Notes on the history of quantification in sociology: Trends, sources and problems,' *Isis* 52 pp277–333.
26. Charles Davenant (1771a) 'Discourses on the public revenues, and on the Trade of England . . . [1698],' in *The Political and Commercial Works of That Celebrated Writer Charles Davenant . . . Collected and Revised by Sir Charles Whitworth* (5 vols., London) Vol. I, p128.
27. Davenant, 'Discourses on the public revenues,' p135.
28. Keith Thomas (1987) 'Numeracy in early modern England,' *Transactions of the Royal Historical Society* 5th series 37 p131.
29. Davenant, 'Discourses on the public revenues,' p136. See also Buck, 'Seventeenth-century political arithmetic,' pp67–68 and Karin Johannisson (1990) 'Society in numbers: The debate over quantification in eighteenth-century political economy,' in Tore Frängsmyr, J. L. Heilbron and R. E. Rider (eds.) *The Quantifying Spirit in the Eighteenth Century* (University of California Press, Berkeley and Los Angeles) p350.
30. Keith Tribe (1978) *Land, Labour and Economic Discourse* (Routledge and Kegan Paul, London) p86, and Robert Schware (1981) *Quantification in the History of Political Thought: Toward a Qualitative Analysis* (Greenwood Press, Westport, CT) p32.
31. Tribe, *Land, Labour and Economic Discourse*.
32. Charles Davenant (1771b) 'An essay upon ways and means [1695],' in *The Political and Commercial Works of That Celebrated Writer Charles Davenant . . . Collected and Revised by Sir Charles Whitworth* (5 vols., London) Vol. I, p13, and Waddell, 'Charles Davenant,' p282.
33. J. L. Heilbron (1990) 'Introductory essay,' in Tore Frängsmyr, J. L. Heilbron and R. E. Rider (eds.) *The Quantifying Spirit in the Eighteenth Century* (University of California Press, Berkeley, and Los Angeles) p2.
34. Davenant, 'Discourses on the public revenues,' p132.
35. Davenant, 'Discourses on the public revenues,' p131.
36. Davenant, 'Discourses on the public revenues,' p147.
37. Tribe, *Land, Labour and Economic Discourse*, p81.
38. Davenant, 'Discourses on the public revenues,' p162. See also p130, pp296–297, and 'An essay upon ways and means,' p16.

39. Davenant, 'Discourses on the public revenues,' p146.
40. Buck, 'Seventeenth-century political arithmetic,' p69; Tribe, *Land, Labour and Economic Discourse*, p82; and Terence W. Hutchinson (1988) *Before Adam Smith: The Emergence of Political Economy, 1662–1776* (Basil Blackwell, Oxford) p53.
41. Buck, 'Seventeenth-century political arithmetic,' p81.
42. Peter Buck (1982) 'People who counted: Political arithmetic in the eighteenth century,' *Isis* 73 pp28–45.
43. See the proposals to Parliament in British Library 816.m.6 ff14, 17, 26, 29, 31, 32, 60 and 76, and in B.L. 1890.e.4 f88 and f90 which are discussed in Beckett, 'Land tax or excise.'
44. Tribe, *Land, Labour and Economic Discourse*, p85, and Mark Blaug (ed.) (1991) *Pre-Classical Economists, Vol. I: Charles Davenant (1656–1714) and William Petty (1623–1687)* (Edward Elgar, Aldershot, UK) x.
45. Davenant, 'An essay upon ways and means,' p16 and p15.
46. Davenant, 'Discourses on the public revenues,' p251.
47. Davenant, 'Discourses on the public revenues,' p145. See also Davenant, 'An essay upon ways and means,' p67.
48. Davenant, 'Discourses on the public revenues,' p232.
49. Davenant, 'An essay upon ways and means,' p62.
50. Davenant, 'An essay upon ways and means,' p80 and p62.
51. Davenant, 'Discourses on the public revenues,' p223, p222 and p224.
52. Davenant, 'An essay upon ways and means,' p62.
53. Davenant, 'Discourses on the public revenues,' p156.
54. Beckett, 'Land tax or excise,' p299.
55. Braddick, *The Nerves of State*, p149.
56. B.L. Harleian Mss 1243 *Some Considerations About an Excise*, f334v.
57. Buck, 'People who counted,' p32, and B.L. Harleian Mss 1243 f339.
58. Brewer, *The Sinews of Power*, p147.
59. Stone, 'Introduction,' p20, and B.L. Harleian Mss 1243 f340.
60. Beckett, 'Land tax or excise.'
61. Brooks, 'Public finance and political stability,' and Beckett, 'Land tax or excise.'
62. Brewer, *The Sinews of Power*, p100.
63. Davenant, 'An essay upon ways and means,' p61.
64. Davenant, 'An essay upon ways and means,' p78, p75, pp77–79 and p71.
65. Davenant, 'An essay upon ways and means,' pp67–68.
66. Davenant, 'Discourses on the public revenues,' p276.
67. Davenant, 'Discourses on the public revenues,' p206. See also p203, p207, p270, p286, and 'An essay upon ways and means,' p68.
68. Davenant, 'Discourses on the public revenues,' p195.
69. Davenant, 'Discourses on the public revenues,' pp176–179.
70. Hughes, *Studies in Administration and Finance*, p164. Waddell, in 'Charles Davenant,' suggests that he may have still been owed a large sum by the previous monarch.
71. Waddell, 'Charles Davenant,' p279, and Blaug, *Pre-Classical Economists*, ix.

72. This account of the first forty years of the Excise is based on Hughes, *Studies in Administration and Finance;* C. D. Chandaman (1975) *The English Public Revenue, 1660–1688* (Clarendon Press, Oxford); Braddick, *Parliamentary Taxation;* and Patrick K. O'Brien and Philip Hunt (1997) 'The emergence and consolidation of excises in the English fiscal system before the Glorious Revolution,' *British Tax Review* 1 pp35–58.
73. Hughes, *Studies in Administration and Finance,* p127.
74. Hughes, *Studies in Administration and Finance,* p138.
75. Chandaman, *The English Public Revenue.*
76. Brewer, *The Sinews of Power,* p95 and p94. See also O'Brien and Hunt, 'The rise of a fiscal state,' p155.
77. Braddick, *The Nerves of State,* p149, and Braddick, *Parliamentary Taxation,* p275.
78. B.L. Harleian Mss 1898 ff64–68 shows a 22.8% improvement in revenues collected on country beer and ale from 1683/1684 to 1688/1689.
79. Braddick, *Parliamentary Taxation,* p209. This administrative geography dates from the 1674 farm; see Davenant, 'Discourses on the public revenues,' p211.
80. B.L. Harleian Mss 4227 *Abstract of the Revenue of the Excise, 1684–1687.* These figures do not include London. Unfortunately no map survives and the geographical information is not sufficiently precise to allow one to be reconstructed.
81. B.L. Harleian Mss 5123 *Management of the Excise.*
82. E.g., Wiltshire was shared between five collections and Devonshire between three; see B.L. Harleian Mss 4227.
83. B.L. Add. Mss 29458 *The State of the Excise, 1662–1786,* ff18–19.
84. Chandaman, *The English Public Revenue,* p73, and Davenant, 'Discourses on the public revenues,' p187.
85. Davenant, 'Discourses on the public revenues,' p177.
86. *Calendar of Treasury Books, 1681–1685* [ed. William A. Shaw] VII 29 December 1683 p1000. Davenant's diaries are B.L. Harleian Mss 4077 *An Account of the Management of the Officers of the West of England, 1685;* B.L. Harleian Mss 5120 and 5121 *Miles Edgar on the Excise;* and B.L. Harleian Mss 5123. For their attribution to Davenant, see Hughes, *Studies in Administration and Finance,* p160; Waddell, 'Charles Davenant'; and 5121 f14. These are each small, handwritten notebooks (the last being a neater copy of one of the early diaries) that offer brief accounts of the work that was undertaken at each place interspersed with some comments on the Excise as a whole and a few personal reflections. They are Davenant's personal memoranda of his journeys rather than an official record.
87. There were two journeys described in his diaries but not mapped here. The first (17 July 1683 to 1 August 1683) took him round London from Bow to Enfield, Edgware and Staines and then east to Hammersmith and south to Guildford and Farnham. The second (16 May 1687 to 23 May 1687) was a circuit north of London from Barnet through Luton and Leighton Buzzard to Bedford, Royston, Bishops Stortford and Hertford.

88. Braddick, *Parliamentary Taxation* and *A Dialogue betwixt an Excise-Man and Death* (London, 1659).

89. In this account of the historical geography of accuracy I have drawn upon Latour, *Science in Action*; John Law (1986) 'On the methods of long-distance control: Vessels, navigation and the Portuguese route to India,' in John Law (ed.) *Power, Action and Belief: A New Sociology of Knowledge?* (Routledge and Kegan Paul, London) pp234–263; Donald Mackenzie (1990) *Inventing Accuracy: A Historical Sociology of Nuclear Missile Guidance* (MIT Press, Cambridge, MA); and Andrew Barry (1993) 'The history of measurement and the engineers of space,' *British Journal of the History of Science* 26 pp459–468.

90. Thomas, 'Numeracy in early modern England.'

91. Cf. Richard Collins (1677) *The Countrey Gaugers Vade Mecum; or, Pocket Companion* . . . (London) and John Brown (1678) *The Practical Gauger, Arithmetical and Instrumental* . . . (London), with Thomas Everard (1684) *Stereography Made Easie: or, The Description and Use of a New Gauging Rod or Sliding Rule* (London) and Robert Shirtcliffe (1740) *The Theory and Practice of Gauging, Demonstrated in a Short and Easy Method* (London).

92. On mathematical teaching and writing, see Thomas, 'Numeracy in early modern England,' and John Money (1993a) 'Teaching in the market-place, or "Caesar adsum jam forte: Pompey aderat": The retailing of knowledge in provincial England during the eighteenth century,' in John Brewer and Roy Porter (eds.) *Consumption and the World of Goods* (Routledge, London) pp335–377. On additional information for excisemen, see John Mayne (1680) *A Companion for Excise-Men, Containing the Excise-Man's Aid & Journal* . . . (London); William Hunt (1683a) *An Abridgement of the Laws of Excise* (York) which was sold with William Hunt (1683b) *Practical Gauging Epitomized, with the Use, and Construction of the Tables of Logarithms* (York); and Charles Leadbetter (1739) *The Royal Gauger; or, Gauging Made Easy, as It Is Actually Practised by the Officers of His Majesty's Revenue of Excise* (London) which even appended tables for working out cumulative salary per day, including leap years!

93. William Hunt (1673) *A Guide for the Practical Gauger, with a Compendium of Decimal Arithmetick* (London) no pagination. On teaching, also see Leadbetter, *The Royal Gauger* and Samuel Clark (1761) *The British Gauger; or, Trader and Officer's Instructor, in the Revenue of the Excise and Customs* (London).

94. Among others Collins, *The Countrey Gaugers Vade Mecum;* Everard, *Stereography Made Easie;* Brown, *The Practical Gauger;* and William Flower (1768) *A Key to the Modern Sliding-Rule* (London) all had an instrument to sell, if possible by getting it recommended by those at the Excise Board. Consequently many of these books were dedicated to the excise commissioners or farmers, although Edward Hatton (1729), author of *The Gauger's Guide; or, Excise-Officer Instructed* (London), dedicated his to Sir Robert Walpole, and Charles Leadbetter, author of *The Royal Gauger,* dedicated his to the officers in the field.

95. Michael Baxendall (1972) *Painting and Experience in Fifteenth-Century Italy: A Primer in the Social History of Pictorial Style* (Clarendon Press, Oxford), pp86–87, shows many of the principles at work in the Renaissance. For different methods of gauging a cask, cf. Collins, *The Countrey Gaugers Vade Mecum* and William Yeo (1749) *The Method of Ullaging and Inching All Sorts of Casks and Other Utensils, Used by Common Brewers, Victuallers, Distillers etc . . .* (London).

96. For slide rules, see Brown, *The Practical Gauger;* Everard, *Stereography Made Easie;* and Leadbetter, *The Royal Gauger.* Logarithmic slide rules allowed division and multiplication to be done by addition and subtraction. They were calibrated for certain sorts of uses, e.g., to calculate in beer gallons, and offered a versatile and convenient instrument although limited in accuracy to a few decimal places. See D. D. Swade (1994) 'Calculating machines,' in I. Grattan-Guiness (ed.) *Companion Encyclopedia of the History and Philosophy of the Mathematical Sciences* (Routledge, London) Vol. I, pp694–700. For tables, see Collins, *The Countrey Gaugers Vade Mecum;* William Hunt (1687) *The Gauger's Magazine . . .;* and Hatton, *The Gauger's Guide.*

97. Collins, *The Countrey Gaugers Vade Mecum,* no pagination.

98. See Leadbetter, *The Royal Gauger,* footnote vi.

99. See the assumptions made by Brown, *The Practical Gauger,* p90; Leadbetter, *The Royal Gauger,* p66 and p125; and Shirtcliffe, *Theory and Practice,* viii.

100. Peter Linebaugh (1991) *The London Hanged: Crime and Civil Society in the Eighteenth Century* (Penguin, Harmondsworth, UK) Chapter 5, and Iain A. Boal (1995) 'The darkening green,' *History Workshop Journal* 39 p129.

101. Thomas, 'Numeracy in early modern England,' p130.

102. Robert K. Hutcheson (1798) *For Maltsters, Brewers, and Hop-Planters: All the Excise Laws and Adjudged Cases* (London) p43, and Julian Hoppit (1993) 'Reforming Britain's weights and measures, 1660–1824,' *English Historical Review* CVIII pp82–103.

103. B.L. Harleian Mss 5121 f14v.

104. Davenant, 'Discourses on the public revenues,' p215.

105. B.L. Harleian Mss 5120 f6v and f49v; 5121 f2v and ff19–19v.

106. B.L. Harleian Mss 5120 f54; 5121 f18v and f50v.

107. B.L. Harleian Mss 4077 f14 and ff16v–17; 5120 f59; 5121 f3v.

108. Davenant, 'Discourses on the public revenues,' p215; B.L. Harleian Mss 4077 f20v; 5120 f20v, f21, f38, f41 and f41v; 5121 f8 and f19.

109. B.L. Harleian Mss 4077 f8 and f52; 5120 f43v and ff59–59v; 5121 f35v, f36v and f40v; 5123 f1v.

110. For the 'semicircular rule,' see J. T. (1667) *The Semicircle on a Sector . . .* (London), and B.L. Harleian Mss 5120 ff11–11v, f21, f30 and f59. These clashes [B.L. Harleian Mss 5120 f29 and f60v] with Everard, who was a general supervisor in Davenant's area, were only part of many problems Davenant had with him; see B.L. Harleian Mss 5120 f56v, f59, f59v and f62v, and 5121 f19. Hatton, in *The Gauger's Guide,* x, later argued that Everard's method was a 'Guess-way of working [which] carries nothing

of Reason or Demonstration along with it,' although it was defended in Flower, *Modern Sliding-Rule,* vii.

111. B.L. Harleian Mss 4077 f13, f20v, f36v and f43v; 5120 f38v; 5121 f19 and f36; 5123 f1v.

112. B.L. Harleian Mss 5120 ff27–27v.

113. B.L. Harleian Mss 5120 f56v and *Excise Board Entry Books of Correspondence with Treasury, 1683–1686* PRO CUST 48/2 22nd July 1684 f51. For his identification of bad practices, see, e.g., B.L. Harleian Mss 5121 f23v, f27v, f36, f36v and f37.

114. Barry, 'The history of measurement.' For a discussion of the problems of replicability in science, see Simon Schaffer (1993) 'The consuming flame: Electrical showmen and Tory mystics in the world of goods,' in John Brewer and Roy Porter (eds.) *Consumption and the World of Goods* (Routledge, London) pp489–526.

115. B.L. Harleian Mss 5120 ff2–2v. For implementation, see PRO CUST 48/2 5 October 1684 f74, and B.L. Harleian Mss 5120 f61 and f63v.

116. B.L. Harleian Mss 5121 ff45–46 and 5120 f24.

117. B.L. Harleian Mss 5120 f11v, f17v and f30v.

118. PRO CUST 48/2 10 April 1684 ff30–32 and 12 May 1685 f112, and B.L. Harleian Mss 5121 f20.

119. Peter Mathias (1959) *The Brewing Industry in England, 1700–1830* (Cambridge University Press, Cambridge), and 'A. Gentleman' (1768) *Every Man His Own Brewer; or, A Compendium of the English Brewery* (London).

120. The backs were preferred to the guile tun; see B.L. Harleian Mss 4077 f26; 5121 f10v and f15v.

121. B.L. Harleian Mss 4077 f20v; 5120 f17v, f22, ff26–27, f39 and f52v; 5121 f5, ff7–7v, f11, f14 and f21.

122. B.L. Harleian Mss 5120 f27v; 5121 f13; and PRO CUST 48/2 10 April 1684 f30.

123. B.L. Harleian Mss 5120 f57.

124. See PRO CUST 48/2 20 March 1683 f29. The discretionary allowance for heat (see B.L. Harleian Mss 4077 f29 and 5120 f33) was replaced by a one-tenth allowance on the duty in 1689; see Davenant, 'Discourses on the public revenues,' p185, and Mathias, *The Brewing Industry,* p364.

125. B.L. Harleian Mss 5120 f50.

126. PRO CUST 48/2 20 March 1683 ff29–30, and B.L. Harleian Mss 5120 ff33–37.

127. B.L. Harleian Mss 5120 f22 and f24.

128. PRO CUST 48/2 20 March 1683 f30.

129. B.L. Harleian Mss 5120 ff34v–35.

130. B.L. Harleian Mss 5120 f1; Kent, 'The centre and the localities'; Braddick, *The Nerves of State,* p168; and Braddick, 'The early modern English state,' p110.

131. Quotations from B.L. Harleian Mss 5120 f26 and f14v; see also B.L. Harleian Mss 5120 f15, f21, f21v, f28v, f31v, f38v and f61; 5121 f5v, f6, f9 and f10.

132. Brooks, in 'Interest, patronage and professionalism,' shows that they also came into conflict.
133. B.L. Harleian Mss 5120 f7, f35v, f40v, ff42v–43, f45 and f50; PRO CUST 48/2 20 March 1683 ff29–30; and *Calendar of Treasury Books, 1681–1685* VII 31 July 1683 p887.
134. PRO CUST 48/2 10 April 1683 ff30–32.
135. Mathias, *The Brewing Industry*, xvii.
136. B.L. Harleian Mss 5120 ff49v–50.
137. B.L. Harleian Mss 5120 ff50–51.
138. B.L. Harleian Mss 5120 ff50v–51. The strategy seems to have worked; see B.L. Harleian Mss 5121 f17v.
139. B.L. Harleian Mss 5120 f58v, and 5121 f15v, f31v and f35.
140. For other cases, see B.L. Harleian Mss 5120 f23, f26, ff32–32v; 5121 f38; and *Calendar of Treasury Books, 1681–1685* VII, 8 July 1684 pp1212–1213.
141. Mixing involved brewing overstrong beer and, after paying the excise on it, mixing it with water or small beer to make more drink. This was advantageous while beer was only taxed at two rates: 'strong' and 'small.' See Mathias, *The Brewing Industry*, p346 and p369, and B.L. Harleian Mss 5120 ff56v–57 and f60.
142. B.L. Harleian Mss 5120 f14, f34 and f39.
143. See Hunt, *Practical Gauging Epitomized*, p103, and *Excise Board Entry Books of Correspondence with Treasury, 1685–1690* PRO CUST 48/3 July 1687 f138.
144. Quotation from B.L. Harleian Mss 4077 f23; see also f36v and f47; 5120 f12 and f36; 5121 f2, f2v, f4, f9, f13v, f34v and f36.
145. B.L. Harleian Mss 5121 f40; see also 5121 f20.
146. B.L. Harleian Mss 5120 f56v.
147. B.L. Harleian Mss 4077 f42v, and 5120 ff13v–14.
148. B.L. Harleian Mss 4077 f6 and f9, and 5120 f12, f14v, f29, f43 and f52v.
149. B.L. Harleian Mss 5120 ff48v–49; see also f59 and f61v.
150. B.L. Harleian Mss 5120 f30.
151. PRO CUST 48/2 12 May 1685 ff112–113.
152. B.L. Harleian Mss 4077 ff42v–43, f45v and ff56–57; 5120 ff63–63v; 5121 f26.
153. Quotation from B.L. Harleian Mss 5121 f6v; see also 4077 f4, f7, f8, f10 and f50v; 5121 f7 and f50.
154. The model for this was Yorkshire; see B.L. Harleian Mss 5120 f51v, f47v, f54 and f56v.
155. Hunt, *Practical Gauging Epitomized*, p106.
156. B.L. Harleian Mss 4077 f22v, 26v and 28v; 5120 f11v and f21v; 5121 f6, f23v and f51.
157. B.L. Harleian Mss 4077 f36; 5120 f4, f31, f54 and f59v; 5121 f8v, f38v, f43v, f47v and f52.
158. B.L. Harleian Mss 5120 f6v; see also 5121 f40v.
159. For alterations, see, e.g., B.L. Harleian Mss 5120 f13 and f48; 5121 ff25–25v and ff51–51v. Rides are tabulated in B.L. Harleian Mss 5123,

and their revenues, in the context of the collection and the country as a whole, are tabulated in B.L. Harleian Mss 4227. For 'compounding,' see B.L. Harleian Mss 5120 f47v and 5121 f8.

160. PRO CUST 48/3 14 December 1687 ff177–178; B.L. Harleian Mss 5120 f1, f7v, ff25v–26, f31 and f59; 5121 f16v and f38v.

161. B.L. Harleian Mss 5120 f7; 5121 f24 and f35.

162. B.L. Harleian Mss 4077 f1–1v, f20v, ff22v–23, f36 and f50v; 5120 f13; 5121 f5 and f52v. Officers were later prevented from working where they had been born or trained; see Brewer, *The Sinews of Power.*

163. The notion of this sort of 'network' is from Latour, *Science in Action.* The term seems more appropriate in this context than 'assemblage,' as suggested in Mitchell Dean (1996) 'Putting the technological into government,' *History of the Human Sciences* 9 pp47–68.

164. Davenant, 'Discourses on the public revenues,' p177.

165. John Ward (1707) *The Young Mathematician's Guide* (London) p34.

166. See the fraud detected in B.L. Harleian Mss 5121 ff44v–46v.

167. Davenant, 'Discourses on the public revenues,' p215.

168. Ezekial Polstead (1697) Καλως τελωνησανται; or, *The Excise Man . . .* (London). The Greek title translates, I'm told, as 'They will take a toll beautifully.' The only other work by Polstead that I have been able to trace is a poem in celebration of Wales written in a classical style, (1702) *Cambria Triumphans; or, A Panegyrick upon Wales. A Pindarick Poem* (London), and dedicated to an excise commissioner, Philip Riley. The only other full exploration of the writings of an excise man that I have found is John Money's interpretation of the journal of John Cannon, in Money, 'Teaching in the market-place.'

169. B.L. Harleian Mss 4077 f47v and f50v; B.L. Harleian Mss 7431 *Names and Salaries of Excise Men, 1688 & 1689,* f26; and *Excise Board Minute Books, 27th January 1695/6 to 25th June 1696* PRO CUST 47/2 15 April 1696 f44 and 5 May 1696 f58.

170. Polstead, *The Excise Man,* p109.

171. For earlier examples of satire on the Excise, see Braddick, *Parliamentary Taxation.*

172. Polstead, *The Excise Man,* Chapter IX.

173. Polstead, *The Excise Man,* p45.

174. Polstead, *The Excise Man,* p56 and p57.

175. Polstead, *The Excise Man,* p58.

176. Polstead, *The Excise Man,* p116.

177. Polstead, *The Excise Man,* p24.

178. John Cannon's journal shows the jostling for position, and for the favourable walks and rides, that characterised the local management of the Excise; see Money, 'Teaching in the market-place,' p375 footnote 61.

179. Polstead, *The Excise Man,* pp28–29. *Ex Mero Motu:* as of their own free will, literally, of their own motion.

180. Polstead, *The Excise Man,* p1 and p30.

181. Polstead, *The Excise Man,* p75.

182. Polstead, *The Excise Man,* pp50–51.

183. Polstead, *The Excise Man,* p53 and p51.

184. Polstead, *The Excise Man,* p54 and p55.

185. This is John Cannon's term; see Money, 'Teaching in the market-place,' p351.

186. Polstead, *The Excise Man,* p110.

187. Polstead, *The Excise Man,* p14. John Cannon also exhibited a joy in the pleasures of mathematics; see Money, 'Teaching in the market-place,' p358.

188. Polstead, *The Excise Man,* p15.

189. Polstead, *The Excise Man,* p16. This professionalised relationship between knowledge and status is quite different from the ways in which it was gentlemanly status that guaranteed the truth of scientific knowledges among seventeenth-century natural philosophers. See Steven Shapin (1994) *A Social History of Truth: Civility and Science in Seventeenth-Century England* (University of Chicago Press, Chicago).

190. Polstead, *The Excise Man,* p13.

191. Thomas, 'Numeracy in early modern England,' p113, and Buck, 'Seventeenth-century political arithmetic.' Their practical activities were also defined as masculine; see Polstead, *The Excise Man,* pp21–22.

192. Polstead, *The Excise Man,* pp80–81 and p88.

193. Polstead, *The Excise Man,* p102. John Cannon also wrote detailed local historical and geographical descriptions. John Money, 'Teaching in the market-place,' p353, refers to them as his 'own mental map of the places where he lived and worked.'

194. Polstead, *The Excise Man,* p11.

195. John Money also uses John Cannon's journal to draw out the implications of 'the separateness of the service and the separateness of the individual officer within it'; see Money, 'Teaching in the market-place,' pp351–352.

196. Polstead, *The Excise Man,* Chapter XIII.

197. This can be seen as living out the 'differentiation' of the modern state; see Braddick, 'The early modern English state.'

198. Polstead, *The Excise Man,* p67.

199. Polstead, *The Excise Man,* pp31–32.

200. B.L. Harleian Mss 4077 f50v and f51v.

201. Polstead, *The Excise Man,* p29.

202. Polstead, *The Excise Man,* pp33–34.

203. The Excise Man's silence can be taken further. It defines his fidelity to the state and the Excise. Polstead notes that he must ensure that superiors know that he will not disclose secrets, or pass on information that he has received except through the proper channels (*The Excise Man,* p60), and he notes that 'we shall find him an absolute Enemy to the talking (tho a great Lover) of the Government, For he knows the Persons as well as the Government of Kings to be Sacred' (*The Excise Man,* p26).

204. Polstead, *The Excise Man,* p35.

205. Polstead, *The Excise Man,* p21.
206. Stone, in his 'Introduction,' p6, calls this the 'Brewer Paradox.'
207. Polstead, *The Excise Man,* p108 and p77.
208. Polstead, *The Excise Man,* p111.
209. This is also abundantly clear in the varied reactions of officers to the Monmouth Rebellion, noted by Davenant, in B.L. Harleian Mss 4077 f3v to f17v *passim,* and in John Cannon's chequered career; see Money, 'Teaching in the market-place.'
210. Mikhail Bakhtin (1962) *Rabelais and His World* (Indiana University Press, Bloomington) p16 and p87. It is also worth noting the differences between the bodies described by Polstead and by Rabelais.
211. Max Weber quoted in Mommsen, ' "Toward the iron cage of future serfdom"?,' p175. See also Erving Goffman (1961) *Asylums: Essays on the Social Situation of Mental Patients and Other Inmates* (Penguin, Harmondsworth, UK) p280.
212. Pocock, 'Modernity and anti-modernity,' p53 and p55. See also Patrick Brantlinger (1996) *Fictions of State: Culture and Credit in Britain, 1694–1994* (Cornell University Press, Ithaca, NY).
213. Brewer, *The Sinews of Power,* p154.
214. These figure do not include officers working at the Excise Office in London. They are calculated from Brewer, *The Sinews of Power,* pp104–105.
215. B.L. Add. Mss 10404 *The Establishment of the Revenue of Excise, 1736–1763.* For 1771, see *Excise Board Entry Books of Correspondence with Treasury, 1767–1774* PRO CUST 48/18 28 November 1771 ff251–256.
216. Davenant, 'Discourses on the public revenues,' p186, and Mathias, *The Brewing Industry,* p540.
217. William Hersee (1829) *The Spirit of the General Letters and Orders Issued by the Honourable Board of Excise . . . from 1700 to 1827 Inclusive* (London).
218. This section is primarily based upon Commissioners of the Excise (1750) *Orders and Instructions for the Management of the London Brewery* (London); (1755a) *Instructions for Surveyors in the London Brewery* (London); (1761) *Instructions for Officers in the London Brewery* (London); and (1775) *Instructions for Officers in the London Brewery* (London). For other commodities, see Commissioners of Excise (1732) *Instructions for Officers Who Survey the Large Dealers in Coffee, Tea and Chocolate, &c. and All the Permit Writers* (London); (1755b) *Instructions for the General-Surveyors of the Distillery* (London); (1762a) *Instructions for Officers Who Survey Distillers for Exportation* (London); (1773) *Instructions for Officers of the London Distillery, Brandy, and Small Dealers in Tea etc.* (London); (1762b) *Instructions to Be Observed by the Officers Employ'd in Charging the Duties on Candles and Soap in London* (London); (1755c) *Instructions for the Tide-Surveyors of the Excise* (London); (1764) *Instructions for the Tide-Waiters of Excise in the Port of London* (London); and (1774) *Instructions to Be Observed by the Officers Concerned in Ascertaining the Duties on Glass* (London). For books of advice and instruction, see Leadbetter, *The Royal Gauger;* Samuel West (1769) *The Exciseman's Pocket-Book: Containing Abstracts of All the Laws Relating to the Cus-*

toms and Excise (London); and Jelinger Symons (1775) *The Excise Laws Abridged . . .* (London).

219. Torrance, 'Social class and bureaucratic innovation'; Paul Langford (1975) *The Excise Crisis: Society and Politics in the Age of Walpole* (Clarendon Press, Oxford); and Kathleen Wilson (1995b) *The Sense of the People: Politics, Culture and Imperialism in England, 1715–1785* (Cambridge University Press, Cambridge) pp117–136.

220. B.L. Lansdowne Mss 1215/38 *Draft of a Presentment to the Lords of the Treasury Concerning the Mismanagement of the London Brewery*, ff135–136.

221. B.L. Add. Mss 29458 f17.

222. Mathias, *The Brewing Industry*, p11.

223. Commissioners of Excise, *Brewery* (1750), p2 and p3.

224. Commissioners of Excise, *Brewery* (1750), p8. This was also the case for other commodities.

225. Hutcheson, *For Maltsters, Brewers, and Hop-Planters*, pp50–51 and p54.

226. Commissioners of Excise, *Brewery* (1755a), p4.

227. Commissioners of Excise, *Brewery* (1750), pp10–11.

228. Rule from 13 October 1753 in Hersee, *The Spirit of the General Letters*, p291.

229. Commissioners of Excise, *Brewery* (1755a), p5, and Commissioners of Excise, *Brewery* (1761), pp14–15 and pp17–18.

230. The General Surveyor was to do the same to the officers; see Commissioners of Excise, *Distillery* (1755b), p7, and *Glass* (1774), p13.

231. Hutcheson, *For Maltsters, Brewers, and Hop-Planters*, pp54–55.

232. Commissioners of Excise, *Brewery* (1755a), p6.

233. Commissioners of Excise, *Brewery* (1761), p8.

234. Commissioners of Excise, *Coffee etc* (1732), p22. See also the legal requirements on how to tie up a packet of starch with string in Hersee, *The Spirit of the General Letters*, p410.

235. Hersee, *The Spirit of the General Letters*, p438.

CHAPTER 6

1. Michael J. Freeman (1983) 'Introduction,' in Derek H. Aldcroft and Michael J. Freeman (eds.) *Transport in the Industrial Revolution* (Manchester University Press, Manchester, UK) p2.

2. William Albert (1983) 'The turnpike trusts,' in Derek H. Aldcroft and Michael J. Freeman (eds.) *Transport in the Industrial Revolution* (Manchester University Press, Manchester, UK) p32 and p38, and Nigel J. Thrift (1990) 'Transport and communication, 1730–1914,' in R. A. Dodgshon and R. A. Butlin (eds.) *An Historical Geography of England and Wales* 2d ed. (Academic Press, London) pp453–486.

3. Albert, 'The turnpike trusts,' p41 and p42. See the maps in Eric Pawson (1977) *Transport and Economy: The Turnpike Roads of Eighteenth-Century Britain* (Academic Press, London) p139, p140, and p151.

4. Paul Langford (1989) *A Polite and Commercial People: England, 1727–1783* (Oxford University Press, Oxford) p396.

5. John A. Chartres and Gerald L. Turnbull (1983) 'Road transport,' in Derek H. Aldcroft and Michael J. Freeman (eds.) *Transport in the Industrial Revolution* (Manchester University Press, Manchester, UK) pp65–66.

6. Langford, *A Polite and Commercial People*, p404.

7. Thrift, 'Transport and communication.'

8. Michael J. Freeman (1986) 'Transport,' in John Langton and R. J. Morris (eds.) *Atlas of Industrializing Britain, 1780–1914* (Methuen, London) p80.

9. Philip S. Bagwell (1974) *The Transport Revolution from 1770* (Batsford, London) p41.

10. Howard Robinson (1948) *The British Post Office: A History* (Princeton University Press, Princeton, NJ) p103 and p106.

11. Derek Gregory (1987) 'The friction of distance? Information circulation and the mails in early nineteenth-century England,' *Journal of Historical Geography* 13 pp130–154.

12. Kenneth Ellis (1958) *The Post Office in the Eighteenth Century: A Study in Administrative History* (Oxford University Press, London) viii.

13. Robinson, *The British Post Office*, p165.

14. David Hancock (1995) *Citizens of the World: London Merchants and the Integration of the British Atlantic Community, 1735–1785* (Cambridge University Press, Cambridge), and Howard Robinson (1964) *Carrying British Mails Overseas* (George Allen and Unwin, London).

15. Ellis, *The Post Office*, viii.

16. Kathleen Wilson (1995b) *The Sense of the People: Politics, Culture and Imperialism in England, 1715–1785* (Cambridge University Press, Cambridge) pp44–45.

17. Ellis, *The Post Office*, p67.

18. John Brewer (1989) *The Sinews of Power: War, Money and the English State, 1688–1783* (Unwin Hyman, London), and Julian Hoppit (1996) 'Political arithmetic in eighteenth-century England,' *Economic History Review* XLIV pp516–540.

19. Brewer, *The Sinews of Power*, p221.

20. Wilson, *The Sense of the People*.

21. Wilson, *The Sense of the People*, pp29–33.

22. This paragraph is based on Jeremy Black (1987) *The English Press in the Eighteenth Century* (Croom Helm, London); G. A. Cranfield (1962) *The Development of the Provincial Newspaper, 1700–1760* (Clarendon Press, Oxford); Michael Harris (1987) *London Newspapers in the Age of Walpole: A Study of the Origins of the Modern English Press* (Associated University Presses, London); and Roy M. Wiles (1965) *Freshest Advices: Early Provincial Newspapers in England* (Ohio State University Press, Columbus).

23. Wilson, *The Sense of the People*, p37.

24. Harris, *London Newspapers in the Age of Walpole*, p33.

25. Wilson, *The Sense of the People*.

26. Kathleen Wilson (1995c) 'The good, the bad, and the impotent: Imperi-

alism and the politics of identity in Georgian England,' in Ann Berming-ham and John Brewer (eds.) *The Consumption of Culture, 1600–1800: Image, Object, Text* (Routledge, London) pp239–240.

27. Hancock, *Citizens of the World*, p25.
28. Christopher Dandeker (1990) *Surveillance, Power and Modernity: Bureaucracy and Discipline from 1700 to the Present Day* (Polity Press, Cambridge, UK) p77, and Paul Kennedy (1988) *The Rise and Fall of the Great Powers: Economic Change and Military Conflict from 1500 to 2000* (Unwin Hyman, London).
29. Hancock, *Citizens of the World*, p29. See also Elizabeth B. Schumpeter (1960) *English Overseas Trade Statistics, 1697–1808* (Clarendon Press, Oxford), and Patrick K. O'Brien and Stanley L. Engerman (1991) 'Exports and the growth of the British economy from the Glorious Revolution to the Peace of Amiens,' in Barbara L. Solow (ed.) *Slavery and the Rise of the Atlantic System* (Cambridge University Press, Cambridge) pp177–209.
30. James Walvin (1997) *Fruits of Empire: Exotic Produce and British Taste, 1660–1800* (Macmillan, Basingstoke, UK) and Elizabeth Kowaleski-Wallace (1997) *Consuming Subjects: Women, Shopping, and Business in the Eighteenth Century* (Columbia University Press, New York).
31. O'Brien and Engerman, 'Exports and the growth of the British economy,' p182.
32. Marcus Rediker (1987) *Between the Devil and the Deep Blue Sea: Merchant Seamen, Pirates and the Anglo-American Maritime World, 1700–1750* (Cambridge University Press, Cambridge) p45, and Hancock, *Citizens of the World*, p175.
33. Paul Gilroy (1993) *The Black Atlantic: Modernity and Double Consciousness* (Verso, London) p58.
34. Gilroy, *The Black Atlantic*, p221.
35. Walvin, in *Fruits of Empire*, also notes the occurrence of a 'consumer revolution' among indigenous North American fur trappers.
36. Hancock, *Citizens of the World*, p37.
37. T. S. Ashton (1960) 'Introduction,' in Elizabeth B. Schumpeter, *English Overseas Trade Statistics, 1697–1808* (Clarendon Press, Oxford) pp1–14; Rediker, *Between the Devil and the Deep Blue Sea*, p21; and Peter Linebaugh (1991) *The London Hanged: Crime and Civil Society in the Eighteenth Century* (Penguin, Harmondsworth, UK) p69.
38. Hancock, *Citizens of the World*, p69, p85, p19 and p132.
39. Hancock, *Citizens of the World*, pp101–102.
40. Rediker, *Between the Devil and the Deep Blue Sea*, p75. Defoe is quoted in Hancock, *Citizens of the World*, p35.
41. Peter Linebaugh (1982) 'All the Atlantic mountains shook,' *Labour/Le Travailleur* 10 p109 and p112.
42. Gilroy, *The Black Atlantic*, p16.
43. Peter Linebaugh and Marcus Rediker (1990) 'The many-headed Hydra: Sailors, slaves, and the Atlantic working class in the eighteenth century,' *Journal of Historical Sociology* 3 pp225–252. See also the writings of Olau-

dah Equiano and Quobna Ottabah Cugaono in Adam Potkay and Sandra Burr (1995) *Black Atlantic Writers of the Eighteenth Century: Living the New Exodus in England and the Americas* (Macmillan, Basingstoke, UK).

44. Linebaugh, *The London Hanged*, p70 and p119.
45. Charles W. J. Withers (1996) 'Encyclopaedism, modernism, and the classification of geographical knowledge,' *Transactions of the Institute of British Geographers* 21 pp275–298.
46. Brewer, *The Sinews of Power*.
47. Anthony Giddens (1990) *The Consequences of Modernity* (Polity Press, Cambridge, UK) p174 and p140.
48. David Harvey (1989) *The Condition of Postmodernity* (Basil Blackwell, Oxford, UK).
49. Anthony Giddens (1985) *The Nation-State and Violence* (Polity Press, Cambridge, UK) p178 and p181, and Giddens, *The Consequences of Modernity*, p77.
50. Giddens, *The Nation-State and Violence*, p174.
51. Giddens, *The Consequences of Modernity*, p33, p87 and p4.
52. Walvin, *Fruits of Empire*, pp194–195.
53. Rosalind H. Williams (1993) 'Cultural origins and environmental implications of large technological systems,' *Science in Context* 2 p382.
54. The date is given here according to the New Style Gregorian calendar.
55. [Henry Fielding] (1752) *A Plan of the Universal Register Office, Opposite Cecil Street in the Strand, and of That in Bishopsgate-Street, the Corner of Cornhill*, 2d ed. (London) pp9–10. I have used the second edition throughout since it repeats what is in the first edition (1751) with some useful additions. For textual commentary, see Henry Fielding (1988) *'The Covent-Garden Journal' and 'A Plan of the Universal Register-Office,'* ed. Bertrand A. Goldgar (Clarendon Press, Oxford). See also *London Daily Advertiser,* 31 October 1751.
56. [Henry Fielding], *Plan of the Universal Register Office,* p14.
57. The Bishopsgate Office was run by John Fielding and opened on 6 April 1752, while the Dublin Office was an independent venture that shared information with the Universal Register Offices in London. See R. Leslie-Melville (1934) *The Life and Work of Sir John Fielding* (Lincoln Williams, London) and *A Plan of the Universal Register Office Now Open'd Opposite to the Parliament-House in College-Green* (Dublin, 1751).
58. [John Fielding] (1755a) *A Plan of the Universal Register Office, Opposite Cecil Street in the Strand, and of That in Bishopsgate-Street, the Corner of Cornhill* 8th ed. (London) p2, and Michel de Montaigne, Essay 35: 'Something lacking in our civil administrations,' in (1991) *The Essays of Michel de Montaigne,* trans. and ed. M. A. Screech (Penguin, Harmondsworth, UK) bk1, pp251–252.
59. M. Dorothy George (1926–1929) 'The early history of registry offices,' *Economic Journal: Economic History Supplement* 1 pp570–590.
60. Henry Robinson (1650) *The Office of Addresses and Encounters . . .* (London) p6.

61. Robinson, *The Office of Addresses and Encounters*, p4.
62. Williams, 'Cultural origins,' p382.
63. Williams, 'Cultural origins,' p382.
64. [Henry Fielding], *Plan of the Universal Register Office*, pp5–6.
65. [Henry Fielding], *Plan of the Universal Register Office*, p5.
66. [Henry Fielding], *Plan of the Universal Register Office*, p5.
67. [Henry Fielding], *Plan of the Universal Register Office*, pp6–7; see also Chapter 4 this book.
68. [Henry Fielding], *Plan of the Universal Register Office*, p7.
69. *Plan of the Universal Register Office [Dublin]*, p3.
70. *Plan of the Universal Register Office [Dublin]*, p4.
71. [Henry Fielding], *Plan of the Universal Register Office*, pp7–8.
72. *Plan of the Universal Register Office [Dublin]*, pp4–5.
73. [Henry Fielding], *Plan of the Universal Register Office*, p9 and p10.
74. [Henry Fielding], *Plan of the Universal Register Office*, p3.
75. [Henry Fielding], *Plan of the Universal Register Office*, p3.
76. *Plan of the Universal Register Office [Dublin]*, p4.
77. *London Daily Advertiser*, 3 June 1751.
78. The advertisements are quoted in Leslie-Melville, *The Life and Work of Sir John Fielding*.
79. *Plan of the Universal Register Office [Dublin]*, p16, and [Henry Fielding], *Plan of the Universal Register Office*, p17 and p19.
80. [John Fielding], *Plan of the Universal Register Office*, p19 and p14.
81. [Henry Fielding], *Plan of the Universal Register Office*, p19.
82. Robinson, *The Office of Addresses and Encounters*, p5.
83. Kowaleski-Wallace, *Consuming Subjects*.
84. [Henry Fielding], *Plan of the Universal Register Office*, p15. The Universal Register Office was recommended on these grounds at the end of Henry Fielding (1751) *An Inquiry into the Causes of the Late Increase of Robbers . . .* (London).
85. *Plan of the Universal Register Office [Dublin]*, p13.
86. [John Fielding], *Plan of the Universal Register Office*.
87. [Henry Fielding], *Plan of the Universal Register Office*, pp6–7.
88. [Henry Fielding], *Plan of the Universal Register Office*, p11 and p12. See also *London Daily Advertiser*, 3 June 1751.
89. *Plan of the Universal Register Office [Dublin]*, p15, and [Henry Fielding], *Plan of the Universal Register Office*, pp16–17.
90. *Plan of the Universal Register Office [Dublin]*, p5, and *London Daily Advertiser*, 31 October 1751.
91. *Plan of the Universal Register Office [Dublin]*, p7.
92. Williams, 'Cultural origins,' p384.
93. Robinson, *The Office of Addresses and Encounters*, p4.
94. Robinson, *The Office of Addresses and Encounters*, p3.
95. John Styles (1983) 'Sir John Fielding and the problem of criminal investigation in eighteenth-century England,' *Transactions of the Royal Historical Society* 5th series 33 p128.

96. John Fielding (1758b) *An Account of the Origin and Effects of a Police Set on Foot by His Grace the Duke of Newcastle in the Year 1753, upon a Plan Presented to His Grace by the Late Henry Fielding, Esq* (London) p37.

97. Leon Radzinowicz (1956) *A History of the English Criminal Law and Its Administration from 1750. Vol. 3: Cross-currents in the Movement for the Reform of the Police* (Stevens & Sons, London) pp46–47, and John Fielding (1768) *Extracts from Such of the Penal Laws, as Particularly Relate to the Peace and Good Order of This Metropolis* (London) p4.

98. Fielding, *Account of the Origin and Effects of a Police*, p30 and p34.

99. Fielding, *Account of the Origin and Effects of a Police*, p38, and Fielding, *Extracts from . . . the Penal Laws*, p6.

100. John Bender (1987) *Imagining the Penitentiary: Fiction and the Architecture of Mind in Eighteenth-Century England* (University of Chicago Press, Chicago) p171.

101. Fielding, *Account of the Origin and Effects of a Police*, x–xi, and Linebaugh, *The London Hanged*.

102. John Fielding (1776) *Some Proper Cautions to the Merchants, Tradesmen and Shopkeepers of the Cities of London and Westminster* (London) p83, p86 and p87; see also *Thieving Detected; Being a True and Particular Description, of the Various Methods and Artifices, Used by Thieves and Sharpers, to Take In and Deceive the Public* (London, 1777).

103. 'Report of the Committee of the House of Commons on Sir John Fielding's Plan for Preventing Burglaries and Robberies' [10 April 1770], in *The Parliamentary History of England from the Earliest Period to the Year 1803*, ed. William Cobbett (London, 1813) Vol. XVI, columns 930–931.

104. Fielding, *Account of the Origin and Effects of a Police*, p39.

105. Bertrand A. Goldgar (1988) 'General introduction,' in Henry Fielding, *'The Covent-Garden Journal' and 'A Plan of the Universal Register-Office'* (Clarendon Press, Oxford) xv.

106. Martin C. Battestin with Ruth R. Battestin (1989) *Henry Fielding: A Life* (Routledge, London) p561, and Styles, 'Sir John Fielding.'

107. Fielding, *Extracts from . . . the Penal Laws*, and Fielding, *Some Proper Cautions to the Merchants*. The anonymous author of *Thieving Detected*, which was addressed to Sir John Fielding, claimed that he had gathered all his knowledge during a three months' stay in Newgate prison.

108. Fielding, *Extracts from . . . the Penal Laws*, vi and v.

109. The plan also included better street lighting, a foot patrol, a regiment of light horse to police the turnpikes out of London, and a newspaper 'established by law, in which every Thing, relative to the Discovery of Offenders, should be advertised.' See 'Abstract of Sir John Fielding's Plan of Police,' in *Liverpool Papers* CXLV, British Library Add. Mss 38334 f75v.

110. Styles, 'Sir John Fielding.'

111. Circular from Sir John Fielding, 19 October 1772; reprinted in Appendix 1 of Radzinowicz, *A History of the English Criminal Law, Vol. 3*, p482.

112. Styles, 'Sir John Fielding,' p129.

113. Circular from Sir John Fielding, 22 September 1772; reprinted in Appen-

dix 1 of Radzinowicz, *A History of the English Criminal Law, Vol. 3*, p480. These circulars—the 'Quarterly Pursuit of Criminals' and the 'Weekly or Extraordinary Pursuit'—eventually became the *Police Gazette*. For examples of the descriptions, see Radzinowicz, *A History of the English Criminal Law, Vol. 3*, footnote 12 p52.

114. Letter from Sir John Fielding to the Acting Magistrates for the County of Essex, n.d.; reprinted in Appendix 1 of Radzinowicz, *A History of the English Criminal Law, Vol. 3*, pp481–482.

115. Fielding, 22 September 1772 in Radzinowicz, *A History of the English Criminal Law, Vol. 3*, p480. Fielding also planned other similar schemes: associations of tradesmen and shopkeepers; 'a select Body of Pawnbrokers'; and an association of gentlemen to prevent highway robberies; see Fielding, *Extracts from . . . the Penal Laws*, pp267–270 and p272, and John Fielding (1755b) *A Plan for Preventing Robberies within Twenty Miles of London* (London).

116. Leslie-Melville, *The Life and Work of Sir John Fielding*, p11.

117. Fielding, 19 October 1772, in Radzinowicz, *A History of the English Criminal Law, Vol. 3*, p482.

118. Bender, *Imagining the Penitentiary*, p140.

119. Fielding, 19 October 1772, in Radzinowicz, *A History of the English Criminal Law, Vol. 3*, p483.

120. Joseph Reed (1761) *The Register Office: A Farce of Two Acts* (London). Except where indicated the text that I have used is the second edition of 1771.

121. Reed quoted in George Winchester Stone Jr and George M. Kahrl (1979) *David Garrick: A Critical Biography* (University of Southern Illinois Press, Carbondale) p599.

122. David M. Little and George M. Kahrl (eds.) (1963) *The Letters of David Garrick, Vol. II* (Oxford University Press, London) Letter 450, 5 April 1767.

123. *Dictionary of National Biography* (Hereafter DNB).

124. *DNB*

125. Stone and Kahrl, *David Garrick*, p599, and *DNB*

126. George Winchester Stone (ed.) (1962) *The London Stage, 1660–1800. Part 4: 1747–1776* (University of Southern Illinois Press, Carbondale), and Stone and Kahrl, *David Garrick*, p599.

127. George, 'The early history of registry offices.'

128. Fielding, *Extracts from . . . the Penal Laws*, p141, and Goldgar, 'General introduction,' xxii and xxvii.

129. Reed, *The Register Office*, p7.

130. Reed, *The Register Office*, p21, stresses that 'A Register-Office, under the Management of an honest Man, must certainly be very serviceable to the Publick.'

131. Reed, *The Register Office*, p8.

132. Reed, *The Register Office*, p8, p9 and p13.

133. Reed, *The Register Office*, p11. On the cultural politics of late-eighteenth-

century hairdressers and their pretensions, see Don Herzog (1996) 'The trouble with hairdressers,' *Representations* 53 pp21–43.

134. Reed, *The Register Office,* pp16–17, p19, p22, p29 and p36; and Reed, *The Register Office,* 1st ed., p37. Inducing the poor and unwary to going to the plantations as indentured labour was widely thought to be one of the dangers of the seventeenth- and eighteenth-century intelligence and register offices; see George, 'The early history of registry offices,' and Leslie-Melville, *The Life and Work of Sir John Fielding.*

135. Reed, *The Register Office,* p22.

136. This, it appears, is another reference to Henry Fielding. See Henry Fielding (1753) *A Clear State of the Case of Elizabeth Canning* (London).

137. Reed, *The Register Office,* p38 and p43.

138. Reed, *The Register Office,* p46.

139. Reed, *The Register Office,* p31 and p32.

140. Reed, *The Register Office,* p7.

141. Reed, *The Register Office,* 1st ed., p21.

142. Joseph Reed (1769) *Tom Jones: A Comic Opera* (London) no pagination.

143. Reed, *The Register Office,* p16 and p11.

144. Reed, *The Register Office,* p19.

145. Reed, *The Register Office,* p23.

146. Reed, *The Register Office,* p20, p39, p32 and p33.

147. Reed, *Tom Jones,* no pagination.

148. Reed, *The Register Office,* p9 and pp10–11.

149. Reed, *The Register Office,* p33.

150. Reed, *The Register Office,* p36.

151. Reed, *The Register Office,* 1st ed., p20. See also Lord Brilliant's description of his wife as a tradesman's daughter 'ten Times more haughty and impertinent, than if she had been born a Woman of Quality,' in Reed, *The Register Office,* p36.

152. Reed, *The Register Office,* p8.

153. Harvey, *The Condition of Postmodernity,* p240.

154. Giddens, *The Consequences of Modernity,* p90.

155. Reed, *The Register Office,* 1st ed., p44.

156. Reed, *The Register Office,* p47.

157. Reed, *The Register Office,* p48.

CHAPTER 7

1. Henri Lefebvre (1991) *The Production of Space* (Basil Blackwell, Oxford, UK) p86.

2. Kathleen Wilson (1995a) 'Citizenship, empire, and modernity in the English provinces, c 1720–1790,' *Eighteenth-Century Studies* 29 p71.

3. Most of the material here is taken from the newspaper accounts and prints collected together in *Remarkable Characters; Exhibitions; Fireworks in the Green Park, 1749,* Vol. 5 in the Fillinham Collection in the British Library.

4. *A Description of the Machine for the Fireworks . . . Published by Order of His Majesty's Board of Ordnance* (London, 1749) p3.
5. David Cressy (1989) *Bonfires and Bells: National Memory and the Protestant Calendar in Elizabethan and Stuart England* (Weidenfeld and Nicolson, London).
6. John Brewer (1997) *The Pleasures of the Imagination: English Culture in the Eighteenth Century* (Harper Collins, London) uses this example to argue for the vibrancy of the commercialised and public 'arts' rather than those sponsored by royalty.
7. The military connections are evident in Robert Jones (1765) *A Treatise on Artificial Fireworks* (London) which is dedicated to Charles Frederick, and in R. A. Jones (1776) *Artificial Fireworks Improved to the Modern Practice . . . . Also Mr Muller's Fireworks, for Sea and Land Service* (London).
8. *A Letter from a Gentleman in London . . . Concerning the Treaty at Aix-La Chapelle, Concluded on 8th of October 1748* (London, 1748).
9. Fillinham Collection, f73.
10. *The Green-Park Folly; or, The Fireworks Blown Up; A Satire* (London, 1749) p13, p24 and p28.

Bibliography

ARCHIVAL SOURCES

British Library

B.L. Add. Mss 10404   *The Establishment of the Revenue of Excise, 1736–1763.*

B.L. Add. Mss 29458   *The State of the Excise, 1662–1786.*

B.L. Add. Mss 38334   Abstract of Sir John Fielding's Plan of Police, *Liverpool Papers* CXLV.

B.L. Harleian Mss 1243   *Some Considerations About an Excise.*

B.L. Harleian Mss 1898   *Gross and Neat Produce of the Excise*

B.L. Harleian Mss 4077   *An Account of the Management of the Officers of the West of England, 1685.*

B.L. Harleian Mss 4227   *Abstract of the Revenue of the Excise, 1684–1687.*

B.L. Harleian Mss 5120 & 5121   *Miles Edgar on the Excise.*

B.L. Harleian Mss 5123   *Management of the Excise.*

B.L. Harleian Mss 7431   *Names and Salaries of Excise Men, 1688 & 1689.*

B.L. Lansdowne Mss 1215/38   *Draft of a Presentment to the Lords of the Treasury Concerning the Mismanagement of the London Brewery.*

Burn Collection   *A Collection of Tickets, Bills of Performance, Pamphlets, Ms. Notes, Engravings and Extracts and Cuttings from Books and Periodicals Relating to Vauxhall Gardens. Originally Made by Jacob Henry Burn.*

Fillinham Collection   *Volume 5: Remarkable Characters; Exhibitions; Fireworks in the Green Park, 1749.*

Duchy of Cornwall Office

Print Collection. Folder 28: *A Collection of Newspaper Cuttings and Other Papers Relating to the History of the New Spring Gardens, Popularly Known as Vauxhall.*
Folder 4: *Vauxhall.*
Folder 5: *Cartoons and Caricatures of Vauxhall.*

Minet Library, Lambeth

Vauxhall Gardens Archive. *Bound Volume 5 (1785–1835).*
Vauxhall Gardens Archive. *Press Cuttings, 1732–1823.*

Public Record Office

CUST 47/2   *Excise Board Minute Books, 27 January 1695/6 to 25 June 1696.*
CUST 48/2   *Excise Board Entry Books of Correspondence with Treasury, 1683–1686.*
CUST 48/3   *Excise Board Entry Books of Correspondence with Treasury, 1685–1690.*
CUST 48/18   *Excise Board Entry Books of Correspondence with Treasury, 1767–1774.*

ACTS OF PARLIAMENT

13 &14 Car. II cap 2 [1662]. *An Act for Repairing the Highways and Sewers, and for Paving and Keeping Clean of the Streets, in and about the Cities of London and Westminster. . . .*
2 William and Mary session 2 cap 8 [1690]. *An Act for Paving and Cleansing the Streets in the Cities of London and Westminster. . . .*
2 Geo. II cap 11 [1728]. *An Act for Better Paving and Cleansing the Streets in the City and Liberty of Westminster. . . .*
2 Geo. III cap 21 [1762]. *An Act for Paving, Cleansing, and Lighting the Squares, Streets, and Lanes, within the City and Liberty of Westminster. . . .*
4 Geo. III cap 39 [1764]. *An Act to Explain, Amend and Render More Effectual, . . . Acts of Parliament . . . for Paving, Cleansing, and Lighting the Squares, Streets, and Lanes, within the City and Liberty of Westminster. . . .*
5 Geo. III cap 13 [1765]. *An Act for Empowering the Commissioners for Putting in Execution the Several Acts passed for Paving, Cleansing, and Lighting the Squares, Streets, and Lanes, within the City and Liberty of Westminster. . . .*
5 Geo. III cap 50 [1765]. *An Act for Enlarging Powers. . . .*
9 Geo. III cap 13 [1769]. *An Act for the Better Paving, Cleansing, Lighting, and Watching, the Liberty of St. Martin Le Grand, within the City and Liberty of Westminster. . . .*

9 Geo. III cap 31 [1769]. *An Act for the Establishing and Well Governing a Hospital for the Reception, Maintenance, and Employment, of Penitent Prostitutes.*

11 Geo. III cap 22 [1771]. *An Act to Amend and Render More Effectual Several Acts Made Relating to Paving, Cleansing, and Lighting the Squares, Streets, and Lanes, within the City and Liberty of Westminster. . . .*

PERIODICALS

Applebee's Journal
British Magazine
Connoisseur
Gentleman's Magazine
Grub Street Journal
London Daily Advertiser
London Magazine
Macaroni, Scavoir Vivre, and Theatrical Magazine
Matrimonial Magazine
Oxford Magazine
Rambler
Spectator
Town and Country Magazine
Universal Magazine
Universal Spectator and Weekly Journal
Weekly Register

PUBLISHED SOURCES

A. B. [Nathaniel Lardner] (1758). *A Letter to Jonas Hanway Esq; In Which Some Reasons Are Assigned, Why Some Houses for the Reception of Penitent Women, Who Have Been Disorderly in Their Lives, Ought not to Be Called Magdalen-Houses* (London).

'A Gentleman.' (1768). *Every Man His Own Brewer; or, A Compendium of the English Brewery* (London).

An Alphabetical Index of the Streets, Squares, Lanes, Alleys, &c. Contained in the Plan of the Cities of London and Westminster, and the Borough of Southwark . . . (London, 1747).

A Member of Parliament. (1769?). *An Explanation of the Proposed Scheme for Better Paving, Repairing, Cleaning and Lighting the Squares, Streets and Lanes of the City and Liberty of Westminster . . .* (London).

Authentic Memoirs of George Robert Fitzgerald, Esq; With a Full Account of His Trial and Execution for the Murder of Patrick Randall McDonnell, Esq (London, 1786).

Bentham, J. (1791). *Panopticon; or, The Inspection House* (London).

A Bill for Paving, Cleansing, Enlightening and Keeping in Repair the Street Called Pall Mall . . . Read 22nd May 1751.

A Brief Description of the Cities of London and Westminster, the Public Buildings, Palaces, Gardens, Squares, &c. With an Alphabetical List of All the Streets, Squares, Courts, Lanes, and Alleys, &c. within the Bills of Mortality (London, 1776).

Brown, J. (1678). *The Practical Gauger, Arithmetical and Instrumental . . .* (London).

Cibber, T. (1733). *The Harlot's Progress; or, The Ridotto Al' Fresco: A Grotesque Pantomime Entertainment* (London).

Clark, S. (1761). *The British Gauger; or, Trader and Officer's Instructor, in the Revenue of the Excise and Customs* (London).

Cobbett, W. (ed.) (1806–1820). *The Parliamentary History of England from the Earliest Period to the Year 1803* (London).

Collins, R. (1677). *The Countrey Gaugers Vade Mecum; or, Pocket Companion . . .* (London).

Colman, G. (1770). *Man and Wife: Or, The Shakespeare Jubilee. A Comedy, of Three Acts* (London).

Commissioners of Excise. (1732). *Instructions for Officers Who Survey the Large Dealers in Coffee, Tea and Chocolate, &c. and All the Permit Writers* (London).

Commissioners of the Excise. (1750). *Orders and Instructions for the Management of the London Brewery* (London).

Commissioners of the Excise. (1755a). *Instructions for Surveyors in the London Brewery* (London).

Commissioners of the Excise. (1755b). *Instructions for the General-Surveyors of the Distillery* (London).

Commissioners of the Excise. (1755c). *Instructions for the Tide-Surveyors of the Excise* (London).

Commissioners of the Excise. (1761). *Instructions for Officers in the London Brewery* (London).

Commissioners of the Excise. (1762a). *Instructions for Officers Who Survey Distillers for Exportation* (London).

Commissioners of the Excise. (1762b). *Instructions to Be Observed by the Officers Employ'd in Charging the Duties on Candles and Soap in London* (London).

Commissioners of the Excise. (1764). *Instructions for the Tide-Waiters of Excise in the Port of London* (London).

Commissioners of the Excise. (1773). *Instructions for Officers of the London Distillery, Brandy, and Small Dealers in Tea etc.* (London).

Commissioners of the Excise. (1774). *Instructions to Be Observed by the Officers Concerned in Ascertaining the Duties on Glass* (London).

Commissioners of the Excise. (1775). *Instructions for Officers in the London Brewery* (London).

A Congratulatory Epistle from a Reformed Rake, to John F———g, Esq; Upon the New Scheme of Reclaiming Prostitutes (London, 1758).

Considerations on the New Paving Bill. (London, 1769).

Davenant, C. (1771a). 'Discourses on the Public Revenues, and on the Trade of England . . . [1698].' In Sir C. Whitworth (ed.), *The Political and Commercial Works of That Celebrated Writer Charles Davenant . . . Collected and Revised by Sir Charles Whitworth* (London) Vol. I, pp 125–303.

Davenant, C. (1771b). 'An essay upon ways and means [1695].' In Sir C. Whitworth (ed.), *The Political and Commercial Works of That Celebrated Writer Charles Davenant . . . Collected and Revised by Sir Charles Whitworth* (London) Vol. I, pp1–81.

Defoe, D. (1722). *The Fortunes and Misfortunes of the Famous Moll Flanders* 3d ed. (London).

Defoe, D. (1724–1727). *A Tour Thro' the Whole Island of Great Britain* (London).

A Description of the Machine for the fireworks . . . Published by Order of His Majesty's Board of Ordnance (London, 1749).

A Description of Vaux-Hall Gardens. Being a Proper Companion and Guide for All Who Visit That Place (London, 1762).

A Dialogue Betwixt an Excise-Man and Death (London, 1659).

Dingley, R. (1758). *Proposals for Establishing a Public Place of Reception for Penitent Prostitutes, &c* (London).

Dodd, W. (ed.). (n.d.). *The Magdalen; or, History of the First Penitent* (London).

Edwards, J. (1789). *Description of Southwark, Lambeth, Newington, &c* (London).

The Evening Lessons. Being the First and Second Chapters of the Book of Entertainments (London, 1742).

Everard, T. (1684). *Stereography Made Easie; or, The Description and Use of a New Gauging Rod or Sliding Rule* (London).

Fashion: A Poem (Bath, 1775).

[Fielding, H.] 'Lemuel Gulliver.' (1728). *The Masquerade; A Poem Inscribed to C——t H——d——g—r* (London).

Fielding, H. (1751). *An Inquiry into the Causes of the Late Increase of Robbers . . .* (London).

[Fielding, H.] (1752). *A Plan of the Universal Register Office, Opposite Cecil Street in the Strand, and of That in Bishopsgate-Street, the Corner of Cornhill.* 2d ed. (London).

Fielding, H. (1753). *A Clear State of the Case of Elizabeth Canning* (London).

Fielding, H. (1988). *'The Covent-Garden Journal' and 'A Plan of the Universal Register-Office,'* ed. B. A. Goldgar (Clarendon Press, Oxford).

Fielding, J. (1755a). *A Plan of the Universal Register Office, Opposite Cecil Street in the Strand, and of That in Bishopsgate-Street, the Corner of Cornhill.* 8th ed. (London).

Fielding, J. (1755b). *A Plan for Preventing Robberies within Twenty Miles of London* (London).

Fielding, J. (1758a). *A Plan for a Preservatory and Reformatory, for the Benefit of Deserted Girls, and Penitent Prostitutes* (London).

Fielding, J. (1758b). *An Account of the Origin and Effects of a Police Set on Foot by His Grace the Duke of Newcastle in the Year 1753, upon a Plan Presented to His Grace by the Late Henry Fielding* (London).

Fielding, J. (1768). *Extracts from Such of the Penal Laws, as Particularly Relate to the Peace and Good Order of This Metropolis* (London).

Fielding, J. (1776). *Some Proper Cautions to the Merchants, Tradesmen and Shopkeepers of the Cities of London and Westminster* (London).

The First Part of the Rural Lovers Delight . . . (London, no date).

Flower, W. (1768). *A Key to the Modern Sliding-Rule* (London).

The Frisky Songster (London, no date).

Gay, J. (1716). *Trivia; or, The Art of Walking the Streets of London* (London).

The Gree-Park Folly; or, The Fireworks Blown Up; A Satire (London, 1749).

Gwynn, J. (1749). *An Essay on Design: Including Proposals for Erecting a Public Academy . . . for Educating the British Youth in Drawing* (London).

Gwynn, J. (1766). *London and Westminster Improved* (London).

Hanway, J. (1754). *A Letter to Mr John Spranger, on His Excellent Proposal for Paving, Cleansing and Lighting the Streets of Westminster* (London).

Hanway, J. (1756). *An Essay on Tea: Considered as Pernicious to Health; Obstructing Industry; and Impoverishing the Nation . . .* (London).

Hanway, J. (1758a). *A Plan for Establishing a Charity-House, or Charity-Houses, for the Reception of Repenting Prostitutes. To Be Called the Magdalen Charity* (London).

Hanway, J. (1758b). *Thoughts on the Plan for a Magdalen House for Repentant Prostitutes* (London); 2d ed., 1759.

Hanway, J. (1758c). *Letter V to Robert Dingley* (London).

Hanway, J. (1761). *Reflections, Essays and Meditations on Life and Religion* (London).

Hanway, J. (1775). *The Defects of Police, the Cause of Immorality* (London).

Hanway, J. (1776). *Solitude in Imprisonment* (London).

Hanway, J. (1781). *Distributive Justice and Mercy* (London).

Harrison, W. (1775). *A New and Universal History, Description and Survey of the Cities of London and Westminster . . .* (London).

Hatton, E. (1729). *The Gauger's Guide; or, Excise-Officer Instructed* (London).

Hercules Mac-Sturdy, Esq. (1737). *A Trip to Vauxhall; or, A General Satyr on the Times* (London).

Hersee, W. (1829). *The Spirit of the General Letters and Orders Issued by the Honourable Board of Excise . . . from 1700 to 1827 Inclusive* (London).

The Histories of Some of the Penitents in the Magdalen House, as Supposed to Be Related by Themselves (London, 1760).

Hitchcock, R. (1773). *The Macaroni: A Comedy* (York, UK).

Hume, D. (1758). *Essays and Treatises on Several Subjects* (London).

Hunt, W. (1673). *A Guide for the Practical Gauger, with a Compendium of Decimal Arithmetick* (London).

Hunt, W. (1683a). *An Abridgement of the Laws of Excise* (York, UK).

Hunt, W. (1683b). *Practical Gauging Epitomized, with the Use, and Construction of the Tables of Logarithms* (York).

Hunt, W. (1687). *The Gauger's Magazine . . .* (London).

Hutcheson, R. K. (1798). *For Maltsters, Brewers, and Hop-Planters: All the Excise Laws and Adjudged Cases* (London).

J. T. (1667). *The Semicircle on a Sector . . .* (London).

Jones, R. (1765). *A Treatise on Artificial Fireworks* (London).

Jones, R. A. (1776). *Artificial Fireworks Improved to the Modern Practice. . . . Also Mr Muller's Fireworks, for Sea and Land Service* (London).

Journals of the House of Commons.

Leadbetter, C. (1739). *The Royal Gauger; or, Gauging Made Easy, as It Is Actually Practised by the Officers of His Majesty's Revenue of Excise* (London).

A Letter from a Gentleman in London . . . Concerning the Treaty at Aix-La Chapelle, Concluded on 8th of October 1748 (London, 1748).

The Life of George Robert Fitzgerald, Esq (London, 1786).

Lockman, J. (1750). *The Vast Importance of the Herring Fishery &c to These Kingdoms . . . in Three Letters Addressed to a Member of Parliament* (London).

Lockman, J. (1751). *The Shetland Herring and Peruvian Gold Mine: A Fable* (London).

[Lockman, J.] (1752). *A Sketch of the Spring-Gardens, Vaux-Hall, in a Letter to a Noble Lord* (London).

The Macaroni Jester, and Pantheon of Wit; Containing All that Has Lately Transpired in the Regions of Politeness, Whim and Novelty (London, 1773?).

Magdalen Hospital (1758). *The Plan of the Magdalen House for the Reception of Penitent Prostitutes* (London).

Magdalen Hospital. (1759). *The Rules, Orders and Regulations, of the Magdalen House, for the Reception of Penitent Prostitutes* 2d ed. (London). 4th ed., 1769.

Magdalen Hospital. (1770). *An Account of the Rise, Progress and Present State of the Magdalen Hospital* 4th ed. (London). 5th ed., 1776.

Maitland, W. (1739). *History of London from Its Foundation by the Romans to the Present Time* (London).

Mandeville, B. (1705). *The Grumbling Hive* (London).

Mandeville, B. (1714). *The Fable of the Bees; or, Private Vices Publick Benefits* (London).

Marchant, Mr. (1758). *Observations on Mr Fielding's Plan for a Preservatory and Reformatory* (London).

Massie, J. (1758). *A Plan for the Establishment of Charity-Houses for Exposed or Deserted Women and Girls, and for Penitent Prostitutes* (London).

Mayne, J. (1680). *A Companion for Excise-Men, Containing the Excise-Man's Aid & Journal . . .* (London).

Noorthouck, J. (1773). *A New History of London* (London).

Observations on the Bill for Paving, Cleansing, Lighting and Regulating the Squares, &c. within the City and Liberty of Westminster . . . (London, 1767).

Observations upon the Considerations on the New Paving Bill (London, 1769).

The Paving of Westminster Was Originally Begun upon Public Money . . . (London, 1769).

A Plan of the Universal Register Office Now Open'd Opposite to the Parliament-House in College-Green (Dublin, 1751).

Polstead, E. (1697). Καλως τελωνησανται; or, *The Excise Man . . .* (London).

Polstead, E. (1702). *Cambria Triumphans; or, A Panegyrick upon Wales. A Pindarick Poem* (London).

Pugh, J. (1787). *Remarkable Occurrences in the Life of Jonas Hanway* (London).

Queries against the Intended Daily Toll for Paving the Streets of Westminster (London, 1766?).

Reasons for the Petition for Better Paving, Cleansing and Lighting the Streets of Westminster (London, 1753).

Reed, J. (1761). *The Register Office: A Farce of Two Acts* (London). 2d ed., 1771.

Reed, J. (1769). *Tom Jones: A Comic Opera* (London).

Robinson, H. (1650). *The Office of Addresses and Encounters* . . . (London).

Scott, S. (1762). *Millenium Hall* (London).

A Second Holiday for John Gilpin; or, A Voyage to Vauxhall . . . (London, 1785).

Shaftesbury, 3rd Earl, A. A. Cooper. (1711). *Characteristics of Men, Manners, Opinions, Times* (London).

Shaw, W. A. (ed.) (1935). *Calendar of Treasury Books, 1681–1685. Vol. VII* (H. M. S. O., London).

Shirtcliffe, R. (1740). *The Theory and Practice of Gauging, Demonstrated in a Short and Easy Method* (London).

Smart, C. (1751). *A Solemn Dirge, Sacred to the Memory of His Royal Highness Frederick Prince of Wales. As It Was Sung by Mr Lowe, Miss Burchell, and Others, at Vaux-Hall* (London).

The Songster's Magazine (London, no date).

Spranger, J. (1754). *A Proposal or Plan for an Act of Parliament for the Better Paving, Cleansing and Lighting of the Streets, Lanes, Courts and Alleys, and Other Open Passages, and for the Removal of Nuisances, as well within the Several Parishes of the City and Liberty of Westminster* . . . (London).

Symons, J. (1775). *The Excise Laws Abridged* . . . (London).

Thieving Detected: Being a True and Particular Description, of the Various Methods and Artifices, Used by Thieves and Sharpers, to Take In and Deceive the Public (London, 1777).

Toupee, S. (1739a). 'An Evening at Vaux-Hall.' *Scots Magazine* 1 pp322–324 and pp 363–364.

Toupee, S. (1739b). 'An Evening at Vauxhall.' *Scots Magazine* 12 pp409–410.

The Trials of George Robert Fitzgerald, Esq; And Timothy Brecknock . . . (Dublin, 1786).

Twigem, F. (1773). *The Macaroni: A Satire* (London).

The Vauxhall Affray; or, The Macaronies Defeated: Being a Compilation of All the Letters, Squibs etc. on Both Sides of That Dispute 2d ed. (London, 1773).

Vaux-Hall: A Poem (Dublin, 1750).

Walcot, C. (1763). *Considerations for the More Speedy and Effectual Execution of the Act, for Paving, Cleansing, and Lighting the City and Liberty of Westminster, and for Removing Annoyances Therein* (London).

Ward, J. (1707). *The Young Mathematician's Guide* (London).

Ward, N. (1709). *The London Spy Compleat in Eighteen Parts* (London).

Welch, S. (1758). *A Proposal to Render Effectual a Plan, to Remove the Nuisance of Common Prostitutes from the Streets of this Metropolis; to Prevent the Innocent from Being Seduced* . . . (London).

West, S. (1769). *The Exciseman's Pocket-Book: Containing Abstracts of All the Laws Relating to the Customs and Excise* (London).

Whitworth, C. (1771). *Observations on the New Westminster Paving Act* (London).

Wood, R. (1753). *Ruins of Palmyra, Otherwise Tedmor, in the Desart* (London).

Yeo, W. (1749). *The Method of Ullaging and Inching All Sorts of Casks and Other Utensils, Used by Common Brewers, Victuallers, Distillers etc* . . . (London).

Zeal, Z. (1764?). *A Seasonable Alarm to the City of London, on the Present Important Crisis, Shewing by Most Convincing Arguments, That the New Method of Paving the Streets with Scotch Pebbles and the Pulling Down of the Signs, Must*

Be Both Equally Pernicious to the Health and Morals of the People of England (London).

SECONDARY WORKS

Adorno, T., Horkheimer, M. (1979, orig. 1944). *Dialectic of Enlightenment* (Verso, London).

Agnew, J-C. (1993). 'Coming up for air: Consumer culture in historical perspective.' In J. Brewer and R. Porter (eds.), *Consumption and the World of Goods* (Routledge, London) pp19–39.

Albert, W. (1983). 'The turnpike trusts.' In D. H. Aldcroft and M. J. Freeman (eds.), *Transport in the Industrial Revolution* (Manchester University Press, Manchester, UK) pp31–63.

Allen, B. (1983). 'The landscape.' In T. J. Edelstein (ed.), *Vauxhall Gardens* (Yale Center for British Art, Yale University Press, New Haven, CT) pp17–24.

Altick, R. D. (1978). *The Shows of London: A Panoramic History of Exhibitions* (Belknap Press of Harvard University Press, Cambridge, MA).

Anderson, P. (1984). 'Modernity and revolution.' *New Left Review* 144 pp96–113.

Andrew, D. T. (1989). *Philanthropy and Police: London Charity in the Eighteenth Century* (Princeton University Press, Princeton, NJ).

Appleby, J. H. (1992). 'Mills, models and Magdalens: The Dingley brothers and the Society of Arts.' *Journal of the Royal Society of Arts* 140 pp267–273.

Armstrong, N. (1987). *Desire and Domestic Fiction: A Political History of the Novel* (Oxford University Press, Oxford).

Ashton, T. S. (1960). 'Introduction.' In E. B. Schumpeter, *English Overseas Trade Statistics, 1697–1808* (Clarendon Press, Oxford) pp1–14.

Aylmer, G. E. (1980). 'From office-holding to civil service: The genesis of modern bureaucracy.' *Transactions of the Royal Historical Society* 5th series 30 pp91–108.

Bagwell, P. S. (1974). *The Transport Revolution from 1770* (Batsford, London).

Bakhtin, M. (1962). *Rabelais and His World* (Indiana University Press, Bloomington).

Barker-Benfield, G. J. (1992). *The Culture of Sensibility: Sex and Society in Eighteenth-Century Britain* (University of Chicago Press, Chicago).

Barrell, J. (1992). 'Introduction.' In J. Barrell (ed.), *Painting and the Politics of Culture: New Essays on British Art, 1700–1850* (Oxford University Press, Oxford) pp1–11.

Barry, A. (1993). 'The history of measurement and the engineers of space.' *British Journal of the History of Science* 26 pp459–468.

Bate, J. (1989). *Shakespearean Constitutions: Politics, Theatre, Criticism, 1730–1830* (Clarendon Press, Oxford).

Battestin, M. C., with Battestin, R. R. (1989). *Henry Fielding: A Life* (Routledge, London).

Bauman, Z. (1989). *Modernity and the Holocaust* (Polity Press, Cambridge, UK).

Bauman, Z. (1991). *Modernity and Ambivalence* (Polity Press, Cambridge, UK).

Baxendall, M. (1972). *Painting and Experience in Fifteenth-Century Italy: A Primer in the Social History of Pictorial Style* (Clarendon Press, Oxford).

Beckett, J. V. (1985). 'Land tax or excise: The levying of taxation in seventeenth- and eighteenth-century England.' *English Historical Review* 100 pp 285–308.

Bender, J. (1987). *Imagining the Penitentiary: Fiction and the Architecture of Mind in Eighteenth-Century England* (University of Chicago Press, Chicago).

Bender, J. (1992). 'A new history of the Enlightenment?' *Eighteenth-Century Life* 16 pp1–20.

Berman, M. (1983). *All That Is Solid Melts Into Air: The Experience of Modernity* (Verso, London).

Berman, M. (1984). 'The signs in the street: A response to Perry Anderson.' *New Left Review* 144 pp114–123.

Bermingham, A. (1995). 'Introduction. The consumption of culture: Image, object, text.' In A. Bermingham and J. Brewer (eds.), *The Consumption of Culture, 1600–1800: Image, Object, Text* (Routledge, London) pp1–20.

Bermingham, A., and Brewer, J. (eds.) (1995). *The Consumption of Culture, 1600–1800: Image, Object, Text* (Routledge, London).

Berry, C. J. (1994). *The Idea of Luxury: A Conceptual and Historical Investigation* (Cambridge University Press, Cambridge).

Besant, W. (1902). *London in the Eighteenth Century* (Adam & Charles Black, London).

Black, J. (1987). *The English Press in the Eighteenth Century* (Croom Helm, London).

Black, J. (1993). *The Politics of Britain, 1688–1800* (Manchester University Press, Manchester, UK).

Blaug, M. (ed.). (1991). *Pre-Classical Economists, Vol. I: Charles Davenant (1656–1714) and William Petty (1623–1687)* (Edward Elgar, Aldershot, UK).

Blomley, N. (1994). *Law, Space, and the Geographies of Power* (The Guilford Press, New York).

Boal, I. A. (1995). 'The darkening green.' *History Workshop Journal* 39 pp124–135.

Borsay, P. (1989). *The English Urban Renaissance: Culture and Society in the Provincial Town, 1660–1770* (Clarendon Press, Oxford).

Borsay, P. (1990). 'Introduction.' In P. Borsay (ed.), *The Eighteenth-Century Town: A Reader in English Urban History, 1688–1820* (Longman, London) pp1–38.

Boucé, P-G. (1980). 'Aspects of sexual tolerance and intolerance in eighteenth-century England.' *British Journal for Eighteenth-Century Studies* 3 pp 173–191.

Boucé, P-G. (1982). 'Some sexual beliefs and myths in eighteenth-century Britain.' In P.-G. Boucé (ed.), *Sexuality in Eighteenth-Century Britain* (Manchester University Press, Manchester, UK) pp28–46.

Braddick, M. J. (1994). *Parliamentary Taxation in Seventeenth-Century England: Lo-*

cal Administration and Response Royal Historical Society Studies in History 70 (Boydell Press, Woodbridge, UK).

Braddick, M. J. (1996a). *The Nerves of State: Taxation and the Financing of the English State, 1558–1714* (Manchester University Press, Manchester, UK).

Braddick, M. J. (1996b). 'The early modern English state and the question of differentiation, from 1550 to 1700.' *Comparative Studies in Society and History* 38 pp92–111.

Brantlinger, P. (1996). *Fictions of State: Culture and Credit in Britain, 1694–1994* (Cornell University Press, Ithaca, NY).

Bravo, M. (1996). 'The great South Sea caterpillar.' *Journal of Historical Geography* 22 pp484–488.

Breen, T. H. (1993). 'The meanings of things: Interpreting the consumer economy in the eighteenth century.' In J. Brewer and R. Porter (eds.), *Consumption and the World of Goods* (Routledge, London) pp249–260.

Brewer, J. (1983). 'Commercialisation and politics.' In N. McKendrick, J. Brewer and J. H. Plumb (eds.), *The Birth of a Consumer Society: The Commercialisation of Eighteenth-Century England* (Hutchinson, London) pp197–262.

Brewer, J. (1989). *The Sinews of Power: War, Money and the English State, 1688–1783* (Unwin Hyman, London).

Brewer, J. (1994). 'The eighteenth-century British state: Contexts and issues.' In L. Stone (ed.), *An Imperial State at War: Britain from 1689 to 1815* (Routledge, London) pp52–71.

Brewer, J. (1995). '"The most polite age and the most vicious": Attitudes towards culture as a commodity, 1660–1800.' In A. Bermingham and J. Brewer (eds.), *The Consumption of Culture, 1600–1800: Image, Object, Text* (Routledge, London) pp341–361.

Brewer, J. (1997). *The Pleasures of the Imagination: English Culture in the Eighteenth Century* (Harper Collins, London).

Brewer, J., and Porter, R. (eds.) (1993). *Consumption and the World of Goods* (Routledge, London).

Brooks, C. (1974) 'Public finance and political stability: The administration of the land tax, 1688–1720.' *Historical Journal* 17 pp281–300.

Brooks, C. (1987). 'Interest, patronage and professionalism: John, 1st Baron Ashburnham, Hastings and the revenue services.' *Southern History* 9 pp51–70.

Buck, P. (1977). 'Seventeenth-century political arithmetic: Civil strife and vital statistics.' *Isis* 68 pp67–84.

Buck, P. (1982). 'People who counted: Political arithmetic in the eighteenth century.' *Isis* 73 pp28–45.

Bullough, V. (1987). 'Prostitution and reform in eighteenth-century England.' In R. P. Maccubbin (ed.), *'Tis Nature's Fault: Unauthorized Sexuality during the Enlightenment* (Cambridge University Press, Cambridge) pp61–74.

Burkitt, I. (1992). 'Beyond the "iron cage": Anthony Giddens on modernity and the self.' *History of the Human Sciences* 5 pp71–79.

Byrd, M. (1978). *London Transformed: Images of the City in the Eighteenth Century* (Yale University Press, New Haven, CT).

Calhoun, C. (ed.) (1992). *Habermas and the Public Sphere* (MIT Press, Cambridge, MA).

Campbell, C. (1987). *The Romantic Ethic and the Spirit of Modern Consumerism* (Basil Blackwell, Oxford, UK).

Castle, T. (1986). *Masquerade and Civilization: The Carnivalesque in Eighteenth-Century English Culture and Fiction* (Methuen, London).

Castle, T. (1987). 'The culture of travesty: Sexuality and masquerade in eighteenth-century England.' In G. S. Rousseau and R. Porter (eds.), *Sexual Underworlds of the Enlightenment* (Manchester University Press, Manchester, UK) pp156–180.

Castle, T. (1995). *The Female Thermometer: Eighteenth-Century Culture and the Invention of the Uncanny* (Oxford University Press, Oxford).

Chandaman, C. D. (1975). *The English Public Revenue, 1660–1688* (Clarendon Press, Oxford).

Chard, C. (1994). 'Effeminacy, pleasure and the classical body.' In G. Perry and M. Rossington (eds.), *Femininity and Masculinity in Eighteenth-Century Art and Culture* (Manchester University Press, Manchester, UK) pp142–181.

Chartres, J. A., and Turnbull, G. L. (1983). 'Road transport.' In D. H. Aldcroft and M. J. Freeman (eds.), *Transport in the Industrial Revolution* (Manchester University Press, Manchester, UK) pp64–99.

Clark, J. C. D. (1984). 'Eighteenth-century social history.' *Historical Journal* 27 pp773–788.

Clark, J. C. D. (1985). *English Society, 1688–1832: Ideology, Social Structure and Political Practice during the Ancien Regime* (Cambridge University Press, Cambridge).

Clark, J. C. D. (1986). *Revolution and Rebellion: State and Society in England in the Seventeenth and Eighteenth Centuries* (Cambridge University Press, Cambridge).

Clark, J. C. D. (1989). '1688 & all that.' *Encounter* 72 pp14–17.

Clark, J. C. D. (1992). 'Reconceptualising eighteenth-century England.' *British Journal for Eighteenth-Century Studies* 15 p135–139.

Clery, E. J. (1991). 'Women, publicity and the coffee-house myth,' *Women: A Cultural Review* 2 pp168–177.

Cohen, M. (1996). *Fashioning Masculinity: National Identity and Language in the Eighteenth Century* (Routledge, London).

Coke, D. (1984). 'Vauxhall Gardens.' In M. Snodin (ed.), *Rococo: Art and Design in Hogarth's England* Victoria and Albert Museum Exhibition Catalogue (Victoria and Albert Museum, London) pp74–98.

Colley, L. (1986). 'The politics of eighteenth-century British history.' *Journal of British Studies* 25 pp359–379.

Colley, L. (1992). *Britons: Forging the Nation, 1707–1837* (Yale University Press, New Haven, CT).

Compston, H. F. B. (1917). *The Magdalen Hospital: The Story of a Great Charity* (SPCK, London).

Cook, D. (1990). 'Remapping modernity.' *British Journal of Aesthetics* 30 pp35–45.

Coole, D. (1992). 'Modernity and its other(s).' *History of the Human Sciences* 5 pp81–91.

Copley, S. (1992). 'The fine arts in eighteenth-century polite culture.' In J. Barrell (ed.), *Painting and the Politics of Culture: New Essays on British Art, 1700–1850* (Oxford University Press, Oxford) pp13–37.

Corfield, P. J. (1982). *The Impact of English Towns, 1700–1800* (Oxford University Press, Oxford).

Corfield, P. J. (1990). 'Walking the streets: The urban odyssey in eighteenth-century England.' *Journal of Urban History* 16 pp132–174.

Cranfield, G. A. (1962). *The Development of the Provincial Newspaper, 1700–1760* (Clarendon Press, Oxford).

Cressy, D. (1989). *Bonfires and Bells: National Memory and the Protestant Calendar in Elizabethan and Stuart England* (Weidenfeld and Nicholson, London).

Dandeker, C. (1990). *Surveillance, Power and Modernity: Bureaucracy and Discipline from 1700 to the Present Day* (Polity Press, Cambridge, UK).

Daniels, S. J. (1993). 'The country and the city.' *Journal of Historical Geography* 19 pp453–462.

Daniels, S. J. (1996). 'On the road with Humphrey Repton.' *Journal of Garden History* 16 pp170–191.

Darlington, I., and Howgego, J. (1964). *Printed Maps of London circa 1553–1850* (George Philip & Son, London).

Darnton, R. (1984). *The Great Cat Massacre and Other Episodes in French Cultural History* (Penguin, Harmondsworth, UK).

Dean, M. (1996). 'Putting the technological into government.' *History of the Human Sciences* 9 pp47–68.

de Bolla, P. (1995). 'The visibility of visuality: Vauxhall Gardens and the siting of the viewer.' In S. Melville and B. Readings (eds.), *Vision and Textuality* (Macmillan, Basingstoke, UK) pp282–295.

de Bolla, P. (1996). 'The visibility of visuality.' In T. Brennan and M. Jay (eds.), *Vision in Context: Historical and Contemporary Perspective on Sight* (Routledge, London) pp63–81.

de Cauter, L. (1993). 'The panoramic ecstasy: On world exhibitions and the disintegration of experience.' *Theory, Culture and Society* 10 pp1–23.

De Certeau, M. (1984). *The Practice of Everyday Life* (University of California Press, Berkeley and Los Angeles).

Dennis, R. (1994). 'Interpreting the apartment house: Modernity and metropolitanism in Toronto, 1900–1930.' *Journal of Historical Geography* 20 pp305–322.

Dickson, P. G. M. (1967). *The Financial Revolution in England: A Study in the Development of Public Credit* (Macmillan, London).

Donald, D. (1996). *The Age of Caricature: Satirical Prints in the Age of George III* (Yale University Press, New Haven, CT).

Duffy, M. (ed.) (1980). *The Military Revolution and the State, 1500–1800* Exeter Studies in History 1 (University of Exeter, Exeter, UK).

Earle, P. (1994). *A City Full of People: Men and Women of London, 1650–1750* (Methuen, London).

Eaves, T. C. D., and Kimpel, B. D. (1971). *Samuel Richardson: A Biography* (Clarendon Press, Oxford).

Edelstein, T. J. (1983). 'The paintings.' In T. J. Edelstein (ed.), *Vauxhall Gardens* (Yale Center for British Art, Yale University Press, New Haven, CT) pp25–35.

Eisenstadt, S. N. (ed.) (1987). *Patterns of Modernity. Vol. I: The West* (Francis Pinter, London).

Elias, N. (1978). *The History of Manners, vol. 1 of The Civilizing Process* (Pantheon Books, New York).

Elias, N. (1982). *State Formation and Civilisation, vol. 2 of The Civilizing Process* (Basil Blackwell, Oxford, UK).

Elias, N. (1991). *The Society of Individuals* (Basil Blackwell, Oxford, UK).

Ellis, K. (1958). *The Post Office in the Eighteenth Century: A Study in Administrative History* (Oxford University Press, London).

Ellis, M. (1996). *The Politics of Sensibility: Race, Gender and Commerce in the Sentimental Novel* (Cambridge University Press, Cambridge).

Elvin, M. (1986). 'A working definition of "modernity"?' *Past and Present* 113 pp209–213.

Ertman, T. (1994). 'The sinews of power and European state-building theory.' In L. Stone (ed.), *An Imperial State at War: Britain from 1689 to 1815* (Routledge, London) pp33–51.

Evans, R. (1982). *The Fabrication of Virtue: English Prison Architecture, 1750–1840* (Cambridge University Press, Cambridge).

Falkus, M. E. (1976). 'Lighting in the dark ages of English economic history: Town streets before the Industrial Revolution.' In D. C. Coleman and A. H. John (eds.), *Trade and Economy in Pre-Industrial England: Essays Presented to F. J. Fisher* (Wiedenfeld and Nicolson, London) pp248–273.

Fehér, F. (1990). *The French Revolution and the Birth of Modernity* (University of California Press, Berkeley and Los Angeles).

Felski, R. (1995). *The Gender of Modernity* (Harvard University Press, Cambridge, MA).

Foucault, M. (1977). *Discipline and Punish: The Birth of the Prison* (Allen Lane, London).

Foucault, M. (1979). *The History of Sexuality. Vol. 1: An Introduction* (Allen Lane, London).

Foucault, M. (1988). 'The political technology of individuals.' In L. H. Martin, H. Gutman, and P. H. Hutton (eds.), *Technologies of the Self* (Tavistock, London) pp145–162.

Fraser, N. (1992). 'Rethinking the public sphere: A contribution to the critique of actually existing democracy.' In C. Calhoun (ed.), *Habermas and the Public Sphere* (MIT Press, Cambridge, MA) pp109–142.

Freeman, M. J. (1983). 'Introduction.' In D. H. Aldcroft and M. J. Freeman (eds.), *Transport in the Industrial Revolution* (Manchester University Press, Manchester, UK) pp1–30.

Freeman, M. J. (1986). 'Transport.' in J. Langton and R. J. Morris (eds.), *Atlas of Industrializing Britain, 1780–1914* (Methuen, London) pp80–93.

Friedland, R., and Boden, D. (eds.) (1994). *NowHere: Space, Time and Modernity* (University of California Press, Berkeley and Los Angeles).

Gascoigne, J. (1994). *Joseph Banks and the English Enlightenment: Useful Knowledge and Polite Culture* (Cambridge University Press, Cambridge).

George, M. D. (1926–1929). 'The early history of registry offices.' *Economic Journal: Economic History Supplement* 1 pp570–590.

George, M. D. (1935). *Catalogue of Political and Personal Satires Preserved in the Department of Prints and Drawings in the British Museum, Vol. V: 1771–1783* (Trustees of the British Museum, London).

George, M. D. (1987, orig. 1925). *London Life in the Eighteenth Century* (Penguin, Harmondsworth, UK).

Giddens, A. (1985). *The Nation-State and Violence* (Polity Press, Cambridge, UK).

Giddens, A. (1990). *The Consequences of Modernity* (Polity Press, Cambridge, UK).

Giddens, A. (1991). *Modernity and Self-Identity: Self and Society in the Late Modern Age* (Polity Press, Cambridge, UK).

Gillis, J. R. (1987). 'Married but not churched: plebeian sexual relations and marital nonconformity in eighteenth-century Britain.' In R. P. Maccubbin (ed.), *'Tis Nature's Fault: Unauthorized Sexuality during the Enlightenment* (Cambridge University Press, Cambridge) pp31–42.

Gilroy, P. (1993). *The Black Atlantic: Modernity and Double Consciousness* (Verso, London).

Glanville, P. (1972). *London in Maps* (Connoisseur, London).

Glennie, P. D., and Thrift, N. J. (1992). 'Modernity, urbanism and modern consumption,' *Environment and Planning D: Society and Space* 10 pp423–443.

Glennie, P. D., and Thrift, N. J. (1996). 'Consumers, identities and consumption spaces in early-modern England.' *Environment and Planning A* 28 pp25–45.

Goffman, E. (1961). *Asylums: Essays on the Social Situation of Mental Patients and Other Inmates* (Penguin, Harmondsworth, UK).

Goldgar, B. A. (1988). 'General introduction.' In H. Fielding, *'The Covent-Garden Journal' and 'A Plan of the Universal Register-Office'* (Clarendon Press, Oxford) xv–liv.

Goldsmith, M. M. (1976). 'Public virtue and private vices: Bernard Mandeville and English political ideologies in the early eighteenth century.' *Eighteenth-Century Studies* 9 pp477–510.

Goodman, D. (1992). 'Public sphere and private life: Toward a synthesis of current historiographical approaches to the old regime.' *History and Theory* 31 pp1–20.

Goodman, D. (1995). 'Introduction: The public and the nation.' *Eighteenth-Century Studies* 29 pp1–4.

Goodman, J. (1992). '"Altar against altar": The Colisée, Vauxhall utopianism and symbolic politics in Paris (1769–77).' *Art History* 15 pp434–469.

Gordon, C. (1987). 'The soul of the citizen: Max Weber and Michel Foucault on rationality and government.' In S. Lash and S. Whimster (eds.), *Max Weber, Rationality and Modernity* (Allen & Unwin, London) pp293–316.

Gordon, S. P. (1995). 'Voyeuristic dreams: Mr Spectator and the power of the spectacle.' *The Eighteenth Century: Theory and Interpretation* 36 pp3–23.

Gowing, L. (1953). 'Hogarth, Hayman, and the Vauxhall decorations.' *Burlington Magazine* 95 pp4–19.

Gregory, D. (1987). 'The friction of distance? Information circulation and the mails in early nineteenth-century England.' *Journal of Historical Geography* 13 pp130–154.

Gregory, D. (1989). 'The crisis of modernity? Human geography and critical social theory.' In R. Peet and N. Thrift (eds.), *New Models in Geography: The Political Economy Perspective. Vol. II* (Unwin Hyman, London) pp348–385.

Gregory, D. (1991). 'Interventions in the historical geography of modernity: Social theory, spatiality and the politics of representation.' *Geografiska Annaler* 73B pp17–44.

Gregory, D. (1994). *Geographical Imaginations* (Basil Blackwell, Oxford, UK).

Gruffudd, P. (1994). 'Back to the land: Historiography, rurality and the nation in interwar Wales.' *Transactions of the Institute of British Geographers* 19 pp61–77.

Habermas, J. (1984a). *The Theory of Communicative Action, Vol. I: Reason and the Rationalisation of Society* (Heinemann, London).

Habermas, J. (1984b). *The Theory of Communicative Action, Vol. II: Lifeworld and System: A Critique of Functionalist Reason* (Polity Press, Cambridge, UK).

Habermas, J. (1985). 'Modernity—an incomplete project.' In H. Foster (ed.), *Postmodern Culture* (Pluto Press, London) pp3–15.

Habermas, J. (1987). *The Philosophical Discourse of Modernity: Twelve Lectures* (Polity Press, Cambridge, UK).

Habermas, J. (1989). *The Structural Transformation of the Public Sphere: An Inquiry into a Category of Bourgeois Society* (Polity Press, Cambridge, UK).

Hall, J. A., and Jarvie, I. C. (eds.). (1992). *Transition to Modernity: Essays on Power, Wealth and Belief* (Cambridge University Press, Cambridge).

Hancock, D. (1995). *Citizens of the World: London Merchants and the Integration of the British Atlantic Community, 1735–1785* (Cambridge University Press, Cambridge).

Haraway, D. (1989). *Primate Visions: Gender, Race, and Nature in the World of Modern Science* (Routledge, London).

Harding, P,. and Mandler, P. (1993). 'From "fiscal–military" state to laissez-faire state, 1760–1850.' *Journal of British Studies* 32 pp44–70.

Harris, B. (1996). '"American idols": Empire, war and the middling ranks in mid-eighteenth-century Britain.' *Past and Present* 150 pp111–141.

Harris, M. (1987). *London Newspapers in the Age of Walpole: A Study of the Origins of the Modern English Press* (Associated University Presses, London).

Harris, R. C. (1991). 'Power, modernity, and historical geography.' *Annals of the Association of American Geographers* 81 pp671–683.

Harvey, D. (1989). *The Condition of Postmodernity* (Basil Blackwell, Oxford, UK).

Heilbron, J. L. (1990). 'Introductory essay.' In T. Frängsmyr, J. L. Heilbron, and

R. E. Rider (eds.), *The Quantifying Spirit in the Eighteenth Century* (University of California Press, Berkeley and Los Angeles) pp1–23.

Henderson, A. (1992). *Female Prostitution in London, 1730–1830* (Unpublished PhD diss., University of London).

Herzog, D. (1996). 'The trouble with hairdressers.' *Representations* 53 pp21–43.

Highfall, P. H. Jr. (1980). 'Performers and performing.' In R. D. Hume (ed.), *The London Theatre World, 1660–1800* (University of Southern Illinois Press, Carbondale) pp143–180.

Hill, C. (1967). *Reformation to Industrial Revolution: A Social and Economic History of Britain, 1530–1780* (Wiedenfeld and Nicolson, London).

Hitchcock, T. (1997). *English Sexualities, 1700–1800* (Macmillan, Basingstoke, UK).

Hjort, A. M. (1991). 'Mandeville's ambivalent modernity.' *Modern Language Notes* 106 pp951–966.

Hoppit, J. (1993). 'Reforming Britain's weights and measures, 1660–1824.' *English Historical Review* CVIII pp82–103.

Hoppit, J. (1996). 'Political arithmetic in eighteenth-century England.' *Economic History Review* XLIV pp516–540.

Howell, P. (1993). 'Public space and the public sphere: Political theory and the historical geography of modernity.' *Environment and Planning D: Society and Space* 11 pp303–322.

Howson, G. (1973). *The Macaroni Parson: A Life of the Unfortunate Dr Dodd* (Hutchinson, London).

Hughes, E. (1934). *Studies in Administration and Finance, 1558–1825, with Special Reference to the History of Salt Taxation in England* (Manchester University Press, Manchester, UK).

Hundert, E. J. (1995). 'Bernard Mandeville and the Enlightenment's maxims of modernity.' *Journal of the History of Ideas* 56 pp577–593.

Hunt, J. D. (1985). *Vauxhall and London's Garden Theatres* (Chadwyck Healey, Cambridge, UK).

Hunt, L. (ed.) (1993). *The Invention of Pornography: Obscenity and the Origins of Modernity* (Zone Books, New York).

Hunt, L. (1994). 'The virtues of disciplinarity.' *Eighteenth-Century Studies* 28 pp1–7.

Hutchinson, T. W. (1988). *Before Adam Smith: The Emergence of Political Economy, 1662–1776* (Basil Blackwell, Oxford, UK).

Hyde, R. (1982). 'The making of John Rocque's map.' In *The A–Z of Georgian London* London Topographical Society Publication 126 (London Topographical Society, London).

Hyland, P. (ed.) (1993). *The London Spy: Ned Ward's Classic Account of Underworld Life in Eighteenth-Century London* (Colleagues Press, East Lansing, MI).

Ignatieff, M. (1978). *A Just Measure of Pain: The Penitentiary in the Industrial Revolution, 1750–1850* (Pantheon Books, New York).

Innes, J. (1987a). 'Jonathan Clark, social history and England's "ancien regime."' *Past and Present* 115 pp165–200.

Innes, J. (1987b). 'Prisons for the poor: English Bridewells, 1555–1800.' In F. Snyder and D. Hay (eds.), *Labour, Law and Crime: An Historical Perspective* (Tavistock, London) pp42–122.

Innes, J. (1994). 'The domestic face of the military-fiscal state: Government and society in eighteenth-century Britain.' In L. Stone (ed.), *An Imperial State at War: Britain from 1689 to 1815* (Routledge, London) pp96–127.

Jarrett, D. (1986). *England in the Age of Hogarth* (Yale University Press, New Haven, CT).

Jenner, M. (1995). 'The politics of London air: John Evelyn's *Fumifugium* and the Restoration.' *Historical Journal* 38 pp535–551.

Jesse, J. H. (1843). *George Selwyn and His Contemporaries* (Richard Bentley, London).

Johannisson, K. (1990). 'Society in numbers: The debate over quantification in eighteenth-century political economy.' In T. Frängsmyr, J. L. Heilbron and R. E. Rider (eds.), *The Quantifying Spirit in the Eighteenth Century* (University of California Press, Berkeley and Los Angeles) pp343–361.

Johnson, C. L. (1995). *Equivocal Beings: Politics, Gender, and Sentimentality in the 1790s. Wollstonecraft, Radcliffe, Burney, Austen* (University of Chicago Press, Chicago).

Jones, C. (1978). 'Prostitution and the ruling class in eighteenth-century Montpellier.' *History Workshop Journal* 6 pp7–28.

Jones, E. L., and Falkus, M. E. (1990). 'Urban improvement and the English economy in the seventeenth and eighteenth centuries.' In P. Borsay (ed.), *The Eighteenth-Century Town: A Reader in English Urban History, 1688–1820* (Longman, London) pp116–158.

Jordan, G., and Rogers, N. (1989). 'Admirals as heroes: Patriotism and liberty in mid-Hanoverian England.' *Journal of British Studies* 28 pp201–224.

Jordanova, L. (1987). 'The popularisation of medicine: Tissot on onanism.' *Textual Practice* 1 pp68–79.

Keane, J. (1988). 'Despotism and democracy: The origins and development of the distinction between civil society and the state, 1750–1850.' In J. Keane (ed.), *Civil Society and the State* (Verso, London) pp35–71.

Kennedy, P. (1988). *The Rise and Fall of the Great Powers: Economic Change and Military Conflict from 1500 to 2000* (Unwin Hyman, London).

Kent, J. R. (1995). 'The centre and the localities: State formation and parish government in England, circa 1640–1740.' *Historical Journal* 38 pp363–404.

Keymer, T. (1995). 'Smollett's Scotlands: Culture, politics and nationhood in *Humphrey Clinker* and Defoe's *Tour*.' *History Workshop Journal* 40 pp118–132.

Kiaer, C. H. (1993). 'Professional femininity in Hogarth's *Strolling Actresses Dressing in a Barn*.' *Art History* 16 pp239–265.

Klein, L. E. (1984–1985). 'The Third Earl of Shaftesbury and the progress of politeness.' *Eighteenth-Century Studies* 18 pp186–214.

Klein, L. E. (1989). 'Liberty, manners and politeness in early eighteenth-century England.' *Historical Journal* 32 pp583–605.

Klein, L. E. (1993). 'Gender, conversation and the public sphere in early eighteenth-century England.' In J. Still and M. Worton (eds.), *Textuality and Sexuality: Reading Theories and Practices* (Manchester University Press, Manchester, UK) pp100–115.

Klein, L. E. (1994). *Shaftesbury and the Culture of Politeness: Moral Discourse and Cultural Politics in Early Eighteenth-Century England* (Cambridge University Press, Cambridge).

Klein, L. E. (1995a). 'Gender and the public/private distinction in the eighteenth century: Some questions about evidence and analytical procedure.' *Eighteenth-Century Studies* 29 pp97–109.

Klein, L. E. (1995b). 'Politeness for plebes: consumption and social identity in early eighteenth-century England.' In A. Bermingham and J. Brewer (eds.), *The Consumption of Culture, 1600–1800: Image, Object, Text* (Routledge, London) pp362–382.

Koselleck, R. (1981). 'Modernity and the planes of historicity.' *Economy and Society* 10 pp166–183.

Koselleck, R. (1988). *Critique and Crisis: Enlightenment and the Pathogenesis of Modern Society* (Berg, Oxford, UK).

Kowaleski-Wallace, E. (1997). *Consuming Subjects: Women, Shopping, and Business in the Eighteenth Century* (Columbia University Press, New York).

Kubek, E. B. (1995). 'Women's participation in the urban culture of early modern London: Images from fiction.' In A. Bermingham and J. Brewer (eds.), *The Consumption of Culture, 1600–1800: Image, Object, Text* (Routledge, London) pp440–454.

Landau, N. (1988–1989). 'Eighteenth-century England: Tales historians tell.' *Eighteenth-Century Studies* 22 pp208–218.

Landers, J. (1993). *Death and the Metropolis: Studies in the Demographic History of London, 1670–1830* (Cambridge University Press, Cambridge).

Landes, J. B. (1988). *Women and the Public Sphere in the Age of the French Revolution* (Cornell University Press, Ithaca, NY).

Langford, P. (1975). *The Excise Crisis: Society and Politics in the Age of Walpole* (Clarendon Press, Oxford).

Langford, P. (1989). *A Polite and Commercial People: England, 1727–1783* (Oxford University Press, Oxford).

Langford, P. (1991). *Public Life and the Propertied Englishman, 1689–1798* (Clarendon Press, Oxford).

Latour, B. (1987). *Science in Action: How to Follow Scientists and Engineers through Society* (Open University Press, Milton Keynes, UK).

Latour, B. (1993). *We Have Never Been Modern* (Harvester Wheatsheaf, Hemel Hempstead, UK).

Laugero, G. (1995). 'Infrastructures of enlightenment: Road-making, the public sphere, and the emergence of literature.' *Eighteenth-Century Studies* 29 pp45–67.

La Vopa, A. J. (1992). 'Conceiving a public: Ideas and society in eighteenth-century Europe.' *Journal of Modern History* 64 pp79–116.

Law, J. (1986). 'On the methods of long-distance control: Vessels, navigation and the Portuguese route to India.' In J. Law (ed.), *Power, Action and Belief:*

A New Sociology of Knowledge? (Routledge and Kegan Paul, London) pp234–263.

Lawrence, H. W. (1993). 'The greening of the squares of London: Transformation of urban landscapes and ideals.' *Annals of the Association of American Geographers* 83 pp90–118.

Lazarfeld, P. F. (1961). 'Notes on the history of quantification in sociology: Trends, sources and problems.' *Isis* 52 pp277–333.

Lefebvre, H. (1991). *The Production of Space* (Basil Blackwell, Oxford, UK).

Lefebvre, H. (1995). *Introduction to Modernity: Twelve Preludes, September 1959–May 1961* (Verso, London).

Leslie-Melville, R. (1934). *The Life and Work of Sir John Fielding* (Lincoln Williams, London).

Lewis, W. S. (ed.) (1937–1983). *Horace Walpole's Correspondence* 48 vols (Yale University Press, New Haven, CT).

The Life and Times of George Robert Fitzgerald, Commonly Called Fighting Fitzgerald (1852). (Dublin).

Linebaugh, P. (1982). 'All the Atlantic mountains shook.' *Labour/Le Travailleur* 10 pp87–121.

Linebaugh, P. (1991). *The London Hanged: Crime and Civil Society in the Eighteenth Century* (Penguin, Harmondsworth, UK).

Linebaugh, P., and Rediker, M. (1990). 'The many-headed Hydra: Sailors, slaves, and the Atlantic working class in the eighteenth century.' *Journal of Historical Sociology* 3 pp225–252.

Little, D. M., and Kahrl, G. M. (eds.). (1963). *The Letters of David Garrick, Vol. II* (Oxford University Press, London).

Livingstone, D. N., and Withers, C. W. J. (eds.) (forthcoming). *Geography and Enlightenment* (University of Chicago Press, Chicago).

Lloyd, S. (1996). '"Pleasure's golden bait": Prostitution, poverty and the Magdalen Hospital in eighteenth-century London.' *History Workshop Journal* 41 pp50–70.

Lovell, T. (1995). 'Subjective powers? Consumption, the reading public and domestic women in early eighteenth-century England.' In A. Bermingham and J. Brewer (eds.), *The Consumption of Culture, 1600–1800: Image, Object, Text* (Routledge, London) pp23–41.

MacCarthy, M. (1930). *Fighting Fitzgerald and Other Papers* (Martin Secker, London).

Macfarlane, A. (1978). *The Origins of English Individualism: The Family, Property and Social Transition* (Basil Blackwell, Oxford, UK).

Macfarlane, A. (1987). *The Culture of Capitalism* (Basil Blackwell, Oxford, UK).

Mackenzie, D. (1990). *Inventing Accuracy: A Historical Sociology of Nuclear Missile Guidance* (MIT Press, Cambridge, MA).

Macpherson, C. B. (1967). *The Political Theory of Possessive Individualism: Hobbes to Locke* (Clarendon Press, Oxford).

Mann, M. (1980). 'State and society, 1130–1815: An analysis of English state finances.' In M. Zeitlin (ed.), *Political Power and Social Theory: A Research Annual* (JAI Press, Greenwich, CT) pp165–208.

Mann, M. (1984). 'The autonomous power of the state: Its origins, mechanisms and results.' *Archives Européenes de Sociologie* 25 pp185–213.

Marshall, B. L. (1994). *Engendering Modernity: Feminism, Social Theory and Social Change* (Polity Press, Cambridge, UK).

Marx, K., and Engels, F. (1971, orig. 1848). *The Communist Manifesto* (Penguin, Harmondsworth, UK).

Mathias, P. (1959). *The Brewing Industry in England, 1700–1830* (Cambridge University Press, Cambridge).

McClintock, A. (1995). *Imperial Leather: Race, Gender and Sexuality in the Colonial Contest* (Routledge, London).

McKee, F. (1988) 'Early criticism of *The Grumbling Hive.*' *Notes and Queries* 35 pp176–177.

McKendrick, N. (1983a). 'Introduction.' In N. McKendrick, J. Brewer and J. H. Plumb (eds.), *The Birth of a Consumer Society: The Commercialisation of Eighteenth-Century England* (Hutchinson, London) pp1–6.

McKendrick, N. (1983b). 'The consumer revolution of eighteenth-century England.' In N. McKendrick, J. Brewer and J. H. Plumb (eds.), *The Birth of a Consumer Society: The Commercialisation of Eighteenth-Century England* (Hutchinson, London) pp9–33.

McKendrick, N., Brewer, J. and Plumb, J. H. (eds.) (1983). *The Birth of a Consumer Society: The Commercialisation of Eighteenth-Century England* (Hutchinson, London).

Melossi, D., and Pavarini, M. (1981). *The Prison and the Factory: Origins of the Penitentiary System* (Macmillan, Basingstoke, UK).

Miller, D. (1981). *Philosophy and Ideology in Hume's Political Thought* (Clarendon Press, Oxford).

Miller, D. P., and Reill, P. H. (eds.) (1996). *Visions of Empire: Voyages, Botany, and Representations of Nature* (Cambridge University Press, Cambridge).

Miller, P. (1992). 'Accounting and objectivity: The invention of calculating selves and calculable spaces.' *Annals of Scholarship* 9 pp61–86.

Mitchell, C. (1944). 'Benjamin West's "Death of General Wolfe" and the popular history piece.' *Journal of the Warburg and Courtauld Institutes* 7 pp20–33.

Mollenauer, R. (ed.) (1965). *Introduction to Modernity: A Symposium on Eighteenth-Century Thought* (University of Texas Press, Austin).

Mommsen, W. J. (1980). '"Toward the iron cage of future serfdom"? On the methodological status of Max Weber's ideal-typical concept of bureaucratisation,' *Transactions of the Royal Historical Society* 5th series 30 pp 157–181.

Money, J. (1993a). 'Teaching in the market-place, or "Caesar adsum jam forte: Pompey aderat": The retailing of knowledge in provincial England during the eighteenth century.' In J. Brewer and R. Porter (eds.), *Consumption and the World of Goods* (Routledge, London) pp335–377.

Money, J. (1993b). 'The Masonic moment; or, Ritual, replica, and credit: John Wilkes, the Macaroni Parson, and the making of the middle-class mind.' *Journal of British Studies* 32 pp358–395.

Montaigne, M. de (1991). *The Essays of Michel de Montaigne,* translated and edited by M. A. Screech (Penguin, Harmondsworth, UK).

Nash, C. (1996). 'Men again: Irish masculinity, nature, and nationhood in the early twentieth century.' *Ecumene* 3 pp427–453.

Nash, S. (1984). 'Prostitution and charity: The Magdalen Hospital, a case study.' *Journal of Social History* 17 pp617–628.

Nicolson, E. E. C. (1996). 'Consumers and spectators: The public of the political print in eighteenth-century England.' *History* 81 pp5–21.

Norton, R. (1992). *Mother Clap's Molly House: The Gay Subculture in London, 1700–1830* (Gay Men's Press, London).

Nussbaum, F. A. (1990). 'The politics of difference.' *Eighteenth-Century Studies* 23 pp375–386.

Nussbaum, F. A. (1995). *Torrid Zones: Maternity, Sexuality, and Empire in Eighteenth-Century English Narratives* (Johns Hopkins University Press, Baltimore).

O'Brien, P. K., and Engerman, S. L. (1991). 'Exports and the growth of the British economy from the Glorious Revolution to the Peace of Amiens.' In B. L Solow (ed.), *Slavery and the Rise of the Atlantic System* (Cambridge University Press, Cambridge) pp177–209.

O'Brien, P. K., and Hunt, P. A. (1993). 'The rise of a fiscal state in England, 1485–1815.' *Historical Research* 66 pp129–176.

O'Brien, P. K., and Hunt, P. A. (1997). 'The emergence and consolidation of excises in the English fiscal system before the Glorious Revolution.' *British Tax Review* 1 pp35–58.

O'Donoghue, E. G. (1929). *Bridewell Hospital: Palace, Prison, Schools from the Death of Elizabeth to Modern Times* (John Lane, London).

Oestreich, G. (1982). *Neostoicism and the Early Modern State* (Cambridge University Press, Cambridge).

Ogborn, M. (1995). 'Knowing the individual: Michel Foucault and Norbert Elias on *Las Meninas* and the modern subject.' In S. Pile and N. Thrift (eds.), *Mapping the Subject: Geographies of Cultural Transformation* (Routledge, London) pp57–76.

Oostindie, G. (ed.) (1995). *Fifty Years Later: Antislavery, Capitalism and Modernity in the Dutch Orbit* (KITLV Press, Leiden).

Osborne, P. (1995). *The Politics of Time: Modernity and Avant-Garde* (Verso, London).

Outram, D. (1995). *The Enlightenment* (Cambridge University Press, Cambridge).

Paulson, R. (1975). *Emblem and Expression: Meaning in English Art of the Eighteenth Century* (Thames & Hudson, London).

Pawson, E. (1977). *Transport and Economy: The Turnpike Roads of Eighteenth-Century Britain* (Academic Press, London).

Perry, G., and Rossington, M. (eds.) (1994). *Femininity and Masculinity in Eighteenth-Century Art and Culture* (Manchester University Press, Manchester, UK).

Perry, R. (1991). 'Colonising the breast: Sexuality and maternity in eighteenth-century England.' *Journal of the History of Sexuality* 2 pp204–234.

Phillips, H. (1952). 'John Rocque's career.' *London Topographical Record* xx pp9–25.

Pile, S., and Thrift, N. (eds.) (1995). *Mapping the Subject: Geographies of Cultural Transformation* (Routledge, London).

Plumb, J. H. (1950). *England in the Eighteenth Century* (Penguin, Harmondsworth, UK).

Plumb, J. H. (1983). 'The acceptance of modernity.' In N. McKendrick, J. Brewer and J. H. Plumb (eds.), *The Birth of a Consumer Society: The Commercialisation of Eighteenth-Century England* (Hutchinson, London) pp316–334.

Pocock, J. G. A. (1975). *The Machiavellian Moment: Florentine Political Thought and the Atlantic Republican Tradition* (Princeton University Press, Princeton, NJ).

Pocock, J. G. A. (1985). *Virtue, Commerce, and History: Essays on Political Thought and History, Chiefly in the Eighteenth Century* (Cambridge University Press, Cambridge).

Pocock, J. G. A. (1987). 'Modernity and anti-modernity in the anglophone political tradition.' In S. N. Eisenstadt (ed.), *Patterns of Modernity, Vol. 1: The West* (Frances Pinter, London) pp44–59.

Pollock, G. (1988). *Vision and Difference: Femininity, Feminism and the Histories of Art* (Routledge, London).

Porter, R. (1982). 'Mixed feelings: The Enlightenment and sexuality in eighteenth-century Britain.' In P.-G. Boucé (ed.), *Sexuality in Eighteenth-Century Britain* (Manchester University Press, Manchester, UK) pp1–27.

Porter, R. (1988). 'Seeing the past.' *Past and Present* 118 pp186–205.

Porter, R. (1990). *English Society in the Eighteenth Century* 2nd ed. (Penguin, Harmondsworth, UK).

Porter, R. (1992). 'Georgian Britain: An ancien regime?' *British Journal for Eighteenth-Century Studies* 15 pp141–144.

Porter, R. (1993). 'Consumption: Disease of the consumer society?' In J. Brewer and R. Porter (eds.), *Consumption and the World of Goods* (Routledge, London) pp58–81.

Porter, R. (1994). *London: A Social History* (Hamish Hamilton, London).

Porter, R. (1996). 'Material pleasures in the consumer society.' In R. Porter and M. M. Roberts (eds.), *Pleasure in the Eighteenth Century* (Macmillan, Basingstoke, UK) pp19–35.

Porter, R. (1997). 'The new eighteenth-century social history.' In J. Black (ed.), *Culture and Society in Britain, 1660–1800* (Manchester University Press, Manchester, UK) pp29–50.

Porter, R., and Teich, M. (1981). *The Enlightenment in National Context* (Cambridge University Press, Cambridge).

Potkay, A., and Burr, S. (1995). *Black Atlantic Writers of the Eighteenth Century: Living the New Exodus in England and the Americas* (Macmillan, Basingstoke, UK).

Pred, A. (1990). *Lost Words and Lost Worlds: Modernity and the Language of Everyday Life in Late Nineteenth-Century Stockholm* (Cambridge University Press, Cambridge).

Pred, A. (1995). *ReCognizing European Modernities: A Montage of the Present* (Routledge, London).

Pred, A., and Watts, M. J. (1992). *Reworking Modernity: Capitalisms and Symbolic Discontent* (Rutgers University Press, New Brunswick, NJ).

Price, J. V. (1982). 'Patterns of sexual behaviour in some eighteenth-century novels.' In P.-G. Boucé (ed.), *Sexuality in Eighteenth-Century Britain* (Manchester University Press, Manchester, UK) pp159–175.

Pringle, P. (1955). *Hue and Cry: The Birth of the British Police* (Museum Press, London).

Prostko, J. (1989). '"Natural conversation set in view": Shaftesbury and moral speech.' *Eighteenth-Century Studies* 23 pp42–61.

Rabinow, P. (1989). *French Modern: Norms and Forms of the Social Environment* (MIT Press, Cambridge, MA).

Radzinowicz, L. (1956). *A History of the English Criminal Law and Its Administration from 1750, Vol. 3: Cross-Currents in the Movement for the Reform of the Police* (Stevens & Sons, London).

Raeff, M. (1975). 'A well-ordered police state and the development of modernity in seventeenth- and eighteenth-century Europe.' *American Historical Review* 80 pp1221–143.

Raeff, M. (1983). *The Well-Ordered Police State: Social and Institutional Change through Law in the Germanies and Russia, 1600–1800* (Yale University Press, New Haven, CT).

Rashid, S. (1985). 'Mandeville's *Fable:* Laissez-faire or libertinism?' *Eighteenth-Century Studies* 18 pp313–330.

Raven, J. (1992). *Judging New Wealth: Popular Publishing and Responses to Commerce in England, 1750–1800* (Clarendon Press, Oxford).

Raven, J. (1995). 'Defending conduct and property: The London press and the luxury debate.' In J. Brewer and S. Staves (eds.), *Early Modern Conceptions of Property* (Routledge, London) pp301–319.

Rediker, M. (1987). *Between the Devil and the Deep Blue Sea: Merchant Seamen, Pirates and the Anglo-American Maritime World, 1700–1750* (Cambridge University Press, Cambridge).

Rengger, N. J. (1995). *Political Theory, Modernity and Postmodernity: Beyond Enlightenment and Critique* (Basil Blackwell, Oxford, UK).

Robinson, H. (1948). *The British Post Office: A History* (Princeton University Press, Princeton, NJ).

Robinson, H. (1964). *Carrying British Mails Overseas* (George Allen & Unwin, London).

Rodgers, B. (1949). *The Cloak of Charity: Studies in Eighteenth-Century Philanthropy* (Methuen, London).

Rogers, N. (1978). 'Popular protest in early Hanoverian London.' *Past and Present* 79 pp70–100.

Rogers, N. (1991). 'Policing the poor in eighteenth-century London: the vagrancy laws and their administration.' *Histoire Sociale/Social History* XXIV pp127–147.

Rogers, P. (1974). *The Augustan Vision* (Wiedenfeld and Nicolson, London).

Rossiaud, J. (1985). 'Prostitution, sex and society in French towns in the fifteenth century.' In P. Ariès and A. Béjin (eds.) *Western Sexuality: Practice and Precept in Past and Present Times* (Basil Blackwell, Oxford, UK) pp76–94.

Rousseau, G. S., and Porter, R. (eds.) (1987). *Sexual Underworlds of the Enlightenment* (Manchester University Press, Manchester, UK).

Rudé, G. (1959). 'The London "mob" of the eighteenth century.' *Historical Journal* 2 pp1–18.

Russett, A. (1994). 'Peter Monamy's marine paintings for Vauxhall Gardens.' *Mariner's Mirror* 80 pp79–84.

Ryan, J. (1994). 'Women, modernity and the city.' *Theory, Culture and Society* 11 pp35–63.

Ryan, M. P. (1992). 'Gender and public access: Women's politics in nineteenth-century America.' In C. Calhoun (ed.), *Habermas and the Public Sphere* (MIT Press, Cambridge, MA) pp259–288.

Sack, R. D. (1992). *Place, Modernity, and the Consumer's World: A Relational Framework for Geographical Analysis* (Johns Hopkins University Press, Baltimore).

Sands, M. (1946). *Invitation to Ranelagh, 1742–1803* (John Westhouse, London).

Schabert, T. (1983). 'Modernity and history.' *Diogenes* 123 pp110–124.

Schaffer, S. (1993). 'The consuming flame: Electrical showmen and Tory mystics in the world of goods.' In J. Brewer and R. Porter (eds.), *Consumption and the World of Goods* (Routledge, London) pp489–526.

Schama, S. (1988). *The Embarrassment of Riches: An Interpretation of Dutch Culture in the Golden Age* (Fontana, London).

Schivelbusch, W. (1988). *Disenchanted Night: The Industrialisation of Light in the Nineteenth Century* (Berg, Oxford, UK).

Schorske, C. E. (1981). *Fin de Siècle Vienna: Politics and Culture* (Cambridge University Press, Cambridge).

Schumpeter, E. B. (1960). *English Overseas Trade Statistics, 1697–1808* (Clarendon Press, Oxford).

Schware, R. (1981). *Quantification in the History of Political Thought: Toward a Qualitative Analysis* (Greenwood Press, Westport, CT).

Schwarz, L. D. (1992). *London in the Age of Industrialisation: Entrepreneurs, Labour Force and Living Conditions, 1700–1850* (Cambridge University Press, Cambridge).

Scobey, D. (1992). 'Anatomy of the promenade: The politics of bourgeois sociability in nineteenth-century New York.' *Social History* 17 pp203–227.

Secretan, P. (1984). 'Elements for a theory of modernity,' *Diogenes* 126 pp71–90.

Sekora, J. (1977). *Luxury: The Concept in Western Thought, Eden to Smollett* (Johns Hopkins University Press, Baltimore).

Sellin, T. (1944). *Pioneering in Penology: The Amsterdam Houses of Correction in the Sixteenth and Seventeenth Centuries* (University of Philadelphia Press, Philadelphia).

Semple, J. (1993). *Bentham's Prison: A Study of the Panopticon Penitentiary* (Clarendon Press, Oxford).

Sennett, R. (1974). *The Fall of Public Man* (Cambridge University Press, Cambridge).

Shammas, C. (1980). 'The domestic environment in early modern England and America.' *Journal of Social History* 14 pp3–24.

Shapin, S. (1994). *A Social History of Truth: Civility and Science in Seventeenth-Century England* (University of Chicago Press, Chicago).

Sherman, S. (1995). 'Credit, simulation, and the ideology of contract in the early eighteenth century.' *Eighteenth-Century Life* 19 pp86–102.

Shevelow, K. (1989). *Women and Print Culture: The Construction of Femininity in the Early Periodical* (Routledge, London).

Shoemaker, R. B. (1987). 'The London "mob" in the early eighteenth century.' *Journal of British Studies* 26 pp273–304.

Simmel, G. (1971, orig. 1903). 'The metropolis and mental life.' In D. Levine (ed.), *Georg Simmel on Individuality and Social Forms* (University of Chicago Press, Chicago) pp324–339.

Smart, B. (1990). 'Modernity, postmodernity and the present.' In B. S. Turner (ed.), *Theories of Modernity and Postmodernity* (Sage, London) pp14–30.

Solkin, D. H. (1992). 'ReWrighting Shaftesbury: The air pump and the limits of commercial humanism.' In J. Barrell (ed.), *Painting and the Politics of Culture: New Essays on British Art, 1700–1850* (Oxford University Press, Oxford) pp73–99.

Solkin, D. H. (1993). *Painting for Money: The Visual Arts and the Public Sphere in Eighteenth-Century England* (Yale University Press, New Haven, CT).

Spadafora, D. (1990). *The Idea of Progress in Eighteenth-Century Britain* (Yale University Press, New Haven, CT).

Speck, W. A. (1980). 'The harlot's progress in eighteenth-century England.' *British Journal for Eighteenth-Century Studies* 3 pp127–139.

Speck, W. A. (1992). 'The eighteenth century: England's ancien régime?' *British Journal for Eighteenth-Century Studies* 15 pp131–133.

Spierenburg, P. (1984). 'The sociogenesis of confinement and its development in early modern Europe.' In P. Spierenburg (ed.), *The Emergence of Carceral Institutions: Prisons, Galleys and Lunatic Asylums, 1550–1900* (Centrum Voor Maatschappij Geschiedenis, Erasmus Universiteit, Rotterdam) pp9–77.

Spierenburg, P. (1987). 'From Amsterdam to Auburn: An explanation for the rise of the prison in seventeenth-century Holland and nineteenth-century America.' *Journal of Social History* 20 pp439–461.

Spierenburg, P. (1991). *The Prison Experience: Disciplinary Institutions and Their Inmates in Early Modern Europe* (Rutgers University Press, New Brunswick, NJ).

Stafford, B. M. (1991). *Body Criticism: Imaging the Unseen in Enlightenment Art and Medicine* (MIT Press, Cambridge, MA).

Stafford, B. M. (1994). 'Redesigning the image of images: A personal view.' *Eighteenth-Century Studies* 28 pp9–16.

Stallybrass, P., and White, A. (1986). *The Politics and Poetics of Transgression* (Methuen, London).

Statt, D. (1995). 'The case of the Mohocks: Rake violence in Augustan London.' *Social History* 20 pp179–199.

Staves, S. (1982). 'A few kind words for the fop.' *Studies in English Literature, 1500–1900* 22 pp413–428.

Steele, V. (1985). 'The social and political significance of Macaroni fashion.' *Costume* 19 pp94–109.

Stevenson, J. (1979). *Popular Disturbances in England* (Longman, London).

Stewart, A. (1995). 'The early modern closet discovered.' *Representations* 50 pp76–100.

Stewart, M. A. (1996). 'Inexhaustible generosity: The fictions of eighteenth-century British imperialism in Richard Cumberland's *The West Indian*.' *The Eighteenth-Century: Theory and Interpretation* 37 pp42–55.

Stone, G. W. (ed.) (1962). *The London Stage, 1660–1800. Part 4: 1747–1776* (University of Southern Illinois Press, Carbondale).

Stone G. W. Jr, and Kahrl, G. M. (1979). *David Garrick: A Critical Biography* (University of Southern Illinois Press, Carbondale).

Stone, L. (1977). *The Family, Sex and Marriage in England, 1500–1800* (Wiedenfeld and Nicolson, London).

Stone, L. (1994). 'Introduction.' In L. Stone (ed.), *An Imperial State at War: Britain from 1689 to 1815* (Routledge, London) pp1–32.

Straub, K. (1992). *Sexual Suspects: Eighteenth-Century Players and Sexual Ideology* (Princeton University Press, Princeton, NJ).

Styles, J. (1983). 'Sir John Fielding and the problem of criminal investigation in eighteenth-century England.' *Transactions of the Royal Historical Society* 5th series 33 pp127–149.

Summerson, J. (1991, orig. 1945). *Georgian London* (Penguin, Harmondsworth, UK).

Swade, D. D. (1994). 'Calculating machines.' In I. Grattan-Guiness (ed.), *Companion Encyclopedia of the History and Philosophy of the Mathematical Sciences* (Routledge, London) Vol. I, pp694–700.

Sweet, R. (1996). 'The production of urban histories in eighteenth-century England.' *Urban History* 23 pp171–188.

Tanner, T. (1979). *Adultery and the Novel: Contract and Transgression* (Johns Hopkins University Press, Baltimore).

Taylor, J. S. (1985). *Jonas Hanway, Founder of the Marine Society: Charity and Policy in Eighteenth-Century Britain* (Scolar Press, London).

Tester, K. (1994). *The Flâneur* (Routledge, London).

Thomas, K. (1987). 'Numeracy in early modern England.' *Transactions of the Royal Historical Society* 5th series 37 pp103–132.

Thrift, N. J. (1990). 'Transport and communication, 1730–1914.' In R. A. Dodgshon and R. A. Butlin (eds.), *An Historical Geography of England and Wales* 2d edition (Academic Press, London) pp453–486.

Tilly, C. (ed.) (1975). *The Formation of National States in Western Europe* (Princeton University Press, Princeton, NJ).

Tilly, C. (1990). *Coercion, Capital and European States, AD 990–1990* (Basil Blackwell, Oxford, UK).

Torrance, J. (1978). 'Social class and bureaucratic innovation: The Commissioners for Examining the Public Accounts, 1780–1787.' *Past and Present* 78 pp56–81.

Toulmin, S. (1990). *Cosmopolis: The Hidden Agenda of Modernity* (University of Chicago Press, Chicago).

Tribe, K. (1978). *Land, Labour and Economic Discourse* (Routledge and Kegan Paul, London).

Trumbach, R. (1987a). 'Modern prostitution and gender in *Fanny Hill:* Libertine and domesticated fantasy.' In G. S. Rousseau and R. Porter (eds.), *Sexual Underworlds of the Enlightenment* (Manchester University Press, Manchester, UK) pp69–85.

Trumbach, R. (1987b). 'Sodomitical subcultures, sodomitical roles, and the gender revolution of the eighteenth century: The present historiography.' In R. P. Maccubbin (ed.), *'Tis Nature's Fault: Unauthorized Sexuality during the Enlightenment* (Cambridge University Press, Cambridge) pp109–121.

Trumbach, R. (1991). 'Sex, gender, and sexual identity in modern culture: Male sodomy and female prostitution in Enlightenment London.' *Journal of the History of Sexuality* 2 pp186–203.

Tully, J. (1993a). 'After the Macpherson thesis.' In J. Tully (ed.), *An Approach to Political Philosophy: Locke in Contexts* (Cambridge University Press, Cambridge) pp71–96.

Tully, J. (1993b). 'Governing conduct: Locke on the reform of thought and behaviour.' In J. Tully (ed.), *An Approach to Political Philosophy: Locke in Contexts* (Cambridge University Press, Cambridge) pp179–241.

Turner, B. S. (ed.) (1990a). *Theories of Modernity and Postmodernity* (Sage, London).

Turner, B. S. (1990b). 'Periodization and politics in the postmodern.' In B. S. Turner (ed.), *Theories of Modernity and Postmodernity* (Sage, London) pp1–13.

Varley, J. (1948). 'John Rocque: Engraver, surveyor, cartographer and map-seller.' *Imago Mundi* 5 pp83–91.

Velody, I. (1992). 'Rationality deferred: An introduction to the politics of modernity.' *History of the Human Sciences* 5 pp1–7.

Waddell, D. (1958–1959). 'Charles Davenant (1656–1714): A biographical sketch.' *Economic History Review* 2d series 11 pp279–288.

Wagner, P. (1994). *A Sociology of Modernity: Liberty and Discipline* (Routledge, London).

Walvin, J. (1997). *Fruits of Empire: Exotic Produce and British Taste, 1660–1800* (Macmillan, Basingstoke, UK).

Wanko, C. (1994). 'The eighteenth-century actress and the construction of gender: Lavinia Fenton and Charlotte Charke.' *Eighteenth-Century Life* 18 pp75–90.

Watt, I. (1957). *The Rise of the Novel: Studies in Defoe, Richardson and Fielding* (Chatto & Windus, London).

Watt, I. (1969). '*Robinson Crusoe,* individualism and the novel.' In F. H. Ellis (ed.), *Twentieth Century Interpretations of Robinson Crusoe* (Prentice Hall, Englewood Cliffs, NJ) pp39–54.

Webb, S., and Webb, B. (1922). *English Local Government: Statutory Authorities for Special Purposes* (Longmans, Green and Co., London).

Weber, M. (1967). 'Bureaucracy.' In H. H. Gerth and C. Wright Mills (eds.), *From Max Weber: Essays in Sociology* (Routledge & Kegan Paul, London) pp196–244.

Weber, M. (1976, orig. 1904–1905). *The Protestant Ethic and the Spirit of Capitalism* (Allen & Unwin, London).

Weitzman, A. J. (1975). 'Eighteenth-century London: Urban paradise or fallen city?' *Journal of the History of Ideas* 38 pp469–480.

Wheatley, H. B. (1914). 'Rocque's plan of London.' *London Topographical Record* ix pp15–28.

Whitney, C. (1986). *Francis Bacon and Modernity* (Yale University Press, New Haven, CT).

Wiles, R. M. (1965). *Freshest Advices: Early Provincial Newspapers in England* (Ohio State University Press, Columbus).

Williams, R. H. (1993). 'Cultural origins and environmental implications of large technological systems.' *Science in Context* 2 pp377–403.

Williams, R. H. (1982). *Dream Worlds: Mass Consumption in Late Nineteenth-Century France* (University of California Press, Berkeley and Los Angeles).

Wilson, E. (1987). *Adorned in Dreams: Fashion and Modernity* (University of California Press, Berkeley and Los Angeles).

Wilson, E. (1992). 'The invisible flâneur.' *New Left Review* 191 pp90–110.

Wilson, K. (1988). 'Empire, trade and popular politics in mid-Hanoverian Britain: The case of Admiral Vernon.' *Past and Present* 121 pp74–109.

Wilson, K. (1994). 'Empire of virtue: The imperial project and Hanoverian culture, c. 1720–1785.' In L. Stone (ed.), *An Imperial State at War: Britain from 1689 to 1815* (Routledge, London) pp128–164.

Wilson, K. (1995a). 'Citizenship, empire, and modernity in the English provinces, c. 1720–1790.' *Eighteenth-Century Studies* 29 pp69–96.

Wilson, K. (1995b). *The Sense of the People: Politics, Culture and Imperialism in England, 1715–1785* (Cambridge University Press, Cambridge).

Wilson, K. (1995c). 'The good, the bad, and the impotent: Imperialism and the politics of identity in Georgian England.' In A. Bermingham and J. Brewer (eds.), *The Consumption of Culture, 1600–1800: Image, Object, Text* (Routledge, London) pp237–262.

Withers, C. W. J. (1996). 'Encyclopaedism, modernism and the classification of geographical knowledge.' *Transactions of the Institute of British Geographers* 21 pp275–298.

Wolff, J. (1985). 'The invisible *flâneuse:* Women and the literature of modernity.' *Theory, Culture and Society* 2 pp37–46.

Wood, E. M. (1991). *The Pristine Culture of Capitalism: A Historical Essay on Old Regimes and Modern States* (Verso, London).

Wrigley, E. A. (1967). 'A simple model of London's importance in changing English society and economy, 1650–1750.' *Past and Present* 37 pp44–70.

Wrigley, E. A. (1994). 'Society and the economy in the eighteenth century.' In L. Stone (ed.), *An Imperial State at War: Britain from 1689 to 1815* (Routledge, London) pp72–95.

Wroth, W. W. (1896). *The London Pleasure Gardens of the Eighteenth Century* (Macmillan, London).

Index

Absolutism, 144, 171
Addison, Joseph, 82
Africa, 138, 205–207
Aix-la-Chapelle, Treaty of (1748), 236–238
Allen, Ralph, 203
America, 61, 138, 142, 203, 205–207, 223, 237
Amherst, General Jeffrey, 143–146
Amsterdam, 43–44
Ancien regime, 23–24, 41, 236–238
Athens, 83–84, 90
Atlantic world, 16, 35, 134, 203, 206–209

B

Banks, Joseph, 134, 137
Bate, Henry, 116–118, 147, 148–149, 154, 155, 156
Bauman, Zygmunt, 4, 7, 17, 18, 40
Beer, 177
    brewing of, 179, 195
    different from ale, 180–181
    taxation of, 160, 166–167, 172, 178–183, 195–198
Berman, Marshall, 5, 11–12, 17, 18–19, 39–40
Bickham Jr., George, 128
Billingsgate, 107, 192–193
Blackfriars Bridge (1769), 34, 61

Brewer, John, 30, 127, 128, 158, 161, 167, 171
Bucknall, Sir William, 170
Bureaucracy, 1, 3, 4, 5–6, 10, 11, 13, 20, 158, 161, 171, 187–188, 191, 198, 199, 231
Bureaucratic identity, 187–188, 192–194
Bureaucratic network, 27, 162
Bureaucratisation, 19, 21, 25, 161, 195

C

Canada, 142–144
Capitalism, 39, 76. *See also* Modernity, and capitalism
Caribbean, 138, 142, 143, 203, 206
Charity, 47, 48, 57, 61, 109, 110, 144, 217
    sensibility and, 52–54
Charles I, 170
Charles II, 92, 170–171, 236
Chelsea, 99, 123
Cibber, Theophilius, 132, 223
Circulation, 94, 164–165, 211, 215
    ideology of, 212–213, 218, 223, 228
City, The. *See also* Knowledge, of the city; Space, urban
    improvements to, 76, 91–104, 109, 113, 115
    planning of, 98–101
    representations of, 31, 77, 90, 104–114, 234

Civility, 79, 81, 88, 110–111, 113, 115.
    See also Politeness
Clark, Jonathan C. D., 23–24, 41
Class, 78, 89, 110–111, 119, 126, 129,
    134, 140, 228
    and gender, 139, 153–154, 192,
    217–218, 219
Clive, Robert, of India, 144–147
Closterman, John, 82
Coffee and Coffeehouses, 36, 78, 106,
    117, 138–139, 194, 198, 205
Collins, Richard, 176
Colman, George, 139–140
Commerce, 75, 84–85, 87, 112–113, 115,
    138–139, 212, 213, 215, 229, 234
    as gendered conversation, 88–89
    global, 12–13, 201, 205–209, 214, 237
    and morality, 216–217, 227–228
Commercial society, 82–83, 85, 90, 110,
    114–115, 124–125, 213
Commercialisation, 35, 118, 237
    of leisure, 112–118
    of Shakespeare, 139
Commodification, 1, 9, 10, 19, 20, 21–22,
    30–31, 37, 115, 156, 209, 227, 232,
    237
    of cultural production, 118–119, 123
    of masculinity, 139, 155, 210
    and sexuality, 128–142
    at Vauxhall Gardens, 122–128
Consumption, 5, 43, 85, 115, 217–218
    of commodities, 116, 125, 127, 157
    culture of, 119, 127–128
    and global trade, 138–139, 141
    spaces of, 127–28
Covent Garden, 49, 93, 112, 116, 219,
    221–222
Credit, 154, 155
Cumberland, Duke of, 30

D

Darly, Matthew and Mary, 134, 137
Davenant, Charles, 162–163, 185,
    199–200, 234
    and excise administration, 170–185
    and political arithmetic, 163–170
    travels of, 172–175, 287n87
Defoe, Daniel, 31, 42, 208
Dingley, Robert, 45, 47, 52, 53
Dodd, William, 72, 134, 282n193

Dreaming, 126, 127–128, 129, 132–133
Dublin, 120, 212, 214, 218
Dummer, Edward, 203

E

East Indies, 138, 205–207, 209
Effeminacy, 115, 134, 140–142, 145, 153,
    155. *See also* Masculinity
Elizabeth I, 236
Empire, 20, 21, 32–33, 36, 46, 52, 99,
    122, 158–160, 166, 201, 203,
    205–206, 210, 214
    herrings and, 143
    masculinity and, 144–147, 153, 154
    at Vauxhall Gardens, 142–148
Englishness, 139–142
    and song, 143
Enlightenment, 22, 26–27, 77–78, 152
Excise Board, 172, 178
Excise commissioners, 163, 169,
    171–172, 179, 184, 194
Excise Crisis (1733), 195, 204
Excise taxation, 28, 33, 37, 158–200,
    204
    administrative geography of, 171–172,
    182–184, 195–198
    Charles Davenant's arguments for,
    165–170, 231
    farming of, 170–171
    general excise, 167–168
    justices of the peace and, 180–181,
    185
    in London, 194–198
    management of, 168–170, 170–185
    modernity of, 160–162
    patronage and, 161, 180, 199
Excisemen, 162, 167, 169, 170, 176, 179,
    185–194, 233. *See also* Polstead,
    Ezekial, *The Excise Man*
    as national officers working locally,
    191–193
    number of in London, 194
    'removes' of, 181–183, 185, 190–191
    self-fashioning of, 185–194, 199
    skills and training of, 177–178,
    180–181, 182, 185, 189–190, 197.
    See also Gauging
    social status of, 187–188
    suspicion of, 173
Everard, Thomas, 178, 189

F

Fashion, 10, 34, 36, 85, 117, 119, 123,
133, 139, 140
macaronis and, 135–138, 153
Felski, Rita, 7, 8, 11, 16
Femininity, 7, 128, 206, 217. *See also*
Gender
Fielding, Henry, 42, 45, 129, 201, 224,
229, 234
on luxury, 125–128
and policing, 219–221
on Universal Register Office,
211–215, 217
Fielding, John, 106, 234
and Magdalen Hospital, 45, 47–48, 52,
72
and policing, 221–223
and Universal Register Office, 211,
212, 216, 217, 224
Financial revolution, 160, 171
Fireworks, 236–238
Fitzgerald, George Robert, 116–118,
148–149, 153–157
Flamsteed, John, 184
Flâneur, The, 16–17, 113
Foucault, Michel, 39, 48
Foundling Hospital, 30, 47
Fox, Charles, 134, 137
Fox, Stephen, 134
France, 33, 96, 140–141, 143, 155, 164,
166, 207, 212, 225–226, 236–237.
See also Paris
Frederick, Charles, 237–238
Frederick, Prince of Wales, 30, 120, 142,
273n23, 279n127
Frederick St. John, 2nd Viscount
Bolingbroke, 135–137

G

Garrick, David, 139–140, 143, 223
Gauging, 158, 176–185, 195–197.
accuracy of, 173–178, 199
the 'method,' 181–182, 183
in the worts, 179–180, 182, 183
Gay, John, 42, 104–114
Trivia, 104–114
Gender, 10. 14–17, 49, 73–74, 119, 129,
140–142, 228. *See also* Class and
gender; Femininity; Masculinity

government of the self and, 88–89,
189–193
men looking at women, 117, 147,
148–50, 151, 155, 282n167
public sphere and, 78, 83–84, 89,
110–111, 114, 149
rationality and, 70–72, 192
subjectivity and, 42–43
George II, 236
George III, 144
George, M. Dorothy, 34, 35, 97, 134
Giddens, Anthony, 8–10, 17–18,
210–211
Gilroy, Paul, 3, 10, 14–16, 17, 18, 22,
207–208
Gravelot, Hubert François, 128
Gwynn, John, 98–101, 103, 114–115

H

Habermas, Jürgen, 76, 77–79, 90, 114
Halley, Edmond, 184
Handel, George Frederick, 122, 151, 236,
237
Hanway, Jonas, 234
and Magdalen Hospital, 43–45, 47,
50–52, 53, 58, 61, 64–72
and paving, 74, 91, 96–97
Hartley, Elizabeth, 116–117, 147,
148–150, 155, 157
Hayman, Francis, 120–122, 123, 143–145
Heidegger, John James, 129
Hitchcock, Robert, 134, 140–141
Hoare, Sir Richard, 30
Hogarth, William, 30
The Harlot's Progress, 53, 55, 57, 132
Hume, David, 77, 79, 82, 87–91, 111,
114, 124–125
Hunt, William, 189

I

Identity, 15, 22, 37, 40–43, 60, 79, 91,
128, 129, 155, 233, 235. *See also*
Bureaucratic identity
consumption and, 119, 127, 157
excisemen and, 186–194, 199–200
vision and, 66–70, 72, 151–152 *See also*
Self, self-reflection and
India, 142, 144, 206, 237. *See also* East
Indies

Individual, The, 48, 52, 58, 93, 103–104, 200
Individualisation, 1, 14, 19, 20, 37, 74, 111, 232. *See also* Private interests
Individualism, 24, 39, 41–42
Industrial revolution, 23, 32
Information, 37, 64, 210, 215. *See also* Knowledge
    and empire, 205–206, 207
    management of, 201, 203–204, 206–211, 229–230, 232
    politics of, 201, 203–204, 208–210, 219, 229–230
Ireland, 116, 209, 225. *See also* Dublin
Isle of Wight, 177
Italy, 33, 132, 140, 143

J

James II, 171, 236
Johnson, Samuel, 223

K

Kent, 171, 181
King, Gregory, 163
Knowledge, 4, 7–8, 18, 22, 26, 39, 160, 199, 228. *See also* Information
    of the city, 108, 113–114, 220, 221
    control of, 178, 197–198, 200
    geographies of, 27
    mathematical, 163–165, 170, 176–178, 182–183, 188–189, 197. *See also* Gauging; Political arithmetic

L

Latour, Bruno, 6, 7–8, 12, 14
Leadbetter, Charles, 176–177
Lefebvre, Henri, 21–22, 27, 235
Lockman, John, 123, 124, 126–128, 143, 151, 152
London, 1, 22, 25, 28–36, 57, 74, 83, 86–87, 101–114, 137, 138, 141, 145, 166, 201, 202, 205, 219, 232
    as a capital city, 33, 35, 163, 184
    excise taxation in, 194–198
    growth of, 33–36
    as a port, 34, 35–36, 207–208, 209
    rudeness of inhabitants, 109
Luxury, 82, 85, 87–88, 89, 90, 111, 115, 119, 124–128, 132, 134–135, 138–139, 145, 153, 213, 218, 234, 237–238
    aristocratic government and, 134, 142, 145
Lyttelton, Thomas, 116, 155–156, 270*n*2

M

Macaronies, 116–118, 128, 133–142, 145, 147, 148–149, 152–157, 210, 233
Magdalen Hospital, 27, 28, 32–33, 37, 43–74, 88, 151, 230, 232, 233, 234, 251*n*37
    organisation of space in, 60–70
Maitland, William, 30
Mandeville, Bernard, 49, 77, 79, 84–87, 90, 96, 114, 124–125
Marx, Karl, 6, 9, 40, 127
Masculinity, 42, 118, 128, 206, 217, 232. *See also* Gender
    commodification of, 152–155, 210
    and empire, 142–148, 153, 156
    and Englishness, 140–142
    excisemen and, 189–190, 192
    macaronies and, 137–142, 155–156
Masquerade, 120, 123, 140, 141, 153. *See also* Ridotto al Fresco
Merchants, 34, 35, 206–208
Modernisation theory, 11, 19, 25
Modernity
    as 'Big Ditch' or 'Great Divide,' 3, 6–9, 12
    and capitalism, 5–6, 9, 10–13, 21, 23, 32, 119, 210, 214, 234–235
    and the city, 40, 115, 232
    and commodified fashion, 119
    as contingent, 162, 199–200
    and difference, 2, 4, 6, 9, 11, 12, 14–17, 20, 24, 26, 28, 36, 238
    and discourse, 7–8, 10–11
    and the eighteenth century, 22–28, 231, 238
    and experience, 9–10, 11–12, 15, 26, 28, 74, 233
    geography of, 1–2, 7, 9–10, 14, 16–17, 17–22, 24, 26–27, 28, 32, 37–38, 42, 232–233, 234–236
    as global, 9. 10, 16, 19–22, 33, 40, 207, 210

Modernity *(continued)*
and hybridity, 19–20, 21, 26–27, 28, 36, 206
and institutions, 8–10, 12, 15, 17–18, 26, 28, 210, 233
and laughter, 193–194, 199–200
as local, 19–22
as multiple modernities, 9–11, 12, 14, 17, 19, 20, 25, 233–234
and 'networks,' 8, 20, 21, 37, 162, 183–184, 199, 232
as the 'new,' 2, 14, 23, 28, 271*n*12
and periodisation, 2, 6–8, 12, 22, 26–27
as a 'project,' 28, 215, 236
and rationality, 2, 3–5, 7–8, 10, 12, 13–14, 20, 21, 22–23, 77, 234–235
as rural, 32–33, 37
and Shaftesbury, 82–83
and the state, 160–162, 171, 199–200, 210
temporality, history and, 3, 11–12, 16, 17–22, 27–28, 321–326
theories of, 2–22, 25, 38, 231–232, 234–235
and totalisation, 2–3, 5, 10–11, 14–15, 17, 25–26, 38, 233, 238
and vision, 150
Money, 112, 124, 125–127, 152, 164
and sex, 128–133, 217, 227–228
Montagu, Lady Barbara, 53
Morgan, William, 30

N

Nation-state, 9, 10, 14, 160, 164, 184
Netherlands, 30, 43–44, 84, 164, 203, 207. *See also* Amsterdam
Newspapers, 23, 204–206, 209, 221

P

Panopticon, 150, 152
Paris, 5, 16, 18, 22, 31, 32, 33, 34, 91, 96, 120, 126
Paving, 27, 34, 37, 76–77, 79, 90–91, 91–104
Paving commissioners, 94–96, 97–98, 100, 101–103

Pedestrians, 104–114, 233
Penitence, 52, 64, 67–70, 72, 233
and self-reflection, 58–60
Petty, William, 163–164, 165
Pine, John, 30, 36
Pleasure, 125–126, 132–133, 157, 217
commodification of, 127
and the dirty city, 107
Goddess of, 132
and politeness, 118, 122, 126, 128, 130–131
visual, 151–152
Police, 46, 48, 49–51, 73, 76, 77, 96–97, 219–223
Politeness, 24, 75, 81, 82–83, 84, 88–91, 113, 115, 233. *See also* Civility
and consumption, 125, 139
and pleasure, 118, 126, 128–129, 130–131
Political arithmetic, 31–32, 46–48, 158, 199
Charles Davenant on, 163–170
Political philosophy, 79–91
Pollock, Griselda, 2, 16, 17, 22
Polstead, Ezekial, 185–194
The Excise Man, 185–194
Postmodernity, 236
Post office, 202–204, 205, 209
Power, 4, 8–9, 14–17, 18, 22, 24, 26, 31, 39, 41, 79, 91–92, 144–145, 158, 181, 199–200, 220–221, 228, 229, 232, 244*n*105
Price, Richard, 165
Print culture, 10, 34, 221, 227, 229. *See also* Newspapers
Private interests, 77, 80–81, 86, 88–89, 90, 94, 97–98, 99, 101–103, 114, 125, 204, 229
Prostitution, 45–53, 56, 71, 72, 73, 112, 128, 228, 232
geography of, 49–50
and sentimental fiction, 53–54
Public. *See also* Space, public
defined by Hume, 88–90
defined by Mandeville, 85–87
defined by Shaftesbury, 81–84
Public sphere, 1, 10, 21, 30–31, 37, 50, 52, 74, 115, 151, 231
and empire, 144–145
gender and, 78, 83–84, 89, 149
Habermas on, 76, 77–79

and the parish, 101–104
of private individuals, 78–79, 87,
  90–91, 93, 103–104, 106, 111,
  113–115. *See also* Private interests
and Vauxhall Gardens, 118

R

Race, 14–15, 75, 89, 208–209
Ranelagh Gardens, 123, 125, 126–127,
  142–143
Rationalisation, 37, 41
Rationality, 32, 42, 57, 61, 77–78, 94,
  161, 191, 231, 234–235. *See also*
  Modernity, and rationality
and gender, 70–72, 192
Reason, 59, 88, 192
Reed, Joseph, 211, 223–224, 227, 229
  The Register Office, 211, 223–230
Religion, 23, 52, 57, 67–68
and sexuality, 48
Richardson, Samuel, 53–54
Richmond, Duke of, 30
Ridotto al Fresco, 120, 128–133, 142
Roads, 23, 94, 201–202
Robinson, Henry, 212, 217, 219
Rocque, John, 28–36
  Map of London (1746), 28–36
Ruggieri, Gaetano, 236
Russia Company, 43, 45, 47

S

Sargent, John, 203, 208
Sarti, Guiseppi, 236
Scotland, 24, 225–228
Scott, Sarah, 53
Self, The, 12, 26, 81, 155. *See also*
  Identity; Individualisation; Sexuality;
  Solitude
contingency of, 161, 193–194
dissolution of, 127, 129
in the eighteenth century, 41–43
government of, 48, 75, 86, 88–89,
  112–113, 186, 193, 232. *See also*
  Self, self-fashioning; Self,
  transformation of
lost and found, 54–60
modern, 14, 39–41, 44, 70, 72, 73–74,
  154, 231, 233
narcissism and, 148, 151–152, 154–155

self-fashioning, 185, 188–194
self-interest, 84–85, 88, 103, 107, 111,
  125, 169. 191, 228. *See also* Private
  interests
self-reflection and, 58–60, 61, 66–70,
  88, 151–152, 232
sentimental fiction and, 53–60
transformation of 61–70, 73
Selwyn, George, 135–137
Servandoni, Jean-Nicholas, 236–238
Sexuality, 42, 73, 79, 119, 149–150,
  233
and commodification, 128–142
regulation of, 48–49
and the self, 58–59
and transgression, 119, 122, 129, 132
Shaftesbury, Anthony Ashley Cooper, 3rd
  Earl of, 77, 79–84, 86, 87, 90, 114,
  124
Slavery, 15, 32. 35, 206–207, 209
Sloane, Hans, 30
Smith, Adam, 125
Solitude, 42, 44, 61, 68–70, 73, 81, 89,
  108, 151
Solkin, David, 82, 118, 125–126, 128,
  144
Southwark, 50. 61, 91, 99, 224
Space. *See also* Modernity, geography of
bureaucratisation of, 195
as calculable spaces, 160, 164, 177
production of, 17, 21–22, 36–37, 103,
  113, 160–161, 162, 199–200,
  231–233, 235
private, 43, 84, 96, 149, 196
public, 35, 75–77, 79, 83–84, 86–87,
  90–91, 93, 96, 101, 103–104,
  108–110, 111, 113
and the public sphere, 78–79
and subjectivities, 42–43
urban, 83–84, 89–90, 106–114,
  233–234, 235
Spectacle
fireworks as, 237–238
imperialism and, 142–148
London as, 108–109, 113
men as, 137, 145–147, 152–154
and Vauxhall Gardens, 115, 123, 132,
  150–152
women as, 117, 148–150
Spranger, John, 93–97, 103, 109,
  114–115, 234

State, The, 17–18, 46, 77, 88, 114, 185,
    198, 199–200, 204, 219, 237. *See also*
    Modernity, and the state; Nation-
    state; State formation
    'fiscal-military' state, 158–160, 168,
      171, 192, 199, 232
    geography of, 161, 181, 184, 194, 200,
      232
    legitimacy and, 160, 162, 170, 173,
      177, 184–185, 191–192, 199
State formation, 1, 3, 20, 21, 37, 158, 232
Stratford-upon-Avon, 139–140
Stratton, Richard, 203
Steele, Richard, 82
Street lighting, 51, 76, 90–91, 92, 95–96
Streets, 28, 37, 90–91, 138–139, 232. *See
    also* Paving
    and dirt, 75–76, 86–87
    of Westminster, 75–76, 91–104, 233
Surveillance, 66–67, 160–161, 169, 182,
    196–197, 217, 228, 236

T

Taxation, 46, 165–168, 199, 204,
    237–238. *See also* Excise taxation
    direct, 162, 168, 170
    parliamentary control of, 167–169, 170
    reorganisation of, 170–171
Tea, 36, 138–139, 194, 198, 205, 206
Tetbury, 179–180
Thames, River, 31, 99, 116, 207
Time-space
    distanciation, 9, 17, 161, 232
    transformation of, 1, 3, 5, 10, 37,
      201–211, 215, 219, 223, 229–230,
      231
Tinney, John, 30
Toulmin, Stephen, 6, 13–14, 15, 22, 40
Trust, 210–211, 216–217, 220, 229–230,
    232
Tyers, Jonathan, 120–124, 128–129, 133,
    142–143, 151

U

Universal Register Office, 27, 28, 37,
    201, 211–219, 221, 222–223, 224,
    229–230, 233, 234

Urban improvement. *See* City,
    improvements to

V

Vauxhall Gardens, 27, 28, 33, 37,
    116–133, 142–148, 150–157, 218,
    231, 232, 237
Vernon, Admiral Edward, 142
Vision
    culture of, 148–155
    sexual politics and, 149–150. *See also*
      Gender, men looking at women
Visual illusion, 118–119, 127–128, 129,
    150, 152–153, 157, 231
    masculinity and, 153–155
    sexual pleasure, money and,
      132–133

W

Walcot, Charles, 98
Wales, 172, 181, 185–186, 190
Walpole, Horace, 30, 133
Walpole, Robert, 116, 128
Wapping, 99, 107
Ward, John, 184
Ward, Ned, 104–114
    The London Spy, 104–114
Warfare, 34, 35, 46, 85, 141–142,
      143–145, 154, 158–160, 174, 166,
      167–168, 194, 199, 201, 205–206,
      209, 229, 237
    English Civil War, 165
    Seven Years War, 142–147, 203
    Thirty Years War, 12–13
    War of the Austrian Succession, 236
    War of the Spanish Succession, 203
Weber, Max, 4, 6, 9, 161
Welch, Saunders, 45, 47, 50–52, 216
West, The, 4, 7, 9, 10, 11, 14, 19, 32, 36
Westminster, 2, 37, 109, 218. *See also*
    Streets, of Westminster
    bridge (1750) 34, 99
Whitechapel, 43, 49, 60, 64
Wilson, Kathleen, 25–26, 145, 235–236
Wren, Sir Christopher, 99